T0265572

THE
50 GREATEST PLAYERS
IN
CLEVELAND BROWNS
HISTORY

ROBERT W. COHEN

LYONS PRESS

ESSEX, CONNECTICUT

An imprint of Globe Pequot, the trade division of
The Rowman & Littlefield Publishing Group, Inc.
4501 Forbes Blvd., Ste. 200
Lanham, MD 20706
www.rowman.com

Distributed by NATIONAL BOOK NETWORK

British Library Cataloguing in Publication Information available

Library of Congress Cataloging-in-Publication Data available

ISBN 978-1-4930-6279-9 (cloth)
ISBN 978-1-4930-6936-1 (electronic)

CONTENTS

ACKNOWLEDGMENTS

I wish to thank Troy Kinunen of MEARSonlineauctions.com, Kate of RMYauctions.com, Erik Drost, George A. Kitrinos, and Jeffrey Beall, each of whom generously contributed to the photographic content of this work.

INTRODUCTION

THE BROWNS LEGACY

A charter member of the short-lived All-America Football Conference (AAFC) that lasted just four seasons, the Cleveland Browns came into being in 1945 when taxi-cab magnate Arthur B. "Mickey" McBride secured the rights to a Cleveland franchise in the newly formed league. Heeding the advice of *Cleveland Plain Dealer* sportswriter John Dietrich, McBride, who earlier tried unsuccessfully to purchase the NFL's Cleveland Rams, hired former Massillon (Ohio) High School and Ohio State Buckeyes head coach Paul Brown to run his team, giving the 36-year-old Ohio native an ownership stake in the franchise and ceding to him full power in making all player personnel decisions.

After receiving his discharge from the military at the end of World War II, Brown assumed head coaching duties in Cleveland prior to the start of the AAFC's inaugural season of 1946. Taking up residence in the league's Western Division, which they shared with the San Francisco 49ers, Los Angeles Dons, and Chicago Rockets, the Browns, who took their name from their head coach and general manager and played their home games at Cleveland Municipal Stadium, a 78,000-seat ballpark that had served as home to the Cleveland Indians since 1931, proved to be practically unbeatable during the AAFC's brief four-year run, compiling an overall record of 47-4-3, en route to winning the division title and league championship each season. Particularly dominant in 1948, the Browns posted a perfect 14-0 record during the regular season, outscoring their opponents by a combined margin of 389–190, before routing the Buffalo Bills 49–7 in the AAFC Championship Game.

Absorbed by the NFL, along with the 49ers and the original Baltimore Colts, when the AAFC folded following the conclusion of the 1949 campaign, the Browns joined the New York Giants, Philadelphia Eagles, Pittsburgh Steelers, Chicago Cardinals, and Washington Redskins in the league's American (Eastern) Division, where they continued to experience a considerable amount of success the next six years, even as ownership of the team passed from McBride to a group of prominent Cleveland businessmen headed by David R. Jones, who had once served as director of the Cleveland Indians. Winning six more division titles and another three league championships from 1950 to 1955, the Browns laid claim to their first NFL championship by edging out the Los Angeles Rams 30–28 in the 1950 title tilt. After losing to the Rams (24–17) and the Detroit Lions (17–7 and 17–16) the next three years, the Browns captured consecutive league championships in 1954 and 1955 by manhandling the Lions 56–10 in the first of those campaigns, before defeating the Rams 38–14 in the second.

Certainly, the brilliant coaching mind of Paul Brown, who became the first coach to call plays for his quarterback, give players IQ and personality tests, use game film to evaluate opponents, and sign Black players, helped the Browns establish themselves as one of the greatest dynasties in the history of pro sports, with the team setting a North American major professional sports record by appearing in the league championship game in each of their first 10 years of existence. An exceptional judge of talent, Brown assembled a roster that included several future Hall of Famers, with talented wide receivers Mac Speedie and Dante Lavelli, bruising fullback Marion Motley, standout center Frank Gatski, legendary kicker / offensive tackle Lou Groza, and superb defensive linemen Bill Willis and Len Ford all making huge contributions to the success the Browns experienced during their period of dominance. However, Brown would not have been able to lead his team to as many division titles and league championships as he did without quarterback Otto Graham, who did a magnificent job of directing Cleveland's offense from 1946 to 1955. One of the greatest winners in the history of the game, Graham led the Browns to an overall record of 105-17-4, earning in the process league MVP honors on six separate occasions. And, some 65 years after Graham appeared in his last game, only Tom Brady has quarterbacked his team to as many league championships.

Graham's importance to the Browns became quite evident when his retirement prior to the start of the 1956 campaign resulted in the first losing season in franchise history. Help was on the way, though, in the form of Jim Brown, who the team selected with the sixth overall pick of the 1957 NFL Draft. Arguably the greatest running back ever to play the game, Brown went on to lead the league in rushing in eight of the next nine seasons, setting several NFL records along the way. And, with Brown serving as the focal point of their offense, perennial All-Pro offensive linemen Mike McCormack, Gene Hickerson, Dick Schafrath, and Jim Ray Smith providing exceptional blocking up front, wide receivers Ray Renfro and Gary Collins gathering in passes from quarterback Frank Ryan, and linebacker Jim Houston and linemen Bill Glass and Bob Gain starring on defense, the Browns won three division titles and one league championship from 1957 to 1965, experiencing much of that success under a new regime.

Purchased for nearly $4 million by a group of investors headed by 35-year-old New York advertising and television executive Art Modell in March 1961, the Browns continued to be run by Paul Brown until 1963, when complaints made by many of the team's players about the coach's dictatorial ways prompted Modell to replace him at the helm with former chief assistant, Blanton Collier. Hailed by many as "the father of modern football," Brown left Cleveland having led his team to an overall record of 157-48-8, 11 division titles, and seven league championships. A strong proponent of signing the best players, regardless of the color of their skin, Brown later received high praise for the advancements he made in that area from one of his harshest critics, Jim Brown, who said, "Paul Brown integrated pro football without uttering a single word about integration. He just went out, signed a bunch of great black athletes, and started kicking butt. That's how you do it. You don't talk about it. . . . In his own way, the man integrated football the right way—and no one was going to stop him."

Far less autocratic than Brown, under whom he had served as an assistant on both offense and defense, Collier reenergized the Browns, who ended up winning five division titles and their eighth league championship in his eight years in charge. After finishing a close second to the Giants in the NFL East in 1963, the Browns edged out the St. Louis Cardinals for the division title the following year, before defeating the heavily favored Baltimore Colts 27–0 in the NFL championship game. The Browns advanced to the title game once again in 1965, but this time lost 23–12 to Vince Lombardi's Green Bay Packers. The Browns subsequently failed to advance to the playoffs in 1966 even though they posted a record of 9-5. After the NFL adopted a new four-division setup and expanded its playoff format to two rounds in 1967, the Browns moved to the Century Division, which they shared with the Giants, St. Louis Cardinals, and Pittsburgh Steelers. Easily the strongest of the four teams, the Browns captured the division title three straight times and advanced to the NFL championship game twice, although they lost to the Baltimore Colts 34–0 in 1968 and suffered a 27–7 defeat at the hands of the Minnesota Vikings the following year.

Following the NFL/AFL merger in 1970, the Browns, Pittsburgh Steelers, and Baltimore Colts moved to the new American Football Conference, where they joined the 10 teams of the old AFL. Slotted in the AFC Central Division, along with the Steelers, Houston Oilers, and Cincinnati Bengals, the Browns finished just 7-7 in 1970, after which the 64-year-old Collier announced his retirement. In addition to leading the Browns to five division titles and one league championship in his eight years as head coach, Collier guided the team to an overall regular-season record of 76-34-2 and helped oversee the development of standout performers such as running back Leroy Kelly, wide receiver Paul Warfield, tight end Milt Morin, and defensive lineman Walter Johnson.

The Browns continued to perform well under new head coach Nick Skorich in 1971 and 1972, advancing to the playoffs twice and winning one division title, although they failed to make it past the opening round of the postseason tournament both years, losing to the Baltimore Colts 20–3 in 1971, before falling to the Miami Dolphins 20–14 the following season. But, following the retirements of many of the team's veteran players, the Browns spent the remainder of the decade toiling in mediocrity, never finishing any higher than third in their division, as Skorich, Forrest Gregg, Dick Modzelewski, and Sam Rutigliano all took turns coaching the team. Nevertheless, several outstanding performers graced the Browns' roster during this period of mediocrity, with Greg Pruitt and Mike Pruitt starring at running back, Doug Dieken providing consistently strong play at left tackle on offense, and lineman Jerry Sherk, safety Thom Darden, and cornerback Clarence Scott all excelling on defense.

The Browns experienced something of a resurgence under Rutigliano in 1980, thanks to the efforts of quarterback and league MVP Brian Sipe, who engineered a series of last-minute touchdown drives that led to the team being nicknamed the "Kardiac Kids." But, after winning their first division title in nine years, the Browns came up short in the playoffs, suffering a heartbreaking 14–12 defeat at the hands of the eventual Super Bowl champion Oakland Raiders in the opening round. With the Browns failing to perform at the same level under Rutigliano the next three seasons, Art Modell replaced him with defensive coordinator Marty Schottenheimer, who, after experiencing very little success his first year in charge, led the team to three straight division titles, four consecutive playoffs appearances, and two trips to the AFC Championship Game, both of which they lost in stunning fashion to the Denver Broncos.

After recording a 23–20 overtime victory over the Jets in the divisional round of the 1986 postseason tournament, the Browns appeared to be headed to Super Bowl XXI when they entered the latter stages of the final period of the AFC Championship Game holding a 20–13 lead over Denver. But, with less than six minutes remaining in the fourth quarter and the Broncos gaining possession of the football at their own 2 yard line, Denver quarterback John Elway led his team on a 98-yard, 15-play touchdown drive that tied the score at 20–20 with just 37 seconds left in regulation. The Broncos subsequently won the game in overtime on a 33-yard field goal by Rich Karlis, with "The Drive" making Elway a household name.

The Browns once again came oh so close to advancing to the Super Bowl the following year, when, after defeating the Indianapolis Colts 38–21 in the opening round of the playoffs, they seemed poised to send the AFC Championship Game into overtime. But, with the Browns trailing Denver 38–31 with just 1:12 left on the clock and in possession of the football at their opponent's 8 yard line, cornerback Jeremiah Castille stripped running back Earnest Byner of the ball just before he crossed the goal line and the Broncos recovered, allowing them to run down the clock before intentionally taking a safety that gave them a 38–33 victory.

Although the Browns advanced to the playoffs once again in 1988, they lost to the Houston Oilers 24–23 in the wild card round, prompting Art Modell to replace Schottenheimer with former Pittsburgh Steelers, Los Angeles Rams, and New York Jets defensive coordinator Bud Carson. Leaving Cleveland having led the Browns to four straight playoff appearances and an overall record of 44-27, Schottenheimer had the good fortune of coaching some of the AFC's finest players, with quarterback Bernie Kosar, running back Kevin Mack, tight end Ozzie Newsome, linebacker Clay Matthews, and cornerbacks Hanford Dixon and Frank Minnifield all gaining Pro Bowl recognition during his 4½-year stint as head coach.

Returning to the AFC Championship Game their first year under Bud Carson after winning the division title and defeating the Buffalo Bills 34–30 in the divisional round of the 1989 playoffs, the Browns faced Denver for the third time in four seasons. However, they again came up short against the Broncos, losing to them by a score of 37–21. Carson remained in Cleveland through the midway point of the ensuing campaign, before being replaced by offensive coordinator Jim Shofner after the Browns won only two of their first nine games.

Choosing to go in a different direction after the Browns finished the 1990 season with a record of 3-13, Modell named former New York Giants defensive coordinator Bill Belichick the team's new head coach. Although

Belichick later experienced a tremendous amount of success in New England, he struggled somewhat in his first head-coaching gig, leading the Browns to just one winning record and one playoff appearance in his five years at the helm, before leaving the organization at the end of 1995 when Art Modell announced his intentions to move the team to Baltimore.

Taken aback by Modell's announcement, the City of Cleveland threatened him with legal action. However, Modell reached a compromise with the city and the NFL early in 1996 that allowed him to establish the Baltimore Ravens as a new franchise and retain the contracts of all Browns personnel. In turn, the Browns' intellectual property, including team name, logos, training facility, and history, were kept in trust. Additionally, after suspending operations for three seasons, the Browns would resume play in 1999 with a roster consisting of players acquired via an expansion draft, free agency, and the regular NFL Draft.

After considering several other candidates, a seven-member NFL expansion committee awarded the new Browns franchise to Baltimore banking and real estate executive Al Lerner for $530 million in September 1998. The 65-year-old Lerner held a majority share, while Carmen Policy, who had helped build the 49ers dynasty of the 1980s, owned 10 percent of the team. After hiring former 49ers wide receiver Dwight Clark to serve as the team's operations director in December 1998, Lerner and Policy signed then Jacksonville Jaguars offensive coordinator Chris Palmer as the reactivated team's first head coach.

Meanwhile, behind the scenes, demolition of Cleveland Municipal Stadium, which had served as home to the Browns since their inception in 1946, began in November 1996. Nearly three years later, newly constructed Cleveland Browns Stadium opened to the public. Erected on the same site as the old ballpark, at 1085 West 3rd Street in Cleveland, Browns Stadium, which has since been renamed FirstEnergy Stadium, occupies 17 acres and seats 73,000 patrons.

Unfortunately, after resuming operations in 1999, the Browns experienced very little success over the course of the next two decades, posting just two winning records and making only one playoff appearance from 1999 to 2019. Noted for their organizational instability throughout the period, the Browns hired 11 different head coaches, with only Butch Davis (2001–2004), Romeo Crennel (2005–2008), and Hue Jackson (2016–2018) lasting more than two seasons. Several changes in ownership and upper management also prevented the Browns from fielding a competitive squad, with Al Lerner, who died of brain cancer in October 2002, leaving the team to his son, Randy, who sold the club to businessman Jimmy Haslam in 2012. Meanwhile, Carmen Policy (1999–2003), John Collins (2004–2009), Tom Heckert (2010–2012), Michael Lombardi (2013), Ray Farmer (2014–2015), Sashi Brown (2016–2017), John Dorsey (2017–2019), and Paul DePodesta (2020–) all assumed the role of primary decision-maker in the front office. With so much volatility within the organization, the Browns ended up posting an overall record of 101-234-1 from 1999 to 2019, reaching their nadir from 2015 to 2017, when they compiled an embarrassing three-year mark of just 4-44.

However, things began to turn around in Cleveland after Jimmy Haslam relieved GM John Dorsey and head coach Freddie Kitchens of their duties and elevated chief strategy officer Paul DePodesta's role within the organization following the conclusion of the 2019 campaign. After hiring former Minnesota Vikings offensive coordinator Kevin Stefanski as their new head coach, the Browns named Philadelphia Eagles vice president of football operations (and former Browns front office executive) Andrew Berry executive vice president and general manager, making him, at 32 years of age, the youngest GM in NFL history. And, with Stefanski installing a new offense in Cleveland, quarterback Baker Mayfield, the first overall pick in the 2018 NFL Draft, posted the best numbers of his young career in 2020, with his strong play behind center leading the Browns to a regular-season record of 11-5 that earned them their first playoff berth in 18 years. Displaying that they had truly arrived as a force to be reckoned with during the postseason tournament, the Browns defeated the Pittsburgh Steelers 48–37 in the wild card round, before losing a hard-fought 22–17 decision to the defending Super Bowl champion Kansas City Chiefs in the divisional round.

Unfortunately, the Browns took a step backward in 2021, compiling a record of just 8-9 that failed to earn them a return trip to the playoffs. Nevertheless, with a strong defense anchored by All-Pro end Myles Garrett and a potentially explosive offense led by newly acquired quarterback Deshaun Watson and Pro Bowl running back Nick Chubb, the Browns figure to be perennial contenders in the AFC North in the years ahead. Their next division title will be their 23rd. The Browns have also won eight league championships and four NFL titles. Featuring a plethora of exceptional performers through the years, the Browns have inducted 17 players into their Ring of Honor and retired the numbers of five different men. Meanwhile, 21 members of the Pro Football Hall of Fame spent at least one full season in Cleveland, 16 of whom wore a Browns uniform during many of their peak seasons.

FACTORS USED TO DETERMINE RANKINGS

It should come as no surprise that selecting the 50 greatest players ever to perform for a team with the rich history of the Cleveland Browns presented quite a challenge. Even after narrowing the field down to a mere 50 men, I still needed to devise a method of ranking the elite players that remained. Certainly, the names of Jim Brown, Otto Graham, Leroy Kelly, Lou Groza, Ozzie Newsome, and Joe Thomas would appear at, or near, the top of virtually everyone's list, although the order might vary somewhat from one person to the next. Several other outstanding performers have gained general recognition through the years as being among the greatest players ever to wear a Browns uniform, with Marion Motley, Gene Hickerson, Dante Lavelli, Dick Schafrath, Clay Matthews, and Michael Dean Perry heading the list of other Browns icons. But how does one compare players who lined up on opposite sides of the ball with any degree of certainty? Furthermore, how does one differentiate between the pass-rushing and run-stopping skills of front-seven defenders such as Clay Matthews and Myles Garrett and the ball-hawking skills of defensive backs such as Hanford Dixon and Frank Minnifield? And, on the offensive end, how can a direct correlation be made between the contributions made by standout linemen such as Mike McCormack and Frank Gatski and skill-position players such as Greg Pruitt and Nick Chubb? After initially deciding whom to include on my list, I then needed to determine what criteria I should use to formulate my final rankings.

The first thing I decided to examine was the level of dominance a player attained during his time in Cleveland. How often did he lead the league in a major statistical category? Did he ever capture league MVP honors? How many times did he earn a trip to the Pro Bowl or a spot on the All-Pro Team?

I also chose to assess the level of statistical compilation a player achieved while wearing a Browns uniform. I reviewed where he ranks among the team's all-time leaders in those statistical categories most pertinent to his position. Of course, even the method of using statistics as a measuring stick has its inherent flaws. Although the level of success a team experiences rushing and passing the ball is impacted greatly by the performance of its offensive line, there really is no way to quantifiably measure the level of play reached by each individual offensive lineman. Conversely, the play of the offensive line affects tremendously the statistics compiled by a team's quarterback and running backs. Furthermore, the NFL did not keep an official record of defensive numbers such as tackles and quarterback sacks until the 1980s (although the Browns kept their own records prior to that). In addition, when examining the statistics compiled by offensive players, the era during which a quarterback, running back, or wide receiver competed must be factored into the equation.

To illustrate my last point, rules changes instituted by the league office have opened up the game considerably over the course of the last two decades. Quarterbacks are accorded far more protection than ever before, and officials have also been instructed to limit the amount of contact defensive backs are allowed to make with wide receivers. As a result, the game has experienced an offensive explosion, with quarterbacks and receivers posting numbers players from prior generations rarely even approached. That being the case, one must place the numbers Baker Mayfield compiled during his time in Cleveland in their proper context when comparing him to earlier Browns quarterbacks such as Frank Ryan and Brian Sipe. Similarly, the statistics posted by Jarvis Landry must be viewed in moderation when comparing him to previous Browns wideouts Mac Speedie and Gary Collins.

Other important factors I needed to consider were the overall contributions a player made to the success of the team, the degree to which he improved the fortunes of the club during his time in Cleveland, and the manner in which he impacted the team, both on and off the field. While the number of championships and division titles the Browns won during a player's years with the team certainly factored into the equation, I chose not to deny a top performer his rightful place on the list if his years in Cleveland happened to coincide with a lack of overall success by the club. As a result, the names of players such as Mike Pruitt and Josh Cribbs will appear in these rankings.

One other thing I should mention is that I only considered a player's performance while playing for the Browns when formulating my rankings. That being the case, the names of Hall of Fame players such as Bobby Mitchell and Paul Warfield, both of whom had many of their finest seasons for other teams, may appear lower on this list than one might expect. Meanwhile, the names of fellow Hall of Famers Len Dawson and Willie Davis are nowhere to be found.

Having established the guidelines to be used throughout this book, the time has come to reveal the 50 greatest players in Browns history, starting with number 1 and working our way down to number 50.

1

JIM BROWN

Despite the brilliance of Otto Graham, who started at quarterback for Browns teams that won seven league championships, Jim Brown stands far and above all others as the greatest player in franchise history. Generally considered to be the greatest running back ever to play the game, Brown proved to be the dominant figure of his era, winning eight rushing titles over the course of his nine-year Hall of Fame career. Blessed with the perfect combination of power and speed, Brown gained more than 1,000 yards on the ground seven times, en route to amassing the most yards rushing, yards from scrimmage, all-purpose yards, rushing touchdowns, and total TDs in team annals. The central figure on Browns teams that won three division titles and one NFL championship, Brown earned nine Pro Bowl selections, nine All-Pro nominations, and four league MVP trophies, before being further honored by being named to the NFL's 75th Anniversary Team and the NFL 100 All-Time Team, receiving a top two ranking by both the *Sporting News* and the NFL Network on their respective lists of the 100 Greatest Players in NFL History, and having his #32 retired by the Browns.

Born in St. Simons Island, Georgia, on February 17, 1936, James Nathaniel Brown grew up not knowing his father, a professional boxer who left the family about two weeks after his birth. Raised primarily by his great-grandmother after his mother moved north to seek employment, Brown spent his early years attending school in a segregated two-room shack, before moving to Long Island, New York, at the age of eight after his mom sent for him.

Eventually establishing himself as a star athlete at mostly white Manhasset High School, Brown earned 13 letters in football, basketball, baseball, lacrosse, and track. An outstanding student as well, Brown gained membership to the honor society for scholastic achievement, becoming so popular that he was elected chief justice of the high school court. Yet, despite being recognized as a model student athlete, Brown later admitted

Jim Brown led the NFL in rushing in eight of his nine years in the league.
Courtesy of RMYAuctions.com

to serving as president of a gang called "The Gaylords" that engaged in fist-fights, although he made it clear that they used only their fists as weapons.

Recruited by several colleges, Brown ultimately accepted a full athletic scholarship to New York's Syracuse University, where he went on to have a storied career in multiple sports, earning varsity letters in football, basketball, lacrosse, and track and field, qualifying for the Olympic Games after placing fifth nationally in the 1956 decathlon competition. Experiencing similar success in football and lacrosse, Brown earned First-Team All-America honors in both sports his senior year, concluding his college career on the gridiron in fine fashion by rushing for 329 yards, scoring nine touchdowns, and kicking 10 extra points in his final two games.

After finishing a disappointing fifth in the 1956 Heisman Trophy balloting, Brown entered the 1957 NFL Draft, where the Browns selected him in the first round, with the sixth overall pick. Establishing himself as a dominant force his first year in Cleveland, Brown gained Pro Bowl and All-Pro recognition for the first of nine straight times and earned NFL MVP and Rookie of the Year honors by leading the league with 942 yards rushing, nine rushing touchdowns, and 10 total TDs, while also placing among the leaders with 997 yards from scrimmage, 1,133 all-purpose yards, and an average of 4.7 yards per carry. Performing even better in 1958, Brown began a fabulous eight-year run during which he posted the following numbers:

YEAR	YDS RUSHING	RECS	REC YDS	YDS FROM SCRIMMAGE	TDS
1958	**1,527**	16	138	**1,665**	18
1959	**1,329**	24	190	**1,519**	14
1960	**1,257**	19	204	1,461	11
1961	**1,408**	46	459	**1,867**	10
1962	996	47	517	1,513	18
1963	**1,863**	24	268	**2,131**	15
1964	**1,446**	36	340	**1,786**	9
1965	**1,544**	34	328	**1,872**	21

* Please note that any numbers printed in bold throughout this book indicate that the player led the NFL in that statistical category that year.

Making Brown's 1958–1960 statistics even more impressive is the fact that he compiled them in a 12-game season (the NFL did not expand its schedule to 14 games until 1961). In addition to leading the NFL in rushing in seven of those eight seasons, Brown topped the circuit in yards from scrimmage six times, all-purpose yards five times, rushing touchdowns and total TDs four times each, and yards per rushing attempt twice, earning in the process league MVP honors three more times (1958, 1963, and 1965). Meanwhile, the Browns won the division title in 1964 and 1965 and the NFL championship in 1964.

Rivaling Johnny Unitas as the NFL's most recognizable figure during that time, Brown clearly established himself as the greatest player in the game, with his size, strength, speed, and incredible balance making him the scourge of defenders throughout the league. Virtually impossible for one man to bring down, the 6'2", 232-pound Brown earned the respect and admiration of even the league's meanest defenders, with Philadelphia Eagles legendary linebacker Chuck Bednarik saying, "You gang-tackled him. You did everything—give him extra-curriculars—and he'd get up slow, look at you, and walk back to that huddle and wouldn't say a word, and just come at you again, and again. You'd just say, 'What the hell! What's wrong with this guy? For Heaven's sake, when is he gonna stop carrying the ball? How much more can he take?'"

Dick Butkus, whose rookie campaign coincided with Brown's final season, stated, "I played against Jim Brown once when I was with the college All-Stars, and there was talk, and I had heard about Jim Brown, the great Jim Brown, blah, blah, blah. So, I thought, 'Here's my shot at getting this legend.' So, some way or other, my arm got caught under his, and he started rolling the other way, and it hyper-extended my arm, and I'm like, 'Hey, you son-of-a-bitch!' And I thought, 'Damn, this guy is not bad.'"

Colts Hall of Fame defensive end Gino Marchetti recounted the following scene that took place in the Baltimore locker room one day: "After the game in our locker room, [head coach] Weeb Ewbank says, 'They think Jim Brown is so good. If they'd have taken that 60-yard run away from him, if they'd have taken that 32-yard run away from him, if they'd have taken that 18-yard run away from him, he wouldn't have done anything.' . . . That's the trouble with a guy like Jim Brown. He always gets those 60-yard runs and those 30-yard runs. That's what makes Jim Brown what he is."

Marchetti then added, "The only thing that I could say about Jim Brown is that he might not have been the best blocker in the world. But who cares about that when you could run and do the things that he could do?"

Deacon Jones is another Hall of Fame defensive end who had high praise for Brown, saying, "You can't measure his greatness on yards. But you gotta measure it on impact. What you had to do when you faced him. This is one man, and you couldn't stop him."

The level of dominance that Brown attained caused him to be revered by his teammates, with Bobby Mitchell, who spent four seasons starting alongside him in the Cleveland backfield, claiming, "Until you lined up next to this guy and watched him, time after time, in very tough, crucial situations, make it come out alright for the Cleveland Browns, you can't fully respect how good he was. If we had the capabilities today to show him from 15 different angles, people would say, 'That was not a human.'"

Former Browns owner Art Modell stated, "He did things on a football field that I have never seen since. Did it continually. He'd go against the grain against the Giants and just cut across the field shedding tacklers."

Certainly, Brown's tremendous physique, which he used to dole out almost as much punishment as he received, contributed greatly to the success he experienced on the field, as he suggested when he said, "I had a great body. That was given to me by my mother and father, and by God."

Agreeing with his former teammate's assessment, Paul Warfield stated, "Here was an individual who had a torso that was sculpted, obviously, by God Himself. Jim was perhaps the perfect instrument to run a football. . . . The Creator said, 'I'm only going to do this one time in a very secial player.'"

Brown also knew how to use his powerful frame and penetrating stare to intimidate his opponent, creating an aura surrounding him that left everyone believing he had the ability to accomplish almost anything, with Paul Hornung claiming, "I think he's the only guy who probably could have challenged Ali in his heyday."

Meanwhile, Deacon Jones said, "He had the perfect body—built just like a V. He had the perfect body, and he used it. I mean, he could look at you and you'd think he was looking straight through you."

Hornung added, "I've always felt that Jim Brown's the only guy I've ever known who, at 50 years old, I would have bet he could have gained 1,000 yards in the NFL."

In discussing the manner with which Brown carried himself before each contest, Pat Summerall stated, "He warmed up by himself, not with the rest of the team. And we sort of stood with our hands on our hips, watching him warm up. It was almost like Superman or Captain Marvel."

An extremely intelligent player, Brown entered each game well prepared for anything that might transpire during the contest, with Paul Warfield saying, "There was more to it than just physical ability. There was a very shrewd, very intimate intellectual approach to everything that he did. So, the combination of physical, as well as mental, preparation was of the essence to him, and he did not slack off on the mental application of it one iota, even though he could have accomplished all the things that he accomplished just from a physical standpoint."

Brown also learned how to channel the inner rage he felt over the racial discrimination he encountered to his opponent, stating, "I'll tell you why I am the way that I am. It doesn't start on the field. It starts as a person. I was dealing with race since I was born. And in my inner-self, my strength was unbending when it came to accepting that B.S.—racial discrimination.

Because I was never going to let anybody make me feel that I was not top shelf. And that was a battle that raged, and I could use a lot of that on the field."

Brown's strong will and belief in himself caused him to share a somewhat uneasy relationship with dictatorial Browns head coach, Paul Brown, with the Hall of Fame running back recalling, "Paul was Julius Caesar. He was a ruler. And I was a very determined person, set in my ways to a certain degree, so we always had a little edge in our relationship."

With the differences between the two men worsening by 1962, Brown led a players' revolt after the team finished just 7-6-1, telling Art Modell at season's end, "Either Paul Brown goes, or I quit." Choosing his star running back over his head coach, Modell handed the elder Brown his walking papers prior to the start of the 1963 campaign, replacing him with offensive assistant Blanton Collier, who subsequently led the Browns to the NFL title his second year in charge. Recalling how the change in coaches affected him personally, Brown said, "When Paul left, I went to a different emotional and mental level because I didn't want people to think that my career was based on Paul Brown. I wanted it so bad that I thought about it all the time. I practiced, I think, harder than I ever did in my life. I got to a level where I could go 80 yards and wouldn't be tired at all. I had so much under my command that year that that was like putting almost everything you had into football. That was like my life was just that. That year was an awesome kind of experience for me."

Posting arguably the finest overall numbers of his career in 1963, Brown earned NFL MVP honors for the third time by leading the league with 1,863 yards rushing, 2,131 yards from scrimmage, and 15 touchdowns, before serving as the central figure on Cleveland's 1964 NFL championship team, once again topping the circuit in yards rushing (1,446) and yards from scrimmage (1,786). Although the Browns failed to repeat as league champions in 1965, suffering a 23–12 defeat at the hands of the Green Bay Packers in the NFL title game, Brown had another exceptional season, earning NFL MVP honors for the fourth and final time by leading the league with 1,544 yards rushing, 1,872 yards from scrimmage, and 21 touchdowns, with the last figure setting a single-season franchise record that still stands. But, with Brown still at the top of his game, a series of events transpired in the summer of 1966 that prompted him to abruptly announce his retirement at only 30 years of age.

Due to production delays during the filming of the movie *The Dirty Dozen*, Brown found his return to the Browns in time for the start of training camp being compromised somewhat. Unhappy with the situation, Art

Modell told the media that he intended to fine Brown $1,500 for every week of training camp he missed, releasing a statement that read: "No veteran Browns player has been granted or will be given permission to report late to our training camp at Hiram College—and this includes Jim Brown. Should Jim fail to report to Hiram at check-in time deadline, which is Sunday, July 17, then I will have no alternative but to suspend him without pay. I recognize the complex problems of the motion picture business, having spent several years in the industry. However, in all fairness to everyone connected with the Browns—the coaching staff, the players, and, most important of all, our many faithful fans—I feel compelled to say that I will have to take such action should Jim be absent on July 17."

Not one to be given ultimatums, Brown, who had already said that he did not intend to play past 1966, announced his retirement while still on the set of the movie, saying at the time that he wanted to devote more time to his movie career and improving race relations. Looking back on his decision years later, Brown said, "When I quit, I was happy. I had nine good years. I did all the things I wanted to do. I went into movies. I started talking to pretty girls. So, I never looked back."

Meanwhile, Modell later admitted in the book *When All the World Was Browns Town*, that he had perhaps made an error in judgment in dealing with Brown, saying, "I may have acted hastily in 1966. If I had told him to just forget training camp and show up when he could, I think he would have returned. But it wasn't fair to the coaches and players [for him to miss camp]."

Expressing the sentiments of every defensive player in the league upon learning of Brown's decision to call it quits, Deacon Jones recalled, "We were all happy, and anybody who said they weren't happy had to be on the Cleveland Browns team. But I think all the defensive personnel in the league were very, very delighted that he decided to go into the movie business."

Ending his nine-year playing career with 12,312 yards rushing, 262 receptions, 2,499 receiving yards, 14,811 yards from scrimmage, 648 kickoff-return yards, 15,459 all-purpose yards, 106 rushing touchdowns, 126 total touchdowns, and a rushing average of 5.2 yards per carry, Brown retired as the NFL's all-time leader in rushing yards, rushing touchdowns, total touchdowns, yards from scrimmage, and all-purpose yards. The only player in NFL history to average more than 100 yards per game on the ground for his career, Brown also holds the league record for most rushing titles (eight).

In summarizing his career, Brown said, "I played nine seasons, and I never missed a game. And I never laid out on the football field. I might not have the greatest ability of everybody, but the one thing that stands out is that, when it was time to play, I was there."

Following his playing days, Brown continued his movie career, appearing in nearly 50 feature films and several television shows, while also remaining active in sports for decades as an occasional color analyst for football, boxing, and UFC matches. Brown has also spent the last 15 seasons serving as a special advisor for the Browns, helping to build relationships with the team's players and assisting with the organization's various player programs.

A social activist and strong proponent for the advancement of minorities, Brown helped form the Negro Industrial Economics Union, which began assisting Black-owned businesses during the 1960s. In 1988, Brown created the Amer-I-Can program to turn gang members from destructive to productive members of society. An outspoken critic of the modern African American athlete for what he perceives as a lack of involvement in the Black community, Brown has called individuals such as Charles Barkley, Magic Johnson, and Michael Jordan "basically prima donnas."

Yet, despite his greatness on the football field and good intentions off it, Brown has shown through the years a dark side to his persona that has frequently caused him to run afoul of the law. Accused of several violent crimes, primarily against women, Brown has been arrested for allegedly forcing himself on an 18-year-old girl in 1965, throwing a model from a balcony in 1966, beating and raping a woman in 1985, assaulting his fiancée one year later for flirting with another man, and beating up a golfing partner, although, in most cases, he has either been found innocent or had the charges against him dropped. However, after being convicted in 1999 of smashing the window of his wife's car, Brown had his driver's license suspended for a year, received a three-year probation sentence, and had to attend special counseling for domestic batterers.

Nevertheless, Brown remains a football legend more than half a century after he appeared in his last game, even to those men who never saw him perform. After calling Brown "the most dominant player to ever step on any athletic field," Ray Lewis stated, "When you talk about Bo Jackson, Marcus Allen, Eric Dickerson, Tony Dorsett, Walter Payton, there's not one trait that they had that he didn't have."

Terrell Davis said, "Jim Brown is the greatest back to ever play. He was a bad man, and not only on the field. Jim Brown, being an activist, had an impact on me as well."

In explaining why he considers Brown to be the greatest player in NFL history, Jerry Rice stated, "It's everything he brought to the game. He didn't play as long as other running backs, but he had the speed and physicality, and it's just the way he played the game."

Ceding the title of greatest all-time running back to Brown, Emmitt Smith said, "He's one. [Walter] Payton two. I fall to three."

In examining Brown's place in history, social activist Dr. Harry Edwards suggested, "His principal legacy is going to be what he accomplished as a football player. But Jim Brown was not principally a great football player. Jim Brown was a great man who just also happened to play a great game of football."

Kareem Abdul-Jabbar expressed similar sentiments when he said, "Jim Brown really represented achievement for the black community. And he was so good that it didn't matter what color they were; they had to acknowledge him as the best in his field. And that meant a lot to black Americans in the 60s, when everything that any black person achieved was questioned as to whether it was significant. But there were no question marks about Jim Brown."

Preferring to focus on Jim Brown, the football player, former Colts, Steelers, and Redskins defensive back Johnny Sample stated, "Jim Brown's the greatest running back that has ever breathed."

Former Browns teammate Bill Glass took it one step further, proclaiming, "Jim Brown was the greatest player that ever played the game of football."

CAREER HIGHLIGHTS

Best Season

There are so many great seasons from which to choose, with the 1958, 1961, 1963, and 1965 campaigns heading the list. But, while any of those seasons would make an excellent choice, I ultimately settled on 1963, since, en route to earning NFL Player of the Year honors and one of his four MVP trophies, Brown led the league in six different categories, establishing career-high marks with 1,863 yards rushing, 2,131 yards from scrimmage, 2,131 all-purpose yards, and an average of 6.4 yards per carry, with his 1,863 yards rushing and 2,131 yards from scrimmage both setting single-season franchise records that still stand.

Memorable Moments/Greatest Performances

Brown went over 100 yards rushing for the first time in his career during a 21–17 win over the Washington Redskins on November 3, 1957, finishing the game with 21 carries for 109 yards and two touchdowns.

Brown led Cleveland to a 45–31 victory over the Los Angeles Rams on November 24, 1957, by carrying the ball 31 times for 237 yards and four touchdowns, the longest of which came on a 69-yard run.

Brown victimized the Rams again in the 1958 regular-season opener, rushing for 171 yards and two touchdowns during a 30–27 Browns win.

Brown rushed for 129 yards and three touchdowns during a lopsided 45–12 victory over the Steelers on October 5, 1958, with the longest of his TD runs covering 59 yards.

Brown followed that up by rushing for 182 yards and three touchdowns during a 35–28 win over the Chicago Cardinals on October 12, 1958.

After rushing for 153 yards and scoring two touchdowns during a 27–10 win over the Steelers the previous week, Brown concluded October 1958 with another fabulous performance on the 26th of the month, gaining 180 yards on the ground and scoring four touchdowns during a 38–24 victory over the Cardinals, with the longest of his TDs coming on a 62-yard run.

Brown continued to torment the Cardinals on October 4, 1959, rushing for 147 yards and two touchdowns during a 34–7 Browns win.

Brown defeated the Baltimore Colts almost singlehandedly on November 1, 1959, rushing for 178 yards and five touchdowns during a 38–31 win, scoring one of his TDs on a 70-yard run.

Brown starred in defeat on October 23, 1960, rushing for 167 yards, amassing 224 yards from scrimmage, and scoring a touchdown on a 71-yard run during a 31–29 loss to the Eagles.

Brown turned in an extraordinary all-around effort on November 13, 1960, rushing for 173 yards, returning two kickoffs for 55 yards, amassing 237 all-purpose yards, and scoring two touchdowns during a 28–27 victory over the St. Louis Cardinals.

Brown turned in a similarly impressive performance on December 4, 1960, amassing 252 all-purpose yards and scoring a touchdown during a 27–16 win over the Redskins, with 135 of his yards coming on the ground, 64 through the air, and 53 on special teams.

Brown topped both those efforts, though, on November 19, 1961, when he rushed for 237 yards, amassed 313 all-purpose yards, and scored four TDs during a 45–24 victory over the Eagles.

Although Brown gained only 79 yards on the ground during a 38–14 win over the Cardinals on November 18, 1962, he scored four touchdowns, the longest of which came on a 16-yard run.

Brown followed that up by rushing for 110 yards, making five receptions for 56 yards, and scoring three touchdowns during a 35–14 win over the Steelers, with the longest of his TDs coming on a 34-yard pass from Frank Ryan.

Brown helped the Browns begin the 1963 campaign on a positive note by rushing for 162 yards, accumulating 262 yards from scrimmage, and scoring three touchdowns during a 27–14 win over the Redskins in the regular-season opener, with one of his TDs coming on an 83-yard catch-and-run and another on an 80-yard run.

Brown continued his exceptional play in Week 2, carrying the ball 20 times for 232 yards and two touchdowns during a 41–24 victory over the Dallas Cowboys on September 22, 1963, scoring his TDs on runs of 71 and 62 yards.

Brown helped lead Cleveland to a 35–24 win over the Giants on October 13, 1963, by rushing for 123 yards, amassing 209 yards from scrimmage, and scoring three touchdowns, the longest of which came on a 72-yard catch-and-run.

Brown starred during a 23–17 win over the Eagles on November 3, 1963, rushing for 223 yards and one touchdown, which came on a 62-yard run.

Brown contributed to a 20–16 victory over the Cowboys on October 18, 1964, by carrying the ball 26 times for 188 yards.

Brown proved to be too much for the Lions to handle on November 15, 1964, rushing for 147 yards, gaining another 47 yards on five pass receptions, and scoring two touchdowns during a 37–21 Browns win.

Brown led Cleveland to a 35–17 victory over the Eagles on October 3, 1965, by rushing for 133 yards and three touchdowns, all of which came on short runs.

Brown followed that up by gaining 168 yards on the ground and scoring two touchdowns during a 24–19 win over the Steelers on October 9, 1965.

Brown displayed his entire offensive arsenal during a 38–14 win over the Giants on October 24, 1965, rushing for 177 yards, making three receptions for 18 yards and one touchdown, and throwing a 39-yard TD pass to Gary Collins.

Brown led Cleveland to a 38–34 victory over Philadelphia on November 7, 1965, by rushing for 131 yards, gaining another 60 yards on five pass receptions, and scoring three touchdowns, the longest of which came on a 32-yard pass from Frank Ryan.

Brown scored another three touchdowns during a 34–21 win over the Giants on November 14, 1965, also finishing the game with 156 yards rushing.

Brown contributed to a 42–21 win over the Steelers on November 28, 1965, by rushing for 146 yards and scoring four TDs, the longest of which came on a 27-yard pass from Jim Ninowski.

Notable Achievements

- Rushed for more than 1,000 yards seven times, topping 1,500 yards on three occasions.
- Surpassed 40 receptions twice and 500 receiving yards once.
- Amassed more than 1,500 yards from scrimmage seven times, topping 2,000 yards once.
- Scored at least 10 touchdowns eight times, topping 20 TDs once.
- Scored more than 100 points three times.
- Averaged more than 5 yards per carry five times.
- Led NFL in rushing attempts six times, yards rushing eight times, yards from scrimmage six times, all-purpose yards five times, rushing touchdowns five times, touchdowns three times, points scored once, and rushing average twice.
- Finished second in NFL in rushing attempts twice, yards from scrimmage twice, all-purpose yards twice, touchdowns three times, points scored once, and rushing average twice.
- Holds Browns single-season records for most yards rushing (1,863 in 1963), yards from scrimmage (2,131 in 1963), rushing touchdowns (17 twice), touchdowns scored (21 in 1965), and points scored (126 in 1965).
- Holds Browns career records for most yards rushing (12,312), yards from scrimmage (14,811), all-purpose yards (15,549), rushing touchdowns (106), and touchdowns scored (126).
- Ranks fourth in franchise history with 756 points scored.
- Ranks among NFL career leaders in yards rushing (11th), rushing touchdowns (6th), touchdowns scored (10th), and rushing average (5th).
- Three-time division champion (1957, 1964, and 1965).
- 1964 NFL champion.
- Four-time NFL MVP (1957, 1958, 1963, and 1965).

- 1963 Bert Bell Award winner as NFL Player of the Year.
- Nine-time Pro Bowl selection (1957, 1958, 1959, 1960, 1961, 1962, 1963, 1964, and 1965).
- Eight-time First-Team All-Pro selection (1957, 1958, 1959, 1960, 1961, 1963, 1964, and 1965).
- 1962 Second-Team All-Pro selection.
- Nine-time First-Team All–Eastern Conference selection (1957, 1958, 1959, 1960, 1961, 1962, 1963, 1964, and 1965).
- Pro Football Reference All-1960s First Team.
- NFL 1960s All-Decade Team.
- Member of NFL's 75th Anniversary Team.
- Named to NFL 100 All-Time Team in 2019.
- Number one on the *Sporting News*' 1999 list of the 100 Greatest Players in NFL History.
- Number two on the NFL Network's 2010 list of the NFL's 100 Greatest Players.
- #32 retired by Browns.
- Member of Cleveland Browns Ring of Honor.
- Elected to Pro Football Hall of Fame in 1971.

2

OTTO GRAHAM

An original member of the Browns, Otto Graham spent his entire 10-year professional career in Cleveland, establishing himself during that time as the greatest quarterback of his era. A deadly accurate passer and creative playmaker who also excelled as a runner, Graham earned the nickname "Automatic Otto" for his consistency and toughness, which made him the unquestioned leader of Browns teams that won 10 consecutive division titles and seven league championships. Performing brilliantly in both the AAFC and the NFL, Graham led his league in touchdown passes three times, completion percentage four times, and passing yards and passer rating five times each, with his superb play earning him six league MVP awards, five Pro Bowl nominations, and seven First-Team All-League selections. A member of both the NFL's 75th Anniversary Team and the NFL 100 All-Time Team, Graham received the additional honors of being ranked number seven by the *Sporting News* on its 1999 list of the 100 Greatest Players in NFL History and number 16 by the NFL Network on that station's 2010 list of the NFL's 100 Greatest Players, having his #14 retired by the Browns, and gaining induction into the Pro Football Hall of Fame in his very first year of eligibility.

Born in Waukegan, Illinois, on December 6, 1921, Otto Everett Graham Jr. displayed a passion for music and sports while growing up with his three brothers in the Midwest. The son of two schoolteachers who both loved music and encouraged their children to play instruments, Graham, who weighed 14 pounds and 12 ounces at birth, became proficient in violin, cornet, piano, and French horn while attending Waukegan High School, winning the Illinois French horn state championship one year. Successful in his athletic pursuits as well, Graham starred in football, baseball, basketball, and track, earning All-State honors in both football and basketball his senior year.

Continuing to compete in multiple sports after accepting a basketball scholarship to Northwestern University, Graham excelled as a center fielder

Otto Graham led the Browns to 10 division titles and seven league championships.
Courtesy of RMYAuctions.com

on the diamond, served as team captain on the basketball court, and starred as a passing tailback on the gridiron, all while waiting to be called into active duty after enlisting in the Navy following the Japanese attack on Pearl Harbor on December 7, 1941. Particularly outstanding in basketball and football, Graham gained All-America recognition in both sports as a senior in 1943, when he also earned conference MVP honors and a third-place finish in the Heisman Trophy voting by setting a new Big Ten single-season passing record.

After obtaining his degree, Graham enrolled in the Navy's V-5 cadet program, a pilot training course offered at Colgate University in Hamilton, New York, before moving to North Carolina Pre-Flight, where he became cadet regional commander and learned how to quarterback in the new "T" formation (where the QB stood directly behind the center) under Cloudbusters head coach Paul "Bear" Bryant. Once the war ended, Graham spent one season playing for the NBA's Rochester Royals, before joining the Cleveland Browns in the newly formed All-America Football Conference, spurning in the process the Detroit Lions, who had selected him with the fourth overall pick of the 1944 NFL Draft. Looking back on his decision to play for the Browns, Graham recalled, "I was getting a naval cadet's pay in World War II when [Paul] Brown came out to the station and offered me a two-year contract at $7,500 per. He also offered me a $1,000 signing bonus and $250 a month for the duration of the war. All I asked was, 'Where do I sign?' Old Navy men say I rooted for the war to last forever."

Laying claim to the starting quarterback job shortly after he arrived in Cleveland in the spring of 1946, Graham, who had been more of a runner than a passer in college, adapted quickly to coach Brown's innovative offense, leading the Browns to the AAFC championship for the first of four straight times by topping the circuit with 17 touchdown passes and a passer rating of 112.1, while also finishing second in the league with 1,834 passing yards and a 54.6 pass-completion percentage. Meanwhile, Graham exhibited his superior athletic ability by also performing well on defense and special teams, amassing 129 punt-return yards and recording five interceptions, which he returned for a total of 102 yards and one touchdown. Graham followed that up with three more outstanding seasons, leading the Browns to another three championships by posting the following numbers:

YEAR	YDS PASSING	TD PASSES	INTS	COMP. %	QBR
1947	2,753	25	11	60.6	109.2
1948	2,713	25	15	52.0	85.6
1949	2,785	19	10	56.5	97.5

Establishing himself as the finest signal-caller in the game, Graham led the AAFC in passing yards all three years, topped the circuit in passer rating twice, and ranked among the leaders in TD passes and completion percentage each season, with his exceptional play earning him First-Team All-AAFC recognition and league MVP honors each season.

Developing into a superb passer under Paul Brown's tutelage, Graham, who employed a modified sidearm technique, delivered the ball accurately to his receivers and did an excellent job of taking something off his long passes, with star wide receiver Dante Lavelli recalling, "I used to catch a lot of them one-handed. He had great touch in his hands."

In describing himself as a passer, Graham said, "I could throw hard if I had to, I could lay it up, I could drill the sideline pass. . . . I could throw a pass to a spot as well as anyone who ever lived—But that's a God-given talent. I could never stand back and flick the ball 60 yards downfield with my wrists like Dan Marino does."

However, the 6'1", 200-pound Graham proved to be far more mobile than Marino, using the skills he learned on the basketball court to excel at spinning and moving in the pocket, with Don Shula, who grew up right outside Cleveland rooting for the Browns, noting years later, "Otto was a guy that had great athletic ability. He was a running back at Northwestern. Paul Brown made him into a quarterback. When the pass broke down and he didn't have anybody open, he could always take off and run with it and be a great runner with the ball. And then, along with that, he was just a prolific passer—a guy that was uncanny as far as his accuracy throwing the ball. He just had such great ability, and he was just very relaxed with the way he handled the great ability that he had."

Agreeing somewhat with Shula's last statement, Graham said, "My personality was such that I think I was always kind of cool under pressure. But I've always said that you have to have the confidence that you will do good, but, at the same time, inside have the fear that you might fail."

Graham then revealed how his fear of failure affected him before each contest, disclosing, "Before we played every game, I could never digest the pre-game meal. I would have a couple of oranges and apples, but the food itself, I couldn't eat. I was just too nervous. My stomach was turning over and over and over."

Continuing to perform at an elite level after the Browns joined the NFL in 1950, Graham led the team to its fifth straight league championship by throwing for 1,943 yards and 14 touchdowns, completing 54.2 percent of his passes, and running for a team-high six touchdowns, earning in the process the first of his five consecutive Pro Bowl nominations. Although the Browns failed to capture the title in any of the next three seasons, Graham earned First-Team All-Pro and NFL MVP honors in both 1951 and 1953 by leading his team to a composite regular-season record of 21-2 those two years. Particularly outstanding in 1953, Graham led all NFL quarterbacks with 2,722 yards passing, a career-high 64.7 pass-completion percentage, and a passer rating of 99.7.

Helping to shift the emphasis in football from running to passing, Graham once said, "What I loved was that we were a passing team in an era of the run."

Nevertheless, Graham often had to subjugate his ego to maintain a good working relationship with Paul Brown, who insisted on calling all the plays from the sideline. In discussing how he ceded full authority to Brown, Graham told Paul Zimmerman of *Sports Illustrated* in 1998, "On the Browns, there was room for only one ego, and it wasn't mine. I never criticized the coach. He was the admiral, the general, the CEO."

Providing further insight into his relationship with Brown during an interview with sportswriter Mickey Herskowitz one year later, Graham said, "We had the greatest coach in the game and an esprit de corps you find very seldom on a football team today. It didn't matter who got the credit, who made the headlines, who scored. . . . Paul Brown was just light-years ahead of everybody. I'm grateful I got to play under him. I learned a lot about football, about organization, about life. There were times when I hated his guts. I could have killed him. Other times, I felt something close to love."

Graham remained with the Browns for two more years, guiding them to the NFL title in both 1954 and 1955, with his strong play and outstanding leadership earning him First-Team All-Pro honors both years and league MVP honors in 1955, when he threw for 15 touchdowns, ran for six others, and topped the circuit with a pass-completion percentage of 53.0 and a passer rating of 94.0. But, after leading the Browns to a convincing 38–14 victory over the Los Angeles Rams in the 1955 NFL championship game, Graham announced his retirement, ending his career with 23,584 passing yards, 174 touchdown passes, 135 interceptions, 882 rushing yards, 44 rushing touchdowns, a pass-completion percentage of 55.8, a passer rating of 86.6, and a winning percentage of .810 as a starter that ranks as the best in NFL history.

Following his playing days, Graham began a career in coaching, where he adopted many of Brown's techniques, later saying, "I found myself doing and saying the same things that used to make me so mad at him."

In addition to coaching the Collegiate All-Stars for many years in their annual game against the defending NFL champions, Graham served as athletic director and head football coach for the US Coast Guard Academy for seven seasons, before coaching the Washington Redskins for three years. After being relieved of his duties in Washington, Graham returned to the

Coast Guard Academy, where he spent the next 16 years serving as athletic director, before retiring from football in 1984.

Relocating to Sarasota, Florida, Graham spent most of his time playing golf and tennis, before serious health issues forced him to adopt a more sedentary lifestyle. Diagnosed as being in the early stages of Alzheimer's disease in 2001, Graham died two years later of a heart aneurysm, passing away at the age of 82 on December 17, 2003.

In discussing Graham's impact on the game of football some years earlier, NFL writer Mike Tanier stated, "Modern quarterbacking dates back to what Otto Graham did with those Browns. He was the first guy to take drop-backs and to be throwing to wide receivers who are running pattern combinations to get open."

Meanwhile, Don Shula expressed his admiration for Graham when he said, "Otto certainly has to be one of the best of all time. All you gotta do is look at his accomplishments. I mean, you go and look at Otto's record, and all he ever did was win championships. And how else do you judge a quarterback. Every season that he lined up the Browns were in a championship game. It's hard to pick anybody better."

Paul Brown also had high praise for his longtime signal-caller, stating, "Otto was my greatest player. He had the finest peripheral vision I had ever seen, and that is a big factor in a quarterback. He was a tremendous playmaker. He had unusual eye-and-hand coordination, and he was bigger and faster than you thought."

Brown added, "Otto was really the greatest of all the players. No man ever took a team into the final game of the season as many times as he did. . . . The test of a quarterback is where his team finishes. By that standard, Otto Graham was the best of all time."

CAREER HIGHLIGHTS

Best Season

Graham had several superb seasons for the Browns, performing especially well from 1947 to 1949, and in 1953. Earning NFL MVP honors in the last of those campaigns, Graham led the league with 2,722 yards passing, a 64.7 pass-completion percentage, and a passer rating of 99.7. However, he completed just 11 touchdown passes and threw nine interceptions. Furthermore, the Browns failed to win the NFL championship. On the other hand, Cleveland captured the AAFC title in 1947, 1948, and 1949, with Graham gaining First-Team All-League recognition each year. That being the case, we'll go with 1947, a season in which Graham led the AAFC with 2,753 yards passing, 25 touchdown passes, a pass-completion percentage of 60.6, and a passer rating of 109.2, while also throwing just 11 interceptions.

Memorable Moments/Greatest Performances

Graham threw the first touchdown pass of his career during a 44–0 rout of the Miami Seahawks in the 1946 regular-season opener when he connected with Dante Lavelli from 39 yards out.

Graham led the Browns to a lopsided 51–14 victory over the Chicago Rockets on November 17, 1946, by completing 7 of 16 pass attempts for 131 yards and four touchdowns, hooking up twice each with Dante Lavelli and Mac Speedie.

Graham scored the first points of a 34–0 win over the Miami Seahawks on December 3, 1946, when he returned an interception 37 yards for a touchdown.

Graham led the Browns to a 14–9 win over the New York Yankees in the 1946 AAFC championship game by intercepting a pass on defense and throwing for 213 yards and one touchdown, which came on a 16-yard pass to Dante Lavelli.

Graham directed the Browns to a 14–7 win over the San Francisco 49ers on October 26, 1947, by passing for 293 yards and two touchdowns, the longest of which went 42 yards to Mac Speedie.

Graham followed that up by throwing for 274 yards and three TDs during a 28–7 victory over the Buffalo Bills on November 2, 1947, collaborating with Speedie on a 99-yard scoring play.

Graham led the Browns to a 37–14 win over the 49ers on November 16, 1947, by passing for 301 yards and three touchdowns, all of which went to Dante Lavelli.

Graham made good use of both his arm and his legs during a 28–17 victory over the Chicago Rockets on September 17, 1948, running 12 yards for one touchdown and hooking up with Bob Cowan on scoring plays that covered 39 and 40 yards.

Graham had a huge game against the New York Yankees on October 24, 1948, running 22 yards for one score and throwing for 310 yards and four touchdowns during a 35–7 Browns win, with the longest of his TD passes going 63 yards to Bob Cowan.

Graham threw another four touchdown passes during a 31–28 win over the 49ers on November 28, 1948, with his longest TD pass of the day being a 41-yard connection with Dante Lavelli.

Graham performed brilliantly during the latter stages of a 28–28 tie with the Buffalo Bills in the 1949 regular-season opener, bringing the Browns back from a 28–7 deficit by throwing three fourth-quarter touchdown passes, delivering the last of those in the closing moments. Graham finished the game with 330 yards passing and four TD passes.

Graham led the Browns to a 42–7 rout of the Los Angeles Dons on October 2, 1949, by throwing for 325 yards and four TDs, the longest of which came on a 74-yard hookup with Bill Boedeker.

Graham victimized the Dons again two weeks later, passing for 362 yards and a career-high six touchdowns during a 61–14 Browns win on October 14, 1949, connecting four times with Dante Lavelli and once each with Dub Jones and Mac Speedie.

Graham led the Browns to a 31–0 win over the New York Yankees on November 20, 1949, by throwing for 382 yards and one touchdown, which came on a 23-yard pass to Bill Boedeker.

Although Graham threw two interceptions during a 31–21 win over the Buffalo Bills in the divisional round of the 1949 AAFC playoffs, he also passed for 326 yards and two touchdowns, collaborating with Dante Lavelli and Dub Jones on scoring plays of 51 and 49 yards.

Graham excelled in his first NFL game, running for one score and throwing for 346 yards and three touchdowns during a 35–10 victory over the Philadelphia Eagles in the 1950 regular-season opener that he later called "the highlight of my whole career."

Graham also performed extremely well in the final game of the 1950 regular season, completing 23 of 32 passes for 321 yards and four touchdowns during a 45–21 drubbing of the Redskins.

Graham subsequently led the Browns to a 30–28 win over the Los Angeles Rams in the 1950 NFL championship game by throwing for 298 yards and four touchdowns, hooking up twice with Dante Lavelli and once each with Dub Jones and Rex Bumgardner.

Graham led the Browns to a 49–7 thrashing of the Eagles on October 19, 1952, by passing for 290 yards and four touchdowns, which included a 47-yard strike to Pete Brewster and a 63-yard connection with Dub Jones.

In addition to throwing for 292 yards during a 27–0 win over the Packers in the opening game of the 1953 regular season, Graham scored a pair of touchdowns on short runs.

Graham followed that up by passing for 310 yards and three touchdowns during a 27–7 victory over the Chicago Cardinals on October 4, 1953.

Graham led the Browns to a lopsided 56–10 victory over the Detroit Lions in the 1954 NFL championship game by running for three touchdowns and throwing for three others.

Graham starred again in the 1955 NFL championship game, running for two scores and passing for two others, in leading the Browns to a 38–14 win over the Los Angeles Rams.

Notable Achievements

- Passed for more than 2,500 yards five times.
- Threw more than 20 touchdown passes three times.
- Completed more than 60 percent of passes twice.
- Posted touchdown-to-interception ratio of better than 2–1 twice.
- Posted passer rating above 90.0 five times, finishing with mark above 100.0 twice.
- Led league in passing yards five times, touchdown passes three times, completion percentage four times, and passer rating five times.
- Finished second in league in passing yards twice, touchdown passes three times, and completion percentage three times.
- Holds Browns career record for most touchdown passes (174).
- Ranks among Browns career leaders with 1,464 pass completions (3rd), 23,584 yards passing (2nd), passer rating of 86.6 (6th—minimum 100 attempts), 44 rushing touchdowns (5th), and 46 touchdowns (10th).
- Holds NFL career record for most yards per pass attempt (9.0).
- Ten-time division champion (1946, 1947, 1948, 1949, 1950, 1951, 1952, 1953, 1954, and 1955).
- Four-time AAFC champion (1946, 1947, 1948, and 1949).
- Three-time NFL champion (1950, 1954, and 1955).
- 1955 Hickock Belt Award winner as Professional Athlete of the Year.
- Three-time AAFC MVP (1947, 1948, and 1949).
- Three-time NFL MVP (1951, 1953, and 1955).
- Five-time Pro Bowl selection (1950, 1951, 1952, 1953, and 1954).
- Three-time First-Team All-AAFC selection (1947, 1948, and 1949).
- Four-time First-Team All-Pro selection (1951, 1953, 1954, and 1955).
- 1952 Second-Team All-Pro selection.
- NFL 1950s All-Decade Team.
- Member of NFL's 75th Anniversary Team.

- Named to NFL 100 All-Time Team in 2019.
- Number 7 on the *Sporting News*' 1999 list of the 100 Greatest Players in NFL History.
- Number 16 on the NFL Network's 2010 list of the NFL's 100 Greatest Players.
- #14 retired by Browns.
- Member of Cleveland Browns Ring of Honor.
- Elected to Pro Football Hall of Fame in 1965.

3

JOE THOMAS

Known for his quickness, athleticism, and extraordinary durability, Joe Thomas established himself as the premier left tackle of his era over the course of his 11-year career, which he spent entirely in Cleveland. Starting every game that the Browns played his first 10½ years in the league, Thomas appeared in 167 consecutive contests, amazingly never missing a snap on offense. The only offensive lineman in NFL history to be named to 10 consecutive Pro Bowls, Thomas received numerous individual accolades despite playing for mostly losing teams, also earning eight All-Pro selections and seven First-Team All-AFC nominations. Further honored by being accorded a spot on the NFL 2010s All-Decade Team and being ranked on NFL.com as the seventh greatest offensive tackle of all time and the third greatest player in Browns history, Thomas is likely to gain the additional distinction of being inducted into the Pro Football Hall of Fame the first time his name appears on the ballot in 2023.

Born in the Milwaukee suburb of Brookfield, Wisconsin, on December 4, 1984, Joseph Hayden Thomas acquired his strong sense of responsibility and tremendous work ethic from his father, Eric, a banker who never missed a day in 39 years of work. Claiming that her son's remarkable durability could also be credited to his father, Thomas's mother, Sally, stated, "He does have the constitution of a horse. He was never really sick as a kid. He's got his dad's bones, which are freakishly thick. He's just a healthy kid, and always has been."

A fan of the Green Bay Packers and University of Wisconsin football in his youth, Thomas recalled, "I grew up in the '90s in Wisconsin, so Brett Favre and Reggie White were guys that I loved. And I loved watching Ron Dayne and the run the Badgers had with Brent Moss and Terrell Fletcher and Darrell Bevell and Joe Panos—some of those great names from Rose Bowl teams in the '90s."

After getting his start in football in the local Pop Warner leagues at the age of 12 as a 6'3", 139-pound fullback / outside linebacker, Thomas

Joe Thomas started 167 consecutive games for the Browns at left offensive tackle.
Courtesy of Erik Drost

eventually enrolled at Brookfield Central High School, where he starred in multiple sports, earning All-Conference honors in basketball four straight times, while also finishing first in both the shotput and discus competition at the 2003 Wisconsin track and field championships. However, Thomas experienced his greatest success on the gridiron, excelling on both sides of the ball for the Lancers, with his 85 tackles and 12 sacks as a defensive end his senior year gaining him recognition as the Wisconsin Football Coaches Association Defensive Player of the Year. Also performing extremely well at right tackle on offense, Thomas earned Second-Team All-State honors from the *Milwaukee Journal Sentinel* and Second-Team All-America honors from *USA Today*.

Describing his play at Brookfield Central, Thomas said, "High school players tend to get more recognition when you play on defense. I didn't really know much about offense at the time, didn't know a lot about the technique. I was just over there because I was a good player and could play both ways, but I definitely enjoyed defense more, and I thought I was better at it."

Recruited by several major colleges, including Nebraska, Colorado, and Notre Dame, Thomas recalled, "I never really expected to get a scholarship. And then, the college coaches started calling. That's when I realized, 'Hey, maybe I'm good enough to get a scholarship.' I never looked too far ahead. I always tried to enjoy the moment and do as well as I could where I was. I feel like I was always the last to know that I was pretty decent in football."

Ultimately choosing to remain close to home and attend the University of Wisconsin, Thomas, in the process, chose a football career on offense, rather than defense, later saying, "Some other schools recruited me as a defensive lineman. Wisconsin was very clear from the beginning that they thought being an offensive tackle was the best long-term position for me."

After serving the Badgers primarily as a blocking tight end his freshman year, Thomas moved to left tackle, where he started every contest in each of the next three seasons despite tearing his anterior cruciate ligament in the final game of his junior year. Recalling how hard he worked after the injury to get ready for the ensuing campaign, Thomas said, "It really motivated me to rehab as hard as I could and put everything into it knowing that potentially, if I didn't, it might be the end of my career, and I might never be the same player again."

Fully healthy by the start of his senior year, Thomas had the finest season of his college career, helping to lead the Badgers to a 12-1 record and a number seven ranking in the final AP poll with his exceptional play up front. In addition to earning First-Team All-America honors and his second straight All–Big Ten Conference selection, Thomas won the Outland Trophy, presented annually to college football's best interior lineman. In summarizing Thomas's play at Wisconsin, former Badgers head coach Barry Alvarez stated, "He is the best lineman to ever come through here. Everything came easy to him. He was such a good athlete. His hand placement. His feet. He was always right on."

Subsequently selected by the Browns with the third overall pick of the 2007 NFL Draft, Thomas revealed that he learned of his selection while fishing on Lake Michigan, saying, "I didn't want to involve myself in all the craziness that goes on [with the draft]. I knew it was going to be an exciting enough time where I didn't need to go to New York."

Installed at left tackle immediately upon his arrival in Cleveland, Thomas ended up making huge contributions to a Browns team that compiled a record of 10-6 in 2007 by allowing just one sack and helping Jamal Lewis rush for 1,304 yards and nine touchdowns, earning in the process the first of his 10 straight Pro Bowl selections, a spot on the NFL All-Rookie Team, and a runner-up finish to Adrian Peterson in the NFL Offensive Rookie of the Year voting. Thomas followed that up with another outstanding season, earning Second-Team All-Pro honors in 2008, before being named to the First Team for the first of six times the following year.

In discussing the evolution of his play at the end of the 2009 season, Thomas said, "I was pleased with the way I played. I felt like I grew as a player from the year before, which is always my goal. I think this was my best season. I improved in a lot of areas that needed improvement, and I stayed good and even improved in the areas I thought I was already solid. . . . I understand the game a lot better. I understand the offense, and I understand defenses. Coming in, you're so concerned about learning your job and the things you need to do to be successful individually. Once that's good, you can start to focus on learning about the guys around you and learning defenses and what they're trying to do to you."

After earning First-Team All-Pro honors once again in 2010, Thomas signed a seven-year contract extension with the Browns worth $84 million that promised to keep him in Cleveland through 2017. Praising Thomas after he inked his long-term deal with the team, Browns head coach Pat Shurmur stated, "Joe is a steady guy, which you need from an offensive lineman. He's a guy that comes out here everyday and works. Every once in a while, he can be vocal, although I wouldn't say that it's his nature to exert himself verbally. There's time within a practice or within a day when something needs to get said, and he'll step right to the front and say it. I have a great appreciation for what he is as a player and a man."

Gradually emerging as the league's foremost player at his position even though he employed a somewhat unorthodox style at the line of scrimmage that saw him utilize a "shotput" technique to break out of his stance, the 6'6", 312-pound Thomas made good use of his 32½-inch arms, with Baltimore Ravens (and future Browns) linebacker Paul Kruger saying, "With his long arms, you've got to defend yourself earlier because he's going to be able to touch you a lot sooner than other guys would."

Fellow Ravens linebacker Terrell Suggs added, "One thing about going against Joe is he's very deceptive. He's more athletic than he looks. . . . He's one of the best tackles in the league. He always gives me trouble. He's a phenomenal player."

Meanwhile, former Browns head coach Mike Pettine spoke of Thomas's remarkable consistency and dedication to his profession, saying, "He's just so consistent. He works just as hard in practice as he does in the game, and it shows up. I always talk about, 'It's you against the grade sheet.' He's well into the 90s every single game."

Continuing to perform at an elite level from 2011 to 2016, Thomas earned six more Pro Bowl selections and five more All-Pro nominations, prompting former offensive lineman and ESPN football analyst Damien Woody to say, "From Day One, he stepped in and has been one of the top left tackles, and I'd say that right now, he's the top left tackle in the game."

Yet, despite Thomas's individual brilliance, the Browns failed to post a winning record in any of his final 10 seasons, causing many to wonder why he never requested a trade. In explaining his loyalty to the organization, Thomas identified his love of Cleveland and its fans as the primary reason, once saying, "It's a blue-collar city, and for a blue-collar guy like myself, it's easy to fall in love with the people and kind of the chip on the shoulder that a lot of people have because they feel like they've been slighted for so long. It's so important for me to be here for the turnaround. I don't want to just get a Super Bowl ring by being traded to a dream team. It would feel unsatisfying. Unfulfilling."

After manning his familiar position of left tackle for the first seven games of the 2017 season, Thomas saw his string of 167 consecutive starts come to an end when he tore the triceps tendon in his left arm during a 12–9 overtime loss to the Tennessee Titans in Week 7. Subsequently forced to undergo season-ending surgery, Thomas chose to announce his retirement following the conclusion of the campaign, ending his career having taken the field for 10,363 consecutive snaps on offense and allowed just 30 sacks on 6,680 blocking attempts.

Making his decision known to the public on March 14, 2018, Thomas said at the time, "This was an extremely difficult decision, but the right one for me and my family. Playing in the NFL has taken a toll on my body, and I can no longer physically compete at the level I need to. . . . As a competitor, you always think that you can still do it, but there's a point in your career that you get to that crossroads, and you say, 'I just can't do it anymore. I just don't have it in my body.' My mind is good, but my body is not willing, and I think that's where I am."

Thomas continued, "As your body fills up with inflammation, your muscles shut down, it's a protection mechanism that your body has.

Specifically, in my knee, which is the main reason I feel like I had to retire. For me, looking down the barrel of a knee replacement, I think that definitely becomes a decision where you're like, 'Hey, this football has been amazing, it's been more than I could ever have expected.' But you have to take other things into consideration if you're deciding if you're going to be able to play football anymore. . . . The last two to three years of my career, it's been almost impossible for me to practice. I would be the first guy in the building and the last guy to leave because it took me all day, literally, to get my body somewhat ready to be able to play on Sundays, and that's only tenable for so long. . . . As much as I want to play and be a part of this new regime in Cleveland and the exciting things that are happening with the Browns, my body has just said no, and I just don't have it anymore."

Thomas then added, "From the moment I was drafted, the city embraced me in a way that I could never fully describe. I am proud to call Cleveland home. The loyalty and passion of the fans is unmatched, and it was an honor to play in front of them for the past 11 years. I would like to thank all of the coaches, teammates, staff, fans, and everyone who has shown me support throughout my career. Even though I will be hanging up my cleats, I will always be a Cleveland Brown."

Expressing their appreciation to Thomas for everything he brought to the organization, Browns owners Dee and Jimmy Haslam issued a statement that read: "Joe has been a pillar of our organization and one of the greatest to put on a Cleveland Browns uniform. We want to thank him for everything he has done for the Browns and the Northeast Ohio community. We should all strive for the standard Joe has set to always be available, put the team above yourself, and always give maximum effort."

Browns head coach Hue Jackson also thanked Thomas for his contributions to the team, saying, "Joe means so much to me both personally and professionally. Joe has been not just a tremendous Cleveland Brown, but one of the best ever to play in the National Football League. I appreciate everything he had done for this organization, and not just on the field, but his leadership and what he brought to the locker room. As a coach, you couldn't ask for a better captain than Joe Thomas. He earned the respect of teammates and peers around the league for the way he worked."

Pro Football Focus also had high praise for Thomas when it named him to its 2010s All-Decade Team two years later, calling him, "Unquestionably, one of the best players in NFL history," and adding, "He was the gold standard for pass protection from the moment he entered the NFL."

Since retiring from football, Thomas, who has lost more than 50 pounds through a ketogenic diet, intermittent fasting, and swimming, has been an analyst for the NFL Network, appearing on that station's pregame and postgame *Thursday Night Football* shows. He also co-hosts with former Browns wide receiver Andrew Hawkins a podcast called "The ThomaHawk Show."

CAREER HIGHLIGHTS

Best Season

Thomas earned All-Pro honors eight straight times from 2008 to 2015, gaining First-Team All-Pro recognition on six separate occasions. While Thomas performed brilliantly in each of those seasons, the 2015 campaign stands out above all others since, at the end of the year, he received from Pro Football Focus the Bruce Matthews Award for being the league's best overall offensive lineman and the Anthony Munoz Award for being the league's best pass protector.

Memorable Moments/Greatest Performances

Thomas anchored an offensive line that enabled the Browns to amass 554 yards of total offense during a 51–45 win over the Cincinnati Bengals on September 16, 2007.

Thomas's strong play up front helped the Browns amass 475 yards of total offense during a 20–17 victory over the Oakland Raiders on December 2, 2012, with 353 of those yards coming through the air.

Thomas performed magnificently during a 31–27 win over the Vikings on September 22, 2013, contributing to a Browns offense that threw for 306 yards and amassed a total of 409 yards by pitching a shutout against perennial Pro Bowl defensive end Jared Allen, who finished the game with no sacks and no tackles.

Thomas helped the Browns amass 460 yards of total offense during a 29–28 win over the Tennessee Titans on October 5, 2014, with 176 of those yards coming on the ground and the other 284 through the air.

Thomas's superior blocking at the point of attack helped the Browns gain 313 yards through the air and amass 475 yards of total offense during a 26–24 win over Atlanta on November 23, 2014.

Thomas and his line-mates dominated the opposition once again on October 11, 2015, with the Browns amassing 505 yards of total offense during a 33–30 overtime victory over the Ravens.

Notable Achievements

- Started 167 consecutive games, playing every snap on offense during that time.
- Member of 2007 NFL All-Rookie Team.
- Finished second in 2007 NFL Offensive Rookie of the Year voting.
- 2015 Pro Football Focus Bruce Matthews Award winner as NFL's best offensive lineman.
- 2015 Pro Football Focus Anthony Munoz Award winner as NFL's best pass protector.
- Ten-time Pro Bowl selection (2007, 2008, 2009, 2010, 2011, 2012, 2013, 2014, 2015, and 2016).
- Six-time First-Team All-Pro selection (2009, 2010, 2011, 2013, 2014, and 2015).
- Two-time Second-Team All-Pro selection (2008 and 2012).
- Seven-time First-Team All-AFC selection (2009, 2010, 2011, 2013, 2014, 2015, and 2016).
- NFL 2010s All-Decade Team.
- Member of Cleveland Browns Ring of Honor.

4

LEROY KELLY

Following a legend is never easy. However, Leroy Kelly did better than anyone could possibly have anticipated when he replaced Jim Brown as the primary running back in Cleveland after the latter unexpectedly announced his retirement prior to the start of the 1966 campaign. Establishing himself as one of the NFL's premier offensive weapons over the course of the next several seasons, Kelly won two rushing titles, amassed more than 1,000 yards from scrimmage six times, and scored at least 10 touchdowns five times, earning in the process six Pro Bowl selections and four All-Pro nominations. A member of teams that won six division titles and one league championship, Kelly ranks among the franchise's all-time leaders in several offensive categories, trailing only Brown in yards rushing, yards from scrimmage, rushing touchdowns, and touchdowns scored, with his brilliant all-around play earning him a spot on the NFL 1960s All-Decade Team and a place in the Pro Football Hall of Fame.

Born in Philadelphia, Pennsylvania, on May 20, 1942, Leroy Kelly, whose younger brother, Pat, went on to play 15 seasons in the major leagues as an outfielder for five different teams, starred in multiple sports at Simon Gratz High School, lettering in football, baseball, and basketball. Particularly outstanding on the gridiron, Kelly displayed his tremendous versatility by playing quarterback on offense and linebacker on defense, while also punting, kicking, and returning kickoffs. Commenting on the varied skill set of his team's best player, head coach Louis DeVicaris once said, "Leroy was the best football player I'd ever seen. Besides being a great runner and a leader, he also was the most vicious tackler on the squad."

Recruited by only a handful of colleges since he had studied mechanics in high school and, therefore, had not taken a college preparatory class, Kelly accepted a half scholarship for football from Morgan State University, a historically black school located in Baltimore, Maryland, that also offered him a part-time job. Moved to running back by head coach Earl Banks following his arrival at Morgan State, Kelly went on to star at that post for

Leroy Kelly rushed for more yards, amassed more yards from scrimmage, and scored more touchdowns than anyone else in franchise history, with the exception of Jim Brown.

the Bears, with the help of Baltimore Colts halfback George Taliaferro, who Kelly claimed offered him the following piece of advice after watching him practice one day: "He told me to keep my eyes open after getting through the line and always to watch for that avenue of escape. George showed me how to run under control, and then to have that burst of energy when the opening appears."

Heeding Taliaferro's advice, Kelly led Morgan State to the Central Intercollegiate Athletic Association championship as a junior, before earning MVP honors of the Orange Blossom Classic game his senior year. Praising Kelly for his exceptional all-around play, Coach Banks stated, "Leroy is one of the finest backs I've ever coached. He has everything it takes."

Weighing only 188 pounds as the 1964 NFL Draft approached, the 6-foot Kelly found himself being projected by many pro scouts as a defensive back. However, with the Colts having plenty of depth in their offensive backfield, Baltimore scout Buddy Young, who had watched Kelly perform at numerous Morgan State practices, used his connections with the Browns to persuade Blanton Collier to draft him as a running back, telling the head coach, "This guy is smaller than Jim Brown. But Kelly has many of the same moves. He's got speed, can cut, and never gives you a full piece of himself. He also keeps those feet close to the ground."

Subsequently selected by the Browns in the eighth round, with the 110th overall pick, Kelly arrived in Cleveland with little chance of making the team solely as a running back, with Jim Brown and Ernie Green firmly entrenched as the starters. However, Kelly made an extremely favorable impression on the coaching staff during training camp with his hustle and ferocious play on special teams, prompting Collier to say when he awarded him a roster spot, "He immediately showed me that he was a very tough tackler. I knew that he would be a good man for the specialty teams."

Seeing very little action at running back his first two seasons, Kelly carried the ball just 43 times for 151 yards and no touchdowns, while also making only nine receptions for 122 yards. But, just as Collier predicted, Kelly proved to be an exceptional performer on special teams, amassing a total of 1,639 yards returning kickoffs and punts, scoring three times on punt returns, and making several outstanding tackles in coverage.

Kelly's role on offense changed dramatically in 1966 after Jim Brown shocked everyone by announcing his retirement just prior to the start of training camp. With Ernie Green sliding over from halfback to fullback, Kelly, who had increased his playing weight to 202 pounds, laid claim to the starting halfback job. Faced with the unenviable task of trying to replace the greatest running back the game had ever seen, Kelly received words of encouragement from Blanton Collier, who said, "I don't expect anyone to replace Jim. Runners like him come along only once in a lifetime. I do expect someone from this squad to make a name for himself, and Leroy is going to get the chance."

Making the most of his opportunity, Kelly began an extraordinary three-year run during which he posted the following numbers:

YEAR	YDS RUSHING	YDS FROM SCRIMMAGE	ALL-PURPOSE YDS	TDS
1966	1,141	1,507	2,014	**16**
1967	**1,205**	**1,487**	1,677	13
1968	**1,239**	**1,536**	1,556	**20**

Establishing himself as arguably the finest all-around back in the game, Kelly finished either first or second in the league in all four categories each year and topped the circuit in yards per carry twice as well, with his exceptional play earning him Pro Bowl and First-Team All-Pro honors each season. Named the winner of the Bert Bell Award as NFL Player of the Year in 1968, Kelly also led the Browns to the division title in each of the last two seasons.

Asked to compare Kelly to Brown at one point, Blanton Collier said, "It's impossible to compare them. Jim played at 222 to 228 and was a fullback type of power runner. Leroy is 200 pounds and a halfback type of runner. Leroy did a lot of things Jim was never asked to do. He played on our special teams. He is a fine team man—good tackler, blocker and pass receiver."

Collier added, "Jim Brown used to say that anyone could run outside, but it took a great one to run inside. Kelly can do that because he has good speed, balance and is quick to sense interior openings and get through."

In explaining how he dealt with the pressure of trying to perform at a level that would not cause the fans of Cleveland to yearn for the return of Brown, Kelly said, "I didn't think about trying to replace Jim Brown. When I was sitting on the bench two years, I used to compare myself to the backs that were starting around the league, and I knew I was as good as most of them. I just wanted to be one of the best backs in the league, not a superman like Jim Brown was."

Kelly continued, "I'm just glad he quit when he did. If he had played a few more years—and he certainly could have done that—I might never have had the chance I had. All I ever wanted to do was to be Leroy Kelly and do the best job I possibly could."

Kelly added, "Jim was the best ever, but I really didn't feel a lot of pressure when I replaced him. We were different kinds of runners. I just tried to be me. . . . When Jim retired, the excellent offensive line was still there. With Gene Hickerson and Schaf [Dick Schafrath], John Wooten, Monte Clark, and John Morrow, they made it very easy for me."

Blessed with good speed, outstanding strength, and tremendous balance, Kelly excelled at breaking tackles, usually making it necessary for more than one man to bring him down. And, as his three punt returns for touchdowns indicate, Kelly possessed the quickness and elusiveness to go the distance once he broke into the open field. Kelly also did an outstanding job of catching the ball out of the backfield and proved to be one of the league's most durable players, missing just four games his entire career, later saying, "A lot of that is just plain luck. Tacklers didn't get in many good shots on me because I was pretty shifty. I wasn't a sprinter, but I was deceptively fast, and I was pretty strong."

Kelly also knew when to employ discretion, saying, "I see runners fight long after it's obvious that they aren't going to get away even for a couple of yards. There is a time to give that second effort and a time to go down. I guess it's instinct as much as anything."

Although Kelly grew a step slower and began to wear down somewhat from all the punishment he took the previous few years, he continued to perform well in 1969, earning the fourth of his six consecutive Pro Bowl selections by rushing for 817 yards, amassing 1,084 yards from scrimmage, and ranking among the league leaders with nine rushing touchdowns and 10 TDs. Remaining a key contributor to the Browns on offense the next three seasons, Kelly gained more than 800 yards on the ground and surpassed 1,000 yards from scrimmage twice each, while also scoring a total of 25 touchdowns. Hampered by knee problems in 1973, Kelly rushed for only 389 yards and amassed just 569 yards from scrimmage, prompting the Browns to place him on waivers during the following offseason. After being picked up and cut by the Oakland Raiders, Kelly signed with the Chicago Fire of the World Football League, with whom he spent one season, before retiring when the league folded at the end of the year. Ending his career with 7,274 yards rushing, 190 receptions, 2,281 receiving yards, 9,555 yards from scrimmage, 12,330 all-purpose yards, 74 rushing touchdowns, and 90 total TDs, Kelly ranked fourth all-time in rushing yards and third all-time in rushing touchdowns at the time of his retirement.

Following his playing days, Kelly invested in a nightclub and a few Burger King franchises that eventually went out of business. He also spent a considerable amount of time traveling across the country, supplementing the $162 per month he receives from his NFL pension by making appearances at country clubs, golf tournaments, and card shows. In addressing the additional income that he earns from his personal appearances, Kelly, who is 80 years old as of this writing, said in 2008, "They give the Hall of Famers a few dollars. It's a hustle for us, really."

CAREER HIGHLIGHTS

Best Season

Kelly performed magnificently for the Browns from 1966 to 1968, earning three consecutive First-Team All-Pro nominations by rushing for more than 1,000 yards, amassing more than 1,500 all-purpose yards, and scoring more than 10 touchdowns each season. Although Kelly accumulated a career-high 2,014 all-purpose yards in the first of those campaigns, the 1968 season would have to be considered his finest, since he earned NFL Player of the Year honors by leading the league in five different offensive categories, topping the circuit with 1,239 yards rushing, 1,536 yards from scrimmage, 16 rushing touchdowns, 20 touchdowns, and 120 points scored.

Memorable Moments/Greatest Performances

Kelly scored the first touchdown of his career on a 68-yard punt return during a 42–20 win over the Giants on October 25, 1964.

Kelly scored again on special teams when he returned a punt 67 yards for a touchdown during a 24–17 victory over the Dallas Cowboys on November 21, 1965.

Kelly contributed to a 42–21 win over the Steelers the very next week by returning a punt 56 yards for a touchdown.

Kelly starred in defeat on September 25, 1966, rushing for 109 yards and scoring three touchdowns during a 34–28 loss to the St. Louis Cardinals, with the longest of his TDs coming on a 57-yard run.

Kelly earned NFL Offensive Player of the Week honors for the first of five times by rushing for 138 yards and one touchdown during a 28–7 win over the Giants on October 2, 1966.

Kelly helped lead the Browns to a 49–17 rout of the Falcons on October 30, 1966, by rushing for 98 yards and scoring two touchdowns, one of which came on a career-long 70-yard run.

Kelly led the Browns to a 49–40 win over the Giants on December 4, 1966, by gaining 125 yards on only 13 carries, making four receptions for 71 yards, and scoring three TDs, all of which came on short runs.

Kelly provided most of the offensive punch during a 14–10 win over the Vikings on November 19, 1967, rushing for 123 yards and scoring both Cleveland touchdowns on short runs.

Kelly earned NFL Offensive Player of the Week honors by amassing 207 yards from scrimmage and scoring two touchdowns during a 42–37 win over the Washington Redskins on November 26, 1967, gaining 163 yards on the ground and another 44 yards on two pass receptions.

Kelly helped the Browns hand the Baltimore Colts their only loss of the 1968 regular season by rushing for 130 yards and two touchdowns during a 30–20 win on October 20, 1968.

Kelly contributed to a 33–21 victory over the San Francisco 49ers on November 3, 1968, by rushing for a career-high 174 yards and one touchdown.

Kelly followed that up by amassing 231 yards from scrimmage and scoring three touchdowns during a 35–17 win over the Saints, gaining 127 yards on the ground and 104 yards on three pass receptions, one of which went for a 68-yard TD.

Kelly displayed his versatility during a 47–13 rout of the Eagles on November 24, 1968, running for 108 yards and two touchdowns, while also throwing a 34-yard TD pass to Paul Warfield.

Although Kelly gained just 56 yards on 16 carries during a 45–10 win over the Giants on December 1, 1968, he earned NFL Offensive Player of the Week honors by scoring a career-high four touchdowns.

Kelly made a huge play against Dallas in the divisional round of the 1968 playoffs, when he gathered in a 45-yard touchdown pass from Bill Nelsen late in the first half that tied the score at 10–10 and completely shifted the momentum of the contest. The Browns went on to post a 31–20 victory, with Kelly scoring again in the third quarter on a 35-yard run.

Kelly proved to be too much for the Giants to handle on November 23, 1969, carrying the ball 18 times for 124 yards and three touchdowns during a 28–17 Browns win, earning in the process NFL Offensive Player of the Week honors for the fifth and final time.

Kelly contributed to a 20–7 victory over the Packers on December 7, 1969, by gaining 151 yards on 22 carries.

Kelly went over 100 yards rushing for the last time in his career during a 26–24 win over the Steelers on November 19, 1972, finishing the game with 21 carries for 107 yards.

Notable Achievements

- Rushed for more than 1,000 yards three times.
- Amassed more than 1,000 yards from scrimmage six times, topping 1,500 yards twice.
- Surpassed 1,500 all-purpose yards three times, topping 2,000 yards once.

- Scored at least 10 touchdowns five times, scoring 20 TDs once.
- Scored more than 100 points once (120 in 1968).
- Averaged more than 5 yards per carry three times.
- Returned three punts for touchdowns.
- Led NFL in rushing attempts twice, yards rushing twice, yards from scrimmage twice, rushing touchdowns three times, touchdowns twice, points scored once, and rushing average twice.
- Finished second in NFL in yards rushing once, yards from scrimmage once, punt-return yards once, all-purpose yards three times, rushing touchdowns twice, touchdowns twice, rushing average once, and punt-return average once.
- Led Browns in rushing seven times.
- Ranks among Browns career leaders with 7,274 yards rushing (2nd), 9,555 yards from scrimmage (2nd), 990 punt-return yards (5th), 1,784 kickoff-return yards (7th), 12,330 all-purpose yards (3rd), 74 rushing touchdowns (2nd), 90 touchdowns (2nd), and 540 points scored (6th).
- Six-time division champion (1964, 1965, 1967, 1968, 1969, and 1971).
- 1964 NFL champion.
- Five-time NFL Offensive Player of the Week.
- 1968 Bert Bell Award winner as NFL Player of the Year.
- Six-time Pro Bowl selection (1966, 1967, 1968, 1969, 1970, and 1971).
- Three-time First-Team All-Pro selection (1966, 1967, and 1968).
- 1969 Second-Team All-Pro selection.
- Three-time First-Team All–Eastern Conference selection (1966, 1967, and 1968).
- 1969 Second-Team All–Eastern Conference selection.
- 1971 Second-Team All-AFC selection.
- NFL 1960s All-Decade Team.
- Member of Cleveland Browns Ring of Honor.
- Elected to Pro Football Hall of Fame in 1994.

5

OZZIE NEWSOME

One of the most prolific pass-receiving tight ends in NFL history, Ozzie Newsome spent 13 seasons in Cleveland, recording more receptions and amassing more receiving yards during that time than any other player in team annals. Making good use of his size, speed, and soft hands, Newsome helped to redefine his position, with his success as a downfield receiver leading to the tight end assuming a more prominent role on offense. Extremely durable as well, Newsome never missed a game due to injury, appearing in a franchise-record 198 consecutive non-strike contests, with his exceptional play and outstanding leadership making him a key contributor to Browns teams that won five division titles. A three-time Pro Bowler and five-time All-Pro, Newsome later received the additional honors of being included on the NFL Network's 2010 list of the 100 Greatest Players in NFL History and gaining induction into the Pro Football Hall of Fame. And following his playing days, Newsome embarked on an equally successful career as an NFL front office executive.

Born in Muscle Shoals, Alabama, on March 16, 1956, Ozzie Newsome Jr. grew up in the South at a time when African Americans throughout the region experienced overt racism in every aspect of their lives. Nevertheless, with attacks against people of color occurring all around him, Newsome asked his parents for permission to take a bus to an elementary school attended mostly by white students. In explaining the reason behind his request years later, Newsome said, "I knew I was going to have to compete with them [white students] academically and athletically eventually, so I wanted to start."

Although Newsome subsequently experienced a considerable amount of racism from classmates and townspeople, he refused to be deterred from pursuing his ultimate goal of making a better life for himself, stating, "I couldn't fight every day. I had to learn to bite my tongue. My parents had it much worse than I did. I was seeing progress."

Ozzie Newsome holds franchise records for most receptions and most receiving yards.
Courtesy of MearsonlineAuctions.com

Eventually emerging as a standout athlete at Colbert County High School in nearby Leighton, Newsome starred in football, basketball, and baseball, earning All-State honors in the first two sports, while also gaining All-America recognition on the gridiron his senior year for his outstanding play at wide receiver. Pursued aggressively by the University of Alabama and Auburn University as graduation neared, Newsome initially considered accepting a football scholarship to Auburn since his high school quarterback had chosen to enroll there when he graduated one year earlier. In the end, though, the prospect of playing for Paul "Bear" Bryant and winning championships as a member of the Crimson Tide convinced him to accept Alabama's offer instead.

Proving that he made the right decision, Newsome went on to start 48 consecutive games at wide receiver for the Crimson Tide, leading them to an overall record of 42-6 and three SEC championships by making a total of 102 receptions for 2,070 yards and 16 touchdowns. In addition to earning All-SEC honors twice, Newsome gained All-America recognition his senior year, when, as team captain, he caught 36 passes, amassed 804 receiving yards, and scored four touchdowns. Yet, Newsome received perhaps his most cherished honor from Bear Bryant, who called him "the greatest end in Alabama history, and that includes Don Hutson." Bryant added, "He is a total team player, fine blocker, outstanding leader, and a great receiver with concentration, speed, and hands."

Meanwhile, Newsome claimed that the life lessons he learned from Bryant helped to make him a better person, saying years later, "He gave me the principles that shaped the rest of my life."

Subsequently selected by the Browns in the first round of the 1978 NFL Draft, with the 23rd overall pick, Newsome moved to tight end as soon as he arrived in Cleveland at the behest of head coach Sam Rutigliano. After adding 20 pounds onto his 6'2" frame, Newsome ended up making a huge impact in his first year as a pro, earning a spot on the NFL All-Rookie Team and Browns Offensive Player of the Year honors by making 38 receptions for 589 yards and two touchdowns, while also carrying the ball 13 times for 96 yards and two TDs. Continuing his outstanding play the next two seasons, Newsome earned First-Team All-AFC and Second-Team All-Pro honors in 1979 by catching 55 passes, amassing 781 receiving yards, and scoring nine touchdowns, before gaining unofficial Second-Team All-Pro recognition from the Newspaper Enterprise Association (NEA) the following year by making 51 receptions for 594 yards and three touchdowns.

Establishing himself as an elite offensive weapon in 1981, Newsome earned Pro Bowl and Second-Team All-Pro honors by leading the Browns with 69 receptions, 1,002 receiving yards, and six TD catches, setting in the process a new single-season franchise record for most pass receptions. After catching another 49 passes and amassing 633 receiving yards during the strike-shortened 1982 campaign, Newsome surpassed his own single-season mark in each of the next two seasons, making 89 receptions in both 1983 and 1984, while totaling 1,971 receiving yards and 11 TD catches.

One of the first tight ends to stretch the field vertically, the 6'2", 235-pound Newsome proved to be a matchup nightmare for opposing defenses. Too fast and nimble for linebackers to guard, and too big and strong for defensive backs to cover, Newsome created a mismatch every time he headed downfield. Add to that his tremendous hands, and Newsome gave the Browns a unique offensive weapon few teams could match.

In discussing the qualities that made Newsome so special, former Cincinnati Bengals Pro Bowl tight end Bob Trumpy said, "He was sensational getting off the line of scrimmage, he was very good in contact down the field, he had good enough speed to beat some safeties, and he had wide receiver hands. . . . He was built like a '70s power forward in basketball, he had a big, long stride, and he was a terrific, terrific receiver down the field."

Trumpy added, "It used to be that the tight end was a number two receiver in the progression . . . you know, flanker one, tight end two. Ozzie made it, tight end one, flanker two. He changed it that much. . . . Back then, nobody wanted to cover Ozzie Newsome. He was beating them to death."

Denver Broncos head coach Dan Reeves also had high praise for Newsome, stating, "He was outstanding. I don't know that there was a better tight end."

Meanwhile, former Browns teammate Bob Golic said, "Hands. The way he ran, the way he got open. There really wasn't too much he couldn't do. That's why they called him 'The Wizard.'"

Perhaps Newsome's only weakness was that he never developed into anything more than a slightly below average blocker. However, with the Browns using him much more as a receiver, that didn't seem to matter much. And, with Newsome, who once said, "I don't like dropping anything. I haven't played this game as long as I have, as well as I have, dropping footballs . . . I guess I'm a perfectionist," focusing mostly on developing his pass-receiving skills, it would be difficult to fault him too much for his shortcomings as a blocker.

Newsome earned Pro Bowl and All-Pro honors for the final time in 1985 by making 62 receptions for 711 yards and five touchdowns, before experiencing a precipitous decline in offensive production the following year, when, plagued by injuries, he caught just 39 passes, amassed only 417 receiving yards, and scored just three touchdowns. Nevertheless, the determination that the injured Newsome displayed by starting all 16 games for the Browns earned him the admiration of his teammates, who voted him the winner of the Ed Block Courage Award, presented annually to the player from each team who serves as a role model of inspiration, sportsmanship, and courage.

Although Newsome's numbers continued to decline in subsequent seasons, his leadership proved to be invaluable to Browns teams that won three division titles and made three AFC Championship Game appearances from 1986 to 1989. But, after making just 23 receptions for 240 yards and two touchdowns in 1990, Newsome announced his retirement, ending his career with 662 receptions, 7,980 receiving yards, 8,115 yards from scrimmage, 8,144 all-purpose yards, 47 touchdown receptions, and 49 total TDs, all of which continue to place him among the Browns' all-time leaders. At the time of his retirement, Newsome also ranked fourth in NFL history in pass receptions, with his 662 catches placing him first among tight ends.

Remaining close to the game after retiring as an active player, Newsome, who spent his offseasons working as an on-campus recruiter in the personnel department of East Ohio Gas Company, scouted for the Browns for a few years, before taking a job in their personnel department. Eventually rising to the position of director of pro personnel under then head coach Bill Belichick, Newsome continued to serve in that capacity until 1995, when owner Art Modell moved the Browns to Baltimore and renamed them "The Ravens." Following the organization to Baltimore, Newsome became the team's first general manager, making him the first African American to occupy that position in the NFL. Faring extremely well under Newsome's leadership the next 23 years, the Ravens made 11 playoff appearances and won five division titles and two Super Bowls. Although Newsome decided to surrender his post following the conclusion of the 2018 campaign, he remains part of the organization as its executive vice president.

In summing up the career of Newsome, who gained induction into the Pro Football Hall of Fame in 1999, former NFL general manager Bill Polian said, "I would make the argument that, if he wasn't in the Hall of Fame as a player, he would be in as a general manager. That's maybe the rarest of occurrences."

CAREER HIGHLIGHTS

Best Season

Newsome performed extremely well for the Browns in 1981 and 1983, concluding the first of those campaigns with 69 receptions, 1,002 receiving yards, and six touchdowns, before setting a single-season franchise record that still stands two years later by making 89 receptions, while also amassing 970 receiving yards and scoring six touchdowns, with his outstanding play those two seasons earning him a pair of Second-Team All-Pro nominations. But Newsome earned First-Team All-Pro honors for the only time in his career in 1984 by finishing second in the NFL with 89 receptions for the second consecutive year, amassing 1,001 receiving yards, and making five TD catches.

Memorable Moments/Greatest Performances

Newsome scored the first touchdown of his career in his first game as a pro when he ran 33 yards to pay dirt after taking a handoff during a 24–7 win over the 49ers in the 1978 regular-season opener.

Newsome went over 100 receiving yards for the first time in his career on November 5, 1978, making four receptions for 124 yards during a 14–10 loss to the Houston Oilers.

Although Newsome made just three receptions during a 13–10 win over the Colts on September 16, 1979, one of them resulted in a career-long 74-yard gain.

Newsome helped lead the Browns to a 28–27 win over Cincinnati on October 21, 1979, by making five receptions for 90 yards and one touchdown, which came on a 27-yard fourth-quarter connection with Brian Sipe that provided the margin of victory.

Newsome gave the Browns a 27–26 win over the Steelers on October 26, 1980, when he gathered in an 18-yard touchdown pass from Brian Sipe late in the final period.

Newsome starred in defeat on September 19, 1982, catching eight passes for 122 yards and two touchdowns during a 24–21 loss to the Eagles, with his TDs coming on hookups of 19 and 34 yards with Sipe.

Newsome helped lead the Browns to a 41–23 victory over the Colts on November 27, 1983, by making eight receptions for 108 yards and one touchdown, which came on a 66-yard connection with Brian Sipe that represented the second-longest reception of his career.

Although the Browns lost to the Jets by a score of 24–20 on October 14, 1984, Newsome earned AFC Offensive Player of the Week honors by establishing career-high marks with 14 receptions and 191 receiving yards.

Newsome helped lead the Browns to a 27–10 win over the Oilers on November 25, 1984, by making 10 receptions for 102 yards and one touchdown, which came on a 12-yard pass from Paul McDonald.

Newsome contributed to the Browns' 23–20 overtime win over the Jets in the divisional round of the 1986 playoffs by gaining 114 yards on six pass receptions.

Notable Achievements

- Appeared in franchise-record 198 consecutive non-strike games over the course of 13 seasons.
- Surpassed 50 receptions six times, topping 80 catches twice.
- Surpassed 1,000 receiving yards twice.
- Made nine touchdown receptions in 1979.
- Finished second in NFL in receptions twice.
- Led Browns in receptions and receiving yards five times each.
- Holds Browns single-season record for most receptions (89 in 1983 and 1984).
- Holds Browns career records for most receptions (662) and receiving yards (7,980).
- Ranks among Browns career leaders with 8,115 yards from scrimmage (5th), 8,144 all-purpose yards (7th), 47 touchdown receptions (5th), and 49 touchdowns (9th).
- Five-time division champion (1980, 1985, 1986, 1987, and 1989).
- Member of 1978 NFL All-Rookie Team.
- 1978 Browns Offensive Player of the Year.
- 1984 Week 7 AFC Offensive Player of the Week.
- 1986 Ed Block Courage Award winner.
- Three-time Pro Bowl selection (1981, 1984, and 1985).
- 1984 First-Team All-Pro selection.
- Four-time Second-Team All-Pro selection (1979, 1981, 1983, and 1985).
- Two-time First-Team All-AFC selection (1979 and 1984).
- Pro Football Reference All-1980s Second Team.
- NFL 1980s All-Decade Second Team.
- Number 73 on the NFL Network's 2010 list of the NFL's 100 Greatest Players.
- Member of Cleveland Browns Ring of Honor.
- Elected to Pro Football Hall of Fame in 1999.

6

GENE HICKERSON

One of the finest pulling guards in NFL history, Gene Hickerson spent 15 seasons in Cleveland, contributing greatly to the success experienced by Hall of Fame running backs Jim Brown, Bobby Mitchell, and Leroy Kelly with his exceptional lead blocking. Blessed with an ideal combination of speed, power, and athletic ability, Hickerson dominated the opposition at the line of scrimmage and beyond, with his strong play up front helping the Browns win six division titles and one NFL championship. Extremely durable as well, Hickerson started 154 consecutive contests from 1963 to 1973, ending his career with the fifth-most games played in franchise history. Along the way, Hickerson earned six Pro Bowl selections, four All-Pro nominations, and a spot on the NFL 1960s All-Decade Team, before being further honored by being inducted into the Browns Ring of Honor and the Pro Football Hall of Fame.

Born in the small town of Trenton, Tennessee, on February 15, 1935, Robert Eugene Hickerson acquired his strong work ethic and compassionate nature from his father, who worked in the lumber business. In discussing his dad, Hickerson said, "When he was in his eighties, he walked to a shopping center every day. He'd buy some candy and then stop at the elementary school during recess. He'd pass out that candy. All the teachers and students knew my daddy's name."

After spending his early teenage years earning money in his spare time by pushing a wheelbarrow full of bricks to a stairway and then carrying them up four flights of stairs, Hickerson enrolled at Trezevant High School, where he first began playing football his senior year, recalling, "I was a fullback in high school, a 226-pound fullback, and a damn good one."

With Hickerson playing only one year of high school ball, he received little interest from major college programs. However, after being visited by an Ole Miss recruiter, Hickerson accepted a scholarship from the University of Mississippi, where he began his first training camp at fullback, remembering, "They started me with the fullbacks, but I got tired of running all

Gene Hickerson earned four All-Pro selections and a spot on the NFL 1960s All-Decade Team with his exceptional lead blocking.
Courtesy of MearsonlineAuctions.com

of those sprints in that sweltering August Mississippi heat. So, I asked to change positions. I said, 'I want a position where I don't have to run as much.' They said, 'What do you have in mind?' I said, 'Make me an offensive guard or a defensive end. Let me play somewhere that I don't have to run in all this Lord-awful heat.' That is how I became a guard."

After redshirting as a freshman, Hickerson spent his sophomore year serving the Rebels primarily as a backup offensive lineman, before breaking into the starting lineup the following year. Excelling at offensive tackle the next two seasons, Hickerson earned All-America, All-SEC, and All-South honors as a senior in 1957.

Recalling their days together at Mississippi, Bobby Franklin, a close friend of Hickerson who played with him in Cleveland as well, said, "I didn't know Gene until my freshman year at Ole Miss, and he took care of me. In those days, the veteran players were pretty rough on the freshmen. We played two years together at Ole Miss and then those years with the Browns. . . . Gene was so much faster than the linemen, and Coach Vaught made him run with the backs."

Another former Rebels teammate Robert Khayat, who later became Ole Miss chancellor, remembered, "In the summer of 1956, I met Gene Hickerson for the first time and immediately thought I would never play football at Ole Miss. He was the finest physical specimen I had seen, and he had remarkable speed."

Impressed with Hickerson's outstanding physical attributes and exceptional play in college, the Browns selected him as a "future" choice in the seventh round of the 1957 NFL Draft, with the 78th overall pick, before he even graduated. Also pursued by the Canadian Football League's Montreal Alouettes, who offered him more money, Hickerson chose to remain in the States, where his friends and family could watch him play on television.

Joining the Browns prior to the start of the 1958 campaign, Hickerson spent his first year in Cleveland serving as one of Paul Brown's "messenger" guards, splitting time with Chuck Noll in delivering plays to quarterback Milt Plum from the sideline. Becoming the full-time starter at right guard the following year, Hickerson spent the next two seasons manning that post, before missing the entire 1961 campaign with a broken leg he sustained during the preseason. Returning to action in 1962, Hickerson reclaimed his starting job from John Wooten, who had replaced him at right guard in his absence.

Retaining his place on the starting unit after Blanton Collier assumed head-coaching duties in 1963, Hickerson began an extraordinary 11-year run during which he appeared in every game the Browns played. Establishing himself during that time as one of the league's finest offensive linemen, Hickerson earned six consecutive Pro Bowl selections from 1965 to 1970, while also gaining All-Pro recognition four times and First-Team All-Conference honors on five separate occasions.

Although the 6'3" Hickerson, who gradually increased his playing weight from 230 to 250 pounds over the course of his playing career, never lifted weights, he possessed great strength, which he used to manhandle his opponent as both a run-blocker and pass-protector. Nevertheless, Hickerson's tremendous quickness and foot speed proved to be his greatest assets, with Jim Brown saying at the time of his former teammate's Hall of Fame induction, "He was one of the best pulling guards that ever played. He had unbelievable speed and mobility and was the best lineman we had. He blocked downfield, something guys today can't do. . . .That's why we had those high averages. You don't get that if you don't have a line that can get downfield and throw blocks when they get down there. . . . Nobody knows blockers better than the guys who ran behind them, and I for one am proud he is in the Hall of Fame."

Bobby Mitchell, who spent three of his four seasons in Cleveland running behind Hickerson, added, "You are looking down the field and making cuts, and all of a sudden you see No. 66. You don't expect to see a lineman that far down the field. . . . For his size, he had exceptional speed. It's refreshing to know the guy who is there to protect you can get to the point of contact and give you some help."

Meanwhile, Leroy Kelly, who once stated that the greatest lesson he learned while serving as Jim Brown's understudy was "to follow Gene Hickerson's butt everywhere he goes," claimed, "Gene is one of the main reasons I'm in the Hall of Fame. I had a hard time catching up to him because he was a great pulling guard. He deserves the honor."

Also greatly appreciated by his fellow offensive linemen, Hickerson drew praise from former guard and NFL assistant coach Howard Mudd, who called him "the consummate guard and a high-quality football player for a long time," adding, "When I came into the league, I said, 'Wow! That's the guy I want to be like.'"

Monte Clark, who spent seven seasons playing alongside Hickerson on the Browns' offensive line, said of his longtime teammate, "He was a hell of a football player. The guy was incredible. He could run like a deer, and he had excellent size for that time. He could go all year and not get beat on a pass. And, when he pulled, his man was on the ground. Show me somebody else like that and I'll kiss your rear."

Meanwhile, former Browns defensive tackle Jim Kanicki suggested that Hickerson's unique approach to practice proved to be one of the keys to his tremendous durability, stating, "Gene always shunned physical contact in practice. He was trying to save his body for the games. And in wind sprints, he was always—without exception—last. But he would say, 'What do I have to prove by running fast here?' . . . Do you notice before games how everyone is out there running and stretching to get warmed up? Well, with Gene, his pregame warm-ups amounted to leaning on the goal post until the game started. He did nothing!"

Kanicki continued, "He was small, especially compared to the guys who are playing today. But I can never remember him even pulling a

muscle, let alone missing a practice or a game. He was a great, great athlete
. . . so quick! He could run like a deer."

After moving to left guard for his final two seasons, Hickerson
announced his retirement following the conclusion of the 1973 campaign,
ending his career having appeared in all but two games the Browns played
while he remained on the team's active roster. Paying tribute to his former
teammate, Doug Dieken, who spent his first three years in Cleveland playing alongside Hickerson on the Browns' offensive line, said, "Even going
into the 1970s and entering his 15th year, he was as good as any guard that
there was. He was our best lineman. They drafted guys to take his place, but
they didn't take his place. Gene left on his own terms."

Following his playing days, Hickerson became a successful businessman, spending many years working in the auto industry as a manufactur-
er's representative, while also getting involved in real estate development
and owning several restaurants, including Hickerson's at the Hanna, a
popular dining spot located on Playhouse Square in Cleveland. Unfortunately, Hickerson developed serious health problems in his later years,
being diagnosed with Alzheimer's disease and vascular dementia in 2007,
the same year he received his long-awaited and much-deserved call to the
Pro Football Hall of Fame. Presented for enshrinement by Bobby Franklin,
Hickerson received the following words of praise from his longtime friend
and former teammate: "Gene was such a great athlete that the Browns
drafted him his junior year. I don't think they drafted a year early unless
it was someone real special. They thought he was real special. Everybody
knew how strong Gene was, had great feet, tremendous speed. . . . Gene
wasn't a guy that talked and bragged about himself. He was a pretty quiet
person. He wasn't an outgoing person. He just did his job and took pride
in doing his job."

After Bob Hickerson spoke for his disabled father during the induction ceremonies, a particularly poignant moment occurred when he said,
"I would ask all of you to please join me in welcoming Gene, who still is
leading the way for Hall of Fame running backs Bobby Mitchell, Leroy
Kelly, and Jim Brown," who subsequently pushed his wheelchair onto the
stage. Hickerson died a little over one year later, passing away at the age
of 73, on October 20, 2008. Following his passing, Jim Brown said in a
statement released by the Browns, "He was a great friend of mine, as well
as a great protector of mine. He was a tremendous guard, a tremendous
pulling guard, but also an outstanding individual. . . . We all eventually
leave this earth at some time, but I am so glad he was able to leave with
his dignity and with the recognition from all of us—his former teammates,

the fans, and writers—who wanted him to go into the Hall of Fame after waiting so long for that honor. I truly respected him as a player and as a human being."

CAREER HIGHLIGHTS

Best Season

Hickerson gained consensus First-Team All-Pro recognition three straight times from 1967 to 1969, turning in the most dominant performance of his career in 1968, when his exceptional play earned him the NFL Outstanding Blocker of the Year Award.

Memorable Moments/Greatest Performances

Hickerson helped the Browns rush for 296 yards and amass 450 yards of total offense during a 28–21 win over the Eagles in the final game of the 1959 regular season.

Hickerson and his line-mates dominated the Eagles at the point of attack once again on October 20, 1963, with the Browns amassing 500 yards of total offense during a 37–7 win.

Hickerson's powerful lead-blocking helped the Browns rush for a season-high 274 yards during a 23–17 victory over the Eagles on November 3, 1963.

Hickerson helped the Browns rush for 250 yards and amass 412 yards of total offense during a 30–17 win over the Pittsburgh Steelers on November 1, 1964.

Hickerson helped pave the way for Browns running backs to gain a season-high 258 yards on the ground during a convincing 28–7 victory over the Giants on October 2, 1966.

Hickerson and his line-mates followed that up with another strong performance, enabling the Browns to rush for 241 yards and amass 467 yards of total offense during a 41–10 mauling of the Steelers on October 8, 1966.

Notable Achievements

- Started 154 consecutive games from 1963 to 1973.
- Ranks among Browns career leaders with 15 seasons played (3rd) and 202 games played (5th).

- Six-time division champion (1964, 1965, 1967, 1968, 1969, and 1971).
- 1964 NFL champion.
- 1968 NFL Outstanding Blocker of the Year Award winner.
- Six-time Pro Bowl selection (1965, 1966, 1967, 1968, 1969, and 1970).
- Three-time First-Team All-Pro selection (1967, 1968, and 1969).
- 1965 Second-Team All-Pro selection.
- Four-time First-Team All–Eastern Conference selection (1966, 1967, 1968, and 1969).
- 1970 First-Team All-AFC selection.
- Pro Football Reference All-1960s Second Team.
- NFL 1960s All-Decade Team.
- Member of Cleveland Browns Ring of Honor.
- Elected to Pro Football Hall of Fame in 2007.

7

LEN FORD

The NFL's first great pass-rusher, Len Ford spent eight seasons in Cleveland terrorizing opposing quarterbacks from his right defensive end position. Starring at that post for the Browns from 1950 to 1957, Ford served as one of the pillars of a defense that helped lead the team to seven division titles and three league championships. A four-time Pro Bowler and five-time All-Pro, Ford recovered more fumbles than anyone else in franchise history, en route to also earning a spot on the NFL 1950s All-Decade Team. And following the conclusion of his playing career, Ford received additional distinctions of being named to the Browns Ring of Honor and gaining induction into the Pro Football Hall of Fame.

Born in Washington, DC, on February 18, 1926, Leonard Guy Ford Jr. grew up during the Great Depression, when young boys often turned to sports to escape their troubles. Developing into an excellent all-around athlete at Armstrong Technical High School, Ford starred in football, basketball, and baseball, earning All-City honors in all three sports his senior year. A monstrous hitter on the diamond, Ford may well have pursued a career in baseball had the major leagues been open to African Americans at the time. Equally proficient on the gridiron, Ford originally aspired to play fullback, but, as he later recalled, "I started to grow, and I grew right out of the backfield."

Having developed his pass-catching and tackling skills under the watchful eye of Armstrong Technical head coach Theodore McIntyre, who later described his protégé as "a boy who dreamed of football instead of cowboys and Indians," Ford enrolled at Morgan State University in Maryland on a football scholarship, although he also played center for the school's basketball team. But, after just one year at Morgan State and a brief stint in the Navy, Ford transferred to the University of Michigan in 1945, in the hope of fulfilling his dream of playing in the Rose Bowl.

Starring for the Wolverines on both sides of the ball his final two seasons at Michigan, Ford excelled at receiver and left defensive end, gaining

Ford starred at right defensive end for Browns teams that won seven division titles and three league championships.
Courtesy of RMYAuctions.com

All-America recognition his senior year, with *Sportfolio* magazine describing him in 1946 as "a great defensive wingman who has sufficient pass-catching ability to handle anything Wolverine halfback Bob Chappuis throws his way."

Nevertheless, with NFL teams reluctant to draft African American players, all 10 clubs bypassed Ford when he became available for selection in 1947, prompting him to sign with the Los Angeles Dons of the infant

All-America Football Conference (AAFC). Ford subsequently spent two years in Los Angeles playing tight end and right defensive end for the Dons, making a total of 67 receptions for 1,175 yards and eight touchdowns, while also intercepting two passes on defense, before being selected by the Browns in the second round of the 1950 AAFC Dispersal Draft after the league disbanded following the conclusion of the 1949 campaign.

Converted into a full-time defensive end by head coach Paul Brown and his assistant Blanton Collier following his arrival in Cleveland, the 6'4" Ford added some 15 pounds onto his frame to increase his playing weight to 260. In explaining the decision to use Ford solely on defense, Collier later said, "He was so devastating on defense, we knew this was his natural spot. Len was very aggressive and had that touch of meanness in him that you find in most defensive players."

After performing well for the Browns at right defensive end during the early stages of the 1950 campaign, Ford ended up missing the final seven games of the regular season with a broken nose and fractured cheekbones he sustained when Chicago Cardinals offensive lineman Pat Harder struck him in the face during an extremely contentious meeting between the two teams. Downplaying the incident afterwards, Ford, who had already gained a reputation for his aggressive style of play, said, "Harder's not to blame. I am—for not getting out of the way of his elbow."

But, after undergoing plastic surgery and sitting out the Browns' divisional playoff win over the Giants, Ford surprised everyone when he suited up for the NFL championship game against the Los Angeles Rams. Playing the final three quarters with a specially designed protective cage on his face-mask, Ford helped lead the Browns to a dramatic 30–28 come-from-behind victory by recording a sack and registering three tackles for loss.

Ford subsequently missed just one game over the course of the next seven seasons—a period during which the Browns established themselves as the NFL's dominant defensive team and Ford rivaled Baltimore's Gino Marchetti as the league's greatest defensive end. Possessing good size, exceptional speed, and tremendous agility, Ford had the strength to discard opposing offensive linemen en route to the quarterback and the quickness to bring down runners before they turned the corner. And if a blocker tried to cut him at the legs, Ford used his superior athleticism to hurdle him.

One of the first defenders to employ an outside pass rush, Ford, who spent most of his career playing as a stand-up defensive end in Cleveland's 4-3 defense, created many of the moves still seen on NFL fields today. In discussing the gusto with which his longtime teammate pursued opposing quarterbacks, Lou Groza said, "Lenny used to delight in running over guys."

Although the NFL did not begin recording sacks as an official statistic until long after he retired, Ford proved to be the league's sack master during the early 1950s. Virtually impossible to block one-on-one, Ford forced opposing teams to alter their strategy on offense, with San Francisco 49ers Hall of Fame offensive tackle Bob St. Clair claiming, "There were things you couldn't do out of certain formations or Lennie was going to break through and make the play."

The Browns also modified their defense to take full advantage of Ford's special talents, with Blanton Collier stating, "We were using a six-man defensive line at the time that Ford joined our club. But he was so outstanding that we knew we had to get him in close where his talents as a pass rusher could be best utilized. So, we moved both tackles into the center and dropped the linebackers slightly back and outside. That might even have been the start of the 4-3 defense that everyone uses today."

Detailing the problems that Ford presented to opposing offenses, a Detroit Lions scouting report issued in the mid-1950s asserted: "LEN FORD—Really blows in. Does a lot of jumping over blockers. Does not predetermine this—if he sees a fellow going very low to block, he will jump over. Plays inside very tough. Must be blocked or he will kill the passer. There is no one in the league who can take him out alone."

Admired and respected by all his teammates as well, Ford, recalled noted *Cleveland Plain Dealer* sportswriter Chuck Heaton, was "a leader, particularly with the black players on the squad."

Although Ford continued to perform at a high level his entire time in Cleveland, his failure to earn Pro Bowl or All-Pro honors in either 1956 or 1957 and the rapid development of young defensive ends Paul Wiggin and Bill Glass prompted the Browns to trade him to the Packers for a draft pick following the conclusion of the 1957 campaign. Ford subsequently spent one season in Green Bay assuming a part-time role, before announcing his retirement with a then–NFL record 20 fumble recoveries to his credit, 19 of which he recorded as a member of the Browns. One of the greatest defensive players of his time, Ford not only made huge contributions to a Cleveland defense that surrendered the fewest points in the league on six separate occasions but helped redefine the position of defensive end.

After retiring as an active player, Ford, who spent his offseasons working in a Detroit real estate office, attended the Detroit College of Law for a year-and-a-half, but never received a degree in law, which, according to Chuck Heaton, typified the Hall of Fame lineman's life after football. Writing that Ford's life was "pretty much downhill" after he retired from professional football, Heaton recalled that, in his later years, Ford seemed in poor physical condition, "only a shadow of the mighty end he once was" and "appeared to have lost the drive which made him such a great football player."

Meanwhile, former major-league pitcher Don Newcombe, a onetime alcoholic who became good friends with Ford, revealed during a 1980 interview that the man who once dominated his opposition on the playing field "became a wino, stumbling around in alleys," adding, "He gave up his life for alcohol."

Ford eventually became assistant recreation director for the City of Detroit, where he spent his time working with inner-city children. But, after serving in that post for 16 months, Ford suffered a heart attack that claimed his life one week later, passing away at only 46 years of age, on March 14, 1972. Four years later, Ford gained induction into the Pro Football Hall of Fame. And just a few years earlier, when the NFL announced its 50th Anniversary Team in 1969, only Gino Marchetti received more votes than Ford for the NFL's all-time greatest defensive end.

BROWNS CAREER HIGHLIGHTS

Best Season

Ford gained Pro Bowl and First-Team All-Pro recognition four straight times from 1951 to 1954, having his finest season for the Browns in 1951, when, in addition to applying constant pressure to opposing quarterbacks, he recovered four fumbles, with football historian John Turney of *Pro Football Journal* writing, "Ford had a monster season in 1951, one of the best-ever by a defensive end."

Memorable Moments/Greatest Performances

Ford led a smothering Browns defense that recorded seven sacks and created five turnovers during a 28–0 shutout of the Pittsburgh Steelers on December 9, 1951.

Ford led the defensive charge again one week later when the Browns recorded 10 sacks and allowed just 73 yards of total offense during a 24–9 win over the Philadelphia Eagles in the 1951 regular-season finale.

Ford scored the only defensive touchdown of his career when he recovered a fumble in the end zone during a 49–7 rout of the Eagles on October 19, 1952.

Ford lit the scoreboard again when he tackled quarterback Zeke Bratkowski in the end zone for a safety during a 39–10 win over the Chicago Bears on November 14, 1954.

Ford recorded two interceptions during the Browns' 56–10 manhandling of the Detroit Lions in the 1954 NFL championship game, returning his two picks a total of 45 yards.

Ford contributed to the Browns' 38–14 victory over the Los Angeles Rams in the 1955 NFL championship game by picking off another pass.

Ford led a swarming Browns defense that recorded nine sacks and forced four turnovers during a 23–12 win over the Steelers on October 5, 1957.

Ford, though, experienced his finest moment in the 1950 NFL championship game, when, after missing the final seven games of the regular season and the Browns' divisional playoff win over the Giants with serious facial injuries, he entered the fray early in the second quarter after the Rams marched down the field 82 yards for a touchdown. Despite having lost 20 pounds after being on a liquid diet for six weeks, Ford starred throughout the remainder of the contest, prompting the *Cleveland Plain Dealer* to later call his effort "one of Len Ford's great moments." Paul Brown, who claimed that Ford represented the team's "only real hope of plugging a hole," stated that the star defensive end "showed me that day he really was a man," and added, "I'll always remember one three-play sequence where he threw Vitamin Smith for a 14-yard loss on a reverse, sacked Bob Waterfield for another big loss, and finally smothered Glenn Davis on an end run. That turned the game around for us."

Notable Achievements

- Scored one touchdown on defense.
- Finished second in NFL in fumble recoveries twice and fumble-return yards once.
- Holds Browns career record for most fumble recoveries (19).
- Seven-time division champion (1950, 1951, 1952, 1953, 1954, 1955, and 1957).
- Three-time NFL champion (1950, 1954, and 1955).
- Four-time Pro Bowl selection (1951, 1952, 1953, and 1954).
- Four-time First-Team All-Pro selection (1951, 1952, 1953, and 1954).
- 1955 Second-Team All-Pro selection.
- Pro Football Reference All-1950s First Team.
- NFL 1950s All-Decade Team.
- Member of Cleveland Browns Ring of Honor.
- Elected to Pro Football Hall of Fame in 1976.

8

BILL WILLIS

Largely responsible for breaking the color barrier in professional football, Bill Willis spent eight seasons in Cleveland, establishing himself during that time as one of the premier defenders in the game. Starring for the Browns primarily at middle guard, the equivalent of middle linebacker in today's game, Willis used his speed, strength, and tremendous anticipation to dominate his opponent at the point of attack, earning Pro Bowl honors three times and All-League honors on seven separate occasions. A member of the Pro Football Hall of Fame 1940s All-Decade Team, Willis helped lead the Browns to eight consecutive division titles and five straight league championships, performing equally well for them in the AAFC and the NFL. Further honored following the conclusion of his playing career by being inducted into the Browns Ring of Honor and the Pro Football Hall of Fame, Willis remains one of the greatest and most influential players in franchise history nearly 70 years after he appeared in his last game.

Born in Columbus, Ohio, on October 5, 1921, William Karnet Willis grew up without his father, who died of pneumonia on April 10, 1923. Raised by his mother and grandfather, young William eventually enrolled at Columbus East High School, where he starred in multiple sports, excelling on both offense and defense in football and as a sprinter and shotputter in track and field. Especially proficient on the gridiron, Willis emerged as one of the finest two-way players in the state after he convinced his coach, Ralph Webster, to allow him to play end and tackle, rather than running back, to prevent him from being constantly compared to his older brother, Claude, who had earned All-City and All-State honors as a fullback at the same institution six years earlier. Gaining similar recognition his senior year for his dominant play on both sides of the ball, Willis proved to be particularly outstanding on defense, with Findlay High School running back Gene Fekete, who later played with Willis in Cleveland, saying of their 1939 encounter on the playing field, "The only recollection I have of that game is that we had a fifth man in our backfield, and it was him."

Bill Willis helped break the color barrier in professional football.

After garnering little interest from major college programs due to the color of his skin, Willis spent one year away from the game, working a regular job, before new Ohio State University head coach Paul Brown recruited him to play football for the Buckeyes. Having been turned down by the Army and classified 4F due to bad varicose veins, Willis accepted Brown's offer and entered OSU on an athletic scholarship in 1941. Picking up right where he left off, Willis went on to earn All-America honors his final two seasons as a tackle on offense and a middle guard on defense, where he typically lined up across from the opposing team's center. Performing especially well his senior year, the 6'2", 202-pound Willis helped lead the Buckeyes to a perfect 9-0 record, with his College Hall of Fame biography claiming, "A sprinter's speed made Willis one of the greatest linemen at running interference, and many an opponent left Ohio Stadium feeling the pains of a Willis pop-block."

Meanwhile, in describing Willis's play on defense, Jack Park wrote in *The Official Ohio State Football Encyclopedia*, "His real claim to fame was that he was just so quick off the ball. He was just through, and into the backfield to break up a play. . . . The Outland Trophy and the Lombardi Award weren't around when Bill was playing at Ohio State. Had they been, I think it's pretty safe to say that Bill Willis would probably have won those, and, if not, been very high in the voting for those awards."

While in college, Willis also competed in the 60- and 100-yard dashes for the school's track team and maintained a high class ranking in business administration.

Yet, despite his excellence on the playing field and in the classroom, Willis knew that the NFL did not represent an option for him due to the league's unwritten rule against signing Black players that had been in existence for more than a decade. As a result, he accepted the position of head coach and athletic director at Kentucky State University, where he remained for one year, before reuniting with Paul Brown after the latter became general manager, part owner, and head coach of the Cleveland Browns in the newly formed All-America Football Conference (AAFC).

Performing brilliantly during his tryout with the Browns, Willis made a strong impression on his future teammates by dominating everyone he faced at the line of scrimmage, with center Mike Scarry recalling, "Everybody got knocked down. We used to just line up over the ball and snap it. With Willis, though, you had to put the ball as far as you could out in front of you, to get as far away from him as you could. He changed the whole way we snapped the ball."

Signed to a contract immediately, Willis became the first African American player to join the AAFC, although the NFL's Los Angeles Rams had inked fellow African Americans Kenny Washington and Woody Strode to deals just days earlier. The Browns also signed powerful fullback Marion Motley to serve as Willis's roommate, leading to the two men becoming the first African American players to appear in a pro football game since 1933 when they took the field against the Miami Seahawks in Cleveland's regular-season opener on September 6, 1946, some seven months before Jackie Robinson broke the color barrier in Major League Baseball.

Willis subsequently spent his first few seasons in Cleveland playing on both sides of the ball, before changes in substitution rules enabled him to focus exclusively on the defensive middle guard position, where he assumed a role akin to the modern-day middle linebacker. Excelling at that post even though he generally tipped the scales at only about 210 or 212 pounds, the 6'2" Willis proved to be a tremendous force on defense, creating havoc in opposing backfields with his extraordinary quickness, while also doing an expert job of pursuing ball-carriers from sideline to sideline and covering backs coming out of the backfield.

Eventually becoming noted more than anything for his amazing quickness and uncanny anticipation that left many opponents believing he had jumped offsides, Willis refuted such claims, recalling, "What I had been doing was concentrating on the ball. The split second the ball moved, or the center's hands tightened, I charged, and I always came at a different angle. . . . I could unleash a pretty good forearm block and a rather devastating tackle too."

In discussing Willis's greatest asset, Paul Zimmerman of *Sports Illustrated* wrote, "The press book had a memo to photographers that Willis must be shot at 1/600th of a second to capture his speed. . . . Willis was, you see, the fastest interior lineman who ever played the game."

Claiming that Willis totally revolutionized defensive play, Paul Brown stated, "He often played as a middle or nose guard on our five-man defensive line, but we began dropping him off the line of scrimmage a yard or two because his great speed and pursuit carried him to the point of attack before anyone could block him. This technique and theory were the beginning of the modern 4-3 defense, and Bill was the forerunner of the modern middle linebacker."

In paying tribute to his frequent foe, Chicago Bears Hall of Fame center Clyde "Bulldog" Turner revealed, "The first guy that ever convinced me that I couldn't handle anybody I ever met was Bill Willis. He didn't look like he should be playing middle guard, but he would jump right over you."

Willis's brilliant play helped lead the Browns to four consecutive AAFC championships and the NFL title in 1950 after they joined the more established league when the AAFC folded. But wherever he competed, Willis had to endure taunts from fans and opposing players alike, recalling years later, "You could hear a lot of, 'Get that black son of a bitch.'" However, much as Jackie Robinson did in baseball, Willis displayed tremendous restraint and allowed his exceptional play on the field to do his talking for him, thereby paving the way for other African Americans to receive the same opportunity the Browns offered him.

In describing how he chose to deal with his tormentors, Willis said, "I knew I was a much better player than they were. Along about the middle of the third quarter when they realized that what they were doing wasn't having any effect and that they couldn't beat me, you'd be surprised how quiet they would get."

After the Browns lost the NFL championship game for the third straight time in 1953, Willis's desire to help others prompted him to announce his retirement at only 32 years of age. Interested in working with young people, especially troubled youth, Willis became assistant commissioner in Cleveland's recreation department. After 10 years in that position, Willis returned to Columbus, where he spent two decades serving as director of the Ohio Department of Youth Services, a state agency created to combat criminal behavior among young people. Following his retirement in 1983, Willis lived another 24 years, before he died of complications from a stroke at the age of 86, on November 27, 2007.

Leaving behind him a legacy that greatly influenced future generations of African Americans, Willis drew high praise from Browns wide receiver Braylon Edwards, who, upon learning of his passing, said, "It meant a lot that he paved the way and showed that guys of our color could play, and that we were disciplined. They gave him a chance, and he ran with it and did well. He basically paved the way for gentlemen like myself. So, I'm very appreciative for him. . . . It had to be hard with him, Jackie Robinson, and those guys. It wasn't just them versus the opposition. It was them versus the players on their team, the fans, organizations. So, to go through, maintain, stay focused, and remain strong through everything says a lot about their character."

Browns head coach Romeo Crennel added, "Bill was a pioneer. Being a black player in a league that had been predominantly white before that, it takes a lot to do that. He blazed the trail for guys like myself to be able to be sitting here talking to you today. We are more than appreciative of everything that he's done."

Browns running back Jason Wright also expressed his appreciation to Willis for the sacrifices he made, saying, "It's something that every player— not just black players in the league, not just minority players—but every player owes a ton of gratitude to him. Because one of the unique things about the football environment is that we really become a family across racial lines and across social-economic lines, and you don't see that in the rest of society. Those guys paved the way for that special atmosphere that we have here."

An inspiration to players of other ethnic backgrounds as well, Willis, said longtime Browns offensive lineman Doug Dieken, "was a great ambassador. Whenever I saw him, I always said, 'Mr. Willis,' because he had that kind of respect. He was just a nice, easygoing, honest guy. If you would have met him, you would have never known what he'd accomplished."

Meanwhile, Cincinnati Bengals owner Mike Brown, who had grown up around his father, Paul's, team, said during his eulogy to Willis, "I had the distinct privilege of hanging around the locker room with all those great players on the early Browns teams. Otto Graham, Lou Groza, Dante Lavelli, and the rest. I looked up to each one of them. But the guy I looked up to the most—the guy I idolized the most—was Bill Willis. He was my hero, and he still is."

CAREER HIGHLIGHTS

Best Season

Although Willis gained First-Team All-AAFC recognition in both 1946 and 1947, he probably played his best ball for the Browns from 1951 to 1953, earning three consecutive First-Team All-Pro nominations. While the unavailability of defensive statistics for that period makes it extremely difficult to determine which season proved to be Willis's best, John Turney of *Pro Football Journal* writes, "In 1952, had there been an award, Bill Willis could have been the NFL Defensive Player of the Year."

Memorable Moments/Greatest Performances

Willis anchored a Browns defense that surrendered just 8 yards rushing and 46 yards of total offense during a 34–0 shutout of the Miami Seahawks on December 3, 1946.

Displaying his ability to dominate his opponent on offense as well, Willis helped the Browns rush for 334 yards and amass 559 yards of total offense during a 42–0 mauling of the Baltimore Colts in the final game of the 1947 regular season.

Willis led a swarming Browns defense that recorded six sacks and forced eight turnovers during a 31–0 manhandling of the New York Yankees on November 20, 1949.

Willis played a huge role in the Browns' 8–3 win over the Giants in the divisional round of the 1950 playoffs. In addition to sacking quarterback

Charlie Conerly in the end zone for a safety, Willis helped preserve the Browns' slim fourth-quarter lead by bringing down New York running back Gene "Choo-Choo" Roberts from behind deep inside Cleveland territory, forcing the Giants to ultimately settle for a field goal. Commenting on the play afterwards, Willis said, "I knew it meant the ball game. I just had to catch him."

Willis led the defensive charge when the Browns recorded six sacks, forced six turnovers, and allowed just 45 yards rushing during a 49–7 rout of the Philadelphia Eagles on October 19, 1952.

Willis and his cohorts turned in another dominant performance on December 7, 1952, forcing five turnovers and surrendering just 52 yards rushing and 150 yards of total offense during a 10–0 win over the Chicago Cardinals.

Notable Achievements

- Missed just three games in eight seasons, appearing in 99 out of a possible 102 contests.
- Eight-time division champion (1946, 1947, 1948, 1949, 1950, 1951, 1952, and 1953).
- Four-time AAFC champion (1946, 1947, 1948, and 1949).
- 1950 NFL champion.
- Three-time Pro Bowl selection (1950, 1951, and 1952).
- Two-time First-Team All-AAFC selection (1946 and 1947).
- Two-time Second-Team All-AAFC selection (1948 and 1949).
- Three-time First-Team All-Pro selection (1951, 1952, and 1953).
- NFL 1940s All-Decade Team.
- Member of Cleveland Browns Ring of Honor.
- Elected to Pro Football Hall of Fame in 1977.

9

LOU GROZA

One of the most beloved players in franchise history, Lou Groza spent his entire 21-year professional career in Cleveland, appearing in more games and scoring more points than anyone else in team annals. Although remembered more for the manner with which he helped transform the art of placekicking, Groza also proved to be an outstanding offensive lineman the first half of his career, with his excellence in both areas making him a significant contributor to Browns teams that won 14 division titles and eight league championships. A nine-time Pro Bowler and six-time All-Pro, Groza later received the additional honors of having his #76 retired by the Browns, being named to the NFL's 50th Anniversary Team in 1969, being included on the *Sporting News'* 1999 list of the 100 Greatest Players in NFL History, and gaining induction into the Pro Football Hall of Fame in 1974.

Born in Martins Ferry, Ohio, on January 25, 1924, Louis Roy Groza grew up in an athletic family that included younger brother Alex, who went on to lead the University of Kentucky to two National Championships in basketball. Starring in multiple sports at Martins Ferry High School, Groza excelled in football, baseball, and basketball, serving as captain of the school's baseball and basketball teams his senior year. Even more proficient on the gridiron, Groza, who learned placekicking from his older brother, Frank, and developed his skills by trying to kick balls over telephone wires when he and his friends played touch football in the street, helped lead Martins Ferry to a share of the state title in his final season, with his outstanding kicking and exceptional play at tackle on both sides of the ball gaining him First-Team All-Ohio recognition from both the Associated Press and United Press International.

Choosing to enroll at Ohio State University on an athletic scholarship following his graduation in 1942, Groza spent his first year at OSU playing tackle and kicking for the school's freshman team, before enlisting in the US Army early in 1943. After basic training, Groza attended Brooks

Lou Groza appeared in more games and scored more points than anyone else in franchise history.

Hospital in San Antonio, Texas, where he received additional training as a battlefield medic. Subsequently sent to Okinawa, Japan, as part of the 96th Infantry Division, Groza spent the next two years serving as a surgical technician in the South Pacific, where he witnessed countless war atrocities, recalling years later, "I saw a lot of men wounded with severe injuries. Lose legs, guts hanging out, stuff like that. It's a tough thing, but you get hardened to it, and you accept it as part of your being there."

While stationed in Okinawa, Groza received a package from former Ohio State head coach Paul Brown that contained footballs, a pair of cleats, and a contract offering him an opportunity to play for the Browns in the newly formed All-America Football Conference when his time in the Army came to an end. After signing the contract, Groza spent the rest of the year in the service, before joining the Browns following his discharge in February 1946.

Making an immediate impact upon his arrival in Cleveland, Groza helped the Browns capture the AAFC championship for the first of four straight times by leading the league with 84 points scored, finishing second in the circuit with a field goal percentage of 44.83, and setting pro football records for most field goals (13) and extra points (45) converted in a season. After a slightly subpar 1947 campaign, the 6'3", 240-pound Groza began spending more time at left tackle on offense the following year, eventually laying claim to the starting job, while retaining his placekicking duties. Continuing to function in both roles for the next 12 seasons, Groza combined with center Frank Gatski and guard Abe Gibron for much of the 1950s to give the Browns a virtually impenetrable left side to their offensive line, with Hall of Fame defensive end Andy Robustelli commenting years later, "Lou never got all the credit he deserved for his tackle play, probably because his great kicking skills got him more notoriety."

Indeed, Groza's exceptional placekicking tended to overshadow his outstanding play along the offensive front, even though he earned All-Pro honors at tackle six straight times. Giving the Browns an advantage over every team they faced with his ability to drive the ball through the goalposts from anywhere inside the 50 yard line, Groza, who acquired the nickname "The Toe" during his time in Cleveland, instilled tremendous confidence in his teammates, with Tommy James, his holder for eight years, saying, "Anywhere from 40 to 50 yards, he was a weapon."

Otto Graham expressed similar sentiments when he stated, "Pressure didn't bother him at all. We always felt if we got within 40 or 50 yards of the goal post, he could make it, and 95 percent of the time he did."

Successfully converting more than 60 percent of his field goal attempts eight times during an era when few kickers approached that mark, Groza led the league in that category on five separate occasions, while also topping the circuit in field goals made six times and points scored twice. Using a head-on style of kicking rarely seen in today's game, Groza approached the football in a straight line and booted it with the top of his foot, aiming for the middle of the ball. Early in his career, Groza attempted to improve the accuracy on his kicks by using his cleats to scrape the ground in a straight line before addressing the football. He also sometimes put a one-inch piece of adhesive tape on the ground for better accuracy. But Groza's uncanny precision, especially from long range, prompted the NFL to adopt the "Lou Groza Rule" in 1950, which banned the use of artificial kicking aids, including tape.

After Groza gained Pro Bowl recognition in nine of the previous 10 seasons, back issues prompted him to announce his retirement following the conclusion of the 1959 campaign. Groza subsequently spent most of 1960 scouting for the Browns and working in the insurance business he founded, later saying, "I was 36, and I thought I had retired." But, with his back feeling better, Browns owner Art Modell coaxed Groza out of retirement in 1961, although he agreed to return to the team strictly as a kicker.

Groza ended up playing for the Browns for seven more years, helping them win three division titles and one NFL championship by consistently ranking among the league leaders in field goal percentage, while also finishing second in the circuit with a career-high 115 points in 1964. Retiring for good at the end of 1967, Groza ended his career having converted 264 of his 481 field goal attempts (54.9 percent), hit on 810 of his 833 extra-point attempts (97.2 percent), and scored a franchise-record 1,608 points, which remains the 21st highest total in NFL history. Yet, despite his many accomplishments as a kicker, Groza later said, "Kicking was something I did because I had the talent. I always considered myself a tackle."

After retiring for a second time, Groza turned down offers to play for the San Francisco 49ers and to return to the Browns as a kicking coach, choosing instead to focus on his insurance business. However, he remained active with the Browns for many more years, retaining his home in Berea, Ohio, near the team's headquarters and training facility, and serving as an ambassador and father figure for the organization, often inviting rookies over for dinner and helping them find apartments. Groza lived until November 29, 2000, when, after battling Parkinson's disease and back and hip problems the previous few years, he suffered a fatal heart attack at the age of 76.

Upon learning of his passing, Browns owner Al Lerner issued a statement that read: "Lou Groza personified the greatness that characterized the Cleveland Browns during its glorious period under the direction of Paul Brown. No one embraced the return of this team to Cleveland with more warmth or commitment than No. 76. Our organization has lost a great ally and a great friend."

Former Browns offensive lineman Doug Dieken paid tribute to one of the franchise's all-time greats by saying, "I don't know if he's the greatest

Cleveland Brown, but he is THE Cleveland Browns. He exemplified what you want in a football player. Lou always had time for everybody. I'm sure every kid that sent a football card to Lou Groza got a Lou Groza card signed and sent back. He was just a big, lovable guy."

Meanwhile, Mike McCormack said of his longtime teammate, "He was a special guy. He was the spirit of the Cleveland Browns."

CAREER HIGHLIGHTS

Best Season

Groza gained recognition from the *Sporting News* as the NFL Player of the Year in 1954, when, in addition to anchoring the Browns' offensive line from his left tackle position, he successfully converted 16 of 24 field goal attempts and all but one of his 38 extra-point attempts, scored 85 points, and compiled a league-best 66.7 field goal percentage. But he performed somewhat better the previous season, earning the second of his four consecutive First-Team All-Pro nominations in 1953 by helping to pave the way for Browns running backs to average 4.2 yards per carry, while also finishing second in the league with 108 points and topping the circuit with 23 field goals and a career-best 88.5 field goal percentage, successfully converting 23 of his 26 attempts.

Memorable Moments/Greatest Performances

Groza contributed to a 44–0 victory over the Miami Seahawks in the 1946 regular-season opener by kicking three field goals in one game for the first time in his career.

In addition to helping the Browns amass 432 yards of total offense from his left tackle position during a 30–17 win over the Brooklyn Dodgers on October 10, 1948, Groza kicked a career-long 53-yard field goal, which represented the longest kick in NFL history at the time.

Groza's superior blocking at the point of attack helped the Browns amass 486 yards of total offense during a 35–7 victory over the New York Yankees on October 24, 1948.

Groza's strong play up front helped the Browns gain 423 yards through the air and amass 607 yards of total offense during a 61–14 rout of the Los Angeles Dons on October 14, 1949.

Groza proved to be the difference in a 13–7 win over the Philadelphia Eagles on December 3, 1950, with his field goals of 35 and 43 yards providing the margin of victory.

Groza scored the only touchdown of his career when he gathered in a 23-yard pass from Otto Graham on a tackle eligible play during a 45–21 win over the Washington Redskins in the 1950 regular-season finale.

Groza gave the Browns a 30–28 victory over the Los Angeles Rams in the 1950 NFL championship game by kicking a 16-yard field goal with just 28 seconds left in regulation.

Although the Browns ended up losing the NFL championship game to the Rams the following year by a score of 24–17, Groza gave them their first points of the contest in the second quarter when he kicked a 52-yard field goal.

Groza gave the Browns a 19–15 win over the Redskins on October 26, 1952, by kicking four field goals in one game for the first time in his career.

Groza's three field goals enabled the Browns to defeat the Giants by a score of 16–7 on November 28, 1954, with the longest of his kicks traveling 38 yards.

Groza scored all the points the Browns registered during a 6–3 win over the Giants in the 1957 regular-season opener, with his 47-yard fourth-quarter kick providing the margin of victory.

Groza helped the Browns forge a 33–33 tie with the St. Louis Cardinals on September 20, 1964, by successfully converting all four of his field goal attempts, the longest of which came from 37 yards out.

Groza proved to be the difference in a 30–21 win over the Dallas Cowboys on October 23, 1966, with his field goals of 39, 30, and 47 yards providing the margin of victory.

Notable Achievements

- Appeared in 108 consecutive games from 1951 to 1959.
- Played in every game in all but two of his 21 NFL seasons.
- Scored more than 100 points twice.
- Converted more than 65 percent of field goal attempts seven times, topping 88 percent once.
- Led league in points scored twice, field goals made six times, and field goal percentage five times.
- Finished second in league in points scored twice, field goals made four times, and field goal percentage four times.

- Holds Browns career records for most points scored (1,608), extra points made (810), seasons played (21), and games played (268).
- Ranks second in franchise history in field goals made (264).
- Fourteen-time division champion (1946, 1947, 1948, 1949, 1950, 1951, 1952, 1953, 1954, 1955, 1957, 1964, 1965, and 1967).
- Four-time AAFC champion (1946, 1947, 1948, and 1949).
- Four-time NFL champion (1950, 1954, 1955, and 1964).
- 1954 *Sporting News* NFL Player of the Year.
- Nine-time Pro Bowl selection (1950, 1951, 1952, 1953, 1954, 1955, 1957, 1958, and 1959).
- Four-time First-Team All-Pro selection (1952, 1953, 1954, and 1955).
- Two-time Second-Team All-Pro selection (1956 and 1957).
- Two-time First-Team All–Eastern Conference selection (1964 and 1965).
- Pro Football Reference All-1950s First Team.
- NFL 1950s All-Decade Team.
- Member of NFL's 50th Anniversary Team.
- #76 retired by Browns.
- Number 99 on the *Sporting News'* 1999 list of the 100 Greatest Players in NFL History.
- Member of Cleveland Browns Ring of Honor.
- Elected to Pro Football Hall of Fame in 1974.

10

MARION MOTLEY

Once called "the greatest all-around football player there ever was" by Hall of Fame running back Joe Perry, Marion Motley starred for the Browns on both offense and defense during the club's formative years in the All-America Football Conference and, later, the NFL. An outstanding blocker and exceptional runner who possessed both size and speed, the powerfully built Motley gained more yards on the ground than any other player in the brief history of the AAFC, ending his eight-year pro career with an average of 5.7 yards per carry that remains a record for fullbacks. Excelling as a linebacker on defense as well during the early stages of his career, Motley gained All-League recognition four times with his superb all-around play. A major contributor to Browns teams that won eight straight division titles and five league championships, Motley later received the additional honors of being named to the NFL's 75th Anniversary Team in 1994 and the NFL 100 All-Time Team in 2019, being ranked number 32 on the *Sporting News*' 1999 list of the 100 Greatest Players in NFL History and number 74 on the NFL Network's 2010 list of the NFL's 100 Greatest Players, and being elected to the Pro Football Hall of Fame in 1968.

Born in Leesburg, Georgia, on June 5, 1920, Marion Motley moved with his family at the age of three to Canton, Ohio, where he starred in football and basketball at McKinley High School. Particularly outstanding on the gridiron, Motley led McKinley to a three-year record of 25-3 while starting at fullback and linebacker, with the school's only losses coming to a Massillon squad coached by Paul Brown.

Following his graduation, Motley enrolled at historically Black South Carolina State University, where he spent one year playing for the Bulldogs, before transferring to the University of Nevada, Reno at the end of his freshman year. Participating in multiple sports for the Wolf Pack over the course of the next three seasons, Motley starred in football and competed in boxing and track as a javelin-thrower. However, Motley failed to earn a

Marion Motley rushed for more yards than any other player in the four-year history of the AAFC.

degree at Nevada, dropping out of school after he suffered a knee injury, and returning to Canton, where he went to work in a steel mill.

Choosing to enter the military following the onset of World War II, Motley ended up playing football at the Great Lakes Naval Training Center for former Massillon head coach, Paul Brown. Impressed with Motley's exceptional all-around play during their time together, Brown later invited him to try out for the Browns of the newly formed AAFC when he assumed head coaching duties in Cleveland at the end of the war (although some accounts claim that Brown eventually signed Motley to a contract because he needed another Black player to room with Bill Willis).

After earning a spot on the Browns' roster, Motley quickly established himself as one of the team's best players, earning Second-Team All-AAFC honors by gaining 601 yards on only 73 carries (averaging in the process an astonishing 8.2 yards per attempt), scoring six touchdowns, and amassing 789 yards from scrimmage and 842 all-purpose yards, while also excelling at linebacker on defense. Improving upon those numbers the following year, Motley once again gained Second-Team All-AAFC recognition by placing near the top of the league rankings with 889 yards rushing, 962 yards from scrimmage, 1,332 all-purpose yards, 10 touchdowns, and a rushing average of 6.1 yards per carry, and returning his lone interception on defense 48 yards for a TD. Continuing to perform at an elite level the next three seasons, Motley posted the following numbers from 1948 to 1950:

YEAR	YDS RUSHING	YDS FROM SCRIMMAGE	ALL-PURPOSE YDS	TDS
1948	**964**	1,156	1,493	7
1949	570	761	1,023	8
1950	**810**	961	961	4

While those numbers might seem modest by today's standards, it must be remembered that Motley compiled them during an era when teams played fewer games and opposing defenses crowded the line of scrimmage to defend against the run, making it extremely difficult for anyone to rush for 1,000 yards in a season. In addition to winning two rushing titles, Motley consistently ranked among the league leaders in yards from scrimmage, all-purpose yards, and yards per rushing attempt, leading the NFL with an average of 5.8 yards per carry in 1950. A First-Team All-Pro selection in both 1948 and 1950, Motley also gained Pro Bowl recognition in the second of those campaigns. More importantly, the Browns continued their five-year run as pro football's dominant team, capturing the AAFC title in 1948 and 1949, before winning the NFL championship in 1950.

Standing 6'1" and weighing 235 pounds at a time when most linemen were not that big, Motley possessed a rare combination of speed and power that made him virtually impossible to bring down one-on-one. Although Motley ran the ball mostly between the tackles, he had the quickness to run outside as well, with Cincinnati Bengals owner Mike Brown describing the star running back of his father's team thusly: "He was a big man. He was 40 or 50 pounds bigger than some of the guys that were playing in his day. He was like Earl Campbell, in more recent times, in that he was a collision runner. He'd hit people, and they'd fall off, and he'd keep going. And in his prime, he had a burst to him."

Brown continued, "He was a great runner, but he was more than a great runner. My dad used to say that Marion was the greatest all-around player ever. He was perhaps the best pass-protecting back ever. He could take these rushers and just stone them. He just stopped them. And he was a willing blocker on runs."

Renowned for his ability to pick up blitzing linebackers and linemen who posed a threat to quarterback Otto Graham, Motley also received high praise from star wide receiver Dante Lavelli for his excellence in that area, with Lavelli recalling, "Motley really built the passing attack for the Browns because of his blocking."

An exceptional defender as well, Motley also starred at linebacker his first few seasons, before injuries began to take their toll on him, with Paul Brown writing in his autobiography, "I've always believed that Motley could have gone into the Hall of Fame solely as a linebacker if we had used him only at that position."

In discussing the totality of Motley's game, Blanton Collier, who served as an assistant under Brown for many years before eventually taking over as head coach, stated, "He had no equal as a blocker. He could run with anybody for 30 yards or so. And this man was a great, great linebacker."

Mike Brown also expressed his appreciation for Motley's all-around brilliance when he said, "The great players of any era can play in any other era, and Marion was one of those. If he walked in today, he'd start for any team in the league. In his era, I think he was the best of the fullbacks. . . . He had great hands. The Browns used to run a lot of wide flares and screens. He was a real threat at that. Beyond that, he was a guy who could go in and play as a linebacker. And the Browns used him as a linebacker in certain yardage situations. He was considered the most talented of the Browns' linebackers. He had the most physical ability."

Brown then added, "We had some great players with those old teams. He ranked up there with Otto Graham—they were the two really key guys at the beginning of the Browns."

Motley's varied skill set has prompted many of his coaches and former teammates to compare him favorably to the great Jim Brown, with Otto Graham saying at a luncheon in Canton in 1964, "There is no comparison between Jim Brown and Marion Motley. Motley was the greatest all-around fullback."

Meanwhile, both Paul Brown and esteemed football writer Paul Zimmerman, who witnessed Motley's entire career, have stated that they considered him to be a better all-around player than Brown, with Zimmerman also identifying Motley as the greatest football player of all time.

Yet, as one of the NFL's first Black players, Motley experienced a tremendous amount of persecution on his way to greatness. Often stepped on by opposing defenders, Motley recalled, "My hands were always bloody. That kind of crap went on for two or three years until they found out what kind of players we [him and teammate Bill Willis] were. They found out that while they were calling us 'niggers,' I was running for touchdowns and Willis was knocking the shit out of them. So, they stopped calling us names and started trying to catch up with us."

Motley continued, "Sometimes I wanted to just kill some of those guys, and the officials would just stand right there. They'd see those guys stepping on us and heard them saying things and just turn their backs. . . . We took a lot of abuse. Anything that they gave out, we took it, but we dished it back to 'em. I'd get my licks in. I kicked butts and took names, I'll tell you that. And it made them respect us too. So, I think I did what I had to do, and did it right."

Unfortunately, age and injuries began to catch up with the 31-year-old Motley in 1951, limiting him to just 61 carries, 273 yards rushing, 325 yards from scrimmage, and one touchdown. Despite being hampered by knee problems in 1952, Motley rebounded somewhat, gaining 444 yards on the ground, scoring three touchdowns, and amassing 657 yards from scrimmage and 745 all-purpose yards, before losing his starting job to Chick Jagade the following year. Motley subsequently chose to sit out the 1954 campaign after Paul Brown told him that he intended to cut him, with Brown saying at the time, "Marion realized that his knee was weak and did not feel that it was coming around. He was one of the truly fine fullbacks in his prime, the type that comes along once in a lifetime. I certainly never will forget some of his runs, and I imagine Cleveland football fans feel the same."

With Motley deciding to attempt a comeback in 1955, the Browns traded him to Pittsburgh for fullback Ed Modzelewski, after which he appeared in six games with the Steelers as a backup linebacker before being released during the season. Subsequently announcing his retirement, Motley ended his career with 4,720 yards rushing, 85 receptions, 1,107 receiving yards, 5,827 yards from scrimmage, 1,122 kickoff-return yards, 6,997 all-purpose yards, 31 rushing touchdowns, 39 total TDs, and a rushing average of 5.7 yards per carry that ranks as the best in pro football history among running backs, although it is not recognized as such because of the years he spent in the AAFC.

After retiring as an active player, Motley pursued his dream of coaching in the NFL. However, he found himself being turned away by the Browns and the other teams he approached, forcing him to eventually take a job with the US Postal Service. Motley subsequently spent many years working for the government, before developing prostate cancer later in life. Losing his battle with the disease on June 27, 1999, Motley died at his son's home in Cleveland at the age of 79, with George Taliaferro, who in 1949 became the first African American drafted by an NFL team, later saying, "Marion Motley died of a broken heart. He should have been the first African American coach in the NFL. But Marion didn't get his degree. No team would hire him to coach. Allegedly, he didn't have the intellect to contribute anything, beyond what he did as a player. That was tragic."

Meanwhile, Mike Brown discussed the fond memories he had of Motley the player, saying, "It's been a long time since he came into pro football, and memories fade, and people probably don't have him in mind like they have later guys. But he was as good as any of them. I'm pretty selective. I don't have so many of them that I consider super. But I consider Marion Motley super."

BROWNS CAREER HIGHLIGHTS

Best Season

Motley had an outstanding year for the Browns in 1950, earning First-Team All-Pro honors by leading the NFL with 810 yards rushing and an average of 5.8 yards per carry, while also scoring four touchdowns and placing near the top of the league rankings with 961 yards from scrimmage. But he performed even better in 1948, gaining consensus First-Team All-AAFC recognition by establishing career-high marks with 964 yards rushing, 1,156 yards from scrimmage, and 1,493 all-purpose yards, scoring seven touchdowns, and averaging 6.1 yards per carry.

Memorable Moments/Greatest Performances

Motley helped lead the Browns to a 20–6 win over the Chicago Rockets on September 13, 1946, by carrying the ball 12 times for 122 yards and scoring the first touchdown of his career on a 20-yard run.

Motley led the Browns to a 31–14 victory over the Los Angeles Dons on October 20, 1946, by gaining 143 yards on just eight carries and scoring two touchdowns, which came on runs of 49 and 68 yards.

Motley recorded a career-long 76-yard TD run during a 42–17 win over the Buffalo Bisons on November 24, 1946, with his 76-yard jaunt representing the longest run in the AAFC all season.

Motley helped lead the Browns to a 14–9 win over the New York Yankees in the 1946 AAFC championship game by carrying the ball 13 times for 98 yards and one touchdown.

Motley displayed his versatility during a 30–14 victory over the Buffalo Bills in the 1947 regular-season opener, rushing for one touchdown and returning an interception 48 yards for another TD.

Motley followed that up by gaining 111 yards on just five carries and scoring two touchdowns during a 55–7 rout of the Brooklyn Dodgers on September 12, 1947, with one of his TDs coming on a 51-yard run.

Motley proved to be a huge factor in the 1947 AAFC championship game, carrying the ball 13 times for 109 yards during a 14–3 win over the New York Yankees.

Motley led the Browns to a lopsided 42–13 victory over the Buffalo Bills on September 12, 1948, by rushing for 136 yards and one touchdown, which came on an 18-yard run.

Motley scored two touchdowns during a 34–21 win over the Yankees on November 21, 1948, with one of his TDs coming on a career-long 78-yard catch-and-run.

Motley helped lead the Browns to a 49–7 rout of the Bills in the 1948 AAFC championship game by carrying the ball 14 times for 133 yards and three touchdowns, the longest of which came on a 31-yard run.

Motley contributed to a 42–7 victory over the Los Angeles Dons on October 2, 1949, by rushing for 139 yards and two touchdowns.

Motley starred again during a 35–2 win over the Chicago Hornets on November 6, 1949, rushing for 118 yards and two touchdowns, one of which came on a 49-yard run.

Motley gave the Browns a 14–0 third-quarter lead over the San Francisco 49ers in the 1949 AAFC championship game when he reeled off a 68-yard touchdown run, finishing the contest, which the Browns won by a score of 21–7, with 75 yards rushing and that one TD.

Motley turned in a record-setting performance during a 45–7 rout of the Steelers on October 29, 1950, gaining 188 yards on just 11 carries, with his average of 17.1 yards per carry setting a single-game mark that lasted more than half a century. Motley also scored two touchdowns during the contest, scoring once on a 69-yard run and again on a sensational 33-yard catch-and-run during which he broke four tackles and had his helmet knocked off, before finally breaking free and lumbering into the end zone.

Motley contributed to a 20–14 victory over the Washington Redskins on November 19, 1950, by carrying the ball 27 times for 178 yards.

Motley gained more than 100 yards on the ground for the final time in his career on October 7, 1951, rushing for 106 yards during a 38–23 win over the Los Angeles Rams.

Notable Achievements

- Rushed for more than 800 yards three times.
- Amassed more than 1,000 yards from scrimmage once.
- Surpassed 1,000 all-purpose yards three times.
- Averaged more than 5 yards per carry six times, topping 6 yards per carry three times and 8 yards per carry once.
- Led league in yards rushing twice, rushing touchdowns once, and rushing average once.
- Finished second in league in rushing average once.
- Finished third in league in yards rushing twice.
- Led Browns in rushing six times.
- Ranks among Browns career leaders with 4,712 yards rushing (7th), 5,819 yards from scrimmage (10th), 6,997 all-purpose yards (8th), and 31 rushing touchdowns (7th).
- Ranks third in NFL history with rushing average of 5.7 yards per carry.
- Eight-time division champion (1946, 1947, 1948, 1949, 1950, 1951, 1952, and 1953).
- Four-time AAFC champion (1946, 1947, 1948, and 1949).
- 1950 NFL champion.
- 1950 Pro Bowl selection.
- 1948 First-Team All-AAFC selection.
- Two-time Second-Team All-AAFC selection (1946 and 1947).
- 1950 First-Team All-Pro selection.
- NFL 1940s All-Decade Team.
- Member of NFL's 75th Anniversary Team.
- Named to NFL 100 All-Time Team in 2019.
- Number 32 on the *Sporting News'* 1999 list of the 100 Greatest Players in NFL History.
- Number 74 on the NFL Network's 2010 list of the NFL's 100 Greatest Players.
- Member of Cleveland Browns Ring of Honor.
- Elected to Pro Football Hall of Fame in 1968.

11

DICK SCHAFRATH

The greatest left tackle in franchise history prior to the arrival of Joe Thomas, Dick Schafrath spent 13 seasons in Cleveland protecting the blind side of Browns quarterbacks and opening holes for Hall of Fame running backs Jim Brown, Bobby Mitchell, and Leroy Kelly. Nicknamed "Mule" for his strength and stubborn determination, Schafrath missed just two games his entire career, appearing in 176 out of 178 regular-season contests and another eight in the postseason. A key member of teams that won six division titles and one NFL championship, Schafrath earned six Pro Bowl selections and four All-Pro nominations, before gaining the additional distinction of being named to Pro Football Reference's All-1960s First Team.

Born in Canton, Ohio, on March 21, 1937, Richard Phillip Schafrath grew up some 33 miles west, in the town of Wooster, where he acquired his incredible work ethic while working alongside his father on the family farm. Developing into an exceptional all-around athlete during his teenage years, Schafrath starred in football and baseball at Wooster High School, earning All-Ohio honors in both sports. Competing in track and basketball as well, Schafrath approached his play on the court with somewhat less enthusiasm, later saying, "The problem with basketball was they just didn't allow you to push and hit. I'd foul out in the third quarter."

Although several major universities recruited Schafrath for football, he initially expressed little interest in going to college, preferring instead to pursue a career in baseball. In fact, after being drafted by the Cincinnati Reds, Schafrath appeared headed to the minor leagues, before, as he put it, "My mom and dad were intercepted by Woody Hayes."

Recalling his family's first meeting with the legendary Ohio State football coach, Schafrath said, "Woody came on Sunday, and he had a trick. He decided he was going to try to see if he could take us all to church. Somehow, he knew we belonged to the Catholic church. So, we all went to church with Woody in his old station wagon. When we got back from

Dick Schafrath missed just two games in his 13 years with the Browns.

church, Woody put on an apron and helped mom cook lunch. After we had lunch, he went down to the barn with dad and talked about all the animals and his farm career. They came back up, Woody kissed mom on the cheek and got in the car and left. Never said a word to me for the five hours he was there. I came in the house a little bit later and I said, 'Boy, mom, I wasn't very impressed with Woody Hayes and Ohio State.' And she said, 'I'll tell you what, son, you're going to Ohio State.'"

Still wishing to play baseball, Schafrath did not work particularly hard in the classroom when he first arrived at Ohio State, remembering, "I tried to get out as fast as I could. I was failing courses, and Woody would make me live with him. I actually lived in Woody's home for three quarters at different times, and his wife, Anne, tutored me."

Having finally learned to focus on his studies, Schafrath turned his attention to football, helping the Buckeyes capture the 1957 National Championship by excelling for them at tackle on offense and end on defense. But, after helping Ohio State earn another top-10 finish in the national rankings in 1958, Schafrath chose to forgo his final year of college eligibility and declare himself eligible for the 1959 NFL Draft.

Subsequently selected by the Browns in the second round, with the 23rd overall pick, Schafrath revealed that he did not learn of his selection until days later. Calling his parents while away from home on a road trip, Schafrath learned from his mother that he had received several phone calls from a man named Paul Brown. Recalling the contents of the conversation, Schafrath said that his mother asked, "Who is he?" Schafrath responded, "He's from Cleveland or something. . . . Why? What did he want?"

Schafrath continued, "So, I called up to Cleveland and Paul said, 'You're one of us, boy.' So, up to Cleveland I came."

Remembering that the team he joined at his first pro training camp possessed a considerable amount of talent, Schafrath said, "The first huddle I was in, there were eight future Hall of Famers, with two other guys who were All-Pro. So, you had a lot of expectations when you stepped in a huddle like that. Groza took me under his wing, along with Mike McCormack."

Weighing only 220 pounds when he first arrived in Cleveland, Schafrath embarked on a serious weight-training program that helped him add more than 40 pounds of bulk onto his 6'3" frame by the end of his first year, recalling, "I started weightlifting, and I was the biggest guy on the Browns for about six, seven years. Paul Brown was mad at me because he didn't believe in weightlifting, he hated it. He liked you to run, run, run and thought weightlifting would tighten you up too much. He accepted it and left me alone because I was doing my job."

Schafrath also increased his weight by competing in various eating contests, stating, "I was in every eating contest across the state. I ate watermelons, hamburgers, eggs, chicken, and I'd eat to win. I never lost."

After spending his first year in Cleveland backing up Lou Groza at left tackle, Schafrath laid claim to the starting job in 1960, beginning in the process a 12-year stretch during which he started virtually every game the Browns played. Yet, during the early part of Schafrath's career, he never fully practiced with the team, since, as a full-time active member of the US Air Force, he spent much of his time serving on the base in Mansfield, Ohio, with Paul Brown mailing him the game plan at the beginning of each week, along with an exercise program.

Paired up at different times with left guards Jim Ray Smith, John Wooten, and John Demarie, Schafrath gradually emerged as one of the league's finest players at his position, earning Pro Bowl honors six straight times from 1963 to 1968, while also gaining First-Team All-Pro recognition on four separate occasions. Outstanding in pass protection, Schafrath helped protect the blind side of quarterbacks Milt Plum, Frank Ryan, and Bill Nelsen, with that trio of signal-callers earning a total of six trips to the Pro Bowl with his assistance. Fast and strong, Schafrath also excelled as a blocker on the Browns' signature running plays, the power sweep, trap, and draw, often driving his man to the turf at the line of scrimmage, before erasing another would-be tackler downfield.

Yet, despite Schafrath's contributions to an extremely talented team, he spent his first five years in Cleveland playing for squads that failed to advance to the playoffs, later saying, "I thought we had really great teams those years. We just lost out on a few of those games that were big games, and we didn't come through. We had the manpower to do it—the attitude I guess was not strong enough."

All that changed, though, shortly after Blanton Collier replaced Paul Brown as head coach prior to the start of the 1963 campaign, with the Browns making the playoffs in six of Schafrath's final eight seasons and winning the NFL championship in 1964. Commenting on the change in offensive philosophy, Schafrath noted, "With Paul Brown, you normally blocked a guy and just stayed with him and tried to drive him in the ground. You pretty much stayed with your man no matter what. That wasn't enough when you played with Blanton in those first three years, which were Jim Brown's last three. It was 'everybody hit.' Once Jimmy would see you start with your hit on one side or the other of a guy, as soon as you hit the guy, you didn't stay with him another two seconds. You tried to go past him because Jim Brown didn't mess around—he was goin'—and get a second block. On that offensive line, we had it going that some guys were always getting two blocks, and three blocks sometimes, on the same play. It became an obsession with the offensive line to make more than one block."

In addition to creating huge holes for Browns running backs, Schafrath became known during his time in Cleveland for his stunts and willingness to take on unusual physical challenges that included wrestling a bear, canoeing across Lake Erie without stopping, and running 62 miles from Cleveland Stadium to his old high school field in Wooster. The last feat, which he accomplished in the summer of 1971 at age 34, proved to be his undoing. Still suffering from the aftereffects of his lengthy trek, Schafrath gradually wore down over the course of the ensuing campaign, causing him to ultimately lose his starting job to 22-year-old rookie Doug Dieken. Choosing to announce his retirement at season's end, Schafrath ended his career with 176 games played, which represents the third-highest total in franchise history among offensive linemen, with only Gene Hickerson and Dieken appearing in more contests.

After retiring as an active player, Schafrath remained away from the game until 1975, when he accepted the position of assistant offensive line coach for the Washington Redskins. Resigning his post at the end of 1977, Schafrath eventually chose to pursue a career in politics, winning a seat in the Ohio State Senate in 1986, which he retained until 2003, when he retired from politics after surviving a bout with cancer and serious heart issues. Three years later, Schafrath released his autobiography, *Heart of a Mule*.

Continuing to be plagued by health problems in his later years, Schafrath lived until August 15, 2021, when he passed away at the age of 84. Shortly thereafter, the Browns released a statement that read: "The Cleveland Browns were saddened to learn of the passing of Dick Schafrath. He was a Cleveland Brown and Ohioan to his core. Schafrath's unmatched work ethic helped establish what it means to be a Cleveland Brown. He was one of the most decorated offensive linemen in team history, earning numerous Pro Bowl and All-Pro honors. He also helped the Browns capture the 1964 NFL Championship and opened holes for three Hall of Fame runners. We send our deepest condolences to his family."

Upon learning of his former teammate's passing, Doug Dieken said, "I played behind Dick for one season, and he was just a pleasure to be around. Not a lot of guys would have taken me under their wing the way he did. He was a great player. His credentials merit the Hall of Fame, but he was also a first-class person."

Meanwhile, Joe Thomas stated, "Right after I was drafted, I learned about the rich history of the left tackle position for the Cleveland Browns. Some of the NFL's all-time greats lined up in that spot—from Lou Groza to Dick Schafrath to Doug Dieken. Dick helped set the standard for left tackles in the NFL, and I am truly saddened to hear of his passing."

Looking back on the time he spent in Cleveland some years earlier, Schafrath said, "I just loved playing in front of that hometown crowd, that was just great. The difference then was you really had a good relationship with them [the fans] because you parked in the parking lot [with them] and walked to the stadium 100 yards, and everybody was signing autographs and taking pictures with you. The fans really were in very close contact with you, so it was like the whole family experience. That stadium was something to play in . . . wow!"

CAREER HIGHLIGHTS

Best Season

Schafrath earned four First-Team All-Pro nominations during his career, accomplishing the feat three straight times from 1963 to 1965. While any of those seasons would make a good choice, I opted to go with 1963 since, en route to earning team MVP honors, Schafrath helped the Browns finish first in the NFL with 2,639 yards rushing, with Cleveland running backs averaging a robust 5.7 yards per carry and Jim Brown gaining a career-high 1,863 yards on the ground.

Memorable Moments/Greatest Performances

Schafrath anchored an offensive line that enabled the Browns to pass for 351 yards and amass 487 yards of total offense during a 34–7 win over the St. Louis Cardinals on October 21, 1962.

Schafrath's superior blocking helped the Browns amass 543 yards of total offense during a 37–14 victory over the Washington Redskins in the 1963 regular-season opener.

Schafrath and his line-mates dominated the opposition at the point of attack once again on October 24, 1965, with the Browns amassing 526 yards of total offense during a lopsided 38–14 win over the Giants.

Schafrath helped the Browns amass 508 yards of total offense during a 49–17 win over the Atlanta Falcons on October 30, 1966.

Schafrath and his cohorts dominated the Falcons at the line of scrimmage once again on October 27, 1968, with the Browns amassing 444 yards of total offense and Atlanta failing to record a single sack of Bill Nelson, who finished the game with 248 yards passing.

Notable Achievements

- Missed just two games in 13 seasons, appearing in 176 out of a possible 178 contests.
- Six-time division champion (1964, 1965, 1967, 1968, 1969, and 1971).

- 1964 NFL champion.
- 1963 Browns MVP.
- Six-time Pro Bowl selection (1963, 1964, 1965, 1966, 1967, and 1968).
- Four-time First-Team All-Pro selection (1963, 1964, 1965, and 1969).
- Three-time First-Team All–Eastern Conference selection (1963, 1964, and 1965).
- Pro Football Reference All-1960s First Team.

12

DANTE LAVELLI

Known for his soft hands, tremendous concentration, and big-play ability, Dante "Gluefingers" Lavelli spent 11 years in Cleveland, establishing himself during that time as one of the most dangerous wide receivers in professional football. Teaming up with quarterback Otto Graham and fellow wideout Mac Speedie to form the most sophisticated passing attack the game had seen prior to the arrival of Johnny Unitas and Raymond Berry, Lavelli starred for the Browns in both the AAFC and NFL, amassing the second-most receptions, receiving yards, and TD catches in franchise history. A key contributor to teams that won 10 division titles and seven league championships, Lavelli earned three Pro Bowl nominations and a berth on the Pro Football Hall of Fame All-1940s Team, before being further honored following the conclusion of his playing career by being inducted into the Browns Ring of Honor and the Pro Football Hall of Fame.

Born to Italian immigrant parents in the small town of Hudson, Ohio, on February 23, 1923, Dante Bert Joseph Lavelli grew up some 30 miles southeast of Cleveland, where his father, Angelo, worked as a blacksmith who made shoes for horses on farms in the area. After spending his early years developing his pass-receiving skills by catching baseballs and ping-pong balls thrown to him by friends, Lavelli enrolled at Hudson High School, where he excelled in multiple sports, starting at quarterback for teams that won three straight county championships, while also starring as a middle infielder in baseball.

Given an opportunity to pursue a career in the big leagues by the Detroit Tigers, who offered him a contract to play second base for them in the minors, Lavelli instead chose to enroll at Ohio State University, also turning down in the process a scholarship from the University of Notre Dame. Switched to wide receiver by head coach Paul Brown shortly after he arrived in Columbus, Lavelli ended up appearing in only three games for the Buckeyes, suffering a knee injury during the early stages of the 1942 campaign that sidelined him for the rest of the year. Subsequently drafted

Dante Lavelli ranks second in franchise history in receptions, receiving yards, and touchdown catches.

into the military, Lavelli spent the next three and a half years serving his country during World War II, seeing action on Omaha Beach (as part of the invasion of Germany-occupied France) and in the Battle of the Bulge as a member of the 26th Infantry Division.

Following his discharge early in 1946, Lavelli elected to forgo his final two years of college eligibility and join his former Ohio State coach and the

Cleveland Browns in the newly formed All-America Football Conference (although he later resumed his studies at OSU, taking classes during offseasons, and eventually earning his degree). Recalling his thought process at the time, Lavelli said, "I had seen a pro game in New York. One of my Ohio State buddies was playing for the Giants. I thought if he could make the grade, so could I. So, when Brown, my old coach, offered me the chance, I was really ready."

Taking the new league by storm, Lavelli earned Second-Team All-AAFC honors as a rookie by topping the circuit with 40 receptions and 843 receiving yards, while also finishing second with eight TD catches and 857 yards from scrimmage. Lavelli followed that up with another outstanding season, helping the Browns capture the second of their five consecutive league championships in 1947 by finishing second in the AAFC with 49 receptions, 799 receiving yards, and nine touchdown receptions. Although Lavelli missed a significant amount of playing time in each of the next two seasons, appearing in only eight games in 1948 after breaking his leg during a preseason contest, he managed to rank among the league leaders in touchdown catches both years, with his seven TD grabs in 1949 placing him second in the league rankings.

Continuing to excel after the NFL absorbed the Browns in 1950, Lavelli made 37 receptions for 565 yards and five touchdowns, before gaining Pro Bowl recognition for the first of three times in 1951 by ranking among the league leaders with 43 receptions, 586 receiving yards, and six touchdown catches.

Certainly, the rules governing the game and the style of play employed at the time helped to greatly reduce Lavelli's offensive numbers. In addition to competing in an era when teams tended to rely heavily on their running game, Lavelli had to contend with defenses that played far more aggressively than they do today, once stating, "They talk about the bump-and-run nowadays. Heck, we had that with one difference. A defender didn't bump you, he knocked you down."

Nevertheless, opposing defenses found it extremely difficult to contain Lavelli, who allegedly acquired his "Gluefingers" nickname when broadcaster Bob Neal commented to Paul Brown during a training camp discussion, "That young guy catches everything. It's like he has glue on his hands."

Later attempting to explain the moniker bestowed upon his star wide receiver, Brown suggested, "The reason was his great concentration on the ball and the best pair of hands I've ever seen on any receiver. They had an almost liquid softness, which seemed to almost slurp the ball into them. He always seemed to catch every ball that was thrown near him, and he took many away from defensive backs who thought he was beaten."

Brown added, "Lavelli had one of the strongest pair of hands I've ever seen. When he went up for a pass with a defender, you could almost always count on him coming back down with the ball. Nobody could take it away from him once he had it in his hands."

Although the 6-foot, 191-pound Lavelli lacked great straight-ahead running speed, he possessed excellent quickness and exceptional route-running ability that he worked on tirelessly with quarterback Otto Graham, who later said, "We had a lot of great receivers on the Browns, but, when it came to great hands, there was nobody like Old Spumoni. There was no better competitor, either. . . . Dante would scratch, claw, and kick to get the ball. He was always coming into the huddle and telling me he was open and that I should throw to him. He wasn't saying that to be a big shot. He just loved to play. If he was open by a few inches, he'd be yelling, 'Otto, Otto.' Many a time when I was stuck and heard that voice, I would throw it in his direction and darned if he didn't come down with it. He had fantastic hands."

Despite being a dedicated route-runner, Lavelli knew how to improvise when things broke down, often taking off downfield and yelling for Graham to throw him the football, with the Hall of Fame signal-caller recalling, "That hollering helped me more than once. Dante had a voice that seemed to penetrate, and it was a welcome sound when a couple of big tackles were bearing down on me. We hit more than once for touchdowns on one of those broken plays."

Extremely clever as well, Lavelli occasionally utilized a trick play that he copied from legendary wideout Don Hutson, who had starred for the Green Bay Packers some years earlier. After racing for the goalposts and swinging around one of them with one hand, he emerged from the other side ready to grab a pass from Graham.

After totaling 66 receptions, 1,119 receiving yards, and 10 TD catches for the Browns from 1952 to 1953, Lavelli caught 47 passes, amassed 802 receiving yards, and scored seven touchdowns for their 1954 NFL championship team, earning in the process his third and final Pro Bowl selection. Lavelli spent two more years in Cleveland, helping the Browns with another NFL title in 1955, before announcing his retirement following the conclusion of the 1956 campaign with career totals of 386 receptions, 6,488 receiving yards, 62 touchdown catches, 6,511 yards from scrimmage, and 6,521 all-purpose yards, with each of the first three figures placing him among pro football's all-time leaders at the time of his retirement.

Following his playing days, Lavelli, who played an important role in the creation of the NFL Players Association his last few years in the league, opened a furniture and appliance store in the Cleveland suburbs that he owned and operated for many years. He also scouted for the Browns and Chicago Bears, briefly served as an assistant coach for the Browns, helped create the NFL Alumni Association, which assists former players in need, and spent a considerable amount of time on the golf course.

Inducted into the Pro Football Hall of Fame in 1975, Lavelli lived until January 20, 2009, when he died at Cleveland's Fairview Hospital from congestive heart failure at the age of 85. Following his passing, Steve Perry, the president and executive director of the HOF, issued a statement that read: "We are deeply saddened to learn of Dante's passing today. He was not only a good friend to all of us at the Pro Football Hall of Fame, but also to the many legions of Cleveland Browns fans across the country. Dante remained loyal to his roots in northeast Ohio, as he spent his life living in the Cleveland area. His devotion to the Browns remained strong through all these years."

CAREER HIGHLIGHTS

Best Season

Lavelli performed exceptionally well his first two years as a pro, leading the AAFC with 40 receptions and 843 receiving yards in 1946, while also finishing second in the league with eight touchdown receptions, before finishing second in the circuit with 49 receptions, 799 receiving yards, and nine TD catches the following year. But Lavelli had his finest all-around season in 1954, when, competing against the superior talent that the NFL had to offer, he placed near the top of the league rankings with 47 receptions, 802 receiving yards, and seven touchdown catches, earning in the process one of his three trips to the Pro Bowl.

Memorable Moments/Greatest Performances

Lavelli scored the first touchdown of his career when he gathered in a 39-yard pass from Otto Graham during a 44–0 rout of the Miami Seahawks in the opening game of the 1946 regular season.

Lavelli collaborated with Graham on a 33-yard scoring play that gave the Browns a 7–0 win over the New York Yankees on October 12, 1946.

Lavelli starred in defeat on October 27, 1946, making eight receptions for 183 yards and one touchdown during a 34–20 loss to the San Francisco 49ers.

Lavelli helped the Browns earn a hard-fought 14–9 victory over the Yankees in the 1946 AAFC championship game by making six receptions for 87 yards and one touchdown, which came on a 16-yard fourth-quarter grab that provided the winning margin.

Lavelli collaborated with Otto Graham on a career-long 72-yard scoring play during a 13–12 victory over the Brooklyn Dodgers on November 9, 1947.

Lavelli helped lead the Browns to a 37–14 win over the 49ers on November 16, 1947, by catching six passes for 127 yards and three touchdowns, the longest of which came on a 64-yard connection with Graham.

Lavelli proved to be too much for the Los Angeles Dons to handle on October 14, 1949, making seven receptions for a career-high 209 yards and four touchdowns during a 61–14 Browns win, with the longest of his scoring plays covering 67 yards.

Lavelli scored the first points of the Browns' 1949 AAFC divisional round playoff game matchup with the Buffalo Bills when he hauled in a 51-yard pass from Otto Graham. Lavelli finished the contest, which the Browns won by a score of 31–21, with five catches for 96 yards and that one TD.

Lavelli helped lead the Browns to a 34–24 victory over the Chicago Cardinals on October 15, 1950, by making six receptions for 131 yards and two touchdowns, which came on passes from Otto Graham that covered 29 and 26 yards.

Lavelli proved to be a huge factor in the 1950 NFL championship game, making 11 receptions for 128 yards and two touchdowns during a 30–28 win over the Los Angeles Rams, with his TDs coming on connections of 37 and 39 yards with Graham.

Lavelli contributed to a 27–7 victory over the Cardinals on October 4, 1953, by making four receptions for 137 yards and two touchdowns, the longest of which covered 55 yards.

Yet, Lavelli always considered the Browns' 35–10 win over the Philadelphia Eagles in the 1950 regular-season opener to be his most memorable game, saying years later, "The game I'll never forget is the first game we played in the National Football League. We beat the Philadelphia Eagles, 35–10. We went back to Cleveland the next day and waiting for us was something else we could be proud of. The press had asked Bert Bell, commissioner of the NFL, what he thought of the game. 'The Browns are the greatest football club I have ever seen,' he said."

Notable Achievements

- Surpassed 40 receptions five times.
- Surpassed 800 receiving yards twice.
- Averaged more than 20 yards per reception once.
- Made nine touchdown receptions in 1947.
- Led league in receptions, receiving yards, and average yards per reception once each.
- Finished second in league in receptions once, receiving yards once, yards from scrimmage once, and touchdown receptions three times.
- Led Browns in receptions and receiving yards four times each.
- Ranks among Browns career leaders with 386 receptions (2nd), 6,488 receiving yards (2nd), 62 touchdown receptions (2nd), 62 touchdowns (4th), 372 points scored (9th), 6,511 yards from scrimmage (7th), and 6,521 all-purpose yards (12th).
- Ten-time division champion (1946, 1947, 1948, 1949, 1950, 1951, 1952, 1953, 1954, and 1955).
- Four-time AAFC champion (1946, 1947, 1948, and 1949).
- Three-time NFL champion (1950, 1954, and 1955).
- 1946 Second-Team All-AAFC selection.
- Three-time Pro Bowl selection (1951, 1953, and 1954).
- NFL 1940s All-Decade Team.
- Member of Cleveland Browns Ring of Honor.
- Elected to Pro Football Hall of Fame in 1975.

13

CLAY MATTHEWS

One of the cornerstones of a defense that ranked among the NFL's best for much of the 1980s, Clay Matthews helped restore the Browns to prominence during the latter half of the decade by providing them with consistently excellent play at the right-outside linebacker position. Excelling as both a run-defender and pass-rusher, Matthews recorded more tackles and forced more fumbles than anyone else in franchise history, while also registering the second most sacks of any player in team annals. Recording more than 100 tackles eight times and more than 10 sacks once, Matthews led the Browns in each of those categories on multiple occasions, making him a key contributor to teams that won five division titles and advanced to the playoffs a total of seven times. Extremely durable, Matthews failed to start just three non-strike games from 1983 to 1993, ending his 16-year stint in Cleveland with only Lou Groza having appeared in more contests as a member of the team. A four-time Pro Bowler and one-time All-Pro, Matthews later received the additional honors of being named to Pro Football Reference's All-1980s Second Team and being inducted into the Browns Ring of Honor.

Born in Palo Alto, California, on March 15, 1956, William Clay Matthews Jr. grew up in a football family that included his father, William Clay Sr., who spent four seasons with the San Francisco 49ers during the early 1950s, and his younger brother, Bruce, who eventually gained induction into the Pro Football Hall of Fame following a brilliant 19-year career with the Houston Oilers/Tennessee Titans. Relocating with his family to Illinois at an early age, Clay Jr. went on to star on the gridiron for New Trier East High School in Winnetka, setting off a recruiting frenzy that included an offer from the University of Southern California. Ultimately choosing to enroll at USC, Matthews spent four seasons playing for the Trojans, gaining All-Conference recognition twice and earning All-America honors as a senior in 1977, with his outstanding play prompting the Browns to select him in the first round of the 1978 NFL Draft, with the 12th overall pick.

Clay Matthews holds franchise records for most tackles and most forced fumbles.
Courtesy of MearsonlineAuctions.com

Following his arrival in Cleveland, Matthews spent his first NFL season performing on special teams and backing up veteran starting outside linebackers Charlie Hall and Gerald Irons, before displacing Irons as the starter on the right side the following year, when he registered 103 tackles, recovered two fumbles, and recorded two sacks. Continuing to perform well in 1980 and 1981, Matthews totaled 10 sacks, three interceptions, three fumble recoveries, and 211 tackles, with his team-high 128 stops in the second of those campaigns representing the highest single-season mark of his career.

After being limited by injury to just two games in 1982, Matthews began a string of eight seasons during which he missed a total of just two games, earning four trips to the Pro Bowl, one All-Pro nomination, and three All-AFC selections during that time. Performing especially well in 1983 and 1984, Matthews recorded 106 tackles, six sacks, and a league-leading four forced fumbles in the first of those campaigns, before earning his lone All-Pro nomination the following year by registering 126 tackles, 12 sacks, and three forced fumbles.

Extremely versatile, the 6'2", 245-pound Matthews excelled in every aspect of linebacker play, with Cincinnati Bengals Hall of Fame offensive tackle Anthony Munoz stating, "Clay is one of the best I've ever played against. He could cover with speed, he rushed the passer as well as any guy, was as smart as any guy. It wasn't just that he could do one of those things. He was so versatile. He wasn't one-dimensional or two-dimensional. He could do everything that they called a linebacker to do, or a linebacker should do. It wasn't like he was playing first and second down and got third downs off. He was there every down."

Sam Rutigliano, the Browns head coach Matthews's first several years in the league, also spoke highly of him in a 2019 interview, saying, "Clay wouldn't come out of the game. He was unique. He had no ego, really just a team player. I can't remember in my seven years with him that I had anything to say that wasn't the best praise I could give a player."

Combining with Chip Banks from 1983 to 1986 to form one of the NFL's top outside linebacker tandems, Matthews gradually emerged as the leader of a defensive unit that helped the Browns win four division titles and earn five straight playoff berths from 1985 to 1989. Commenting on the impact that Matthews made during that period, former Browns QB Gary Danielson, who joined the team in 1985, said, "When I came to the Browns, he and Chip Banks were at the top of their game, and Clay was the best player in the NFL."

Former Browns head coach Marty Schottenheimer also had high praise for Matthews and the rest of the team's linebacking corps, stating, "Our linebacking crew was really, really good. We had Dick Ambrose and Robert Jackson and Chip Banks and, of course, Clay Matthews. Clay was a terrific, terrific player, vastly underrated in my view. One of the best linebackers I've ever been around."

Matthews remained in Cleveland until the end of 1993, when the Browns released him even though he totaled 274 tackles, 21 sacks, eight forced fumbles, and three interceptions over the course of the three previous seasons. Picked up by the Falcons shortly thereafter, Matthews spent the next three years in Atlanta, before announcing his retirement following the conclusion of the 1996 campaign with career totals of 1,595 tackles, 82½ sacks, 27 forced fumbles, 14 fumble recoveries, 16 interceptions, and two touchdowns. As a member of the Browns, Matthews recorded 1,430 tackles, 75 sacks, 24 forced fumbles, 13 fumble recoveries, 14 interceptions, which he returned for a total of 205 yards, and both his TDs.

After retiring as an active player, Matthews returned to his home state of California, where he assumed the position of defensive coordinator at Oaks Christian High School, a co-ed private school located in Westlake Village, not far from his home in Agoura Hills. Matthews later left his post at Oaks Christian to become director of football operations at Carter High School in Tennessee. Matthews also experienced the joy of watching his son, William Clay Matthews III, follow in his footsteps, starring at linebacker for the Green Bay Packers from 2009 to 2018, and winning a Super Bowl as a member of the team at the end of the 2010 season.

Matthews's longevity and outstanding career numbers have prompted many to call for his induction into the Pro Football Hall of Fame, although he has yet to be so honored. Speaking on behalf of his longtime teammate, Ozzie Newsome stated, "Part of my success as a player came from Clay Matthews. I had to practice against him every day since we first came into the league in 1978, and he made me better. Games became easier because of what he did to me in practices. Clay was a complete linebacker. He could set the edge with the best of them, making him a dominant run stopper. He could rush the passer at the Pro Bowl level, and he could cover tight ends and running backs in the passing game. Other Hall of Fame factors are consistency and longevity—Clay had both. To play as long as he did at such a consistently high level says everything."

Too humble to clamor for his own election, Matthews said during a 2019 interview, "Gosh, I would love for that to happen. I just think it is something I am uncomfortable talking about because I realize anything I did as a player really required my teammates to be there. Any height I reached, they helped me get there. I have really become aware of how important that is and how much I feel about that."

Matthews also discussed how much he enjoyed playing in the city of Cleveland, stating, "Playing in Cleveland was a great experience. There are not many distractions, which is good. It's all football. People love the team. They know the game. It really is close to life and death to them. Other teams have good followings, but there is something unique about football in Cleveland, the way the fans embrace the team. I ended my career in Atlanta. I'd go out, and a few people maybe would recognize me. They sold out every game, but it was not like Cleveland. The players mean a lot to the Browns' fans."

BROWNS CAREER HIGHLIGHTS

Best Season

Although Matthews had several outstanding seasons, he turned in his finest all-around performance in 1984, when he earned All-Pro honors for the only time by recording 126 tackles, forcing three fumbles, recovering another, batting away five passes, and registering a career-high 12 sacks, while playing right defensive end in most passing situations.

Memorable Moments/Greatest Performances

Matthews earned AFC Defensive Player of the Week honors for the first of two times by recording a career-high 3½ sacks during a 23–7 win over the Atlanta Falcons on November 18, 1984.

Matthews contributed to a 35–33 victory over the Giants on December 1, 1985, by sacking Phil Simms twice.

Matthews helped lead the Browns to a 34–10 win over the Steelers on September 20, 1987, by recording two interceptions, one of which he returned 26 yards for a touchdown.

In addition to recording two sacks during a 19–3 victory over the Eagles on October 16, 1988, Matthews helped anchor a Browns defense that allowed just 119 yards of total offense.

Matthews scored the Browns' first points of the 1989 campaign when he returned a fumble 3 yards for a touchdown during a 51–0 rout of the Steelers in the regular-season opener.

Matthews made probably the biggest play of his career in the final seconds of the Browns' 34–30 win over the Buffalo Bills in their 1989 divisional round playoff game matchup when he sealed the victory by intercepting a Jim Kelly pass at the Cleveland goal line with just three ticks left on the clock.

Matthews proved to be a thorn in the side of the Steelers once again on October 27, 1991, earning AFC Defensive Player of the Week honors by registering a sack and an interception during a 17–14 Browns win.

Matthews contributed to a 31–0 shutout of the Colts on December 1, 1991, by sacking Jeff George twice.

Notable Achievements

- Scored two defensive touchdowns.
- Recorded more than 100 tackles eight times.
- Finished in double digits in sacks once.
- Led Browns in tackles four times and sacks three times.
- Holds Browns career records for most tackles (1,430) and most forced fumbles (24).
- Ranks among Browns career leaders with 75 sacks (2nd), 13 fumble recoveries (5th), 16 seasons played (2nd), and 232 games played (2nd).
- Five-time division champion (1980, 1985, 1986, 1987, and 1989).
- Two-time AFC Defensive Player of the Week.
- Four-time Pro Bowl selection (1985, 1987, 1988, and 1989).
- 1984 Second-Team All-Pro selection.
- 1984 First-Team All-AFC selection.
- Two-time Second-Team All-AFC selection (1988 and 1989).
- Pro Football Reference All-1980s Second Team.
- Member of Cleveland Browns Ring of Honor.

14

MAC SPEEDIE

A standout performer for the Browns during the club's formative years, Mac Speedie spent seven seasons in Cleveland, amassing the third-most receptions and receiving yards in franchise history. The AAFC's career leader in both categories, Speedie continued to excel for the Browns after they joined the NFL in 1950, surpassing 50 receptions a total of four times, while also topping 1,000 receiving yards twice. A two-time Pro Bowler and five-time All-League selection, Speedie helped lead the Browns to seven division titles and five league championships, prompting the Pro Football Hall of Fame to finally open its doors to him in 2020, the year that marked his 100th birthday.

Born in Odell, Illinois, on January 12, 1920, Mac Curtis Speedie suffered through a difficult childhood that would have discouraged most men from pursuing a career in pro sports. Stricken with Perthes disease, a condition where loss of bone mass in the hip joint affects blood supply to that area, Speedie had to wear a steel brace on his left leg from his hip to his ankle for four years to correct the problem. Although Speedie ultimately recovered from his illness, one leg remained slightly shorter than the other, causing him to walk with something of a limp. Limited to mostly sedentary activities for much of his youth, Speedie later revealed how his disability helped fuel his desire to compete in sports, saying, "I don't suppose I would ever have been ambitious enough to excel at any sport if I hadn't been a cripple as a kid. I spent so much time eating my heart out because I couldn't play normally that when they took the brace off and I found I had legs that matched, it was like turning a frisky colt out to pasture after a year in a box stall. I had such a backlog of athletic ambition that I wanted to play football, basketball, and track all at one time."

Eventually moving with his family to Salt Lake City, Utah, Speedie attended South High School, where he starred in all three sports, starting at center for the school's basketball team, excelling at halfback in football, and performing especially well as a hurdler in track. Later attributing much

Speedie caught more passes for more yards than anyone else in the brief history of the AAFC.

of the success that he experienced on the gridiron to his track background, Speedie suggested, "Hurdling is all speed, balance, and perfect timing. I think that helped me more than anything else in becoming successful in football."

Recruited by several colleges for his athletic prowess, Speedie elected to remain close to home and enroll at the University of Utah, where he continued to compete in all three sports. Especially proficient in track and football, Speedie set or tied conference records in the low and high hurdles and gained All-Conference recognition three straight times at wide receiver.

Selected by the Detroit Lions in the 15th round of the 1942 NFL Draft, with the 135th overall pick, Speedie chose to delay the start of his pro career and enlist in the military to serve his country during World War II. He subsequently spent most of the next three years stationed at Fort Warren in Wyoming, where he played for the base's football team. Discovered by Paul Brown while competing against Brown's Great Lakes Naval Academy squad in 1944, Speedie later received an offer of $7,000 from the future Hall of Fame coach to play for his Cleveland Browns team in the newly formed All-America Football Conference after the war ended.

Joining the Browns prior to the start of the 1946 campaign, Speedie proved to be one of the AAFC's most productive wideouts in the league's inaugural season, making 24 receptions and ranking among the leaders with 564 receiving yards and seven TD catches, before beginning an exceptional three-year run during which he posted the following numbers:

YEAR	RECS	REC YDS	TD RECS
1947	67	1,146	6
1948	58	816	4
1949	62	1,028	7

The infant league's most prolific wideout those three seasons, Speedie led the AAFC in receptions each year and receiving yards twice, earning in the process three consecutive First-Team All-AAFC nominations. More importantly, the Browns compiled an overall regular-season record of 35-2-3, en route to winning three straight league championships.

Blessed with good size and outstanding speed, the 6'3", 203-pound Speedie excelled as both a deep threat and an intermediate receiver. Capable of outrunning even the league's fastest defensive backs, Speedie also possessed the height and leaping ability to outmaneuver his defender in close quarters. Meanwhile, Speedie's unusual running style that resulted from his childhood bout with Perthes disease made him even more difficult to cover, as he later acknowledged when he said that it "gave him an odd gait in which he could fake plays without even trying." A superb blocker and precise route-runner as well, Speedie excelled in every aspect of wide-receiver play, with his outstanding production for the Browns from 1946 to 1949 earning him a spot on the 1940s All-Decade Team.

When asked to compare Speedie and Dante Lavelli in 1949, Paul Brown hedged for a moment, saying, "They've got different styles and different techniques, but each is supreme in his own way."

Then, after singing the praises of Lavelli, Brown stated, "Speedie is perhaps a little more instinctive pass receiver, and a little more deceptive. He's so tall that when he's running at top speed he seems to be gliding easily. His natural ability to change pace and his great speed when he turns it on make it almost impossible to guard him with less than three men. I believe Lavelli does more conscious thinking about his movements than Mac does. He plans his faking, whereas Speedie seems to do his instinctively. They've got two things in common—they can catch anything they can touch, and, after they've caught it, they both run like halfbacks."

Yet, despite the respect that Brown had for Speedie's playing ability, he didn't care much for his independent personality, causing the two men to share a contentious relationship during their time together in Cleveland, with former Browns teammate Ken Carpenter recalling, "He [Speedie] was one of the ones that Paul Brown picked on quite a bit. He'd get on Speedie's case for no particular reason."

In response, Speedie found subtle ways to show his disdain for Brown, such as bringing a skunk with him to training camp one year and naming it "Paul," although he tried to downplay the incident by telling Brown that he named the animal after Paul Revere.

With the relationship between the two men having grown increasingly strained by the time the NFL absorbed the Browns in 1950, Speedie began to look for ways out of Cleveland, even though he continued to perform well on the playing field, totaling 76 receptions and 1,137 receiving yards from 1950 to 1951, before earning Pro Bowl, Second-Team All-Pro, and team MVP honors in 1952 by leading the league with 62 receptions, amassing 911 receiving yards, and scoring five touchdowns. Offered an opportunity to play north of the border by the Saskatchewan Roughriders of the Canadian Football League prior to the start of the 1953 season, Speedie signed for twice as much money as he made with the Browns, causing him to incur the wrath of Brown, who told the Cleveland media, "This was a case of jumping a contract, pure and simple, as this young man morally and ethically had a contract with us."

Speedie, who ended his seven-year stint in Cleveland with career totals of 349 receptions, 5,602 receiving yards, and 34 touchdowns, subsequently spent the next two seasons excelling for the Roughriders at wideout, before announcing his retirement following the conclusion of the 1955 campaign after sustaining an injury early in the year. Following his playing days, Speedie remained away from the game until 1960, when he took a job as receivers coach for the Houston Oilers of the new American Football League. After two years in that post, Speedie joined the coaching staff of the Denver Broncos, who he served as an assistant for more than two years, before assuming head coaching duties for the next two years. After relinquishing his duties as head coach early in 1966, Speedie remained with the Broncos as a scout until 1982, when he retired from football. Speedie lived another 11 years, dying of a heart attack in California at the age of 73, on March 12, 1993.

Not yet having gained induction into the Pro Football Hall of Fame at the time of his death even though football historian Andy Piascik referred to him in a 2002 article as "the best receiver of his era," Speedie once shed some light on his lengthy exclusion when he revealed that Paul Brown told him "He was going to get even" (for his signing with Saskatchewan). Making his former teammate's statement that much more believable, Otto Graham stated in 1991, "Quite honestly, I think Paul Brown is the reason [for Speedie's exclusion]. Paul wasn't the type of guy you crossed. He would never forget it."

Elected to the Hall of Fame as a "senior" candidate in 2020, Speedie finally received his just due nearly 70 years after he appeared in his last game with the Browns.

CAREER HIGHLIGHTS

Best Season

Speedie's final year in professional football proved to be one of his finest, as he led the NFL with 62 receptions in 1952, while also ranking among the leaders with 911 receiving yards and scoring five touchdowns, doing so against a somewhat higher level of competition than the one he faced in the AAFC. Nevertheless, Speedie made a slightly greater overall impact in 1947, earning First-Team All-AAFC honors by catching six TD passes and leading the league with 67 receptions and 1,146 receiving yards.

Memorable Moments/Greatest Performances

Speedie scored the first touchdown in the brief history of the AAFC when he gathered in a 19-yard pass from Cliff Lewis during a 44–0 rout of the Miami Seahawks in the opening game of the 1946 regular season.

Although the Browns lost to the Los Angeles Dons by a score of 17–16 on November 3, 1946, Speedie had a big game, making four receptions for

134 yards and one touchdown, which came on a 79-yard connection with Otto Graham.

Speedie helped lead the Browns to a 31–28 win over the Chicago Rockets on October 19, 1947, by making five receptions for 166 yards and one touchdown, which he scored on a 49-yard pass from Otto Graham.

Speedie followed that up by catching 10 passes for 141 yards and one touchdown during a 14–7 win over the San Francisco 49ers on October 26, 1947.

Although Speedie made just two receptions during a 28–7 victory over the Buffalo Bills on November 2, 1947, one of them went for a career-long 99-yard touchdown on a play that began as a short screen pass from Otto Graham.

Speedie contributed to a lopsided 42–13 victory over the Bills on September 12, 1948, by making 10 receptions for 151 yards and one touchdown.

Speedie continued to torment the Bills in the second meeting between the two teams on October 17, 1948, making seven receptions for 142 yards and two TDs during a 31–14 Browns win.

Speedie had a huge game against the New York Yankees on November 20, 1949, catching 11 passes and setting a franchise record that still stands by amassing 228 receiving yards.

Speedie contributed to a 42–21 win over the Chicago Bears on November 25, 1951, by making six receptions for 144 yards.

Speedie followed that up by making four receptions for 73 yards and three touchdowns during a 49–28 win over the Chicago Cardinals on December 2, 1951.

Speedie had another big game against the Cardinals on November 9, 1952, making 11 receptions for 157 yards and one touchdown during a 28–13 Browns win, with his TD coming on a 43-yard connection with Otto Graham.

Speedie starred in defeat on November 23, 1952, making seven receptions for 156 yards and two touchdowns during a 28–20 loss to the Philadelphia Eagles.

Notable Achievements

- Surpassed 50 receptions four times.
- Topped 1,000 receiving yards twice.
- Averaged more than 20 yards per reception once.

- Led league in receptions four times and receiving yards twice.
- Finished second in league in touchdown receptions once and yards from scrimmage once.
- Led Browns in receptions and receiving yards five times each.
- Holds Browns single-game record for most receiving yards (228 vs. N.Y. Yankees on November 20, 1949).
- Ranks among Browns career leaders with 349 receptions (3rd), 5,602 receiving yards (3rd), 33 touchdown receptions (6th), and 5,602 yards from scrimmage (11th).
- Holds AAFC records for most receptions (221) and receiving yards (3,554).
- Seven-time division champion (1946, 1947, 1948, 1949, 1950, 1951, and 1952).
- Four-time AAFC champion (1946, 1947, 1948, and 1949).
- 1950 NFL champion.
- 1952 Browns MVP.
- Two-time Pro Bowl selection (1950 and 1952).
- Three-time First-Team All-AAFC selection (1947, 1948, and 1949).
- Two-time Second-Team All-Pro selection (1950 and 1952).
- NFL 1940s All-Decade Team.
- Elected to Pro Football Hall of Fame in 2020.

15

MIKE MCCORMACK

dentified by Paul Brown in 1979 as "the finest offensive tackle who ever played pro football," Mike McCormack spent nine seasons in Cleveland, starring on the right side of the Browns' offensive line in eight of those. Acquired from the Baltimore Colts in the spring of 1953 as part of a mammoth 15-player trade that sent four other players to Cleveland, McCormack went on to establish himself as arguably the finest right tackle in the game, earning five trips to the Pro Bowl, three All-Pro nominations, and seven First-Team All–Eastern Conference selections. A member of Browns teams that won three division titles and two NFL championships, McCormack later received the additional honors of being inducted into the Browns Ring of Honor and the Pro Football Hall of Fame.

Born in Chicago, Illinois, on June 21, 1930, Michael Joseph McCormack moved with his family at a very young age to Kansas City, Kansas, where he developed into one of the state's top football prospects while attending De La Salle High School. Continuing to excel on the gridiron at the University of Kansas, McCormack spent three seasons starring for the Jayhawks at tackle on both sides of the ball, gaining First-Team All–Big Seven Conference recognition as a senior in 1950.

Although McCormack originally aspired to become a high school football coach once he earned his degree, he decided to pursue a different career path when the New York Yanks selected him in the third round of the 1951 NFL Draft, with the 34th overall pick. McCormack subsequently spent one year in New York excelling at right tackle for the Yanks, earning Pro Bowl and Second-Team All-Pro honors, before serving in the US Army from 1952 to 1953 during the Korean War. Anticipating an eventual return to New York once his tour of duty ended, McCormack once again had to change his plans when the Browns acquired his services in a huge trade with the Baltimore Colts, who assumed his contract after the Yanks became the Dallas Texans in 1952 and folded one year later. The March 26, 1953, deal, which ranks among the biggest—at least in terms of numbers—in sports

Paul Brown called Mike McCormack the finest offensive tackle he ever saw.
Courtesy of RMYAuctions.com

history, sent McCormack, defensive tackle Don Colo, linebacker Tom Catlin, guard Herschel Forester, and defensive back John Petitbon to Cleveland for a package of 10 players that included kicker/defensive back/return-man Bert Rechichar, guard Art Spinney, and defensive back and future Hall of Fame coach Don Shula.

Joining the Browns following his discharge early in 1954, McCormack spent his first season in Cleveland playing middle guard on defense, a position that the recently retired Bill Willis had manned the previous eight years. But even though McCormack performed well at that post, gaining unofficial Second-Team All-Pro recognition from United Press

International, the return of Bob Gain from the military the following year allowed the Browns to move him back to his more natural position of right tackle.

Immediately asserting himself as one of the NFL's top offensive linemen, McCormack earned All-Pro honors from four different news sources in 1955, with his outstanding play helping the Browns capture their second straight league championship. Continuing to perform at an elite level the following year, McCormack gained Pro Bowl recognition for the first of five times as a member of the Browns and earned the first of his seven consecutive First-Team All–Eastern Conference selections.

Admired throughout the league for his excellence in all phases of offensive line play, McCormick drew praise from former NFL player and executive Bucko Kilroy, who said, "Power combined with great intelligence and 4.8 speed. I've seen him have games where, if you were grading him, he'd score 100. Not one mistake, and his guy would never make a tackle."

Standing 6'2" and weighing more than 250 pounds, McCormack possessed a powerful physique that prompted some to liken him to a block of granite. In describing his father years later, Michael McCormack said, "My high school buddies called him Big Mike. One of them said after meeting him, 'That was like shaking hands with a package of iron hot dogs.' He had a big meaty head that had to be shoe-horned into his helmet, an upper body like a kitchen appliance, and thighs as big as oaks."

An outstanding technician, McCormack expressed what he considered to be the key to good blocking when he stated, "Beat your opponent to the charge and keep your feet."

Respected for his attention to detail and leadership ability as well, McCormack, who served as a team captain from 1956 to 1962, kept such impeccable notes in team meetings according to Paul Brown that the coach made copies and distributed them to the rest of the players, telling them, "This is how it is done."

Meanwhile, fellow Browns offensive lineman John Wooten spoke of McCormack's strong character and leadership ability when he said, "We had a play where Mike was supposed to call out how I was to block. He didn't make the call and I didn't block the way I was supposed to. As I came off the field, Paul Brown ate me alive. Mike stepped in and said it was his fault and Paul didn't say another word. That still resonates because that shows how Mike's character was strong at all times. . . . He's the best captain I've been around on any level of football. I've never seen a captain more committed than Mike. His leadership was outstanding. Of course, he was a great football player, but he was also a man of strong character."

One of the league's most durable players, McCormack started every game the Browns played in seven of his nine seasons in Cleveland, missing a total of just five contests during that time. But, after gaining Pro Bowl recognition in each of the previous three seasons, McCormack decided to announce his retirement following the conclusion of the 1962 campaign, ending his career having started 119 out of a possible 124 contests.

After retiring as an active player, McCormack began a lengthy career in coaching that included stints as an assistant in Washington (1965–1972) and Cincinnati (1976–1979), and as head man in Philadelphia (1973–1975), Baltimore (1980–1981), and Seattle (1982). McCormack also served as president and general manager of the Seahawks from 1983 to 1989. After being relieved of his duties in Seattle, McCormack spent three years working as a consultant to an investment group trying to establish an expansion franchise in Charlotte, North Carolina, before being named president and general manager of the Carolina Panthers in 1993. McCormack continued to function in that dual role until he retired from NFL work in 1997, three years after he received the honor of being named to the *USA Today* NFL 75th Anniversary All-Time Team as one of the three greatest tackles in league history.

McCormack spent the rest of his years living in Palm Desert, California, before dying of heart failure at the age of 83 on November 15, 2013. Upon learning of his passing, the Browns issued a statement that read: "The Cleveland Browns were saddened to learn of the passing of Mike McCormack. His contributions to our history are profound, not only on an individual level, but also with regard to the tremendous success we enjoyed as a team during his career. Both the Browns and the NFL are most fortunate to have shared part of his amazing life. Our deepest condolences go out to his wife, Ann, and his family."

BROWNS CAREER HIGHLIGHTS

Best Season

McCormack gained Pro Bowl recognition in 1956, 1957, 1960, 1961, and 1962. But, while he failed to be so honored in any of the other four seasons, McCormack also earned All-Pro honors in 1957, with the Associated Press awarding him a spot on its Second Team. Furthermore, the Browns placed near the top of the league rankings in both points scored and total yards gained in 1957, making that the most impactful season of McCormack's career.

Memorable Moments/Greatest Performances

Before moving to the offensive side of the ball the following year, McCormack helped lead the Browns to a 6–0 shutout of the Eagles on November 21, 1954, by performing magnificently during a key goal-line stand that kept Philadelphia out of the Cleveland end zone, recalling years later, "They got down to the one-yard line. On the first play, I made the tackle for a yard loss. The second play, I made a tackle for a yard loss again." After revealing that a delay of game penalty pushed the Eagles back 5 more yards, McCormack continued, "I rushed the passer, and he threw incomplete. Then, on fourth down, I pulled out of the line and went into pass defense. I've still got the broken ring finger where I hit the ball and made it incomplete."

McCormack helped the Browns amass 454 yards of total offense during a 41–10 win over the Packers on October 23, 1955, with 204 of those yards coming on the ground and the other 250 through the air.

McCormack helped pave the way for Browns running backs to gain a season-high total of 330 yards on the ground during a 45–31 victory over the Los Angeles Rams on November 24, 1957.

McCormack's strong play up front helped the Browns rush for 298 yards and amass 488 yards of total offense during a 34–28 win over the Giants in the final game of the 1957 regular season.

McCormack's superior blocking at the point of attack helped the Browns amass 428 yards of total offense during a 28–20 win over the Steelers on October 2, 1960, with 296 of those yards coming through the air.

Notable Achievements

- Three-time division champion (1954, 1955, and 1957).
- Two-time NFL champion (1954 and 1955).
- Five-time Pro Bowl selection (1956, 1957, 1960, 1961, and 1962).
- Three-time Second-Team All-Pro selection (1957, 1958, and 1959).
- Seven-time First-Team All–Eastern Conference selection (1956, 1957, 1958, 1959, 1960, 1961, and 1962).
- Named to *USA Today* 75th Anniversary Team in 1994.
- Member of Cleveland Browns Ring of Honor.
- Elected to Pro Football Hall of Fame in 1984.

16

PAUL WARFIELD

Known for his speed, fluidity, grace, soft hands, and exceptional leaping ability, Paul Warfield proved to be one of the finest wide receivers of his era, earning eight Pro Bowl selections and four All-Pro nominations over the course of his 13-year NFL career, more than half of which he spent in Cleveland. A member of the Browns from 1964 to 1969, and again from 1976 to 1977, Warfield contributed to teams that won five division titles and one league championship by surpassing 50 receptions twice, amassing more than 1,000 receiving yards once, and averaging more than 20 yards per reception on four separate occasions, while also recording the third-most touchdown receptions in franchise history. Performing equally well for the Dolphins from 1970 to 1974, Warfield starred on Miami teams that won three conference championships and two Super Bowls, with his total body of work earning him spots on the *Sporting News'* 1999 list and the NFL Network's 2010 list of the 100 Greatest Players in NFL History, a berth on the NFL 100 All-Time Team, and a place in the Pro Football Hall of Fame.

Born in Warren, Ohio, on November 28, 1942, Paul Dryden Warfield grew up rooting for the Cleveland Browns, for whom he hoped to play one day. After getting his start in organized sports in junior high school, Warfield enrolled at Warren G. Harding High School, where he starred in baseball, football, basketball, and track and field. Particularly outstanding in football and track, Warfield won the Ohio High School Athletic Association Class AA broad jump championship in 1958, before setting a Class AA state record in the 180-yard hurdles two years later. Warfield also excelled as a running back and defensive back on the gridiron, scoring 92 points as a junior in 1958, and tallying another 93 points his senior year.

Choosing to remain close to home, Warfield accepted an athletic scholarship to Ohio State University, where he continued to compete in multiple sports, excelling for the Buckeyes' football team at running back and defensive back under head coach Woody Hayes, and lettering twice in track and

Paul Warfield starred at wide receiver for Browns teams that won five division titles and one NFL championship.
Courtesy of MearsonlineAuctions.com

field as a broad jumper, hurdler, and sprinter. Performing brilliantly on the gridiron his senior year, Warfield earned First-Team All-America honors by amassing 526 yards from scrimmage and scoring four touchdowns on offense, while also doing an expert job of blanketing opposing receivers from his cornerback position on defense.

Faced with a difficult decision as graduation neared, Warfield had to choose between preparing himself for the 1964 NFL Draft or competing for a spot as a broad jumper on the US Olympic Team after recording a personal-best leap of 26 feet, 2 inches his senior year. Recalling the dilemma he faced at the time, Warfield said, "It's a chance to represent your country, and a chance to compete on the world basis. If I had been lucky enough to stand on the stand of one of those three places, that's a very special honor."

Ultimately deciding to pursue his dream of playing in the NFL, Warfield ended up being selected by the Browns in the first round, with the 11th overall pick, remembering, "I'm sitting by my radio, and all of a sudden, my name is called. So, I'm elated. My favorite team is going to draft me. This is unbelievable. So, it all worked out."

Although the Buffalo Bills also selected him in the fourth round of that year's AFL Draft, with the 28th overall pick, Warfield wasted little time in signing with the Browns, who initially planned on using him at cornerback. However, after observing Warfield's superior running and pass-catching skills during training camp, the Browns wisely chose to convert him into a wide receiver, with the recently retired Ray Renfro serving as his mentor during the early stages of his rookie campaign.

Learning his lessons well, Warfield went on to earn Pro Bowl and First-Team All–Eastern Conference honors his first year in the league by making 52 receptions, amassing 920 receiving yards, and catching nine touchdown passes for a Browns team that won the NFL championship. However, Warfield ended up appearing in only one game the following year after breaking his collarbone in the annual Chicago All-Star Game that pitted the reigning NFL champions against a team of graduating college all-stars.

Fully healthy by the start of the 1966 campaign, Warfield posted solid numbers the next two seasons, making a total of 68 receptions for 1,443 yards and 14 touchdowns, before gaining Pro Bowl and Second-Team All-Pro recognition in 1968 by leading the NFL with 12 TD catches and placing near the top of the league rankings with 50 receptions and 1,067 receiving yards. Warfield followed that up with another outstanding season, earning Pro Bowl and Second-Team All–Eastern Conference honors in 1969 by making 42 receptions for 886 yards and 10 TDs.

Supremely talented, the 6-foot, 188-pound Warfield possessed outstanding speed, tremendous open-field running ability, and excellent moves that made him a threat to go the distance any time he touched the football. Capable of beating his man deep or using his quickness and acceleration to gain additional yardage after the catch, Warfield averaged more than 20 yards per reception seven times during his career, doing so four times as a member of the Browns. A precise route-runner and exceptional blocker as well, Warfield drew praise from George Allen for his excellence in all aspects of wide receiver play, with the Hall of Fame head coach saying, "He was explosive, dangerous at all times. He didn't catch a lot of balls, but he did a lot with the ones he did catch—talk about a home run hitter. He had sprinter's speed, good hands, great running ability, and boy, could he block. In my book, a receiver who didn't block didn't get a good grade from me, but Warfield was an A+."

A thinking man's receiver, Warfield put a lot of time and effort into his craft, saying, "I don't like going into a situation where I'm going to be surprised by something, so I spent a great deal of time studying strategies employed against me. We knew exactly what to expect, and I would run the adjustment to the pattern."

In addition to his physical and mental gifts, Warfield had an elegance about him that made him a thing of beauty to watch. Employing a smooth, almost effortless running style, Warfield glided down the field gracefully, separating himself from his defender with each step. In discussing his former teammate, Frank Ryan said, "Paul was very fast and very smooth, he looked beautiful running here, there, and yonder, making sharp cuts and stops—and he got his share of passes, that's for sure."

NFL analyst and former Cincinnati Bengals wide receiver Cris Collinsworth said of Warfield, "I think one of the most underrated wide receivers in the history of the game, for my money. You'll never see the numbers because they didn't throw the ball at the time the way they do in the game today, but the routes and the ability to get in and out of cuts was just so effective. One of the greatest receivers of all time."

Further hampered by playing for teams that depended heavily on their potent running attacks to wear down the opposition, Warfield nevertheless found no fault with his team's offensive philosophy, even crediting the Browns for much of the success he experienced when he said, "I came from the Cleveland Browns system. It was greatly advanced in terms of the theory in pass-pattern execution and pass-pattern running, even though the Browns during that era employed great running backs. They had great theoretical ideas about how to throw the football vertically downfield."

Yet, despite the brilliance that Warfield displayed his first six years in the league, the Browns traded him to the Miami Dolphins for the third overall pick in the 1970 NFL Draft, which they subsequently used to select Purdue quarterback Mike Phipps. After completing the deal, Browns owner Art Modell stated, "Paul has played so well for us and is such a high-type person that I hated like the devil to consider any trade involving him.

However, it was the overwhelming consensus of all our combined thinking that we had a pressing need for backup protection behind quarterback Bill Nelsen."

Recalling his feelings at the time, Warfield said, "I had spent six years in Cleveland and felt like my career obviously was headed in the right direction, with me very much a part of the Cleveland offensive philosophy. And when I was called slightly before the draft and informed that I would be going to the Miami Dolphins . . . it was quite a surprise to me."

Warfield continued, "It was a great shock to be going to the Dolphins. They were one of the worst teams in a new league. . . . But 10 days later I began to feel a little bit better after the trade when I learned Don Shula was leaving Baltimore to go to Miami. I had great respect for his contributions to the National Football League. While he hadn't won a Super Bowl to that point, I knew Shula was a great, great coach, and I felt a little at ease."

Warfield added, "Things came together amazingly quickly down there, even in the first year. From that point on, it got better and better. . . . There were some ups and downs in that first year, but it all pulled together. And almost overnight we became a championship team."

And as the Dolphins emerged as one of the strongest teams in pro football, Warfield continued to perform at an elite level, earning five straight Pro Bowl selections and three All-Pro nominations from 1970 to 1974, with his 43 receptions, 996 receiving yards, and league-leading 11 TD catches in 1971 gaining him First-Team All-Pro recognition for the first of two times.

Wowing his new teammates with his superior pass-receiving skills, Warfield later drew praise from three-time Pro Bowl running back Mercury Morris, who stated, "We didn't realize how incredible Warfield was until we saw him in practice, because that's when you got to see a guy who's not just going out to beat another guy, but calculating a way in which to make this guy buy something that he's not selling."

Morris continued, "Many a time I would see Paul count his steps and, as soon as he saw this guy commit to one of the steps that he gave him, he would turn the other way. That's why, when you look at films, you see Paul by himself, because the other guy is still back there wondering what the hell happened. . . . His uniform was always clean. In other words, he didn't get banged around too much, and he was always off the ground. Every catch that he made, it seemed like he always went up and got it just before the ball was supposed to be coming down. He would go up and get it and leave that defender."

After helping the Dolphins win their fourth consecutive division title in 1974, Warfield joined teammates Larry Csonka and Jim Kiick in signing with the Toronto Northmen of the newly formed World Football League. Warfield subsequently spent the 1975 season playing in Memphis after the Northmen moved south of the border and renamed themselves the Southmen, catching 25 passes, amassing 422 receiving yards, and scoring three touchdowns. However, when the WFL folded at the end of the year, Warfield returned to Cleveland, where he spent his final two seasons starting for the Browns at wideout, before announcing his retirement following the conclusion of the 1977 campaign with career totals of 427 receptions, 8,565 receiving yards, 85 touchdown receptions, and 86 total touchdowns. As a member of the Browns, Warfield caught 271 passes, amassed 5,210 receiving yards, made 52 touchdown receptions, and scored 53 TDs, with each of the last three figures placing him among the team's all-time leaders. Meanwhile, Warfield, whose career average of 20.1 yards per reception remains the highest in NFL history among players with at least 300 receptions, ranked tied for third in league history in TD catches at the time of his retirement.

Following his playing days, Warfield, who earned a master's degree in telecommunications from Kent State University in 1977, worked as a sportscaster for WKYC in Cleveland from 1977 to 1980, before assuming the role of director of player relations for the Browns from 1981 to 1987. After spending several years serving as president of a management consulting firm in Moraine, Ohio, Warfield rejoined the Browns in 2004 as a senior advisor to the general manager, a position he held until 2010, when he retired to private life. Now 79 years of age, Warfield is living the quiet life in Rancho Mirage, California.

BROWNS CAREER HIGHLIGHTS

Best Season

Warfield performed brilliantly as a rookie in 1964, earning Pro Bowl and First-Team All–Eastern Conference honors by making a career-high 52 receptions, amassing 920 receiving yards, and scoring nine touchdowns. But he had his finest season for the Browns in 1968, when he earned his lone All-Pro nomination as a member of the team by catching 50 passes, finishing second in the NFL with 1,067 receiving yards, and leading the league with 12 touchdown receptions.

Memorable Moments/Greatest Performances

Warfield helped the Browns forge a 33–33 tie with the St. Louis Cardinals on September 20, 1964, by making three receptions for 63 yards and scoring the first touchdown of his career on a 40-yard pass from Frank Ryan.

Warfield went over 100 receiving yards for the first time as a pro on October 4, 1964, catching five passes for 123 yards and one touchdown during a 27–6 win over the Dallas Cowboys.

Warfield starred in defeat on November 22, 1964, making seven receptions for 126 yards and two touchdowns during a 28–21 loss to the Packers, scoring his TDs on plays of 48 and 19 yards.

Warfield contributed to a 38–10 victory over the Cardinals in the final game of the 1966 regular season by making six receptions for 161 yards.

Warfield torched the Giants' defensive secondary for six receptions, 137 receiving yards, and one touchdown during a 45–10 Browns win on December 1, 1968.

Warfield helped lead the Browns to a 24–3 victory over the Steelers on November 16, 1969, by making five receptions for 132 yards and one touchdown.

Warfield displayed his big-play ability during a 27–21 win over the Cardinals on December 14, 1969, making four receptions for 119 yards and two touchdowns, one of which came on an 82-yard connection with Bill Nelsen.

Notable Achievements

- Surpassed 50 receptions twice.
- Surpassed 1,000 receiving yards once.
- Topped 10 touchdown receptions twice.
- Averaged more than 20 yards per reception four times.
- Led NFL with 12 touchdown receptions in 1968.
- Finished second in NFL in receiving yards once and average yards per reception once.
- Finished third in NFL in touchdown receptions once, touchdowns once, and average yards per reception twice.
- Led Browns in receptions twice and receiving yards four times.
- Ranks among Browns career leaders with 5,210 receiving yards (6th), 52 touchdown receptions (3rd), 53 touchdowns (7th), 318 points scored (12th), and average of 19.2 yards per reception (2nd).
- Five-time division champion (1964, 1965, 1967, 1968, and 1969).

- 1964 NFL champion.
- Three-time Pro Bowl selection (1964, 1968, and 1969).
- 1968 Second-Team All-Pro selection.
- 1964 First-Team All–Eastern Conference selection.
- 1969 Second-Team All–Eastern Conference selection.
- Named to NFL 100 All-Time Team in 2019.
- Number 60 on the *Sporting News*' 1999 list of the 100 Greatest Players in NFL History.
- Number 71 on the NFL Network's 2010 list of the NFL's 100 Greatest Players.
- Member of Cleveland Browns Ring of Honor.
- Elected to Pro Football Hall of Fame in 1983.

17

FRANK GATSKI

A member of the Browns in their inaugural season of 1946, Frank "Gunner" Gatski, so nicknamed for his hard-nosed, rough-and-tumble ways on and off the field, spent all but one of his 12 pro seasons in Cleveland, serving as the bodyguard for Otto Graham much of that time. Starting 110 consecutive games for the Browns at center from 1948 to 1956, Gatski proved to be one of the league's premier players at his position, with his exceptional blocking and tremendous durability making him a key contributor to Browns teams that won 10 division titles and seven league championships. Continuing his winning ways after he left Cleveland, Gatski helped lead the Detroit Lions to the NFL championship in 1957, before announcing his retirement following the conclusion of the campaign. A five-time All-Pro, Gatski later received the additional honors of being inducted into the Browns Ring of Honor and the Pro Football Hall of Fame.

Born to Polish immigrant parents in the coal-mining town of Farmington, West Virginia, on March 18, 1919, Frank Gatski grew up in the Number Nine Coal Mine Camp expecting to follow in the footsteps of his father and grandfather, both of whom spent much of their lives working in the mines. Admitting years later that he never anticipated pursuing a career in pro football, Gatski said, "My football was never planned; I was just in the right place at the right time."

Getting his start on the gridiron at Farmington High School, which played its home games on a cow pasture with no scoreboard, bleachers, or game clock, Gatski started for three years at center and linebacker, while spending his summers working in the mines. After working full-time his senior year, Gatski received an offer to attend Marshall University on a football scholarship. Traveling some 190 miles southwest, to Huntington, West Virginia, Gatski spent his freshman year at Marshall starting at center and linebacker for the school's JV football team, before manning the same positions for the varsity squad the next two seasons. However, following his junior year at Marshall, Gatski enlisted in the military to fight in World

A winner wherever he went, Frank Gatski played for teams that won 11 division titles and eight league championships during his Hall of Fame career.

War II. He subsequently spent the next three years serving his country, primarily in Europe, recalling, "The army reserve unit I was in was activated. After basic training, we were sent to England and later followed the troops through Normandy and into Europe. I wasn't in any heavy fighting."

With Marshall having dropped its football program because of the war, Gatski transferred to Auburn University for his senior year when he returned to the States following his discharge in 1945, later explaining, "Marshall hadn't started back up, and I hadn't played football for two years. I didn't want to sit around and do nothing, so I went to Auburn."

After playing briefly for Auburn in 1945, Gatski received a tryout with the Cleveland Browns of the newly formed All-America Football Conference, with whom he subsequently spent his first two seasons sitting behind veteran center Mike Scarry, while also recording three interceptions and scoring one touchdown on defense as a situational linebacker. Replacing Scarry at center in 1948, Gatski remained at that post for the next nine seasons, a period during which he helped lead the Browns to eight division titles and five league championships. Establishing himself as arguably the league's finest player at his position, Gatski earned All-Pro honors five straight times, being named to the First Team in 1952, 1953, and 1955, while gaining Second-Team recognition in 1951 and 1954.

An excellent pass-protector, the 6'3", 240-pound Gatski drew praise from Browns Hall of Fame quarterback Otto Graham, who said, "You never have to worry about anyone jumping over Frank or bumping him out of the way."

Graham also claimed that Gatski's long legs helped him survey the field better, adding, "When he bends over the ball, I can stand almost straight up and down and still get the snap. If he had short legs, I would be forced to bend over further to take the ball."

An outstanding run-blocker as well, Gatski received praise from Philadelphia Eagles Hall of Fame linebacker Chuck Bednarik, who stated, "He was the best and toughest I ever played against. As a linebacker, I sometimes had to go over the center, but Gatski was the immovable object."

In discussing the degree to which Gatski's skill set impacted the style of play the Browns employed on offense, one reporter wrote, "The way he plants his frame, the enemy has to go around him, never over him. Cleveland's style of offense, splitting the ends and massing the middle of the line, depends on an implanted center like Gatski for down the middle anchorage."

Meanwhile, Dante Lavelli expressed his admiration for his longtime teammate by saying, "He was like a polished stone, very strong in the middle. A very strong man, and a very good player. He was always able to adjust really well to anything. Just a quiet man and a great teammate. I never remember him missing a game."

Extraordinarily consistent and reliable, Gatski never missed a game, or even a practice, prompting his teammates to often refer to him as an "iron man" and a "Rock of Gibraltar." Sporting a perpetual grin, Gatski also earned the nicknames "Li'l Abner" and "Joe Palooka" during his time in Cleveland, in deference to a pair of popular comic strip characters of that era.

After Gatski started every game for them at center in each of the previous nine seasons, the Browns traded him to the Detroit Lions following the conclusion of the 1956 campaign. Coming back to haunt his former team, Gatski helped lead the Lions to the Western Division title in 1957, before anchoring their offensive line during their 59–14 victory over the Browns in the NFL championship game. Gatski subsequently announced his retirement, ending his 12-year career having played for teams that appeared in the league championship game 11 times.

Following his playing days, Gatski initially spent four years working as a scout for the AFL's Boston Patriots, before assuming the dual roles of head football coach and athletic director at the West Virginia Industrial School for Boys in Pruntytown, West Virginia, a correctional facility for juvenile offenders. After 21 years at West Virginia Industrial, Gatski chose to retire to private life, saying at the time, "When I first retired from pro football, I missed it because I played so long. But then I got into the mainstream of life. There's a whole bunch of life after pro football. Having babies and raising kids . . . and getting in the mainstream, that's the real ballgame. Football's easy because you have plays, but there are no plays when you get out in the street."

After leaving Pruntytown, Gatski spent more than two decades living on a mountain in West Virginia, where he spent most of his free time hunting and fishing. Eventually moving into a nursing home in Morgantown, West Virginia, Gatski died of congestive heart failure at the age of 86, on November 22, 2005.

BROWNS CAREER HIGHLIGHTS

Best Season

Gatski gained First-Team All-Pro recognition in 1952, 1953, and 1955, and any of those seasons would make a good choice. But, since the Browns led the league in points scored (349) and placed near the top of the league rankings in yards gained on the ground (2,020) and total yardage (3,970) when they won the NFL title in 1955, we'll identify that as Gatski's finest season.

Memorable Moments/Greatest Performances

Gatski scored the only touchdown of his career when he ran 36 yards to pay dirt after intercepting a pass during a 51–14 rout of the Chicago Rockets on November 17, 1946.

Gatski helped the Browns rush for 268 yards and amass 504 yards of total offense during a 42–13 win over the Buffalo Bills on September 12, 1948.

Gatski anchored an offensive line that enabled the Browns to gain 242 yards on the ground and 550 total yards during a 42–7 manhandling of the Los Angeles Dons on October 2, 1949.

Gatski and his line-mates dominated the opposition at the point of attack once again on November 6, 1949, with the Browns amassing 542 yards of total offense during a lopsided 35–2 victory over the Chicago Hornets, gaining 246 of those yards on the ground and the other 296 through the air.

Gatski helped pave the way for Browns running backs to rush for 338 yards during a 45–7 mauling of the Pittsburgh Steelers on October 29, 1950.

Gatski helped the Browns gain a season-high total of 291 yards on the ground during a 37–7 win over the Los Angeles Rams in the opening game of the 1952 campaign.

Gatski's superior blocking helped the Browns rush for 226 yards and amass 515 yards of total offense during a 62–3 blowout of the Washington Redskins on November 7, 1954.

Notable Achievements

- Intercepted three passes and scored one touchdown on defense.
- Started 110 consecutive games from 1948 to 1956.
- Ten-time division champion (1946, 1947, 1948, 1949, 1950, 1951, 1952, 1953, 1954, and 1955).
- Four-time AAFC champion (1946, 1947, 1948, and 1949).
- Three-time NFL champion (1950, 1954, and 1955).
- 1956 Pro Bowl selection.
- Three-time First-Team All-Pro selection (1952, 1953, and 1955).
- Two-time Second-Team All-Pro selection (1951 and 1954).
- Pro Football Reference All-1950s First Team.
- Member of Cleveland Browns Ring of Honor.
- Elected to Pro Football Hall of Fame in 1985.

18

GREG PRUITT

A n explosive runner who excelled for the Browns on both offense and special teams, Greg Pruitt overcame early questions about his size to establish himself as one of the NFL's most dynamic running backs of the 1970s. A member of the Browns from 1973 to 1981, Pruitt spent parts of seven seasons starting for them at halfback, rushing for more than 1,000 yards three times and amassing more than 1,200 yards from scrimmage on four separate occasions. An excellent punt and kickoff returner as well, Pruitt accumulated more than 1,000 all-purpose yards six times, with his outstanding all-around play earning him four Pro Bowl selections and two All-AFC nominations.

Born in Houston, Texas, on August 18, 1951, Gregory Donald Pruitt developed an affinity for sports from watching them on television, recalling, "We would often watch football, basketball, and baseball, and then go out and play sandlot ball. We would pretend we were the different athletes that we had seen on TV."

Although Pruitt found himself being drawn to baseball first because of his grandfather, Edward Philpot's, background as a professional player in an all-Negro league, Pruitt soon began competing in football as well, oddly enough at the position of center. Describing his initial foray into football, Pruitt said, "We lived in a low-income neighborhood—not ghetto, but low-income. The guys there, who were all black, played sandlot football, and I was the youngest and smallest to go out for it. I was seven or eight years old. Everybody wanted to be a receiver or a running back; nobody wanted to be a lineman. So, I volunteered to be the center, which was the most unpopular position. That gave me an opportunity to play. They usually played four guys against four guys, and I made the ninth guy. So, they made me the center for both sides. It got to the point to where they were used to having me around, and my age didn't matter. After a while, I got to play other positions, and I did very, very well."

Greg Pruitt accumulated more than 1,000 all-purpose yards for the Browns six times.

After Pruitt's parents separated when he was nine years old, the backdrop for his football games became the street where his mother worked as a beautician, with Pruitt remembering, "My friends and I used to play football in the streets, in front of my mother's beauty shop. She felt safer with us out there playing. . . . The street was narrow, three yards wide, if that, and that helped me develop a lot of my moves as a running back. Playing in a narrow street, you had to have some kind of move to get by the defenders. When I went into organized football in high school, I was playing on a field 50 yards wide, which seemed like much more room than I needed. A lot of the moves I used as a running back were developed in that little street right in front of my mother's beauty parlor."

Getting his start in organized football at tiny B.C. Elmore High School, an all-Black school that graduated only 58 students his senior year, Pruitt found that being a star on the gridiron had its perks, recalling, "We had a winning tradition at B.C. Elmore High School, and athletes were accorded a lot of status. . . . It was a big thing to be a football player. To signify that you played football, you would take your chinstrap and put it in your back pocket. Girls were attracted to guys who did that."

After spending his first two years at B.C. Elmore playing quarterback, Pruitt moved to wingback his senior year in the hope of making him more attractive to college scouts, who rarely recruited African American QBs at that time. Yet even though Pruitt caught 87 passes and scored 27 touchdowns in his final year at B.C. Elmore, concerns about his small high school background and smallish 5'8", 145-pound frame tempered the enthusiasm with which scouts recruited him, although Oklahoma, Wyoming, Arizona, and Houston all expressed serious interest in him. Ultimately choosing to enroll at Oklahoma, Pruitt played wide receiver for the freshman team in 1969, before the varsity coaching staff moved him to running back after the Sooners switched to a wishbone offense prior to the start of his sophomore campaign. Upset over the change in positions, Pruitt considered leaving Oklahoma until he spoke to his mother, who told him to write down a telephone number. Then, as Pruitt recalled, "I asked her whose number it was, and she told me it was my uncle. She said, 'I didn't raise any quitters, and if you can't stay with him, you'd better find someplace to go, because you can't stay here when you come home.'"

Deciding to remain at Norman, Pruitt broke into the starting lineup midway through the 1970 season, rushing for 241 yards, gaining another 240 yards on 19 pass receptions, and scoring seven touchdowns, before finishing second in the nation with 1,760 yards rushing his junior year, with his fabulous performance earning him First-Team All–Big Eight Conference and consensus All-America honors and a third-place finish in the Heisman Trophy voting. Pruitt followed that up with another banner year, once again gaining First-Team All–Big Eight Conference and All-America recognition by rushing for 938 yards and scoring 14 touchdowns, this time placing second in the Heisman Trophy balloting to Nebraska's Johnny Rodgers.

After performing so well his last two years at Oklahoma, Pruitt, who had grown to 5'10" and close to 180 pounds while in college, expected to be selected during the early stages of the first round of the 1973 NFL Draft, most likely by former Sooners head coach Chuck Fairbanks, who, as new head man in New England, had three first-round picks at his disposal. But things did not go quite the way Pruitt anticipated, as he admitted years later when he said, "Draft day didn't go the way I thought it would. I was just waiting for it to be official, going to the Patriots in round one, and I actually went out and bought things for a party. But the first round went, and I hadn't gone. And all of those worries I had about whether my size would be a question mark started to become a reality to me. . . . Some reporter found me and told me I had been drafted by the Cleveland Browns in the second round [30th overall pick] . . . . I had no idea where Cleveland, Ohio, was. All I knew was that it was where Jim Brown had played. Jim Brown was one of the players we used to always fuss about when I was a kid. You know, who got to be Jim Brown when he played football. I was a running back, like he had been, and I thought this was a great opportunity."

The choice of Browns owner Art Modell, who overruled head coach Nick Skorich, Pruitt later acknowledged, "I knew a lot of people thought I was too small to play in the NFL. So, when I came to Cleveland after being drafted, before they weighed me, I ate all I could eat and drank as much water as I could drink. Then I got up on the scale and weighed in at 177 pounds. I tell people today, jokingly, that I spent all of my career trying to get to 190 pounds. And now, I'm 225 pounds and trying to get back to 190!"

Following his arrival in Cleveland, Pruitt spent his first year with the Browns backing up Leroy Kelly at halfback and returning kickoffs and punts, amassing a total of 1,112 all-purpose yards and scoring five touchdowns, en route to earning a trip to the Pro Bowl. And, while serving as Kelly's understudy, Pruitt learned from the Hall of Fame running back how to make better use of his size, recalling, "One time, I told Leroy I was running, and I couldn't see around the guard. Leroy told me, 'If you can't see him, he can't see you. You've got the ball. Set him up.'"

Gradually establishing himself as the starter at halfback after Kelly signed with Chicago of the newly formed World Football League prior to the start of the 1974 campaign, Pruitt ended up rushing for a team-high 540 yards, gaining another 274 yards on 21 pass receptions, scoring five touchdowns, one of which came on an 88-yard kickoff return, and finishing fourth in the league with 1,769 all-purpose yards, earning in the process his second consecutive Pro Bowl selection. A full-time starter by 1975, Pruitt played the best ball of his career over the course of the next three seasons, posting the following numbers:

YEAR	YDS RUSHING	RECS	REC YDS	YDS FROM SCRIMMAGE	TDS
1975	1,067	44	299	1,366	9
1976	1,000	45	341	1,341	5
1977	1,086	37	471	1,557	4

In addition to placing in the league's top 10 in yards from scrimmage all three years, Pruitt ranked among the leaders in all-purpose yards twice, amassing a career-high 1,798 in 1975, before surrendering his punt- and kickoff-return duties the following year. Accorded Pro Bowl and Second-Team All-AFC honors in each of the last two seasons, Pruitt also gained unofficial Second-Team All-Pro recognition from the Newspaper Enterprise Association (NEA) in 1977.

Fast and elusive, the 5'10", 190-pound Pruitt proved to be extremely difficult to bring down in the open field, using the outstanding moves he developed on the streets of his hometown to often leave defenders grasping for air. In discussing his running style, Pruitt said, "I think my style prolonged my career because I never let people have good shots at me. I didn't have to take many hard hits."

Blessed with soft hands, Pruitt also excelled as a receiver coming out of the backfield, making him a key contributor to the Browns' passing game. When asked about his versatility, Pruitt said, "I think at first, in college, and later in the pros, I just wanted the opportunity to handle the football. How I got it didn't matter, whether it was running or catching a pass or running back kicks."

Although Pruitt suffered a lower leg injury in 1978 that forced him to miss four games, he had another outstanding season, rushing for 960 yards, gaining another 292 yards on 38 pass receptions, scoring five touchdowns, and finishing second in the league with an average of 5.5 yards per carry. But, after tearing a ligament in his right knee during the early stages of the 1979 campaign, Pruitt ended up appearing in just six games, amassing only 388 yards from scrimmage and scoring just one touchdown. Unable to regain his starting job when he returned to action in 1980 after undergoing surgery on his injured knee, Pruitt spent the next two seasons assuming the role of a third-down specialist, gaining a total of only 241 yards on the ground, but making 115 receptions for 1,080 yards and nine touchdowns, before being traded to the Los Angeles Raiders for an 11th round draft pick prior to the start of the 1982 season.

Upon completion of the deal, Browns head coach Sam Rutigliano said of Pruitt, "In nine years, he was a great player in the NFL with the Cleveland Browns. In the four years I was here, we didn't get his full greatness because of injuries, but we saw some of it. And he's a fine young man . . . . Greg Pruitt's reaction was that he felt very bad about it because he had made Cleveland his home and he has a business here. But this also means he will continue his career, and whenever you're traded, it means that somebody wants you."

Pruitt, who left Cleveland with career totals of 5,496 yards rushing, 323 pass receptions, 3,022 receiving yards, 8,518 yards from scrimmage, 10,700 all-purpose yards, and 43 touchdowns, subsequently spent the next three seasons reviving his career as a return-man with the Raiders, earning the last of his five Pro Bowl selections in 1983 by leading the league with 666 punt-return yards and finishing second in the circuit with 1,270 punt- and kickoff-return yards. After helping the Raiders win two division titles and one Super Bowl, Pruitt announced his retirement following the conclusion of the 1984 campaign, ending his career with 5,672 yards rushing, 328 receptions, 3,069 receiving yards, 8,741 yards from scrimmage, 13,262 all-purpose yards, and 47 touchdowns.

After retiring from football, Pruitt remained in the Cleveland area, where he became involved in several businesses, working for a time as a recreational manager for the city, operating an electronics company, serving as a sports agent, and investing in Cleveland real estate. Today, Pruitt is a consultant to a residential construction company, Pruitt & Associates, that he started many years ago.

Holding the city of Cleveland and its fans close to his heart, Pruitt says, "I've always said I would not have been anything without the fans. I played in front of the greatest pro fans in the world in Cleveland, and I played in front of the greatest college fans at OU. It made a difference in my career. I didn't get to meet all of those people when I was playing, but now, when I get to speak at the Browns Backers events, I truly enjoy it."

BROWNS CAREER HIGHLIGHTS

Best Season

Pruitt earned Pro Bowl honors four times between 1973 and 1977, failing to do so only in 1975 during that five-year period. Yet, despite his Pro Bowl snub, Pruitt had his finest all-around season in 1975, rushing for 1,067 yards, amassing 1,366 yards from scrimmage, and establishing career-high marks with 1,798 all-purpose yards and nine touchdowns.

Memorable Moments/Greatest Performances

Pruitt scored the first touchdown of his career on a 7-yard run during a 16–16 tie with the San Diego Chargers on October 28, 1973.

Pruitt gave the Browns a dramatic 21–16 victory over the Pittsburgh Steelers on November 25, 1973, when he ran the ball in from 19 yards out in the closing moments.

Pruitt went over 100 yards rushing for the first time as a pro during a 20–20 tie with the Kansas City Chiefs on December 2, 1973, finishing the game with 15 carries for 110 yards and one touchdown, which came on a 65-yard fourth-quarter run.

Pruitt provided much of the impetus for a 21–14 victory over the Patriots on November 10, 1974, by returning the game's opening kickoff 88 yards for a touchdown.

Pruitt led the Browns to a 35–23 win over the Cincinnati Bengals on November 23, 1975, by amassing 304 all-purpose yards and scoring two touchdowns, accumulating 77 yards on special teams, 121 yards on the ground, and 106 yards on seven pass receptions.

In what he later called his most memorable game, Pruitt helped lead the Browns to a lopsided 40–14 victory over the Chiefs on December 14, 1975, by carrying the ball 26 times for a career-high 214 yards and three touchdowns.

Pruitt contributed to a 38–17 victory over the Jets in the 1976 regular-season opener by rushing for 124 yards and gaining another 51 yards on four pass receptions.

Pruitt led the Browns to a 20–17 win over the Atlanta Falcons on October 17, 1976, by rushing for 191 yards and two touchdowns, with his longest carry of the day being a 64-yard scamper.

Pruitt helped lead the Browns to a 30–27 overtime victory over the Patriots on September 26, 1977, by rushing for 151 yards and making four receptions for 51 yards and one touchdown, which came on an 8-yard pass from Brian Sipe.

Pruitt starred during a 44–7 rout of the Chiefs on October 30, 1977, rushing for 153 yards and one touchdown, which he scored on a career-long 78-yard run.

Pruitt contributed to a 13–10 overtime victory over the Bengals on September 10, 1978, by carrying the ball 22 times for 120 yards and gaining another 36 yards on five pass receptions.

Pruitt turned in an outstanding all-around effort against the Jets on December 10, 1978, rushing for 138 yards and making six receptions for 69 yards and one TD during a 37–34 overtime win.

Although the Browns lost the 1978 regular-season finale to Cincinnati by a score of 48–16, Pruitt performed brilliantly, rushing for 182 yards and one TD, which came on a 70-yard scamper.

Pruitt helped lead the Browns to a 42–28 win over the Colts on October 25, 1981, by making nine receptions for 104 yards and one touchdown, which came on a 22-yard pass from Brian Sipe.

Notable Achievements

- Rushed for more than 1,000 yards three times.
- Surpassed 50 receptions twice and 400 receiving yards three times.
- Amassed more than 1,000 yards from scrimmage four times, topping 1,500 yards once.
- Surpassed 1,000 all-purpose yards six times, topping 1,500 yards three times.
- Averaged more than 5 yards per carry twice.
- Finished second in NFL with rushing average of 5.5 yards per carry in 1978.
- Finished third in NFL in yards from scrimmage once and rushing average once.
- Led Browns in rushing five times.
- Ranks among Browns career leaders with 5,496 yards rushing (4th), 8,518 yards from scrimmage (3rd), 659 punt-return yards (9th), 1,523 kickoff-return yards (11th), 10,700 all-purpose yards (4th), 323 receptions (5th), 25 rushing touchdowns (9th), and 43 touchdowns (11th).
- 1980 division champion.
- Four-time Pro Bowl selection (1973, 1974, 1976, and 1977).
- Two-time Second-Team All-AFC selection (1976 and 1977).

19

JIM RAY SMITH

An exceptional pulling guard who became known for his tremendous speed, Jim Ray Smith spent seven seasons in Cleveland, combining with Gene Hickerson much of that time to give the Browns the finest pair of guards in the NFL. Helping to pave the way for Hall of Fame running backs Jim Brown and Bobby Mitchell to have several of their finest seasons, Smith contributed significantly to Browns teams that consistently placed near the top of the league rankings in yards rushing and total offense. Outstanding in pass protection as well, Smith earned five Pro Bowl selections and five All-Pro nominations, before being dealt to the Dallas Cowboys following the conclusion of the 1962 campaign.

Born in West Columbia, Texas, on February 27, 1932, James Raye Smith attended West Columbia High School, where he lettered in football, baseball, basketball, and track. Particularly outstanding on the gridiron, Smith excelled at fullback, later drawing praise from former Columbia football coach Charlie Brand, who said of his onetime teammate, "He was a heck of a football player and a great guy. I was a freshman, and he was a senior, but he played in all of the sports and was just a great athlete."

Offered the opportunity to attend Baylor University on an athletic scholarship, Smith recalled years later, "My mother always wanted me to finish high school. No one in my family on either side had gone past the sixth grade. Well, my brother and I and my sister all graduated from high school, and we went on to college and got our degree. If it hadn't been for football, I would never have gone to college without a scholarship. . . . You know, at one point I was thinking about not going to college, and all of a sudden, there you are. I thought I'd be a roughneck or dig ditches for the rest of my life."

Starting at tackle on both sides of the ball for three years at Baylor, Smith earned All-America honors twice, prompting the Browns to select him as a future pick in the sixth round of the 1954 NFL Draft, with the 64th overall pick, even though he had yet to complete his college eligibility. Smith subsequently spent nearly two years in the Army, forcing the Browns to wait

Jim Ray Smith helped pave the way for Jim Brown and Bobby Mitchell to have several of their finest seasons.

until midway through the 1956 season for him to finally arrive in Cleveland. In explaining the lengthy delay, Smith recounted, "I was in the Army for 23 months, from January 1955 through December 1956. I took a 30-day leave during training camp to see if I could make the Browns. I did, but I sprained my ankle during an exhibition game in California. They said, 'Why don't you go back to the Army until you get that well. Then we will bring you on up.' There were six or seven games left when they said, 'Well, we will bring you back now.' I took another leave to finish out the 1956 season."

After appearing in the final six games of the 1956 season as a 6'3",
220-pound defensive end, Smith, anticipating a move to the offensive line,
reported to training camp the following year some 20 pounds heavier. He
subsequently spent the 1957 campaign sharing time at left guard with Herschel Forester, with the two men serving as the team's messenger guards that
delivered play calls from the sideline to quarterbacks Tommy O'Connell
and Milt Plum.

Commenting on his change in positions, Smith recalled, "I had gone to
Cleveland to take Lenny [Ford's] place. I weighed 218 pounds. Of course,
Lenny weighed about 265 and was 6'4" or 6'5". In 1955, I played in the
College All-Star Game, and I played offensive tackle. I was lined up in front
of Don Colo and Lenny Ford. The Browns thought they saw something
there as an offensive lineman instead of a defensive end. When I went to
camp in 1956, I was a defensive end, but they made me learn all of the
offensive guard plays."

A full-time starter by 1958, the now 250-pound Smith soon emerged
as one of the league's top players at his position, earning Pro Bowl and All-
Pro honors for the first of five straight times. Blessed with good size and
strength, Smith proved to be an excellent pass-protector who gave up very
little ground to on-rushing defensive linemen. Even better as a run-blocker,
Smith used his strength and explosion off the ball to push defenders off the
line of scrimmage, and his superior running speed to lead Browns running
backs downfield.

Particularly effective at leading Jim Brown and Bobby Mitchell around
the corners on the famous Cleveland Browns sweep, Smith stated, "I really
didn't have much to do, just get in front of them, and if I could get a block,
they were going to be hard to bring down. Brown was just a powerful runner, and I'd like to think that I helped them make some of those yards."

Developing an especially strong rapport with Brown, Smith recalled
communicating constantly with the team's greatest player, saying, "I was
there in '56 and Jim came in '57. As a pulling guard, you went out to block
for him. We would get together to talk about what we were going to do
in different situations. . . . That's something people don't teach now. The
lineman and the running back need to be talking all the time."

Smith continued, "He'd run out and I'd tell him to slow down a bit. I'd
say, 'Let me knock the guy on his can, and you cut behind me.'"

Smith's tremendous foot speed enabled him to excel as a downfield
blocker. Even after increasing his playing weight to 250 pounds, Smith rou-
tinely finished in a dead heat with speedy wide receiver Ray Renfro, behind
only Brown and Mitchell, in sprints during Cleveland practices. That speed,

coupled with his size and strength, made Smith one of the most devastating blockers of his era.

While still performing at an extremely high level, Smith retired after the 1961 season to devote himself full-time to the successful real estate business he had established in Dallas a few years earlier. Ultimately, though, teammates Ray Renfro and Mike McCormack convinced him to return for one more year. Announcing his retirement once again following the conclusion of the 1962 campaign, Smith later explained, "Our oldest son was going to start school. My wife didn't want to put him in school up there [in Cleveland] for half a year and then bring him down here [to Dallas] for the second half of the year. I was in the real estate business in the offseason, and I was doing decent. I just wanted to stay in the Dallas area, so that is what I did."

Traded to the Dallas Cowboys for offensive tackle Monte Clark prior to the start of the 1963 campaign, Smith decided to resume his playing career, leaving Cleveland having missed a total of just one game the previous six seasons. In addition to earning Pro Bowl and All-Pro honors five times each, Smith gained First-Team All–Eastern Conference recognition six straight times from 1957 to 1962.

Smith subsequently spent two injury-marred seasons in Dallas, starting a total of only 12 games for the Cowboys, before retiring for good at the end of 1964. Recalling his time in Dallas, Smith said, "My first year, I was on a kickoff and got rolled up on my knee. I didn't even see the play. I tore my knee up in the middle of the season and again the second year. I had two knee operations with the Cowboys. I had two broken hands with the Cowboys, and I had two concussions with the Cowboys."

Turning his attention to his real estate business, Smith experienced a considerable amount of success over the course of the next three decades, saying, "I was basically a broker. I ended up meeting Ed Gaylord here in Dallas. He owned Opryland, Oklahoma Publishing, and several television stations. I handled their land in the Dallas area for about 28 years. It was a good relationship. It helped me put three kids through college."

Although Smith, who is 90 years old as of this writing, has since retired to private life, he remained somewhat active in his real estate business until 2014, saying at the time, "I like to call it tiddling. I still do a little bit of real estate. A little bit in the oil business. I bought a little land. I was born and raised about 50 miles south of Houston, in West Columbia. I have a little land down there. Nothing big. Just a few acres. I just watch my retirement portfolio. I try to play a little golf. . . . We have three kids and four grandkids. Hopefully, we will add some more on."

BROWNS CAREER HIGHLIGHTS

Best Season

Smith gained Pro Bowl and All-Pro recognition five straight times from 1958 to 1962, performing his very best in 1960, when he earned one of his three First-Team All-Pro nominations by helping to pave the way for Cleveland running backs to average a robust 5.0 yards per carry, with the Browns also finishing first in the league in points scored (362).

Memorable Moments/Greatest Performances

Smith helped the Browns gain 332 yards on the ground and amass 454 yards of total offense during a 35–28 win over the Chicago Cardinals on October 12, 1958.

Smith performed brilliantly in his two confrontations with Pittsburgh's Ernie Stautner in 1958, with teammates recollecting that the Hall of Fame defensive tackle never even got close to Cleveland quarterbacks Milt Plum and Jim Ninowski during a pair of convincing Browns wins.

Paul Brown recalled in his autobiography that Smith also dominated Hall of Fame defensive tackle Gene "Big Daddy" Lipscomb during a 38–31 win over the Baltimore Colts on November 1, 1959, helping Jim Brown rush for 178 yards and five touchdowns during the contest.

Smith's outstanding lead blocking helped the Browns rush for 329 yards during a 41–24 win over the Philadelphia Eagles in the opening game of the 1960 regular season.

Smith and his line-mates dominated the Eagles at the point of attack once again on November 19, 1961, with the Browns rushing for 259 yards and amassing 505 yards of total offense during a convincing 45–24 victory.

Notable Achievements

- 1957 division champion.
- Five-time Pro Bowl selection (1958, 1959, 1960, 1961, and 1962).
- Three-time First-Team All-Pro selection (1959, 1960, and 1961).
- Two-time Second-Team All-Pro selection (1958 and 1962).
- Six-time First-Team All–Eastern Conference selection (1957, 1958, 1959, 1960, 1961, and 1962).

20

BOB GAIN

One of the finest defensive linemen in the game for nearly a decade, Bob Gain spent his entire 12-year NFL career in Cleveland, starting for the Browns on the interior of their defensive line for nine straight seasons. A model of consistency, Gain appeared in every game the Browns played from 1955 to 1963, with his outstanding defense against the run and ability to apply pressure to opposing quarterbacks up the middle making him a key contributor to teams that won five division titles and three league championships. A five-time Pro Bowler and two-time All-Pro, Gain received the additional honors of gaining All-Conference recognition five times and being named the NFL Defensive Lineman of the Year by the *Los Angeles Times* in 1957.

Born in Akron, Ohio, on June 21, 1929, Robert Gain moved with his mother, aunt, and grandmother to Weirton, West Virginia, at the age of 12 shortly after his father passed away. Eventually emerging as a standout two-way lineman at Weir High School, Gain twice earned First-Team All-OVAC honors and gained All-State recognition as a senior in 1946 for his exceptional play on both sides of the ball.

Recruited by several major colleges as graduation neared, Gain ultimately narrowed his choice down to either Notre Dame or the University of Kentucky. Finally deciding to enroll at Kentucky after Wildcats head coach Bear Bryant told him that he expected him to start his first year, Gain recalled, "Kentucky was closer to home, and I really wanted to play right off, so, for me, there was no question, I went to the University of Kentucky in 1947."

Continuing to perform at an elite level in college, Gain excelled at tackle on both offense and defense, with his brilliant play for the Wildcats earning him All–Southeastern Conference honors three times and All-America honors twice. Also named the winner of the Outland Trophy as the nation's best interior lineman his senior year, Gain capped off his banner year by leading Kentucky to an upset victory over previously undefeated Oklahoma in the Sugar Bowl, handing the Sooners their first loss in three years.

Bob Gain proved to be a pillar of strength on the interior of the Browns' defensive line for more than a decade.

Remembered for more than just his exceptional play at Kentucky, Gain, said former Wildcats basketball coach, Joe B. Hall, who attended the university at the same time, also became known for his exploits around the school's swimming pool, with Hall recalling, "He would go off the tower [diving platform] and land directly on his stomach as a means of toughening himself up."

Hall then went on to praise Gain for the tremendous ability he displayed on the gridiron, saying, "He was 6-foot-3, about 250 pounds, and, back then, that was a big man. We thought he was a giant, but he could move. He loved to leave his feet, dive all out, and tackle you. Bob Gain on the football field was intimidating."

Subsequently selected by Green Bay with the fifth overall pick of the 1951 NFL Draft, Gain failed to come to terms on a contract with the Packers, recalling years later, "I wanted to go there, but they only wanted to give me $7,000, and I thought I should get $8,000."

As a result, Gain chose to travel north of the border and begin his professional career with the Ottawa Rough Riders of the Canadian Football League, who he helped lead to the Grey Cup championship as a rookie, earning in the process First-Team All-CFL honors. But Gain decided to return to the States when the Packers, who still held his NFL rights, traded him to the Browns for four nondescript players prior to the start of the 1952 campaign.

Despite being sidelined for half the season with a broken jaw, Gain made significant contributions to the Browns his first year in the league, starting six games for them at left defensive tackle. However, he subsequently missed the entire 1953 season and most of 1954 while serving in Korea and Japan as a commissioned lieutenant in the US Air Force during the Korean War, even though Browns head coach Paul Brown had reached an agreement with the Air Force to allow him to perform his military service in the United States and fly to Browns games on Sundays.

In explaining his decision not to go along with Brown's special arrangement, Gain stated, "I figured that wasn't such a good idea. . . . I didn't want any special treatment, and I would deck anyone who said I got special treatment. . . . I feel good about it. I feel good when a veteran kisses my cheek or shakes my hand. If I had played football, I couldn't have looked them in the eye. I lost friends in the war, and I had to fulfill my obligation."

After returning to the Browns toward the tail end of 1954, Gain began a string of nine straight seasons during which he appeared in every game they played, gaining general recognition during that time as one of the premier defensive tackles in the league. Extremely versatile, Gain manned virtually every position along Cleveland's defensive front at one time or another, even starting at end for one season, although he spent most of his time at left tackle.

An outstanding run-stuffer who possessed good size and strength, the 6'3", 256-pound Gain did an excellent job of clogging up the middle against opposing ball-carriers, helping the Browns consistently rank among the league leaders in defense against the run. Extremely quick and athletic as well, Gain also proved to be one of the league's better interior pass-rushers, although the NFL did not begin recording sacks as an official statistic until long after he retired.

In discussing Gain's varied skill set, Paul Brown stated, "Bob Gain became an excellent defensive tackle for us. He had such tremendous strength and big hands, he simply tossed aside an opposing lineman. Added to that strength was great quickness and mobility."

Brown also praised Gain for the intangible qualities he possessed, saying, "He was someone who had great instincts and consistently seemed to be in the right place at the right time."

Meanwhile, Hall of Fame guard Dick Stanfel, who played against Gain as a member of the Detroit Lions and Washington Redskins, said of his frequent foe, "He was right in front of me, and we went at it pretty good. Good player. Strong, tough guy. I wished it was somebody else playing in front of me at that time. He was an aggressive, hard-nosed player."

And Mike Peticca later summarized Gain's talents on Cleveland.com, writing, "Listed at 6'3" and usually playing at around 260 pounds, Gain was a first-rate run-stopper and a fine pass-rusher who often drew double-team blocking. He played every position on the line, including middle guard, a position often utilized in those days where the defender would line up in a two-point stance between his tackles, but a couple steps off the line of scrimmage, facing the center. Mostly, though, Gain played left tackle."

Performing especially well for the Browns from 1957 to 1963, Gain earned Pro Bowl and First-Team All–Eastern Conference honors five times each, while also being named Second-Team All-Pro twice. But, after starting every game in each of the previous nine seasons, Gain broke his leg during a 27–6 win over the Dallas Cowboys on October 4, 1964, bringing his playing career to an end. In addition to appearing in 126 games, 117 of which he started, Gain retired with a career total of 15 fumble recoveries that places him fourth in franchise history.

Following his playing days, Gain worked in sales for the companies Cleveland Frog and Pettibone, before serving on the board of trustees for the Freedom House and the Cleveland Touchdown Club. Gain also served as chairman of the Lake County Heart Association for seven years. Eventually retiring to private life, Gain spent most of his leisure time playing golf near his home in Timberlake, Ohio, a village east of Cleveland, where he remained until November 14, 2016, when he died of natural causes at the age of 87. Two years earlier, the *Cleveland Plain Dealer* identified Gain as the 14th greatest player in Browns history in a series it did on the 100 greatest players in team annals.

CAREER HIGHLIGHTS

Best Season

Gain played his best ball for the Browns from 1957 to 1963, gaining Pro Bowl recognition five times during that seven-year stretch, while also earning All-Pro honors in 1962 and 1963. But Gain had the finest season of his career in 1957, when he recovered four fumbles and helped limit opposing runners to 3.8 yards per carry, with his outstanding all-around play prompting the *Los Angeles Times* to accord him NFL Defensive Lineman of the Year honors.

Memorable Moments/Greatest Performances

Gain helped anchor a Browns defense that allowed just 26 yards rushing and 123 yards of total offense during a 30–7 win over the Pittsburgh Steelers on December 4, 1955.

Gain and the rest of the Browns defense turned in another dominant performance on October 13, 1957, surrendering just 63 yards rushing and 107 yards of total offense during a 24–7 victory over the Philadelphia Eagles.

Gain scored the only touchdown of his career when he ran 22 yards to pay dirt after intercepting a pass during a 48–34 win over the Giants in the final game of the 1960 regular season.

Gain and his line-mates dominated the Dallas Cowboys at the point of attack on October 1, 1961, allowing just 52 yards rushing and 152 yards of total offense during a 25–7 Browns win.

Notable Achievements

- Scored one touchdown on defense.
- Started 114 consecutive games from 1955 to 1963.
- Ranks fourth in franchise history with 15 fumble recoveries.
- Five-time division champion (1952, 1954, 1955, 1957, and 1964).
- Three-time NFL champion (1954, 1955, and 1964).

- *Los Angeles Times* 1957 NFL Defensive Lineman of the Year.
- Five-time Pro Bowl selection (1957, 1958, 1959, 1961, and 1962).
- Two-time Second-Team All-Pro selection (1962 and 1963).
- Five-time First-Team All–Eastern Conference selection (1957, 1958, 1959, 1960, and 1963).

21

MICHAEL DEAN PERRY

nown for his remarkable quickness for a man of his proportions, Michael Dean Perry spent seven seasons in Cleveland, establishing himself during that time as one of the most dominant defensive players in team annals. Starring for the Browns at right defensive tackle from 1988 to 1994, Perry provided stout run defense and a strong interior pass rush, with his exceptional all-around play earning him five Pro Bowl selections and four All-Pro nominations. A key contributor to Browns teams that made three playoff appearances and won one division title, Perry continues to rank among the franchise's all-time leaders in sacks, tackles, and forced fumbles nearly three decades after he donned the brown and orange for the last time.

Born in Aiken, South Carolina, on August 27, 1965, Michael Dean Perry grew up with his 11 siblings some 20 miles northeast of Augusta, Georgia, where he learned how to play football from his seven older brothers, one of whom, William, went on to play for the Chicago Bears. Recalling how he got his start on the gridiron, Perry said, "I think I was nine when I started. You had to follow in your brothers' footsteps if you didn't want to be called names."

Developing his competitive nature during his childhood, Perry stated, "I was the youngest of eight boys and most of my brothers pretty much were better athletes than I. Of course, when you're the youngest, you always had to prove yourself. You had to guard those guys and try to get in their end and be competitive, so my competitive nature and skills developed from playing with those guys all my life."

Attributing the tremendous quickness that he later exhibited on the football field to the countless hours he spent on the basketball court, Perry added, "Growing up, I played a lot of basketball, and I always had to guard smaller, quicker guys if I wanted to play. And I think that improved my foot skills and foot speed. I think it's a spinoff from that."

Michael Dean Perry earned five Pro Bowl selections and four
All-Pro nominations during his time in Cleveland.

Developing into a standout two-way lineman at South Aiken High
School, Perry left a lasting impression on Clemson defensive coach Tommy
Harper while attending a summer camp at that university, with Harper
recalling, "Perry was a replica of the enthusiasm, that effervescence that
[older brother] William has that a person can only feel and can't explain.
Those two, when they want to give off a current, you can feel it."

Harper added that he objected vociferously when other Clemson
coaches doubted Perry's playing ability, remembering, "I said, 'You gotta be
crazy. He's super quick. He has the same genetic characteristic as William
Perry. You've got to take him.'"

With Perry standing only 6'1" and having broken his ankle during his
senior year at South Aiken, he received few scholarship offers, with only
Clemson and the University of South Carolina showing significant interest
in him. Choosing to follow in his older brother's footsteps, Perry decided
to enroll at Clemson, where, after redshirting as a freshman, he spent four

years excelling for the Tigers at defensive end and defensive tackle, gaining First-Team All-ACC recognition twice and being named ACC Player of the Year as a senior in 1987, when he also earned All-America honors and was named one of the three finalists for the Outland Trophy Award, presented annually to the nation's best college interior lineman.

Subsequently selected by the Browns in the second round of the 1988 NFL Draft, with the 50th overall pick, Perry spent his first year in Cleveland assuming a part-time role on defense, starting only two games, but earning a spot on the NFL All-Rookie Team by recording six sacks and two forced fumbles. In describing his first year in the league, Perry said, "From the middle to the latter part of that first season, I played a lot. We went to a Bear defense, which is ironically a 4-3. I was the Eagle tackle [3 technique tackle] and got some playing time. I was also a defensive end in pass situations. I was considered a pass-rush specialist at that time."

Perry continued, "I wasn't blown away. I was quick off the ball. I had great speed up the field, so I worked on double teams. I worked on my bull rush. I worked on my skill set that I wasn't very good at. And by doing that, I had more tools in the toolbox so that, if they stopped this one, I'll go to this. That's how it was."

After laying claim to the starting right defensive tackle job the following year, Perry recorded seven sacks, 92 tackles, and two forced fumbles, earning in the process Pro Bowl and All-Pro honors for the first time. Also named AFC Defensive Player of the Year by both United Press International and the Kansas City Committee of 101 (a committee of 101 of the NFL's top sportswriters), Perry helped lead the Browns to the AFC Central Division title, although they ultimately suffered a 37–21 defeat at the hands of the Denver Broncos in the conference championship game. Continuing to perform exceptionally well in each of the next two seasons, Perry gained Pro Bowl and All-Pro recognition in both 1990 and 1991, registering 11½ sacks and 107 tackles in the first of those campaigns, before recording 8½ sacks and 81 tackles in the second.

Although the 6'1", 285-pound Perry's extraordinary quickness proved to be his greatest asset, he also possessed outstanding strength, superb instincts, and a strong work ethic that helped make him equally effective as a pass-rusher and run-stuffer. A perfect fit for the Browns because of both his on-field talents and his ability to connect with the fanbase, Perry stated, "It was like a match made in heaven. From the first day that I put on that Browns uniform and went out and tried to do my very best, Cleveland has always welcomed me. They always showed me a lot of love. And I am so grateful for the love and compassion that you guys had for Michael Dean Perry."

Perry continued his strong play in 1992, recording 8½ sacks and 51 tackles, before earning his fourth Pro Bowl selection the following year by registering six sacks and 81 tackles. However, even though Perry gained Pro Bowl recognition once again in 1994, his numbers slipped to just four sacks and 43 tackles, prompting the salary-strapped Browns to release him at season's end. Perry, who left Cleveland with 51½ sacks, 480 tackles, 10 forced fumbles, seven fumble recoveries, and one touchdown to his credit, signed with the Denver Broncos a few weeks later, remembering, "My time in Cleveland was up. [Bill] Belichick was there at the time. He went in a different direction. [Mike] Shanahan was in Denver, and they were going in another direction and, sure enough, it was a fit."

Perry ended up spending most of the next three seasons in Denver, earning the last of his six Pro Bowl nominations in 1996, before announcing his retirement at only 32 years of age after appearing in one game with the Kansas City Chiefs during the latter stages of the 1997 campaign. Although Perry, who ended his playing career with 61 sacks, 565 tackles, 13 forced fumbles, and eight fumble recoveries, performed well for the Broncos, he later claimed that playing anywhere outside of Cleveland felt more like "work," saying, "My heart was still in Cleveland. It was a job (in Denver). I wanted to stay in Cleveland. I thought I would start and end up in Cleveland, but it didn't work out that way. I enjoyed the city, enjoyed playing for them. And I just loved being there. That's always going to be my favorite."

Perry continued, "That was a great place to play. The fans were tremendous. They were very loyal to the Browns and to me. I had a great experience in Cleveland. What people don't realize is that during that time I was playing, free agency was unheard of. So, the guys stayed on one team a good little while. I had an opportunity to play with the core guys a long time and had a nice relationship with them. That was a great time. We had some great memories. The fans were great. That was a great time in my life. . . . If I could do it all over again, I wouldn't change a thing."

Although several teams tried to talk Perry out of retirement, he never appeared in another NFL game, stating, "It went back to the age-old question: Would I rather have health or wealth? I could have a little of both, without putting my body through a traumatic experience, so that's what I elected to do. When my body started to break down, I said I don't want to be a cripple. I knew the aging process would be accelerated from playing up to that point. I just wanted to preserve as much of my body as I possibly could. So, I retired a little early."

Retiring to Charlotte, North Carolina, Perry owned some Subway restaurants, before operating with his wife the A1 Transportation Company, which specializes in wheelchair transportation.

BROWNS CAREER HIGHLIGHTS

Best Season

Perry performed extremely well when the Browns won the division title in 1989, earning Pro Bowl, All-Pro, and UPI Defensive Player of the Year honors by recording seven sacks, making 92 tackles, forcing two fumbles, and recovering two others. But he had an even better year in 1990, once again gaining Pro Bowl and All-Pro recognition by registering a career-high 11½ sacks and 107 tackles, 12 of which resulted in a loss.

Memorable Moments/Greatest Performances

Perry recorded the first sack of his career when he brought down Chris Chandler behind the line of scrimmage during a 23–17 win over the Indianapolis Colts on September 19, 1988.

Perry recorded two sacks in one game for the first time as a pro during a 27–7 victory over the Steelers on November 20, 1988.

Perry scored the only points of his career when he returned a fumble 10 yards for a touchdown during a 28–23 win over the Houston Oilers in the final game of the 1988 regular season.

Perry anchored a Browns defense that allowed just 36 yards rushing and 53 yards of total offense during a 51–0 shutout of the Steelers in the 1989 regular-season opener.

Perry excelled once again in the opening game of the 1990 regular season, recording two sacks and helping to limit the Steelers to just 49 yards rushing during a 13–3 Browns win.

Perry helped lead the Browns to a 13–10 victory over the Atlanta Falcons on December 16, 1990, by recording 2½ sacks.

Notable Achievements

- Scored one defensive touchdown.
- Finished in double digits in sacks once.
- Recorded more than 100 tackles once.

- Led Browns in sacks three times.
- Ranks among Browns career leaders with 51½ sacks (7th), 480 tackles (7th), and 10 forced fumbles (4th).
- 1989 division champion.
- Member of 1988 NFL All-Rookie Team.
- 1989 UPI and Kansas City Committee of 101 AFC Defensive Player of the Year.
- Five-time Pro Bowl selection (1989, 1990, 1991, 1993, and 1994).
- Two-time First-Team All-Pro selection (1989 and 1990).
- Two-time Second-Team All-Pro selection (1991 and 1994).
- Three-time First-Team All-AFC selection (1989, 1990, and 1991).
- Pro Football Reference All-1990s Second Team.

22

HANFORD DIXON

A true shutdown corner before the term became a regular part of football parlance, Hanford Dixon combined with Frank Minnifield for six seasons to give the Browns one of the greatest cornerback tandems in NFL history. Starting opposite Minnifield from 1984 to 1989, Dixon, who spent a total of nine seasons in Cleveland, joined his teammate in earning Pro Bowl honors three straight times and All-Pro honors twice from 1986 to 1988, while gaining All-Pro recognition a third time by himself. Serving as a defensive cornerstone for teams that won four division titles and made five consecutive playoff appearances, Dixon missed a total of just two games his entire career, with his tremendous durability and exceptional play earning him a place on Pro Football Reference's All-1980s Second Team. Yet Dixon is largely remembered today for being the father of the "Dawg Pound," initiating a practice that led to hundreds of fans barking through dog masks in the end-zone stands at Browns' home games.

Born in Mobile, Alabama, on December 25, 1958, Hanford Lee Dixon grew up with his parents and older sister in a three-bedroom home in nearby Theodore, where he spent his formative years rooting for the Dallas Cowboys. Eventually emerging as a star on the gridiron at Theodore High School, Dixon recalled, "Football started really for me when I was a sophomore in high school. That's when I really started playing football. I played running back, wide receiver, and defensive back. . . . I played football and ran track and played basketball. But football was my best sport. It was the one I really excelled at. I had to choose between playing wide receiver and defensive back. And the reason I chose defensive back was because I didn't like to get hit. I wanted to do the hitting."

Possessing supreme confidence in his abilities, Dixon revealed that he always believed he would play in the NFL one day, saying, "God gave me physical ability, but confidence is an important factor for a cornerback. I played on the varsity team when I was in the ninth grade, and I knew I would turn pro. My friends laughed, but I knew. I told my parents over and

Considered the father of the Dawg Pound, Hanford Dixon spent nine seasons excelling for the Browns at cornerback.

over that someday I would play for the Dallas Cowboys. They laughed, too. But I truly believed it."

Recruited by several Southeastern Conference schools, including Alabama and Auburn, Dixon ultimately chose to enroll at the University of Southern Mississippi, remembering, "Southern Miss recruited me really, really early. I just felt like I had an obligation to them. Then again, I knew—not to say I couldn't have played anywhere else—but I thought it was a place I could go in and play right away. It worked out really, really, really well."

A four-year starter at Southern Miss, Dixon recorded a total of just nine interceptions during his college career, explaining years later, "Coaches and scouts from other teams took notice of my speed and cover ability, and many of them figured the best way to beat me was to throw in someone else's direction. Thus, in my four years, I picked off only nine passes."

Dixon, who gained First-Team All-America recognition from the *Sporting News* as a senior in 1980, also revealed that he changed his way of thinking somewhat while in college, stating, "I had the mindset in college for the first couple of years that, if I got drafted by the fifth round, I knew I could make someone's NFL team. But, after my sophomore year, all that changed. I knew I was good enough to go higher than that, and I knew I could be a first-round draft pick, and that's when my whole mindset changed."

Dixon's plans came to fruition when the Browns selected him in the first round of the 1981 NFL Draft, with the 22nd overall pick. Laying claim to the starting right cornerback job as soon as he arrived in Cleveland, Dixon had a solid rookie season, doing an excellent job of blanketing opposing wide receivers, although he failed to pick off a single pass. However, Dixon began to display his outstanding ball-hawking skills during the strike-shortened 1982 campaign, recording four interceptions in just nine games. Performing extremely well once again in 1983, Dixon picked off three passes, even though opposing teams made every effort to avoid throwing the ball in his direction. But it became impossible for quarterbacks to completely ignore his side of the field after Frank Minnifield began starting opposite him on the left side of Cleveland's defense in 1984, allowing him to record a total of 18 interceptions over the course of the next five seasons, a period during which he earned Pro Bowl and All-Pro honors three times each.

Joining Minnifield in forming one of the top cornerback tandems ever to play the game, the 5'11", 186-pound Dixon combined with his teammate to make the Browns virtually impenetrable deep downfield, with both men possessing the speed and instincts to blanket their man in coverage and the ball-hawking skills to create turnovers. Described in a December 23, 1988, article that appeared in the *New York Times* as "a pair of All-Pro cornerbacks widely regarded as the best duo in the league," Dixon and Minnifield drew further praise from Houston Oilers wide receiver Ernest Givins, who said, "They're the best in the league because they never second-guess themselves. Once they make a commitment to how they're going to make a play, they make it. When you've got two great corners like that, everybody else in the secondary plays more loose because of the cushion they feel they have on the corners. That's a big asset."

In discussing how he and Minnifield prepared themselves for their opponents, Dixon said, "We spend a number of hours preparing, watching film, and taking them with us just about everywhere we go. Receivers have a tendency like anyone to stay with what they do best, and we like to learn that and take it away, or at least make it uncomfortable for them to find their rhythm."

With NFL.com eventually ranking Dixon and Minnifield second only to Lester Hayes and Mike Haynes of the Raiders as the "Best Cornerback Tandem of All-Time," Dixon discussed how he viewed his pairing's place in history, saying, "We were two All-Pro corners, and we were pretty much the best at what we did. But we had those other two guys that we looked up to—talking about Lester Hayes and Michael Haynes. I always had a lot of respect for those guys. . . . . But Frank and I were for a long time the best tandem going. One particular year, I think they only threw the ball to my side like seven times the whole year. That's pretty impressive."

Dixon's exceptional play his first few years in Cleveland made him extremely popular with Browns fans. However, he earned a special place in their hearts in the summer of 1985, when he created the concept of the "Dawg Pound" during training camp. Recalling years later how the idea came to him, Dixon said, "The way this whole thing started, we were at a place called Lakeland Community College for training camp, and at Lakeland Community College the fans could get really close to the field. We always had two great corners, and we had two great linebackers in Clay Matthews and Chip Banks. I was trying to think of something to motivate the defensive line, and I was thinking about down South in my hometown and an old dog chasing a cat."

Dixon continued, "I told those guys, 'Hey man, we're going to bark at you. You guys are the dogs, and when we bark at you, think of that quarterback as the cat and go after him.' So, we started barking. And again, the fans were close to the field, and they just took over the whole thing. Now, not only was the defensive line the dogs, but the whole defense and the whole team became the dogs."

In the more than 35 years since, the Dawg Pound has made its presence felt at Browns' home games, with the team's passionate fanbase serenading its heroes with barking sounds every time a big play is made.

Dixon remained with the Browns until 1989, when, after failing to earn either Pro Bowl or All-Pro honors for the first time in four years, he signed as a free agent with the San Francisco 49ers. However, Dixon never appeared in a regular-season game with the 49ers, announcing his retirement after sustaining a leg injury during the 1990 preseason. Ending his career with 26 interceptions, 225 interception-return yards, four fumble recoveries, and two sacks, Dixon currently ranks 10th in franchise history in picks.

Since retiring as an active player, Dixon has worked as a real estate broker, a player development executive for Horseshoe Casino, and an analyst for the Cleveland Browns Radio Network during the NFL season. Dixon also does color analysis for the high school football game of the week on Fox

Sports Ohio, has served as head coach of the Cleveland Crush in the Lingerie Football League, and has authored a book entitled *Day of the Dawg: A Football Memoir.*

In discussing what playing in front of the fans of Cleveland meant to him, Dixon says, "That energy coming from them came right to us. When we came out and ran through the 'Dawg Pound' to start high-fiving them, it was on. I mean, it was game time. And I just want to tell them, thank you. . . . It didn't take me long to realize when I got here what type of people that Cleveland had. They have the greatest fans anywhere in the world."

CAREER HIGHLIGHTS

Best Season

Dixon gained Pro Bowl, First-Team All-AFC, and consensus First-Team All-Pro recognition in both 1986 and 1987, turning in the finest all-around performance of his career in the second of those campaigns, when his stellar play at cornerback helped the Browns surrender the second-fewest points and third-fewest yards in the league to the opposition.

Memorable Moments/Greatest Performances

Dixon starred during a 10–9 win over the Steelers on December 19, 1982, recording a sack and the first three interceptions of his career, all of which came against Terry Bradshaw. Looking back on his performance years later, Dixon said, "We were playing the Pittsburgh Steelers in a game we really needed to win, and I picked off the first one and I was kind of excited about it, and then I picked off another one, and then I picked off a third one and I was like, 'Wow, you've really arrived in the NFL, you've picked off Terry Bradshaw three times.' But most importantly, we got the win."

Dixon contributed to a 30–0 shutout of the Patriots on November 20, 1983, by recording two interceptions, which he returned a total of 38 yards.

Dixon earned AFC Defensive Player of the Week honors by recovering a fumble, intercepting a Warren Moon pass, and completely shutting down 1,000-yard receiver Drew Hill during a 23–20 win over the Oilers on September 14, 1986, with Hill failing to make a single reception during the contest.

Dixon helped lead the Browns to a 13–10 overtime victory over the Oilers on November 30, 1986, by recording a pair of interceptions.

Notable Achievements

- Missed just two non-strike games in nine seasons, at one point appearing in 89 consecutive contests.
- Intercepted five passes in a season twice.
- Led Browns in interceptions three times.
- Ranks 10th in franchise history with 26 career interceptions.
- Four-time division champion (1985, 1986, 1987, and 1989).
- 1986 Week 2 AFC Defensive Player of the Week.
- Three-time Pro Bowl selection (1986, 1987, and 1988).
- Two-time First-Team All-Pro selection (1986 and 1987).
- 1988 Second-Team All-Pro selection.
- Two-time First-Team All-AFC selection (1986 and 1987).
- Pro Football Reference All-1980s Second Team.

23

FRANK MINNIFIELD

The other half of the Browns' brilliant cornerback tandem, Frank Minnifield spent nine years in Cleveland, establishing himself during that time as one of the NFL's finest one-on-one defenders. A physical corner who typically lined up right near the line of scrimmage, Minnifield did a superb job of shadowing his man all over the field, with his exceptional play making him a significant contributor to four division championship teams. A four-time Pro Bowler and three-time All-Pro, Minnifield also earned a spot on the NFL 1980s All-Decade Second Team, accomplishing all he did after being bypassed by all 28 teams in the 1983 NFL Draft and beginning his pro career with the Chicago Blitz of the United States Football League.

Born in Lexington, Kentucky, on January 1, 1960, Frank LyDale Minnifield grew up in the city's housing projects, where he got his start in sports competing against other neighborhood boys. Eventually emerging as a star football player at Henry Clay High School, Minnifield excelled at tailback and safety, even though he stood just 5'9" and weighed only 140 pounds.

Receiving little interest from major college programs because of his lack of size, Minnifield ultimately chose to remain close to home and enroll at the University of Louisville, whose football team he joined as a walk-on. However, at the end of his freshman year, Minnifield received a scholarship for his final three seasons, during which time he added close to 40 pounds of bulk onto his frame. Excelling for the Cardinals as both a defensive back and return-man, Minnifield, who led the nation with an average of 30.4 yards per kickoff return his junior year, ended his college career with four interceptions and two touchdowns, scoring once on defense and once on special teams.

Yet, despite Minnifield's outstanding play at the collegiate level, his diminutive 5'9" stature caused him to go undrafted by the NFL in 1983, prompting him to sign with the Chicago Blitz, who selected him in the third round of that year's USFL Draft, with the 30th overall pick. Minnifield ended up spending one season in Chicago and another in Arizona after

Frank Minnifield combined with Hanford Dixon to give the Browns
one of the greatest cornerback tandems in NFL history.
Courtesy of MearsonlineAuctions.com

the Blitz moved west and renamed themselves the Wranglers, before suing
to get out of his USFL contract and signing with the Browns for four years
and $1.1 million in the spring of 1984.

Joining the Browns just prior to the start of the 1984 season, Minnifield said at the time, "I should have prepared myself better in relation to
learning the Browns' system. I realize expectations for me are high, and so
are mine. I really want to help this club. So, I'm going to work as hard as I
can. I just finished playing a USFL schedule, so I'm pretty much in shape.
It's just a question of getting my reaction time back to normal."

Meanwhile, Browns head coach Sam Rutigliano welcomed Minnifield with open arms, stating, "Frank has a lot of talent. He's only 5-foot-9, but he can jump, and he can run. He will help us."

Performing well his first year in Cleveland, Minnifield earned a spot on the NFL All-Rookie Team by picking off one pass and recovering two fumbles. After a solid 1985 campaign, Minnifield established himself as one of the NFL's premier corners his third year in the league, gaining Pro Bowl recognition for the first of four straight times by recording three interceptions and two fumble recoveries. Minnifield followed that up by leading the Browns with four interceptions in 1987, earning in the process the first of his three consecutive All-Pro selections. Nevertheless, Minnifield did not particularly enjoy the 1987 campaign since he believed that the strike that occurred early in the season had a negative effect on team chemistry, recalling: "It got real ugly. I think those days are still kind of a little messy for all of us because of how we were all divided. I really believe that it really messed up the chemistry of our team from that point on. It was kind of hard dealing with the fact some guys went back, some didn't, and some guys were financially better off because they went back, versus the guys who stayed together."

Minnifield continued, "We had a special relationship. Our whole team was special. We'd go over each other's house. We actually liked each other. There aren't too many teams that hung out like we did. It was common to go over somebody's house each week and just eat together. Thanksgiving was unbelievable. After that strike, we didn't do it again."

While the Browns eventually overcame any ill feelings that remained from the players' strike to advance to the playoffs in each of the next three seasons, Minnifield continued his string of consecutive Pro Bowl and All-Pro nominations in 1988 and 1989, picking off a total of seven passes those two years.

Although the 5'9", 180-pound Minnifield never recorded more than four interceptions in a season, his elite cover skills could not be measured merely by statistics. Known for his aggressive bump-and-run coverage and hard-hitting style of play, Minnifield hounded his man all over the field, with his ability to stick to opposing wideouts resulting in numerous coverage sacks. One of the best shutdown cornerbacks in the game for much of the 1980s, Minnifield combined with Hanford Dixon to give the Browns a superb pair of corners that helped lead them to four division titles and five straight playoff appearances from 1985 to 1989.

In discussing Minnifield's overall excellence, former Cincinnati Bengals wide receiver and current NBC *Sunday Night Football* color commentator Cris Collinsworth said, "There's a guy I played against, Frank Minnifield, that played with Cleveland that probably never got a vote for the Hall of Fame in his life. I thought he was one of the best guys that I ever played against."

Houston Oilers wide receiver Ernest Givins, who also attended the University of Louisville, shared his thoughts on Minnifield before facing him and the Browns on November 30, 1986, stating, "Frank'll talk a lot to you out there, but distractions are part of the game. Is he good? He can be hell. We try to stay away from each other in Louisville."

Minnifield remained a cornerstone of the Browns defense for three more years, recording another four interceptions, before announcing his retirement following the conclusion of the 1992 campaign with career totals of 20 interceptions, 124 interception-return yards, seven fumble recoveries, and two touchdowns, both of which he scored on special teams.

Since leaving the NFL, Minnifield has experienced a considerable amount of success in the business world, founding Minnifield All-Pro Homes, a home-building company in his hometown of Lexington, Kentucky, becoming in 1993 the first African American executive named to the Lexington Chamber of Commerce Board, and being named chairman of the University of Louisville Board of Trustees in 2011. Minnifield has also given back to the community by helping to create a new chapter of the NFL Players Association in Kentucky that brings together former players to host football clinics for underprivileged youth. It is estimated that Minnifield's work has led to the raising of more than $1 million for youth organizations.

Honored for his philanthropic work in 2014, Minnifield received the Blanton Collier Award for Integrity, with Dr. Kay Collier, daughter of the former Browns head coach, saying during the award ceremony, "Frank Minnifield lives out our father's belief you can accomplish anything so long as you do not care who gets the credit, which explains why he was so surprised to be nominated for this award. . . . Frank is a visionary and humanitarian who almost single-handedly created the KY Pro Football Hall of Fame to benefit children in the commonwealth."

CAREER HIGHLIGHTS

Best Season

Minnifield played his best ball for the Browns from 1986 to 1989, earning four consecutive trips to the Pro Bowl, four All-AFC selections, and three All-Pro nominations by recording a total of 14 interceptions. Although any of those four seasons would make a good choice, the 1988 campaign stands out as Minnifield's finest since he gained consensus First-Team All-Pro recognition for the only time in his career.

Memorable Moments/Greatest Performances

Minnifield recorded the first interception of his career during a 10–6 loss to the Kansas City Chiefs on September 30, 1984.

Minnifield scored the first of his two career touchdowns when he recovered a fumble in the end zone following a blocked punt during a 30–13 loss to the Bengals on September 18, 1986.

Minnifield helped the Browns earn a hard-fought 13–10 overtime victory over the Houston Oilers on November 30, 1986, by recording a pair of interceptions.

Minnifield earned AFC Defensive Player of the Week honors by intercepting three passes during a 40–7 rout of the Oilers on November 22, 1987.

Minnifield punctuated the Browns' 38–21 win over the Colts in the divisional round of the 1987 playoffs by returning his interception of a Sean Salisbury pass 48 yards for a TD in the final period.

Minnifield picked off Randall Cunningham twice during a 19–3 victory over the Philadelphia Eagles on October 16, 1988.

Minnifield contributed to a 27–7 win over the Steelers on November 20, 1988, by recording an interception and returning a blocked punt 11 yards for a touchdown.

Notable Achievements

- Led Browns with four interceptions in 1987.
- Four-time division champion (1985, 1986, 1987, and 1989).
- Member of 1984 NFL All-Rookie Team.
- 1987 Week 11 AFC Defensive Player of the Week.
- Four-time Pro Bowl selection (1986, 1987, 1988, and 1989).
- 1988 First-Team All-Pro selection.
- Two-time Second-Team All-Pro selection (1987 and 1989).
- Three-time First-Team All-AFC selection (1987, 1988, and 1989).
- 1986 Second-Team All-AFC selection.
- NFL 1980s All-Decade Second Team.

24

ABE GIBRON

Although he became better known to football fans for his unsuccessful stint as head coach of the Chicago Bears and his numerous appearances on NFL Films videos, Abe Gibron first made a name for himself as one of the finest guards in the NFL during the 1950s. A major contributor to Browns teams that won six division titles and three league championships, Gibron did an expert job of protecting quarterback Otto Graham and creating holes for Browns running backs to run through during his seven seasons in Cleveland, before splitting his final three years between the Eagles and Bears. A four-time Pro Bowler and three-time All-Pro, Gibron also received the distinction of being named to the Pro Football Reference All-1950s First Team.

Born to Lebanese immigrant parents in Michigan City, Indiana, on September 22, 1925, Abraham Gibron received the following words of advice from his father at an early age: "Dance as fast as you can dance. Run as far as you can run. Drink as much as you can drink. Do what you can. Be as big as you are."

Heeding his father's advice, Gibron starred in football at Isaac C. Elston High School, serving as team captain his senior year, en route to earning All–Northern Indiana Athletic Conference honors. Choosing to enlist in the US Marine Corps following his graduation in 1943, Gibron spent two years serving his country during World War II, before enrolling at Valparaiso University in Valparaiso, Indiana, following his discharge in 1945. After gaining All-Conference recognition and earning honorable mention Little College All-America honors for his outstanding play at guard his freshman year at Valparaiso, Gibron transferred to Purdue University in West Lafayette, Indiana, where he spent the next three seasons starring at guard on offense and tackle on defense, earning honorable mention All-America honors as a senior.

Selected by the Buffalo Bills of the All-America Football Conference (AAFC) in a secret draft held in July 1948, prior to the start of his final

Abe Gibron earned four Pro Bowl selections and three All-Pro nominations as a member of the Browns.

season at Purdue, Gibron later found himself also being selected by the New York Giants in the sixth round of the 1949 NFL Draft, with the 55th overall pick. Choosing to sign with Buffalo, Gibron became an immediate starter at left guard for the Bills, after which he went on to earn Second-Team All-League and AAFC Rookie Lineman of the Year honors.

However, Gibron's stay in Buffalo proved to be short-lived. With the AAFC dissolving following the conclusion of the 1949 campaign and only the Cleveland Browns, San Francisco 49ers, and Baltimore Colts being absorbed by the NFL, Bills owner James Breuil sold Gibron and two other players to the Browns in a deal that gave him a 25 percent share in the team.

Gibron subsequently spent his first season in Cleveland assuming the role of a "messenger guard," alternating with Weldon Humble in delivering play calls from head coach Paul Brown to quarterback Otto Graham. Gibron also saw some action as a defensive lineman during the early stages of his career, recovering three fumbles on defense his first two years with the Browns. Before long, though, it became obvious that Gibron had too much ability to be used so irregularly, prompting Brown to make him the team's full-time starter at left guard.

Making the most of his opportunity, Gibron soon emerged as one of the league's finest players at his position, earning Second-Team All-Pro honors for the first of three times in 1951, before gaining Pro Bowl recognition in each of the next four seasons. Extremely effective as both a run and pass blocker, the 5'11", 243-pound Gibron possessed surprising speed and agility for a man of his proportions, with Paul Brown later saying that he "had the fastest and quickest charge I ever saw."

Brown added, "His shoulder width [54 inches across] made him a fine pass protector, but his greatest attribute was the explosive speed with which he came off the ball. No guard was ever faster for the first five yards, and when he pulled out to lead our sweeps, he could stay in front of our fastest backs until he threw his first block."

Meanwhile, Dante Lavelli spoke of his former teammate's toughness when he stated, "He was really a tough guy. He would go down to the last inch with you."

Finding the Browns' style of play very much to his liking, Gibron said, "The Browns play my type of football. When you play on a team that uses a running game, you get to do straight-ahead blocking, and that's my meat. I block for passing plays, too, but the real fun comes when you split the line for a fullback or halfback."

Gibron's stellar play on the left side of Cleveland's offensive line helped the Browns win six straight division titles and three NFL championships, with the burly guard missing just two games from 1950 to 1955. But, with the team failing to perform at the same lofty level following the retirement of Otto Graham in 1956 and Gibron injuring his leg during a 21–7 loss to the Baltimore Colts in Week 7, the Browns released the 31-year-old veteran to make room on the roster for another player. Signed by the Philadelphia Eagles just two weeks later, Gibron finished the year in Philadelphia, before splitting his final three seasons between the Eagles and Chicago Bears. Announcing his retirement following the conclusion of the 1959 campaign, Gibron ended his career having appeared in every game his team played in eight of his 11 seasons, missing a total of just seven contests.

Following his playing days, Gibron began a lengthy career in coaching that began with a five-year stint as offensive line coach of the Washington Redskins that lasted from 1960 to 1964. From Washington, Gibron moved on to Chicago, where he spent seven seasons serving as an assistant under George Halas (1965–1967) and Jim Dooley (1968–1971), before taking over as head man in 1972. Relieved of his duties in Chicago at the end of the 1974 season after leading the Bears to an overall record of just 11-30-1 in his three years in charge, Gibron subsequently spent one season coaching the Chicago Winds of the ill-fated World Football League, before assuming the role of defensive coordinator for the Tampa Bay Buccaneers from 1976 to 1984. Gibron also later spent five seasons scouting for the Seattle Seahawks.

Although Gibron experienced very little success during his three-year stint as head coach of the Bears, his vivacious personality and willingness to poke fun at himself made him extremely popular with players and fans alike, with the *Chicago Tribune* later describing him as "one of the most recognizable and colorful characters in NFL history."

Meanwhile, the *New York Times*, which described Gibron as a "wise-cracker and gourmand," reported, "His players enjoyed him for his football knowledge and salty honesty. Sportswriters enjoyed him for his sense of humor. At a Monday news conference, he would typically raise a shot of whiskey and say, 'All right, everything is on the record until this touches my lips, and the minute it touches my lips, everything is off the record.' With his love of eating, he weighed well over 300 pounds, and two teammates on the Browns told why. 'Every time you went to dinner,' Lou Groza told the *Chicago Tribune*, 'it was a banquet.' And as Dante Lavelli said, 'He used to eat until 2 o'clock in the morning.'"

Unfortunately, Gibron later developed serious health issues that included a brain tumor that had to be surgically removed and a series of mini strokes that confined him to his home for the last few years of his life. After suffering one such stroke in February 1997, Gibron died at his home in Belle Air, Florida, some seventh months later, passing away on September 23, 1997, just one day after he turned 72 years of age. Following his passing, Gibron's wife, Susie, said, "I know he's happy. He and [George] Halas are up there and have their football game all organized, and Halas is teaching Abe some new words."

BROWNS CAREER HIGHLIGHTS

Best Season

Gibron gained official Second-Team All-Pro recognition from the Associated Press in both 1954 and 1955, helping the Browns win back-to-back NFL championships in the process. But, with the Browns scoring a league-leading 218 points and United Press International (UPI), the Newspaper Enterprise Association (NEA), and the *New York Daily News* all according Gibron unofficial First-Team All-Pro honors in the second of those campaigns, the 1955 season would have to be considered the finest of his career.

Memorable Moments/Greatest Performances

Gibron's strong blocking at the point of attack helped the Browns rush for 293 yards and amass 450 yards of total offense during a 38–23 win over the Los Angeles Rams on October 7, 1951.

Gibron and his line-mates controlled the line of scrimmage once again on November 25, 1951, with the Browns rushing for 273 yards and amassing 516 yards of total offense during a 42–21 victory over the Chicago Bears.

Gibron's powerful lead-blocking helped the Browns gain 234 yards on the ground and amass 507 yards of total offense during a 49–7 rout of the Philadelphia Eagles on October 19, 1952.

Gibron and his cohorts dominated the opposition at the point of attack once again on December 12, 1954, with the Browns rushing for 278 yards and amassing 464 yards of total offense during a 42–7 mauling of the Pittsburgh Steelers.

Notable Achievements

- Missed just two games from 1950 to 1955, appearing in 70 out of 72 contests.
- Six-time division champion (1950, 1951, 1952, 1953, 1954, and 1955).
- Three-time NFL champion (1950, 1954, and 1955).
- Four-time Pro Bowl selection (1952, 1953, 1954, and 1955).
- Three-time Second-Team All-Pro selection (1951, 1954, and 1955).
- Pro Football Reference All-1950s First Team.

25

JERRY SHERK

Considered by many to be the finest interior defensive lineman in franchise history, Jerry Sherk spent 12 seasons in Cleveland, starting for the Browns at right tackle in nine of those. An exceptional pass-rusher and outstanding run-stuffer, Sherk finished in double digits in sacks four times and recorded at least 100 tackles on three separate occasions, earning in the process four Pro Bowl selections, one All-Pro nomination, and Newspaper Enterprise Association (NEA) NFL Defensive Player of the Year honors once. A member of Browns teams that won two division titles, Sherk would have accomplished even more had his career not been cut short by a knee injury and staph infection that nearly cost him his life.

Born in Grants Pass, Oregon, on July 7, 1948, Jerry Martin Sherk wrestled and played football at Grants Pass High School, wrestling for the junior varsity team until his senior year, when, as a member of the varsity squad, he won a district title and finished third in the state at 191 pounds. Meanwhile, after choosing not to try out for the school's football team until his senior year because he considered himself too small, Sherk excelled at defensive end in his final season, helping Grants Pass compile a record of 9-1-1.

Garnering little interest from major college programs, Sherk accepted a work-study scholarship from Grays Harbor College, a community college located in Aberdeen, Washington. Continuing to compete in multiple sports at Grays Harbor, Sherk earned all-conference honors as a two-way lineman on the gridiron and won back-to-back state championships in wrestling, going undefeated and pinning all but two of his opponents. Eventually offered a scholarship to play football and wrestle at Oklahoma State University, Sherk transferred to OSU prior to the start of his junior year, after which he spent two seasons starring for the Cowboys at defensive end, while also winning the 1970 Big Eight heavyweight wrestling championship, en route to earning All-America honors.

Jerry Sherk gained recognition from the NEA as NFL Defensive Player of the Year in 1976.
Courtesy of MearsonlineAuctions.com

Selected by the Browns in the second round of the 1970 NFL Draft, with the 47th overall pick, Sherk learned of his selection while preparing to compete in a wrestling meet for Oklahoma State against Southern Illinois, recalling, "The year before, I didn't even know I would be playing professional football . . . I felt like I had rockets in my shoes, warming up around the mat."

Laying claim to the starting right defensive tackle job immediately upon his arrival in Cleveland, Sherk had a solid rookie season, recording four sacks and 83 tackles, while also recovering two fumbles. Posting extremely similar numbers the following year, Sherk concluded the 1971 campaign with 4½ sacks, 84 tackles, and two fumble recoveries, before helping the Browns make the playoffs as a wild card in 1972 by registering 10½ sacks and 91 tackles. Although the Browns failed to advance to the postseason tournament in any of the next four seasons, Sherk established himself as one of the league's finest players at his position, earning four consecutive Pro Bowl selections and gaining recognition from the NEA as NFL Defensive Player of the Year in 1976, when, in addition to recording 12 sacks, he registered 92 tackles.

Combining with left tackle Walter Johnson to give the Browns arguably the most formidable pair of defensive tackles in the league, Sherk disclosed the contents of a conversation he once had with Johnson, saying, "He actually came up to me late in his career and said, 'Jerry, at first you couldn't do anything. I couldn't believe how terrible you were. But then you got good, and so I really had to work to keep up with you.' So, we were real good for each other."

Complementing Johnson's raw power with his quickness, leverage, and persistence, the 6'4", 258-pound Sherk credited his wrestling background for much of the success he experienced on the gridiron, expressing the belief that the agility and balance he learned and developed as a wrestler served him well on the football field. Sherk also felt that the one-on-one competition he faced on the wrestling mat prepared him for his weekly battles with opposing offensive linemen.

In discussing Sherk's skill set, Browns defensive line coach Dick Modzelewski said, "I don't know what drives him. That's just Jerry. He does everything well. He pursues on every play. He's got good lateral balance. He can stop on a dime. And he anticipates what plays are going to be run."

Modzelewski added, "Take some of the guys I played with and against—like Rosey Grier and Alex Karras. Jerry is much better. He's got them all beat. When I talk to other coaches before and after games on Sundays, all they talk about is Sherk. The other coaches respect him, and the other players respect him."

Sherk's string of four straight Pro Bowl selections and streak of 98 consecutive starts both ended in 1977, when a knee injury he suffered during the preseason limited him to just seven games and three sacks. Although Sherk recorded only three sacks when he returned to action full-time the following year, he turned in a solid all-around performance, registering an unofficial total of 105 tackles. At the top of his game once again by the start of the 1979 campaign, Sherk appeared to be headed toward one of his finest seasons, recording 12 sacks through the first 10 games, before an injury he sustained during a 24–19 win over the Philadelphia Eagles in Week 10 put his career, and life, in jeopardy.

After scraping a boil off his arm on the artificial turf at Philadelphia's Veterans Stadium, Sherk developed a staph infection that traveled through his bloodstream down to his left knee. Experiencing so much pain while driving home to Medina from the Browns' Berea headquarters a few days later that he had to crawl from his car to his front door, Sherk subsequently spent six weeks at the Cleveland Clinic, battling both the staph infection and an allergic reaction he had to the antibiotic he took to treat his malady.

Recalling the circumstances surrounding his lengthy hospital stay years later, Sherk, who lost 40 pounds and nearly lost his leg and his life, said, "They figured it went through my bloodstream, and a bug like that finds the weakest point in your body. For some reason, it settled in my left knee."

Sherk continued, "The reason was, I continued to have a fever. That's a high indication the infection is alive and looking for the next spot. They gave me a really strong antibiotic to fight the infection because they didn't know at first what it was. And I had an allergic reaction to that antibiotic, and it kept my temperature up about 100 degrees."

Unable to mount a successful comeback in 1980, Sherk appeared in just one game, before his aching knee forced him to sit out the rest of the season. Trying once again the following year, Sherk assumed the role of a designated pass-rusher, recording just three sacks and 12 tackles in 15 games, before announcing his retirement at season's end with career totals of 70½ sacks, 864 tackles, and 12 fumble recoveries, all of which place him extremely high in team annals.

Praising Sherk at his retirement press conference, Browns owner Art Modell said, "What Jerry accomplished on the field are achievements that made him the best tackle in Browns history. Those who have had a chance to know him realize what a special person he is."

After retiring from football, Sherk, who dabbled in sports photography during his playing days, decided to pursue a career in that field, selling his work to newspapers and publications such as *Sports Illustrated* and *Pro! Magazine*. In 2010, Sherk even found himself being honored by the Cleveland Touchdown Club Charities, which held a photo show featuring his work called, "Through the Eyes of a Defensive Lineman: The Cleveland Browns as Photographed by Jerry Sherk." After tiring of the freelance photography business, Sherk returned to college, earned a master's degree in counseling psychology, and spent several years working as a school guidance counselor, before founding Mentor Management Systems, a consulting firm based in

Encinitas, California, that provides youth-mentoring programs for state public schools.

Although Sherk, who is 74 years old as of this writing, may well have eventually landed a place in the Pro Football Hall of Fame had his career not been cut short by injury, he does not bemoan the abrupt way his playing days ended, saying, "I really am just happy to be part of that Browns tradition. There were times in mid-career I can remember, during TV timeouts between quarters, just walking from one end of the field thinking, 'This is a really neat place to be.' It was an absolutely incredible experience. It wasn't all good, but it was amazing."

And, as for the connection he felt with the fans of Cleveland, Sherk says, "I loved playing for the people. They were my motivation. I related to the people of Cleveland, the underdogs who were fighting for respect. I tried to immerse myself in their emotions, their cheers. As a defensive tackle, you had to get wound up every game or you would get eaten alive. I had the philosophy that I was a warrior fighting for respect for the people of Cleveland. I wanted to make them happy and proud to be represented by the Cleveland Browns. I saw the town as kind of depressed, and I wanted to help pull them out of the blues."

CAREER HIGHLIGHTS

Best Season

Although Sherk recorded 12 sacks in just 10 games in 1979, he played his best ball for the Browns from 1972 to 1976, finishing in double digits in sacks three times and registering 100 tackles twice over the course of those five seasons. Turning in the finest all-around performance of his career in 1976, Sherk earned one of his four Pro Bowl selections, his lone All-Pro nomination, and AFC Defensive Player of the Year honors by recording 12 sacks, 92 tackles, one interception, and one fumble recovery.

Memorable Moments/Greatest Performances

In addition to recording the first of his three career interceptions during a 31–0 shutout of the Houston Oilers in the 1971 regular-season opener, Sherk helped anchor a smothering Browns defense that registered five sacks, forced six turnovers, and allowed just 35 yards rushing.

Sherk picked off another pass during a 20–13 win over the Washington Redskins in the final game of the 1971 regular season.

Although the Browns lost to the undefeated Miami Dolphins by a score of 20–14 in the divisional round of the 1972 playoffs, Sherk performed well, recording a sack and receiving credit for part of another sack.

Sherk anchored a dominant Browns defense that allowed just 23 yards rushing and 106 yards of total offense during a 42–13 rout of the Oilers on October 21, 1973.

Sherk set a club record by recording four sacks during a 24–3 win over the Philadelphia Eagles on November 14, 1976.

Sherk nearly matched that total when he sacked Roger Staubach three times and recovered a fumble during a 26–7 victory over the Dallas Cowboys on September 24, 1979. Praising Sherk for his effort afterwards, Browns head coach Sam Rutigliano said, "He played the best game of any defensive lineman I ever saw. He controlled the entire middle of the line."

Notable Achievements

- Started 98 consecutive games from 1970 to 1976.
- Finished in double digits in sacks four times.
- Recorded at least 100 tackles three times.
- Led Browns in sacks three times.
- Ranks among Browns career leaders with 70½ sacks (3rd), 864 tackles (3rd), and 12 fumble recoveries (6th).
- Two-time division champion (1971 and 1980).
- 1974 Browns MVP.
- 1976 Newspaper Enterprise Association (NEA) NFL Defensive Player of the Year.
- Four-time Pro Bowl selection (1973, 1974, 1975, and 1976).
- 1976 First-Team All-Pro selection.
- Two-time First-Team All-AFC selection (1975 and 1976).

26

MIKE PRUITT

A swift and powerful runner who spent nine of his 11 NFL seasons in Cleveland, Mike Pruitt served as the focal point of the Browns' running game from 1979 to 1983, leading the team in rushing five straight times. Gaining more than 1,000 yards on the ground four times, Pruitt also surpassed 60 receptions and 400 receiving yards twice each and amassed more than 1,500 yards from scrimmage on three separate occasions, ending his lengthy stint in Cleveland as one of the franchise's all-time leaders in yards rushing, yards from scrimmage, and all-purpose yards. A significant contributor to teams that made two playoff appearances and won one division title, Pruitt earned two Pro Bowl selections and three All-AFC nominations, before splitting his final two seasons between the Buffalo Bills and Kansas City Chiefs.

Born in Chicago, Illinois, on April 3, 1954, Michael L. Pruitt grew up in a crime-ridden area on the city's South Side, where his mother set strict rules for him, insisting that he be home before darkness arrived and the streetlights came on. Excelling in multiple sports as a youth, Pruitt played baseball and football and ran races against his older friends, saying years later, "I was always amazed that none of them could outrun me. It was something that I was blessed with."

Continuing to display his athleticism at Wendell Phillips Academy High School in the Bronzeville District of Chicago, Pruitt ran track and played football, holding the former closest to his heart until one of his football coaches convinced him that pursuing a career on the gridiron would likely prove to be more financially beneficial to him. Recalling the conversation he had with his coach, Pruitt recounted, "'Mike,' he said, 'I don't think you're going to make a whole lot of money at track, but I do think that you have a possibility to make some money at football.'" Pruitt added, "That was the end of my track days."

Ultimately accepting a football scholarship to Purdue University, Pruitt played fullback for the Boilermakers for three years, during which time he

Mike Pruitt rushed for more than 1,000 yards four times as a member of the Browns.
Courtesy of MearsonlineAuctions.com

became known for his unusual combination of speed and strength, posting a personal-best time of 4.4 seconds in the 40-yard dash and bench-pressing 425 pounds. Performing exceptionally well his final two seasons after struggling somewhat as a sophomore, Pruitt rushed for 613 yards and averaged 6.0 yards per carry as a junior in 1974, setting a school record on November 2 of that year by running 94 yards for a touchdown against Iowa. Pruitt then earned Second-Team All–Big Ten Conference honors his senior year by carrying the ball 217 times for 899 yards and three touchdowns.

Entering the 1976 NFL Draft uncertain as to how pro teams valued him, Pruitt did not really know what to expect, recalling, "I did get some interest from the New York Jets. They said, 'Mike, maybe in the later rounds, we may take you.'"

Taking New York's words to heart, Pruitt assumed he had little chance of being selected in the early rounds. Therefore, when his phone rang shortly after the draft began, Pruitt became annoyed, believing that one of his friends, whom he had specifically told not to call him because of the draft, had decided to play a joke on him. Recounting the contents of the conversation that subsequently transpired, Pruitt remembered saying when he answered the phone, "Man, I told you not to call me."

A man on the other end of the phone asked, "Is this Mike Pruitt?"

A somewhat confused Pruitt answered, "Um, yeah. Come on. Don't play with me now."

The man then responded, "This is Art Modell, and we just drafted you."

Selected by the Browns in the first round, with the seventh overall pick, Pruitt still has a difficult time believing that he went so early, saying years later, "To this day, it still shocks me. I was thrilled to no end to know that somebody had that much interest in me to want to put that much stock in me."

Following his arrival in Cleveland in 1976, Pruitt spent his first two seasons backing up Cleo Miller at fullback, gaining only 343 yards on the ground and scoring just one touchdown. However, Pruitt assumed a far more prominent role on offense after Sam Rutigliano took over as head coach in 1978, with Rutigliano saying prior to the start of the regular season, "Mike Pruitt was a No. 1 draft choice out of Purdue. He's a very interesting young man because he has all the redeemable qualities to be an excellent running back in the National Football League. He seems right now to be a little apprehensive, and I think he's lost a little confidence in himself because he hasn't had the opportunity to play. But we very much want to integrate him into our offense, and we feel that we want to use him more and try to get him to realize the talent that he had when he was selected as a No. 1 choice."

His confidence buoyed by Cleveland's new head coach, Pruitt emerged as a potent offensive weapon after he joined the starting unit midway through the 1978 campaign, rushing for 560 yards, amassing 672 yards from scrimmage, and scoring five touchdowns. Establishing himself as the Browns' primary running threat the following year after halfback Greg Pruitt (no relation) sustained a season-ending injury, Pruitt began an outstanding three-year run during which he posted the following numbers:

YEAR	YDS RUSHING	RECS	REC YDS	YDS FROM SCRIMMAGE	TDS
1979	1,294	41	372	1,666	11
1980	1,034	63	471	1,505	6
1981	1,103	63	442	1,545	8

Ranking among the league leaders in yards rushing and yards from scrimmage in each of the first two seasons, Pruitt earned consecutive Pro Bowl and All-AFC nominations, while also helping the Browns win their first division title in nearly a decade in 1980.

Blessed with good size and outstanding speed and strength, the 6-foot, 225-pound Pruitt had the ability to run over, around, or away from opposing defenders, making him extremely effective as both an inside and outside runner. Excelling in particular on plays of the quick-hitting variety, Pruitt often used his speed to burst past defenders at the line of scrimmage, before bowling over defensive backs that tried to bring him down once he reached the secondary.

After performing so well the previous three seasons, Pruitt suffered a minor setback in 1982, gaining only 516 yards on 143 carries and amassing just 656 yards from scrimmage during the strike-shortened campaign. Disappointed in Pruitt's performance, Sam Rutigliano later said that when he returned to action after nearly two months of inactivity, he was "a shell of the guy he had been and was not ready to play, either mentally or physically."

Rebounding in a big way the following year, Pruitt earned All-AFC honors for the third and final time by rushing for 1,184 yards, accumulating 1,341 yards from scrimmage, and scoring a career-high 12 touchdowns. However, after Pruitt lost his starting job to Boyce Green in 1984 due to a series of nagging injuries, the Browns released him just prior to the start of the ensuing campaign. Pruitt, who, upon learning of his release, said, "I'm surprised, but not bitter," left the Browns having rushed for 6,540 yards, made 255 receptions for 1,761 yards, amassed 8,301 yards from scrimmage, accumulated 8,538 all-purpose yards, and scored 52 touchdowns as a member of the team.

Two weeks after being cut by the Browns, Pruitt signed with the Buffalo Bills, for whom he appeared in just four games, before joining the Kansas City Chiefs at midseason. After finishing out the year in Kansas City, Pruitt spent one final season with the Chiefs, starting for them at fullback in 1986, before announcing his retirement at the end of the year with career totals of 7,378 yards rushing, 270 receptions, 1,860 receiving yards, 9,238 yards from scrimmage, 9,475 all-purpose yards, and 56 touchdowns.

Following his playing days, Pruitt started a career in the automotive business, owning during the 1990s a Ford and Lincoln-Mercury-Mazda dealership in Lima, Ohio, that he sold in 2006 and a Honda dealership in Akron, Ohio, that he sold in 2014. After living in Strongsville, Ohio, for many years, Pruitt moved to Cleveland, where he serves as a Jehovah's Witness. Looking back fondly on his years with the Browns, Pruitt says, "I never really had a bad day in Cleveland. It's a great organization. Nobody treats their players like Cleveland does."

BROWNS CAREER HIGHLIGHTS

Best Season

Although Pruitt also performed extremely well in 1980, 1981, and 1983, rushing for more than 1,000 yards and amassing more than 1,300 yards from scrimmage in each of those seasons, he posted the best overall numbers of his career in 1979, earning Pro Bowl and First-Team All-AFC honors by ranking among the league leaders with 1,294 yards rushing, 1,666 yards from scrimmage, and a rushing average of 4.9 yards per carry, while also scoring 11 touchdowns.

Memorable Moments/Greatest Performances

Pruitt contributed to a 44–7 rout of the Kansas City Chiefs on October 30, 1977, by rushing for 96 yards and scoring the first TD of his career.

Pruitt helped lead the Browns to a 41–20 victory over the Bills on October 29, 1978, by carrying the ball 21 times for 173 yards and two touchdowns, one of which came on a 71-yard run.

Pruitt turned in an outstanding all-around effort during a 28–27 win over Cincinnati on October 21, 1979, rushing for 135 yards and scoring a touchdown on a 50-yard pass from Brian Sipe.

Pruitt helped lead the Browns to a 24–19 win over the Eagles on November 4, 1979, by rushing for 104 yards and one touchdown, which came on a 24-yard run in the fourth quarter that provided the margin of victory.

Although the Browns lost to the Seattle Seahawks by a score of 29–24 the following week, Pruitt performed brilliantly, making four receptions for 47 yards, and rushing for 141 yards and two touchdowns, one of which came on a 65-yard run.

Pruitt led the Browns to a 14–7 win over the Houston Oilers on December 2, 1979, by rushing for 111 yards, making four receptions for 67 yards, and scoring both Cleveland touchdowns.

Pruitt followed that up by rushing for 149 yards and two touchdowns during a 19–14 loss to the Oakland Raiders on December 9, 1979, scoring one of his TDs on a career-long 77-yard run.

Pruitt helped lead the Browns to a 27–3 win over Seattle on October 12, 1980, by carrying the ball 24 times for 116 yards and two touchdowns.

Pruitt had another big game against the Bears on November 3, 1980, rushing for 129 yards and two touchdowns during a 27–21 Browns win, with one of his TDs coming on a 56-yard run.

Pruitt starred in defeat on December 3, 1981, rushing for 155 yards and gaining another 58 yards on seven pass receptions during a 17–13 loss to the Oilers.

Pruitt proved to be the difference in a 21–7 victory over Seattle in the 1982 regular-season opener, rushing for 136 yards and two touchdowns.

Pruitt led the Browns to a 31–26 win over the Detroit Lions on September 11, 1983, by rushing for 137 yards and scoring a touchdown on a 6-yard pass from Brian Sipe.

Pruitt contributed to a lopsided 30–0 victory over the Patriots on November 20, 1983, by rushing for 136 yards and one touchdown.

Although the Browns lost to the Oilers by a score of 34–27 on December 11, 1983, Pruitt rushed for 153 yards and scored all three Cleveland touchdowns on short runs.

Notable Achievements

- Rushed for more than 1,000 yards four times.
- Surpassed 60 receptions and 400 receiving yards twice each.
- Scored more than 10 touchdowns twice.
- Amassed more than 1,500 yards from scrimmage three times.
- Led Browns in rushing five times.
- Ranks among Browns career leaders with 6,540 yards rushing (3rd), 8,301 yards from scrimmage (4th), 9,475 all-purpose yards (5th), 47 rushing touchdowns (3rd), and 52 touchdowns (8th).
- 1980 division champion.
- Two-time Pro Bowl selection (1979 and 1980).
- 1979 First-Team All-AFC selection.
- Two-time Second-Team All-AFC selection (1980 and 1983).

27

JIM HOUSTON

One of the few players to achieve the "triple crown" of football, Jim Houston played for championship teams at every level, winning a State Championship in high school, a National Championship in college, and an NFL title with the Browns in 1964. A major contributor to Browns teams that also won six division titles, Houston earned the nickname "Mr. Dependable" for his consistently excellent play and tremendous durability that enabled him to miss just three games over the course of his 13-year professional career, which he spent entirely in Cleveland. One of the bedrocks upon which the Browns built their defense during the 1960s and early 1970s, Houston earned four Pro Bowl selections and one All-Pro nomination as the team's starting left-outside linebacker, after beginning his career as a defensive end.

Born some 50 miles south of Cleveland, in Massillon, Ohio, on November 3, 1937, James Edward Houston spent much of his youth trying to emulate his older brother, Lin, who starred on the gridiron at Massillon Washington High School and Ohio State University, before spending eight seasons playing guard on offense for the Cleveland Browns. Describing the relationship that he shared with the eldest of his five brothers, Houston said: "He never said that we should be playing football or doing anything like that. He left it up to be all our own decision. He just simply talked to us about doing the best you can. He knew that I had to do it myself, that I had to have the determination to do it myself. He was always reliable in a sense that he could get the job done. When you have a person like that, you don't even have to worry about him. You know he's going to carry out his responsibilities and get the job done, whatever that happens to be. We kind of learned that from his example, from the time I was watching him play from my seat that cost 25 cents in Cleveland Stadium."

Revealing that his path to the NFL began somewhat ominously, Houston explained, "I grew up in Massillon, you know. And football was so big a part of life in that community back then, and still is. Well, I went out

Jim Houston earned the nickname "Mr. Dependable" during his time in Cleveland.

for the seventh-grade team when I was old enough to play . . . and got cut. That's right, I got cut from my first football tryout. The coach told me to come back the next year because I was too little. Two years later, I was All-City as a ninth grader."

Eventually establishing himself as a two-way star at Massillon Washington High School, Houston excelled as an end on both offense and defense for three years, with his outstanding play helping the Tigers compile an aggregate record of 27-2-1 and capture back-to-back Ohio state championships in 1953 and 1954. Recruited as a defensive end and receiver by Ohio State head coach Woody Hayes after earning First-Team All-Ohio honors his senior year, Houston continued to star on both sides of the ball for the Buckeyes, leading them in receiving yards once, earning team MVP honors twice, and helping them win the 1957 National Championship. Having also gained All-America recognition as a defensive end his final two years at Ohio State, Houston entered the 1960 NFL Draft as one of the nation's most highly touted prospects. Selected by Cleveland in the first round, with the eighth overall pick, Houston elected to sign with the Browns instead of the Buffalo Bills, who also selected him in the first round of that year's AFL Draft.

Claiming that his decision proved to be an easy one, Houston later said, "The fact that Cleveland was down the road, and I was born in Massillon meant there was no question where I wanted to go."

Following his arrival in Cleveland, the 6'3", 245-pound Houston spent his first three seasons playing left defensive end under head coach Paul Brown, recording an unofficial total of 16 sacks and appearing in every game the Browns played during that time despite being recalled to active duty in the US Army in 1962. Explaining how he juggled his multiple assignments, Houston stated, "I was a first lieutenant in the army in the early part of my pro career . . . I would work during the week and then fly and meet the team and play that weekend. Then, I would hop back on a plane and be back for roll call at 6 a.m. Monday."

Shifted to linebacker prior to the start of the 1963 campaign by new head coach Blanton Collier, who wanted to take advantage of his superior athleticism, Houston embraced his new role, remembering, "Coach Collier needed more talent at the position, and I bought into it. The position change meant all I had to do was stay over the tight end if he was on my side. If he wasn't, I pretty much had free reign. If the tight end was on my side, I'd pretty much beat him up and then go get the running back. That was more fun [compared to defensive end]."

Joining Vince Costello and Galen Fiss on one of the league's stronger linebacking units, Houston displayed a natural affinity for his new position, using his speed to cover opposing tight ends and running backs coming out of the backfield and his size and strength to help stuff the run. Recalling how right-side backer Fiss helped him with his assignments, Houston said, "Fiss would call out the adjustments for us on defense. You'd hear him calling out codes, and you'd hear him yell out 'Blue.' He called me 'Blue' instead of Jim or Houston."

After performing well his first year at linebacker, Houston earned the first of his four Pro Bowl selections in 1964 by intercepting two passes, scoring one touchdown, and averaging seven tackles per game for the eventual NFL champions. Paying tribute to that 1964 squad years later, Houston said, "The essence of the Browns was that '64 team that beat Baltimore. But more, I was never on a team in high school or college that looked out for each other the way the guys on that football team did. It was such a come together thing for us, whether it was '64 when we won, or in '65 when we lost to Green Bay."

Although the Browns failed to capture the NFL title again in 1965, Houston had another outstanding year, earning Pro Bowl, Second-Team All-Pro, and First-Team All–Eastern Conference honors. Continuing to perform at an extremely high level for the next five seasons, Houston gained Pro Bowl recognition another two times, before age and injuries began to take their toll on him. After starting every game that the Browns played for the fourth consecutive time in 1971, Houston assumed a backup role the following year, prompting him to announce his retirement at season's end. Houston, who ended his career with 11 fumble recoveries, 29½ sacks, 14 interceptions, 278 interception-return yards, three defensive touchdowns, and one TD reception, appeared in 177 of the 180 contests the Browns played during his time in Cleveland, starting all but six games from 1963 to 1971.

Looking back on his playing career many years later, Houston said, "I was really lucky. You know, I decided to follow my brother to Ohio State because he played there and really liked it. Things worked out pretty well. I made All-American twice and then played 13 years with the Browns . . . in Pro Bowls . . . and won the championship in 1964. I did all that after getting cut from my seventh-grade team in junior high."

Yet, Houston, who has never come close to gaining induction into the Pro Football Hall of Fame, stated that he considered his omission to be something of an oversight, claiming, "Dave Wilcox [former 49ers linebacker] is in the HOF, and to take nothing away from Dave because he was a great player, but I think I was as good as he was, and I'm not in."

Following his playing days, Houston remained in Ohio, where he entered the business world, selling life insurance, handling securities, running a local machine company, and co-owning a gas station and car wash at different times. He also became involved with various charities, including the Boys and Girls Club.

After being diagnosed with ALS and mixed dementia some years earlier, Houston passed away at the age of 80, on September 11, 2018. An obituary of Houston subsequently stated: "If you knew Jim, he was always ready to stop and carry on a conversation with a willing soul. Jim was full of life and laughter, and always had big smiles, big hugs, and firm handshakes. He loved sitting in his courtyard with his wife, drinking coffee and reading the paper. He followed the Browns and Buckeyes with great enthusiasm."

Concerned about his condition and the future health of his loved ones, Houston donated his brain and spinal cord to the Boston University Concussion Legacy Foundation to help in the diagnosis and treatment of chronic traumatic encephalopathy (CTE). Revealing that researchers discovered that her husband had Stage 3 CTE, Donna Houston told the Associated Press, "He figured something was wrong, and he thought it would be better to find out. His three boys, as well as all four grandsons, played football, and he was just very, very concerned about anything that had to do with head injuries."

CAREER HIGHLIGHTS

Best Season

Houston gained Pro Bowl recognition four times during his career, in 1964, 1965, 1969, and 1970, with his strong play in the first of those campaigns helping the Browns capture the NFL title. But Houston earned All-Pro honors for the only time in 1965, when, in addition to recording two interceptions, he recovered two fumbles.

Memorable Moments/Greatest Performances

Houston recorded the first interception of his career during a 20–6 win over the Los Angeles Rams on September 29, 1963.

Houston scored the first of his four career touchdowns when he ran 42 yards to pay dirt after intercepting a pass during a 38–24 victory over the Philadelphia Eagles on November 29, 1964.

Houston did an exceptional job of defending against John Mackey in the 1964 NFL championship game, combining with defensive back Ross Fichtner to hold the perennial All-Pro tight end to just one reception for 2 yards during a 27–0 Browns win. Looking back on the contest years later, Houston said, "Boy it was exciting, winning that '64 game with Baltimore, because it was such a surprise to everyone. They were supposed to be the team with all the stars. They had Unitas and Raymond Berry and that great defensive unit. We had Jim Brown . . . and some other pretty good players like Ryan, Kelly, and Gary Collins, and a pretty good defense of our own. I just remember as the game went on that all we were concerned about was having enough points to win. I never gave it a thought that we were shutting them out. Afterwards we all thought it was such a remarkable outcome . . . to beat a team that good and hold them scoreless."

Houston picked off two passes in one game for the only time in his career during a 27–24 win over the St. Louis Cardinals on December 19, 1965.

In addition to recording an interception during a 33–21 loss to the Eagles on December 11, 1966, Houston caught a 10-yard touchdown pass from Jim Ninowski on a fake field goal attempt.

Houston lit the scoreboard again when he returned his interception of a Fran Tarkenton pass 79 yards for a touchdown during a 24–14 victory over the Giants on December 3, 1967, earning in the process NFL Defensive Player of the Week honors.

Houston earned that distinction again the following week by returning an interception 18 yards for a touchdown during a 20–16 win over the St. Louis Cardinals on December 10, 1967.

Houston contributed to the Browns' 38–14 win over the Dallas Cowboys in the divisional round of the 1969 playoffs by recording an interception, which he subsequently returned 35 yards.

Notable Achievements

- Missed just three games in 13 seasons, appearing in 177 out of 180 contests.
- Scored three defensive touchdowns.
- Ranks among Browns career leaders with 11 fumble recoveries (tied for 7th) and three touchdown interceptions (tied for 3rd).
- Six-time division champion (1964, 1965, 1967, 1968, 1969, and 1971).
- 1964 NFL champion.
- Two-time NFL Defensive Player of the Week.
- Four-time Pro Bowl selection (1964, 1965, 1969, and 1970).
- 1965 Second-Team All-Pro selection.
- Two-time First-Team All–Eastern Conference selection (1965 and 1966).

28

WARREN LAHR

An outstanding defender who excelled for the Browns at both cornerback and safety, Warren Lahr spent his entire 11-year NFL career in Cleveland, amassing the second-most interceptions and third-most interception-return yards in franchise history. Lahr, who picked off at least five passes in a season six times, also ranks first in team annals in touchdown interceptions, with his larcenous ways earning him Pro Bowl and All–Eastern Conference honors once each. A member of Browns teams that captured eight division titles and four league championships, Lahr also received the distinction of being named to the Pro Football Reference All-1950s Second Team.

Born in Mount Zion, Pennsylvania, on September 5, 1923, Warren Emmett Lahr grew up some 140 miles northeast, in the small town of West Wyoming, Pennsylvania, where he starred in football at West Wyoming High School. Despite his outstanding play at West Wyoming, Lahr received just one scholarship offer, which came from Western Reserve University, a small school in Cleveland, Ohio.

After enrolling at Western Reserve, Lahr began his collegiate career as a reserve under head football coach Tom Davies, for whom he spent one year playing halfback on offense, before enlisting in the US Navy and spending the next three years serving his country during World War II. Following his discharge from the military in 1946, Lahr returned to Western Reserve, where he spent his final two seasons excelling on both offense and defense, transitioning from halfback to quarterback during his senior year.

Ultimately selected by the Pittsburgh Steelers in the 32nd and final round of the 1947 NFL Draft, with the 294th overall pick, Lahr appeared to have little hope of making the Pittsburgh roster when he arrived at his first pro training camp in the summer of 1948. But whatever chance Lahr had disappeared when he injured his knee during the preseason, prompting the Steelers to release him. Subsequently signed by the AAFC's Cleveland Browns, Lahr sat out the entire 1948 campaign while recovering from his

Warren Lahr ranks among the Browns' career leaders in interceptions, interception-return yards, and touchdown interceptions.

injury, before beginning his professional career the following year at the rather advanced age of 26. After nearly being cut by head coach Paul Brown after making a mistake on defense during a preseason game against the 49ers, Lahr ended up serving as a jack-of-all-trades in his first pro season, amassing 56 yards and scoring one touchdown as a halfback on offense, intercepting four passes on defense, returning six punts for 83 yards, and punting the ball four times for 125 yards.

Assuming a starting role in the Browns' defensive secondary after they joined the NFL in 1950, Lahr performed extremely well for the eventual league champions, recording eight interceptions, which he returned for 99 yards and two touchdowns. Lahr followed that up by picking off another five passes, amassing 95 interception-return yards, and recording two more pick-sixes in 1951, en route to earning unofficial All-Pro honors from United Press International (UPI) for the first of five straight times. Continuing to be a thorn in the side of opposing quarterbacks the next four years, Lahr intercepted five passes each season, in helping the Browns win four more division titles and another two NFL championships.

Spending most of his time playing left defensive halfback in an earlier version of what later became known as left cornerback, Lahr proved to be one of the league's most opportunistic defenders, developing a reputation for creating turnovers and making big plays. Although the 5'11", 190-pound Lahr did not possess elite running speed, he made up for whatever he lacked in that area with superior instincts, the ability to track the football well, and outstanding knowledge of the tendencies of opposing quarterbacks and wide receivers. A sure tackler as well, Lahr also excelled in run support, a quality that contributed greatly to the success he experienced at safety when he moved to that position during the latter stages of his career.

Although Lahr recorded just seven interceptions from 1956 to 1959, he remained a solid contributor to one of the league's strongest defenses, earning his lone First-Team All–Eastern Conference nomination in 1956, when the Browns surrendered the fewest points of any team in the NFL. Choosing to announce his retirement following the conclusion of the 1959 campaign, Lahr ended his career with 44 interceptions, 562 interception-return yards, and a franchise-record five pick-sixes. An outstanding postseason performer as well, Lahr recorded five interceptions in 12 playoff games, one of which he returned for a touchdown.

Following his playing days, Lahr settled in Aurora, Ohio, and soon began doing color commentary alongside announcer Ken Coleman for Browns games broadcast on WJW channel 8 in Cleveland. After serving in that role from 1963 to 1967, Lahr took a job as a sales agent for Lax Industries in Cleveland and ran a sporting goods store, before suddenly dying of a heart attack at only 45 years of age on January 19, 1969.

CAREER HIGHLIGHTS

Best Season

Lahr earned his lone Pro Bowl nomination in 1953, when he picked off five passes and amassed a career-high 119 interception-return yards. But he made a slightly greater overall impact in 1950, when he recorded eight interceptions, which he returned for a total of 99 yards and two touchdowns.

Memorable Moments/Greatest Performances

Lahr sealed a 31–21 win over the Buffalo Bills in the divisional round of the 1949 AAFC playoffs when he returned an interception 52 yards for a touchdown in the fourth quarter.

Lahr scored the only touchdown the Browns recorded during a 13–7 victory over the Philadelphia Eagles on December 3, 1950, when he ran 30 yards to pay dirt after picking off a Tommy Thompson pass in the first quarter.

Lahr lit the scoreboard again when he returned an interception 18 yards for a touchdown during a 45–21 win over the Washington Redskins in the final game of the 1950 regular season.

Lahr made a key play during the Browns' 8–3 victory over the Giants in the divisional round of the 1950 playoffs when he picked off a Charlie Conerly pass.

Lahr subsequently recorded two interceptions during the Browns' 30–28 win over the Los Angeles Rams in the 1950 NFL championship game, sealing the victory by picking off a Bob Waterfield pass on the game's final play.

Lahr proved to be a thorn in the side of the Rams once again on October 7, 1951, returning an interception 23 yards for a touchdown during a 38–23 Browns win.

Lahr crossed the opponent's goal line again two weeks later, returning an interception 27 yards for a touchdown during a 17–0 shutout of the Steelers on October 21, 1951.

Lahr scored the last points of his career when he returned his interception of a Zeke Bratkowski pass 27 yards for a touchdown during a 39–10 win over the Bears on November 14, 1954.

Notable Achievements

- Scored five defensive touchdowns.
- Recorded at least five interceptions six times.
- Amassed more than 100 interception-return yards once.
- Finished second in NFL with two non-offensive touchdowns in 1950.
- Led Browns in interceptions three times.
- Holds Browns career record for most touchdown interceptions (5).
- Ranks among Browns career leaders with 44 interceptions (2nd) and 562 interception-return yards (3rd).

- Eight-time division champion (1949, 1950, 1951, 1952, 1953, 1954, 1955, and 1957).
- 1949 AAFC champion.
- Three-time NFL champion (1950, 1954, and 1955).
- 1953 Pro Bowl selection.
- 1956 First-Team All–Eastern Conference selection.
- Pro Football Reference All-1950s Second Team.

29

WALT MICHAELS

Although he is perhaps remembered more for his lengthy coaching career, Walt Michaels previously spent 10 seasons starring for the Browns at outside linebacker. Excelling on both the right and left side of the Cleveland defense at different times, Michaels helped the Browns finish first in the NFL in fewest points allowed on five separate occasions, earning in the process five Pro Bowl selections and two All-Pro nominations. An extremely intelligent player who excelled in all phases of the game, Michaels served as a key member of Browns teams that won five division titles and two NFL championships, before parlaying his vast knowledge of the sport into a career in coaching that lasted more than two decades.

Born to Polish immigrant parents in Swoyersville, Pennsylvania, on October 16, 1929, Walter Edward Michaels acquired a love of football at an early age, even though his father knew little about the game, with Michaels remembering, "He understood two things about football. If you hit, you win. And if you win, you were successful."

Employing the same philosophy when competing in other sports at Swoyersville High School, Michaels became known as an enforcer on the basketball court, with Swoyersville resident Judge Andy Barilla recalling, "If someone was giving one of his teammates a hard time, they would put Walt in the game, and he would take care of it. He would put the guy in the second row of the bleachers."

Even more of a factor on the gridiron, Michaels earned a football scholarship to Washington and Lee College in Virginia with his superb two-way play at Swoyersville, after which he went on to star for the Generals at fullback and guard on offense and linebacker on defense. Particularly outstanding his senior year, Michaels helped lead W&L to the Southern Conference championship, garnering in the process Honorable Mention All-America honors.

Impressed with Michaels's exceptional play at the collegiate level, the Browns made him the 86th overall pick of the 1951 NFL Draft when they

Walt Michaels earned five Pro Bowl selections and two All-Pro nominations as a member of the Browns.
Courtesy of RMYAuctions.com

selected him in the seventh round. However, before the regular season got underway, they included him in an eight-player trade they completed with the Green Bay Packers that landed them the rights to negotiate with future All-Pro defensive lineman Bob Gain. Michaels subsequently spent one year in Green Bay starting at middle linebacker for the Packers, before Paul Brown wisely reacquired him for three offensive linemen prior to the start of the 1952 campaign.

Laying claim to the starting left-outside linebacker job immediately upon his arrival in Cleveland, Michaels recorded a career-high four interceptions for the Browns in 1952, in helping them capture their seventh consecutive division title. Michaels remained on the left side of Cleveland's defense for one more year, before moving to right-outside linebacker in 1954. He subsequently spent all but one of his eight remaining seasons in Cleveland manning that post for the Browns, displaying his versatility by starting for them at middle linebacker in 1956.

Developing a reputation during his time in Cleveland for his consistency, toughness, and durability, the 6-foot, 230-pound Michaels gradually emerged as one of Paul Brown's most reliable players, missing just two games from 1952 to 1961, a period during which the Browns won two NFL championships and Michaels earned Second-Team All-Pro honors twice and five straight trips to the Pro Bowl. Outstanding against the run, Michaels proved to be an aggressive, athletic, and sure tackler who likely would have compiled impressive totals in that category had the league kept track of the statistic at that time. Michaels also excelled in pass coverage and as an occasional blitzer, recording a total of 11 interceptions, which he returned for 139 yards and two touchdowns. Renowned for his football intellect as well, Michaels served as the Browns' defensive signal-caller for most of his 10 seasons with the club.

Recalling Michaels's playing career, Joe Namath, who grew up in western Pennsylvania and later quarterbacked the Jets while Michaels coached the team's defense, said, "I watched Walt when he was in Cleveland. He was a heck of a player."

Although the 32-year-old Michaels continued to perform well for the Browns in 1961, earning First-Team All–Eastern Conference honors from the *Sporting News* for the third time, Paul Brown's unwillingness to pay him what he thought he deserved and his desire to pursue a career in coaching prompted him to announce his retirement at the end of the year. Hired immediately by the AFL's Oakland Raiders, Michaels spent one year serving as the team's defensive backs coach, before beginning a lengthy stint as defensive coordinator for the New York Jets, even appearing in one game with them at linebacker in 1963 due to a rash of injuries. After 10 years with the Jets, Michaels spent three seasons in Philadelphia serving as defensive coordinator for the Eagles. Returning to New York in 1976, Michaels assumed the same role with the Jets for one year, before taking on the position of head coach from 1977 to 1982. After handing in his resignation in New York, Michaels took some time off before he spent his final two seasons (1984–1985) on the sidelines coaching the New Jersey Generals of the United States Football League (USFL).

Eventually retiring to his farm in Shickshinny, Pennsylvania, Michaels lived until July 10, 2019, when he died at a nursing home in Plains, Pennsylvania, at the age of 89. Upon learning of his passing, Jets CEO

Christopher Johnson issued a statement that read: "We are very sad to hear about the passing of Walt Michaels. Walt was a great leader who inspired players to take their games to another level. A defensive mastermind, he had one of his finest moments when he coordinated our unit in the Super Bowl III victory over the Colts. Later, as a head coach, Walt led us to back-to-back playoff berths in 1981–82. Walt had a tireless work ethic and took an honest approach with his players. He will have a lasting impact on our organization, and our thoughts and condolences go out to his family and friends."

Meanwhile, Greg Buttle, who spent seven years playing under Michaels in New York, credited his former coach for his development as a linebacker, telling the *Wilkes-Barre Times Leader*: "Walt was an inordinate genius when it came down to the analysis of his players and how to play the game. I wouldn't have been the football player I was if not for the tutelage of Walt Michaels. Walt never wanted to change you—wanted to make you better. He taught you the game and how to play it the way you could."

BROWNS CAREER HIGHLIGHTS

Best Season

Michaels earned five straight Pro Bowl nominations from 1955 to 1959, with the last of those campaigns representing the finest of his career. In addition to picking off one pass, Michaels ranked among the league leaders with four fumble recoveries, prompting both the Associated Press and United Press International to accord him Second-Team All-Pro honors.

Memorable Moments/Greatest Performances

Michaels scored the first of his two career touchdowns when he ran 34 yards to pay dirt after intercepting a Charlie Conerly pass during a 62–14 rout of the Giants on December 6, 1953.

Michaels contributed to the Browns' lopsided 56–10 victory over Detroit in the 1954 NFL championship game by picking off a pass and recovering a fumble.

Michaels lit the scoreboard for the second and final time in his career when he returned an interception 25 yards for a touchdown during a 24–14 win over the Washington Redskins on October 16, 1955.

Michaels recorded one of the six interceptions the Browns registered against Norm Van Brocklin during their 38–14 victory over the Los Angeles Rams in the 1955 NFL championship game.

Michaels helped anchor a Browns defense that allowed just 71 yards of total offense during a 16–0 shutout of the Philadelphia Eagles on November 18, 1956.

Notable Achievements

- Scored two defensive touchdowns.
- Recorded four interceptions in 1952.
- Five-time division champion (1952, 1953, 1954, 1955, and 1957).
- Two-time NFL champion (1954 and 1955).
- Five-time Pro Bowl selection (1955, 1956, 1957, 1958, and 1959).
- Two-time Second-Team All-Pro selection (1958 and 1959).
- Three-time First-Team All–Eastern Conference selection (1958, 1959, and 1961).
- Pro Football Reference All-1950s Second Team.

30

WALTER JOHNSON

C alled "the best defensive tackle Cleveland has ever had" by Dick Modzelewski, the man he replaced as a starter, Walter Johnson proved to be a pillar of strength on the interior of the Browns defensive line for 12 seasons, never missing a game that entire time. Anchoring the Browns d-line from his left tackle position, Johnson teamed up with Jerry Sherk for much of the 1970s to form one of the top defensive tackle tandems in all of football. An outstanding run-stuffer who also excelled at applying pressure to opposing quarterbacks up the middle, Johnson made significant contributions to Browns teams that won five division titles, earning in the process three Pro Bowl selections. Yet, had Johnson not had the misfortune of playing at the same time as some of the greatest defensive tackles in NFL history, he likely would have earned many more individual accolades.

Born in Cincinnati, Ohio, on November 13, 1942, Walter Johnson attended Robert Taft High School, where he starred in football, basketball, and track and field, setting a Cincinnati Public High School (PHSL) shot-put record with a throw of 55 feet, 3½ inches his senior year. Extremely successful on the court and gridiron as well, Johnson helped his teams win consecutive Cincinnati PHSL championships in both sports, with his outstanding play at fullback making him one of the region's most highly recruited players.

Ultimately accepting a scholarship offer from New Mexico State University, Johnson played briefly for the Aggies, before transferring to California State University during his freshman year. Gradually transitioning from fullback to offensive guard and middle linebacker while at Cal State, Johnson adapted extremely well to his new positions, gaining First-Team Little All-America recognition from the Associated Press and First-Team Little All-Coast recognition from United Press International as a senior in 1964.

Subsequently selected by the Browns in the second round of the 1965 NFL Draft, with the 27th overall pick, Johnson spent his rookie season backing up veterans Dick Modzelewski and Jim Kanicki at defensive tackle,

Walter Johnson ranks among Browns' career leaders in sacks and fumble recoveries.
Courtesy of MearsonlineAuctions.com

before replacing Modzelewski as the team's starting left tackle in 1966. Starting alongside Kanicki the next four years, Johnson emerged as one of the finest players at his position, earning Pro Bowl honors three straight times from 1967 to 1969.

Standing 6'4" and weighing close to 275 pounds, Johnson possessed good size and great strength, making him a stout run-defender who did an excellent job of clogging up the middle. Extremely difficult for any offensive lineman to block one-on-one, Johnson typically found himself being double-teamed, freeing up other Browns' defenders to make tackles. Blessed with exceptional quickness as well, Johnson, who ran the 100-yard dash in 10.0 seconds, also possessed the foot speed to pursue opposing ball-carriers and quarterbacks, who he unofficially sacked a total of 66 times as a member of the Browns. Nevertheless, with Johnson spending most of his time in Cleveland competing against Hall of Fame defensive tackles Bob Lilly, Merlin Olsen, Alan Page, "Mean Joe" Greene, Buck Buchanan, and Alex Karras for postseason honors, he never attained All-Pro status.

After Johnson shed nearly 20 pounds prior to the start of the 1970 campaign to improve his stamina, speed, and agility, rookie Jerry Sherk replaced Jim Kanicki at right tackle, giving the Browns a formidable defensive pairing that remained together for the next seven seasons. During that time, Sherk came to fully appreciate everything Johnson brought to the team, including his outstanding leadership ability and intimidating presence that left a lasting impression on him. In discussing those two aspects of Johnson's persona, Sherk said on www.brownsbacker.com: "When I came to the Browns, Walter Johnson was not only the guy I teamed up with at tackle, but he was the alpha male of the Browns. Guys were in awe of him because of his strength—he could actually hurt people in practice and in the games. My first game was the first Monday night game ever. Each player got four free tickets, and I was only going to use two. Walter knew it and asked if he could buy my other two. I said yes and gave him the tickets. He didn't give me the money, and I was so intimidated by him that I never asked."

Sherk continued, "His strength was legendary on the team. There was a story going around that once Jim Brown called a team meeting, and he was chastising the team for their poor play. During the meeting, he said, 'And if you don't like what I'm saying, I'll kick your ass, and I can kick anyone's ass on the team.' Then he looked over at Walter and said in a lower voice, 'Except maybe for you, Walter!'"

Also known for his tremendous durability, Johnson never missed a game his entire career, appearing in 182 consecutive contests, including 168 as a member of the Browns. Displaying his mental toughness during the Browns' 1969 NFL title game loss to the Vikings in Minnesota, Johnson persevered through sub-zero weather and frostbitten fingers to remain on the field the entire contest.

Johnson continued to perform well for the Browns until 1976, when they decided to waive him at season's end. In addition to leaving Cleveland with an unofficial total of 66 sacks that ranks as the fourth-highest figure in franchise history, Johnson recovered 11 fumbles, which also places him extremely high in team annals.

After being released by the Browns, Johnson signed with the Cincinnati Bengals, with whom he spent the 1977 campaign, before announcing his retirement. Following his playing days, Johnson, who first began wrestling in 1968, continued to compete in that venue until 1984, going up against such notable grapplers as the Masked Destroyer and The Sheik. During his time in the ring, Johnson became known for employing the same head-slap that he used on the football field, launching himself into the ropes, and finishing off his opponent with a painful bear hug.

After retiring from wrestling, Johnson spent his remaining years directing a security alarm firm, until he died of a heart attack at the age of 56 on June 30, 1999, just two days after the passing of another Browns great, Marion Motley. However, Johnson lived long enough to see Art Modell move the Browns out of Cleveland, later expressing his sadness over their departure to NBC's Dick Enberg by saying, "It's as if someone went into my personal biography and took out 11 years of my life and ripped it right out of my book."

BROWNS CAREER HIGHLIGHTS

Best Season

Johnson played his best ball for the Browns from 1967 to 1969, earning three consecutive trips to the Pro Bowl. While any of those campaigns would make a good choice, Johnson's two fumble recoveries, one defensive touchdown, and unofficial total of eight sacks in 1969 prompted me to identify that as the finest season of his career.

Memorable Moments/Greatest Performances

Johnson anchored a smothering Browns defense that forced six turnovers and allowed just 50 yards rushing during a 28–7 win over the Giants on October 2, 1966.

Johnson and his cohorts dominated the opposition once again the following week, with the Browns forcing six turnovers and surrendering just 22 yards on the ground during a 41–10 manhandling of the Pittsburgh Steelers on October 8, 1966.

Johnson scored the first points of his career when he returned a fumble 12 yards for a touchdown during a 27–17 win over the New Orleans Saints on October 12, 1969.

Johnson lit the scoreboard again when he sacked quarterback Virgil Carter in the end zone for a safety during a 30–27 win over the Cincinnati Bengals on October 11, 1970.

Johnson recorded the first of his two career interceptions during a 21–10 victory over the Houston Oilers on December 7, 1970.

Johnson scored what proved to be the game-winning touchdown of a 21–17 victory over the Saints on December 12, 1971, when he recovered an Archie Manning fumble in the end zone early in the fourth quarter.

Johnson recorded the second and last interception of his career during a 26–10 win over the Jets in the 1972 regular-season opener.

Notable Achievements

- Never missed a game in 12 seasons, appearing in 168 consecutive contests.
- Scored two defensive touchdowns.
- Ranks among Browns career leaders with 66 sacks (4th) and 11 fumble recoveries (tied for 7th).
- Five-time division champion (1965, 1967, 1968, 1969, and 1971).
- Three-time Pro Bowl selection (1967, 1968, and 1969).

31

BILL GLASS

The Browns' most consistent pass-rusher for much of the 1960s, Bill Glass spent seven seasons in Cleveland starring at right defensive end for teams that won four division titles and one NFL championship. Acquired by the Browns from the Detroit Lions as part of a huge six-player trade the two teams completed in the spring of 1962, Glass registered more than 10 sacks in a season four times as a member of the Browns, ending his seven-year stint in Cleveland with an unofficial total of 77½ sacks that places him first in franchise history. More than just an outstanding pass-rusher, Glass also did an excellent job of defending against the run, with his exceptional all-around play earning him four Pro Bowl selections and two All-Pro nominations.

Born in Texarkana, Texas, on August 16, 1935, William Sheppeard Glass moved with his family at an early age some 500 miles south, to Corpus Christi, Texas, where his father, Vernon, ran an insurance agency. After getting his start in organized football in junior high school, young Bill suffered a devastating loss when his father passed away, recalling years later, "My dad freely gave his love and blessing to me. And when he passed away, it left a big hole in my heart, and there was no one to bless me."

Fortunately for Glass, he found a mentor in Bill Stages, the head football coach at W.B. Ray High School, who not only taught him how to play defense, but also helped him improve his self-esteem. In discussing the special relationship that he shared with his coach, Glass said, "His parents had died in a car wreck when he was an infant. So, he knew what it was like to grow up without a mother or a father. And he understood the feelings of a kid on the third string sitting on the bench. . . . Coach Stages not only coached me, but he was constantly affirming me and blessing me. I was clumsy and small. You know, it's all right to be small as long as you're fast, but I was slow and clumsy and small."

Aided by Stages's coaching, a six-inch growth spurt, and a weight gain of 60 pounds, Glass eventually emerged as a force-to-be-reckoned-with on

Bill Glass recorded more sacks than anyone else in franchise history.

the football field, stating, "I got to where I couldn't be blocked. The reason is that I had great techniques."

Pursued by several colleges for his skills on the gridiron, the deeply religious Glass ultimately accepted a scholarship offer from Baylor University in Waco, Texas—a Baptist school. Continuing his dominant play at the collegiate level, Glass starred for the Bears at guard on offense and end on defense for three years, gaining unanimous All-America recognition as a senior in 1956, when he recorded 154 tackles in 10 games. While at Baylor, Glass also helped establish the university's chapter of Campus Crusade for Christ.

Impressed with Glass's outstanding play at Baylor, the Detroit Lions made him the 12th overall pick of the 1957 NFL Draft when they selected him late in the first round. However, Glass chose to sign with the Saskatchewan Roughriders of the Canadian Football League, for whom he played one season, before inking a deal with Detroit prior to the start of the 1958 campaign.

After assuming a backup role with the Lions in 1959, Glass spent the next three years starting for them at right defensive end. Establishing himself as one of the league's better pass-rushers during that time, Glass performed well for a defense that also included future Hall of Famers Alex Karras, Joe Schmidt, Yale Lary, and Dick LeBeau. Nevertheless, the Lions chose to include him in a trade they completed with the Browns in late March 1962 that sent Glass, quarterback Jim Ninowski, and running back Howard "Hopalong" Cassady to Cleveland for quarterback Milt Plum, running back Tom Watkins, and linebacker Dave Lloyd.

Proving to be easily the best player involved in the deal, Glass went on to star for the Browns for the next seven seasons, helping them consistently field one of the league's best defenses. Extremely strong, the 6'5", 255-pound Glass possessed good size for a defensive end of the day, with former Browns teammate Frank Ryan stating, "Bill was a great player. He was a humongous human being. I think one of the most fearsome defensive ends in the league during his time."

Doing an outstanding job of applying blind-side pressure to opposing quarterbacks, Glass excelled in that aspect of the game more than any other member of the Cleveland defense. Although the NFL did not begin keeping track of sacks as an official statistic until long after Glass retired, "unofficial" tallies made by pro football reference researchers reveal that he registered at least 15 sacks in a season three times, with his 16½ sacks in 1965 representing the highest single-season mark in team annals. I believe that the researchers work for the NFL in general. Meanwhile, en route to amassing 15 sacks the following year, Glass set another franchise record by bringing down opposing quarterbacks behind the line of scrimmage at least once in seven consecutive games. Extremely effective against the run as well, Glass possessed the size, quickness, and athleticism to stuff the inside run and pursue ball-carriers from sideline to sideline.

Perhaps Glass's most unique talent, though, was his ability to use the psychological concept of autosuggestion to assist him on the playing field, as he revealed when he said, "I would lie on my bed before a game and imagine that I had pulled down a motion picture screen and was watching a film of myself in action, constantly getting past the offensive tackle. This was putting positive pictures into my subconscious—in the same way that performing well in a real game would have done—and it built up my confidence."

One of the league's most durable players, Glass never suffered a major injury until late in his final season, starting 94 consecutive games for the Browns from 1962 to 1968. In explaining his ability to avoid serious injury, Glass said, "I was sort of the aggressor and not the receiver of the body blows. . . . I was a defensive end, where I fought with huge linemen so I could get to the guy with the ball and throw him to the turf. . . . There were some games that were nothing more than brawls, hand-to-hand combat. I'm not talking about dirty play, but hard, physical, demanding—and yes, manly—battles."

Yet, despite his aggressive style of play, Glass always conducted himself with a certain sense of propriety on the field, with one friend recalling, "Quarterbacks told the story on Bill that he would come charging in on you, knock you down, then reach down to pick you up and say, 'Bless you, brother.'"

After earning his fourth Pro Bowl selection and fifth First-Team All–Eastern Conference nomination in 1967, Glass sustained an injury during the latter stages of the ensuing campaign that forced him to miss the season's final four games and ultimately announce his retirement. Glass ended his 11-year career having recorded 87 sacks, recovered nine fumbles, and appeared in 144 of his team's 148 games, 131 of which he started. In addition to registering an unofficial total of 77½ sacks as a member of the Browns, Glass intercepted four passes, recovered five fumbles, and scored two touchdowns.

Following his retirement, Glass used the platform created by his playing career to speak about his greatest passion—his faith in Jesus Christ. Glass, who attended Southwestern Baptist Theological Seminary while living in Fort Worth, Texas, during the 1960s and worked with Reverend Billy Graham while still active in pro football, decided to pursue evangelism as his life's work as a member of the ministry. After founding Bill Glass Ministries in 1969, Glass accepted a challenge from one of his board members three years later to take the gospel to the incarcerated. Beginning in 1972, Glass focused his efforts on preaching the word of the Lord to inmates in all parts of the United States through his "Behind the Walls" prison ministry practice.

Looking back many years later on how the program began, Glass said, "I was thrown into it kicking and screaming, but the response from the inmates was just unbelievable."

Although Glass eventually went into semi-retirement, he remained somewhat active in overseeing the direction of his ministries until he passed away at the age of 86 on December 5, 2021.

BROWNS CAREER HIGHLIGHTS

Best Season

Glass turned in the most dominant performance of his career in 1965, when he earned one of his two Second-Team All-Pro nominations by recording an unofficial total of 16½ sacks that represents the highest single-season mark in franchise history.

Memorable Moments/Greatest Performances

Glass contributed to the Browns' 27–0 win over the Baltimore Colts in the 1964 NFL championship game by recording 1½ sacks.

Glass recorded the first of his four career interceptions during a 17–7 win over the Washington Redskins in the 1965 regular-season opener.

Glass sealed a 49–40 victory over the Giants on December 4, 1966, when he returned a fumble 13 yards for a touchdown late in the fourth quarter.

In addition to picking off a pass during a 24–0 shutout of the Bears on October 22, 1967, Glass led a swarming Browns defense that recorded five sacks and allowed just 20 yards rushing and 136 yards of total offense.

Glass clinched a 24–10 win over the New Orleans Saints in the opening game of the 1968 regular season by returning an interception 17 yards for a touchdown in the fourth quarter.

Notable Achievements

- Scored two defensive touchdowns.
- Finished in double digits in sacks four times, registering at least 15 sacks on three occasions.

- Recorded sacks in seven straight games in 1966.
- Ranks first in franchise history with 77½ career sacks.
- Holds Browns single-season record for most sacks (16½ in 1965).
- Four-time division champion (1964, 1965, 1967, and 1968).
- 1964 NFL champion.
- Four-time Pro Bowl selection (1962, 1963, 1964, and 1967).
- Two-time Second-Team All-Pro selection (1963 and 1965).
- Five-time First-Team All–Eastern Conference selection (1962, 1963, 1964, 1965, and 1967).

32

JOSH CRIBBS

One of the greatest return men in NFL history, Josh Cribbs spent eight seasons in Cleveland, amassing more yards on special teams than any other player in team annals. The NFL record-holder for most kickoff-return touchdowns (eight), Cribbs also scored three times on punt returns, giving him a total of 11 return TDs that places him among the league's all-time leaders in that category as well. The versatile Cribbs also accumulated more than 500 yards from scrimmage twice, ending his eight-year stint in Cleveland with the second-most all-purpose yards in franchise history. A three-time Pro Bowler and two-time All-Pro, Cribbs received the additional honor of being awarded a spot on the NFL 2000s All-Decade First Team, accomplishing all he did after being bypassed by all 32 teams in the 2005 NFL Draft.

Born in Washington, DC, on June 9, 1983, Joshua Cribbs received his introduction to football from his older brother at the age of six, recalling, "We used to play football on concrete, and he used to hit me hard, knock me into the bushes and had me crying. Then, he'd keep me quiet so he wouldn't get in trouble for doing it. My brother made me tougher, and I love him for that. Without the hard work he instilled in me, I probably wouldn't be where I am today."

The nephew of former NFL running back Joe Cribbs, who earned three Pro Bowl nominations while playing for the Buffalo Bills during the 1980s, Josh attended Dunbar High School, where he lettered in football, baseball, basketball, and swimming. Particularly outstanding on the gridiron, Cribbs led Dunbar to three consecutive DC Interscholastic Athletic Association titles, with his strong play at quarterback his senior year earning him First-Team All-Met honors from the *Washington Post*.

Although Cribbs received a considerable amount of interest from Maryland and Syracuse as graduation neared, he chose to enroll at Kent State University in Kent, Ohio, since the other two schools expressed a desire to have him play a position other than quarterback. Cribbs ended up

Josh Cribbs holds the NFL record for most kickoff-return touchdowns.
Courtesy of Erik Drost

starting behind center for the Golden Flashes for four years, setting several school records along the way, including most rushing touchdowns (38), touchdowns scored (41), and total yards accumulated on offense (10,839).

Yet, despite his exceptional play at Kent State, Cribbs's small college background scared off pro scouts, causing him to go undrafted by the NFL in 2005. Subsequently signed by the Browns as a free agent, Cribbs later explained his decision to go to Cleveland by saying, "Well, I wanted to play in the NFL. I tried out for the Redskins, and they wanted me to be on the practice squad. But I wanted to play right away. The Browns told me, 'We want you to be our returner right away. Right now.' So, I ended up taking that. I came out when running quarterbacks weren't as popular, before Kaepernick came and did what he did. I came out back in the days of Seneca Wallace, and

Antwaan Randle El, and those guys. Randle El had to change positions, too. Back then, it was really only pocket passers who were sought after."

Cribbs continued, "I was definitely not confident I would make this team and thrive like I did. I just was confident I was going to give it my best ability. I was confident that, if I had to walk away, if I was forced to walk away, I would be able to look myself in the mirror and say I did everything in my power necessary to allow this dream to come true."

Claiming that his snub by all 32 NFL teams proved to be a blessing in disguise, Cribbs added, "I needed to not get drafted, to give me that chip on my shoulder, that boost of motivation. . . . My potential was there. I was capable, and I was willing. But I needed that extra motivation to put me over the edge, to play in such a way that it would make people think I was drafted. People will even come up to me today and say, 'What round were you drafted in?' . . . Fans couldn't imagine a player like me not being drafted. And I wanted people to just assume that I was drafted, because that means I did a good job."

Making a successful transition from quarterback to return-man following his arrival in Cleveland, Cribbs averaged 24.3 yards per kickoff return as a rookie, amassing in the process 1,106 all-purpose yards. After increasing his output to 1,647 all-purpose yards the following year, Cribbs established himself as arguably the finest returner in the game in 2007, earning Pro Bowl and Second-Team All-Pro honors by accumulating 405 punt-return yards, leading the league with 1,809 kickoff-return yards and 2,312 all-purpose yards, and scoring three times on special teams. Following another strong showing in 2008, Cribbs reached the zenith of his career in 2009, gaining Pro Bowl and First-Team All-Pro recognition by leading the league with 1,994 kickoff- and punt-return yards and four TD returns. Meanwhile, Cribbs, who gained only 239 yards on the ground and caught just 16 passes for 153 yards and one touchdown his first four years in the league, began to see more significant playing time on offense, with his 381 yards rushing and 135 receiving yards giving him a total of 2,510 all-purpose yards that placed him second in the league rankings.

Although the 6'1", 195-pound Cribbs possessed outstanding speed, he differed from most other kick returners in that he ran very much like a running back, punishing would-be tacklers before breaking into the open field. Discussing the problems that Cribbs presented to opposing players on special teams, Buffalo Bills linebacker Jon Corto said prior to a 2009 meeting with the Browns, "He's very physical, runs really hard, and he's just a tough tackle. Guys have to wrap up and really hit him thick. He gets yardage and is really effective at it. He's a playmaker."

Bills receiver Justin Jenkins added, "You've always got dynamic returners inside the NFL, guys like Roscoe Parrish and Darren Sproles—you know, the smaller guys. But you rarely see a bigger guy like Cribbs who can get out just as well as those guys and take the hits, take the pounding as he's running. One-on-one tackles are very hard to come by with him, so you have to make smart decisions and go low. . . . He's going to bring toughness. He sees you and sometimes will try to run through you. Cribbs is that type of guy."

Meanwhile, Buffalo defensive coordinator Tom Jones described the tremendous effort that Cribbs put forth on every play when he stated, "He is elusive. You have to know where he is at every minute or every second of every play. You have to account for him. . . . In his mind, the play is never over. He's going to find a way. If he can't make something happen himself, he's going to try and find a way to get the ball to one of his teammates and have them continue the play. He's a never-say-die guy."

In addition to being one of the game's top return men, Cribbs contributed to the Browns in many other ways, with Cleveland special teams coach Ted Daisher saying prior to the start of the 2008 season, "There really is no one else in the NFL that does all the things that Josh does. There are guys that are great kick returners . . . but you don't see those same guys go down on a kickoff and hit a wedge and make a play or field a punt. Josh has all those skills and those tools. . . . Once he gets in the open field, he's kind of hard to deal with."

And, after spending his first four years in the league serving the Browns almost exclusively on special teams, Cribbs began to assume a far more prominent role on offense as his career progressed, occasionally running the ball from the wildcat formation, and making 41 receptions for 518 yards and four touchdowns as a wide receiver in 2011.

Nevertheless, Cribbs continued to make his greatest impact on special teams, ranking among the league leaders in kickoff- and punt-return yards in both 2011 and 2012, with his total of 1,635 yards in the second of those campaigns earning him the last of his three Pro Bowl selections.

Despite his outstanding play, though, Cribbs did not receive a contract extension from the Browns at the end of 2012, prompting him to sign with the Jets as a free agent. Expressing his sadness to be leaving the city of Cleveland, Cribbs subsequently posted a message on his Instagram account that read: "It's been a blessing to be in Cleveland, wishing the best to the city & the Team. If I could stay, I would."

Shortly after Cribbs signed with the Jets, longtime Cleveland sportswriter Terry Pluto spoke of the toughness he displayed during his time with the Browns, stating, "They line everybody up, somebody kicks the ball, and then you have 22 guys all running at each other like maniacs. This is not a way to have a long career. . . . Eric Mangini, who was the coach in 2010, said Cribbs' toes were almost curled in the last few games. His feet were getting smashed in by people and he just kept playing. Then, Pat Shurmur, his coach last year, said he hardly let Josh practice because that knee was so bad. But Sundays, he was just there."

Cribbs ended up spending just one year in New York, before signing with the Indianapolis Colts prior to the start of the 2014 campaign. Released by the Colts at the end of the year, Cribbs sat out the next two seasons, during which time he considered making a comeback. But, when no team expressed serious interest, Cribbs decided to announce his retirement, saying during an interview with 92.3 The Fan, "I had to wrap my head around the fact that I wasn't able to get on with another team and maintain my skill level to be the Josh Cribbs that everyone knows. I kinda knew internally that I wasn't going to play anymore, but to know it and say it, that's two different things."

Making his decision known to the public on March 22, 2017, Cribbs officially retired as a member of the Browns, ending his career with 11,113 kickoff-return yards, 2,375 punt-return yards, 808 rushing yards, 1,175 receiving yards, 1,983 yards from scrimmage, 15,453 all-purpose yards, 11 return touchdowns, and 20 total TDs, compiling the vast majority of those numbers during his time in Cleveland. Cribbs's 11,113 kickoff-return yards, 13,488 total return yards, and 11 return TDs all place him among the NFL's all-time leaders. Meanwhile, in addition to amassing the second-most all-purpose yards in franchise history (14,065), Cribbs ranks first in team annals in kickoff-return yards (10,015) and punt-return yards (2,154).

Looking back on his playing career, Cribbs said, "Before and after every game, I would look at myself in the mirror and tell myself, 'I'm gonna give it my all. Even if I mess up, I'm gonna do it going full speed.' I was able to live with myself knowing that I gave it my all every single play, every game. I didn't hold back. I wasn't the type of player to step out of bounds early on a play."

Cribbs continued, "It means a lot and confirms to me that not only did I make the NFL, but I exceeded that. I was the best at what I did. The records were confirmation for me and still are confirmation. When people mention the best of the best in returners, they mention my name, and that's good enough for me. . . . I'm at peace in my soul that my NFL career was a great success."

Cribbs also spoke of the special connection he developed with the fans of Cleveland, saying, "Cleveland is a blue-collar city, blue-collar town full of hard workers, and I felt like I embodied that. I felt that I embodied the nature of what it meant to be a Cleveland Browns fan, and I brought that to the field. They gave me energy for games. It was a great relationship with fans that I urge other players to adopt."

Since retiring from football, Cribbs has worked as a motivational speaker and as a spokesman for YMCA charity events. He also spent some time serving as a coaching intern for the Browns and Houston Texans. Blessed with a kind and generous nature, Cribbs created the TeamCribbs Foundation, a nonprofit organization that has been involved in such activities as distributing backpacks to students at a charter school in Cleveland's Central neighborhood and partnering with the Greater Cleveland Salvation Army in providing turkey dinners on its annual Thanksgiving Pantry Day.

In explaining his decision to live in the Cleveland suburbs following his retirement, Cribbs stated, "Had the fans not been so great, I would have easily made the decision to move back east to D.C. or move to another location in a warmer climate. That experience, the fan base, I wouldn't trade it for the world. There's a lot of good fan bases in the country, but none like the Browns."

BROWNS CAREER HIGHLIGHTS

Best Season

Cribbs had a tremendous year for the Browns in 2007, earning Pro Bowl and Second-Team All-Pro honors by leading the NFL with 1,809 kickoff-return yards, 2,214 kickoff- and punt-return yards, 2,312 all-purpose yards, and an average of 30.7 yards per kickoff return. But he posted slightly better overall numbers two years later, gaining First-Team All-Pro and NFL Alumni Special Teams Player of the Year recognition in 2009 by topping the circuit with 1,994 kickoff- and punt-return yards and finishing second in the league with 1,542 kickoff-return yards, 452 punt-return yards, and 2,510 all-purpose yards, with the last figure representing the highest single-season mark in franchise history.

Memorable Moments/Greatest Performances

Cribbs scored the first points of his career when he returned a kickoff 90 yards for a touchdown during a 13–10 loss to the Detroit Lions on October 23, 2005.

Cribbs earned AFC Special Teams Player of the Week honors for the first of four times by returning two kickoffs a total of 118 yards during a 24–21 win over the Oakland Raiders on October 1, 2006.

Although the Browns lost to the Steelers by a score of 24–20 on November 19, 2006, Cribbs scored a touchdown on a 92-yard kickoff return.

Cribbs displayed his explosiveness once again during a 26–24 loss to the Raiders on September 23, 2007, when he returned a kickoff 99 yards for a touchdown.

Although the Browns ended up suffering a 31–28 defeat at the hands of the Steelers on November 11, 2007, Cribbs gave them a 28–24 lead early in the fourth quarter by returning a kickoff 100 yards for a touchdown.

Cribbs scored the first points of a 20–7 win over the 49ers in the 2007 regular-season finale when he returned a punt 76 yards for a touchdown late in the first quarter.

Cribbs lit the scoreboard again when he returned a kickoff 92 yards for a touchdown during a 37–27 loss to the Baltimore Ravens on November 2, 2008.

Although the Browns went on to lose their 2009 regular-season opener to the Vikings by a score of 34–20, Cribbs gave them a 13–10 halftime lead by returning a punt 67 yards for a touchdown late in the second quarter.

Cribbs scored again on special teams when he returned a kickoff 98 yards for a touchdown during a 27–14 loss to the Steelers on October 18, 2009.

Cribbs helped lead the Browns to a 13–6 win over the Steelers on December 10, 2009, by amassing 200 all-purpose yards, gaining 96 of those yards on offense and the other 104 on special teams. Later identifying the victory as the most satisfying of his career, Cribbs, who spent much of the frigid Thursday evening in Cleveland assuming the role of quarterback in the wildcat formation, later said, "Guys still joke today, like Mike Adams will say, 'Yeah, it was Cribbs against the Steelers.' But I say, no, it was everybody. I couldn't have done it without my blockers. The Steelers gave us bulletin board material because they came in saying they were gonna shut us down and stop the wildcat, and we just ran it down their throats. There really was nothing they could do to stop it. We were moving on all cylinders. They were no match for us that game. The defense was working. Our fans were cheering, the 12th man off the bench. You couldn't ask for a greater game, especially against the Steelers. It was like our Super Bowl."

Cribbs turned in another tremendous all-around performance a little over one week later, amassing 316 all-purpose yards and returning two kickoffs for touchdowns during a 41–34 victory over the Kansas City Chiefs on December 20, 2009, with his returns of 100 and 103 yards earning him AFC Special Teams Player of the Week honors.

Cribbs recorded a career-long 65-yard touchdown reception during a 16–14 loss to the Chiefs on September 19, 2010.

In addition to making three receptions for 41 yards during a 27–19 win over the Colts on September 18, 2011, Cribbs earned AFC Special Teams Player of the Week honors for the fourth and final time by returning two kickoffs for 80 yards and two punts for 52 yards.

Cribbs provided one of the few exciting moments of a 20–14 loss to the Baltimore Ravens on December 24, 2011, when he returned a punt 84 yards for a touchdown late in the third quarter.

Notable Achievements

- Returned three punts and eight kickoffs for touchdowns.
- Amassed more than 1,000 all-purpose yards eight times, topping 1,500 yards six times and 2,000 yards twice.
- Led NFL in kickoff-return yards once, kickoff- and punt-return yards twice, all-purpose yards once, and kickoff-return average once.
- Finished second in NFL in kickoff-return yards once, punt-return yards twice, kickoff- and punt-return yards once, and all-purpose yards once.
- Holds NFL record for most kickoff-return touchdowns (eight).
- Ranks among NFL career leaders with 11,113 kickoff-return yards (3rd) and 13,488 kickoff- and punt-return yards (3rd).
- Holds Browns single-season records for most kickoff-return yards (1,809 in 2007) and all-purpose yards (2,510 in 2009).
- Holds Browns career records for most kickoff-return yards (10,015) and punt-return yards (2,154).
- Ranks second in franchise history with 14,065 all-purpose yards.
- Four-time AFC Special Teams Player of the Week.
- Three-time AFC Special Teams Player of the Month.
- 2009 NFL Alumni Special Teams Player of the Year.
- Three-time Pro Bowl selection (2007, 2009, and 2012).
- 2009 First-Team All-Pro selection.
- 2007 Second-Team All-Pro selection.
- NFL 2000s All-Decade First Team.

33

THOM DARDEN

An exceptional ball-hawk who spent his entire career in Cleveland, Thom Darden picked off more passes and amassed more interception-return yards than anyone else in franchise history. Starting at safety for the Browns from 1972 to 1981, Darden recorded at least five interceptions five times, amassed more than 100 interception-return yards four times, and scored three touchdowns on defense, earning in the process one Pro Bowl selection and two All-Pro nominations. Extremely versatile, the hard-hitting Darden, who manned both safety positions at different times in his career, also registered more than 100 tackles once and returned punts his first few years in the league, with his strong all-around play making him a key contributor to Browns teams that made two playoff appearances and won one division title.

Born in Sandusky, Ohio, on August 28, 1950, Thomas Vincent Darden grew up some 65 miles west of Cleveland in a segregated all-Black neighborhood. Frequently engaging in fights with the white residents that lived in a separate neighborhood through which he needed to walk to get to school, Darden dreamed of one day leaving home and playing baseball for the Cleveland Indians. Blessed with the ability to throw the ball with either hand, Darden excelled as a pitcher during his teenage years, with baseball remaining his favorite sport through high school. Failing to develop an affinity for football during that time, Darden, who typically played either halfback or quarterback, objected to the physicality of the game, later saying, "I did not like it because I was getting hit all the time. I could run the ball and do all the options. I just couldn't throw."

However, Darden's attitude toward football began to change shortly after he switched from offense to defense at Sandusky High School, as he revealed when he said, "I started learning how to play the secondary as a freshman in high school, and I enjoyed it. I wasn't getting hit, and I had an opportunity to hit other people. I loved it."

Thom Darden picked off more passes and amassed more interception-
return yards than anyone else in franchise history.
Courtesy of MearsonlineAuctions.com

Excelling as a defensive back and linebacker his three years at Sandusky High, Darden helped lead the Blue Streaks to an overall record of 29-1 and the state championship in 1965. Faced with the dilemma of playing football in college or signing with his beloved Cleveland Indians as graduation neared, Darden chose football because he believed that going to college represented his best path to a better lifestyle. Recalling a conversation he had with his father, Darden revealed that his dad told him, "Look. If you want to go to college, you've got to figure out a way to pay for it, or get it paid for, because we can't afford to send you to college."

After also being recruited by Ohio State, Texas, and Northwestern, Darden accepted a football scholarship from the University of Michigan, where he spent his college career playing defensive back and returning punts for legendary head coach Bo Schembechler. Performing extremely well in his three years as a starter in the Michigan defensive secondary, Darden helped the Wolverines win two Big Ten titles by recording 218 tackles and 11 interceptions, earning in the process two All–Big Ten selections and one All-America nomination.

Subsequently selected by the Browns in the first round of the 1972 NFL Draft, with the 18th overall pick, Darden spent his first year in Cleveland playing strong safety, recording three interceptions, which he returned for a total of 64 yards, while also returning 15 punts for 61 yards. Moved to free safety the following year, Darden spent the remainder of his career at that post, later saying, "I loved that position." Explaining that he enjoyed playing free safety because his ability to call the plays and signals for the defensive backfield made him the quarterback of the unit, Darden said, "There were places where African Americans weren't allowed to play. Blacks didn't play that position. By the time I came into the league, you had Willie Wood over in Green Bay and a couple of others, and I got a chance to play that position, which I knew at that time because I was a fan of the NFL, that there weren't too many African Americans that played that position. And because of that, I felt somewhat of an obligation to do the best I possibly could do."

After picking off just one pass in his first year at his new post, Darden placed among the NFL leaders with eight interceptions and 105 interception-return yards in 1974, while also returning 21 punts for 173 yards and scoring his first touchdown on a 29-yard fumble return. Forced to sit out the entire 1975 campaign with an injured knee he sustained during the preseason, Darden could only watch as the Browns' pass defense, which ranked in the NFL's top 10 in each of his first three seasons, slipped to 23rd in the league. But with Darden returning to action in 1976, the Browns fared much better, finishing 13th in the NFL in passing yards allowed, while also improving their record from 3-11 to 9-5.

Playing the best ball of his career over the course of the next few seasons, Darden recorded 28 interceptions, amassed 505 interception-return yards, and scored two touchdowns on defense from 1976 to 1979, performing especially well in 1978, when he gained Pro Bowl and Second-Team All-Pro recognition by leading the league with 10 interceptions and 200 interception-return yards. And despite being hampered by a bad back the following year, Darden led the Browns with five interceptions and 125 interception-return yards.

Possessing good size and speed, the 6'2", 195-pound Darden proved to be one of the NFL's premier pass defenders, excelling in particular at gauging the flight of the football. Also blessed with soft hands and good timing, Darden placed in the league's top 10 in interceptions four times, leading the Browns in that category on six separate occasions. An extremely hard hitter as well, Darden did an excellent job of defending against the run and made opposing receivers think twice before coming across the middle of the field.

In discussing the many things that Darden brought to the Cleveland defense, former Browns teammate Hanford Dixon, who spent one season playing alongside him in the secondary, said, "He unquestionably was the greatest safety the Browns ever had. . . . He also was ranked fourth among the NFL's hardest hitters by *Sport* magazine. He often was given license to freelance his coverages to wherever he saw the best chance to snare an errant pass."

After picking off a total of five passes the previous two years, Darden chose to announce his retirement following the conclusion of the 1981 campaign, ending his career with 45 interceptions, 820 interception-return yards, nine fumble recoveries, and three touchdowns, with the first two figures both representing franchise records. Darden's 10 picks in 1978 also represent the highest single-season mark in team annals.

Following his playing days, Darden became a professional sports agent, representing, among others, Felix Wright, Chris Calloway, and Tony Boles. He also started a financial services company, the Darden Group, in Cedar Rapids, Iowa, that helps small and midsize businesses find capital, and operated a nonprofit organization that assisted schoolchildren who struggled in basic skills testing.

Now 72 years of age, Darden continues to hold Browns fans close to his heart, saying, "Browns fans, you took a young Ohio kid from a small town, and you really supported him through his growing pains. You helped him become a man. You saw the good and the bad in him and accepted him, so I thank you for that. You constantly treated us like we were family. You showed me how people in this country are supposed to love, not only as sports teams, but as fans and players. So, I thank you from the bottom of my heart."

CAREER HIGHLIGHTS

Best Season

Darden had an outstanding year for the Browns in 1974, finishing third in the NFL with eight interceptions, which he returned for a total of 105 yards, and returning a fumble 29 yards for a touchdown. However, he performed even better in 1978, earning Pro Bowl and consensus All-Pro recognition by leading the league with 10 interceptions and 200 interception-return yards, recording 100 tackles, and recovering two fumbles.

Memorable Moments/Greatest Performances

Darden recorded the first interception of his career during a 27–20 win over the Denver Broncos on October 29, 1972.

Darden helped lead the Browns to a 21–14 victory over the Patriots on November 10, 1974, by picking off two passes and returning a fumble 29 yards for a touchdown.

Darden recorded another two interceptions during a 38–17 win over the Jets in the 1976 regular-season opener.

Darden contributed to a 27–16 victory over the Buffalo Bills on October 23, 1977, by recording two interceptions, which he returned a total of 56 yards.

Darden followed that up by returning his interception of a Mike Livingston pass 18 yards for a touchdown during a 44–7 rout of the Kansas City Chiefs on October 30, 1977.

Darden helped lead the Browns to a 24–16 victory over the Atlanta Falcons on September 17, 1978, by recording a pair of interceptions, which he subsequently returned 46 yards.

Darden followed that up by picking off Terry Bradshaw twice during a 15–9 loss to the Steelers on September 24, 1978.

Darden registered two more interceptions during a 41–20 win over the Bills on October 29, 1978.

Darden helped lead the Browns to a 26–7 victory over the Dallas Cowboys on September 24, 1979, by intercepting Roger Staubach twice, returning one of his picks 39 yards for a touchdown.

Notable Achievements

- Scored three defensive touchdowns.
- Recorded at least five interceptions five times.
- Amassed more than 100 interception-return yards four times, topping 200 yards once.
- Recorded 100 tackles once.
- Led NFL with 10 interceptions and 200 interception-return yards in 1978.
- Finished third in NFL with eight interceptions in 1974.
- Led Browns in interceptions six times.
- Holds Browns single-season record for most interceptions (10 in 1978).
- Holds Browns career records for most interceptions (45) and most interception-return yards (820).
- 1980 division champion.
- 1978 Pro Bowl selection.
- Two-time Second-Team All-Pro selection (1978 and 1979).
- 1978 First-Team All-AFC selection.
- 1979 Second-Team All-AFC selection.

34

BRIAN SIPE

The unquestioned leader of the 1980 "Kardiac Kids," Brian Sipe spent 12 seasons in Cleveland, serving as the Browns' primary starter at quarterback in eight of those. After beginning his career in unheralded fashion as a member of the team's practice squad, Sipe started behind center for the Browns from 1976 to 1983, leading them to two playoff appearances and one division title. Along the way, Sipe threw for more than 3,500 yards and 20 touchdowns four times each, earning in the process one Pro Bowl selection, two All-Pro nominations, and one league MVP trophy. The Browns' single-season record-holder for most pass completions, passing yards, and touchdown passes, Sipe also completed more passes for more yards than any other quarterback in franchise history. Nevertheless, Sipe will always be remembered for error in judgment he made that cost the Browns a chance to advance to the Super Bowl.

Born in San Diego, California, on August 8, 1949, Brian Winfield Sipe got his start in organized sports at an early age, competing in the 1961 Little League World Series for El Cajon, California. Although Sipe spent his early years focusing primarily on baseball, he developed an interest in other sports as well before long, recalling, "When I was young, baseball was the only option because there weren't as many youth sports like there are today. But, as soon as I got a taste of football, I fell in love with it."

Eventually emerging as a standout athlete at Grossmont High School, Sipe excelled in baseball, basketball, and football, proving to be particularly outstanding on the gridiron, where he earned CIF Player of the Year honors for his exceptional play at quarterback his senior year. Offered a football scholarship to San Diego State University, Sipe spent his college career playing for future NFL head coach Don Coryell, under whom he earned honorable mention All-America honors as a senior by leading the Pacific Coast Athletic Association (PCAA) with 2,532 yards passing, 17 touchdown passes, and a 53.1 pass-completion percentage.

Brian Sipe earned NFL MVP honors in 1980.
Courtesy of MearsonlineAuctions.com

Yet, despite the impressive numbers that Sipe compiled during his time at San Diego State, concerns over his somewhat smallish 6'1", 195-pound frame and lack of superior arm strength caused him to fall to the 13th round of the 1972 NFL Draft, where the Browns finally selected him with the 330th overall pick. Sipe subsequently spent the 1972 and 1973 campaigns serving as a member of the Browns' practice squad, before finally being added to the team's roster in 1974.

Sipe ended up seeing very little action over the course of the next two seasons, starting only seven games and throwing for just 1,030 yards and two touchdowns as the backup for Mike Phipps. However, when Phipps went down with an injury in the opening game of the 1976 campaign, Sipe stepped in and did an excellent job the rest of the year, leading the Browns to a 9-5 record (they finished just 3-11 the previous season) by completing 57.1 percent of his passes, throwing for 2,113 yards, and finishing sixth in the league with 17 touchdown passes. Although limited to just nine games in 1977 by a season-ending shoulder injury he sustained during a 35–31 loss to the Pittsburgh Steelers on November 13, Sipe performed well for the Browns behind center, leading them to five wins in their first eight contests by completing 57.4 percent of his passes and throwing for 1,233 yards and nine TDs.

Fully healthy by the start of the 1978 campaign, Sipe had his finest season to date under new head coach Sam Rutigliano, passing for 2,906 yards, throwing 21 touchdown passes and 15 interceptions, completing 55.6 percent of his passes, and posting a passer rating of 80.7 for a Browns team that finished 8-8. Sipe followed that up with another strong season, earning Second-Team All-Pro honors and a third-place finish in the NFL MVP voting in 1979 by leading the league with 28 touchdown passes and finishing second in the circuit with 3,793 passing yards.

Although Sipe lacked great size and a powerful throwing arm, he established himself as one of the NFL's better quarterbacks by making good use of his passing accuracy, soft touch, intelligence, and keen sense of timing. Developing a strong rapport with tight end Ozzie Newsome and wideouts Dave Logan and Reggie Rucker, Sipe seemed to know exactly when to deliver the ball to his intended receiver, more often than not hitting him in stride. Sipe also knew how to take advantage of the pass-receiving skills of running backs Greg and Mike Pruitt, both of whom posted their best receiving totals with Sipe starting behind center. And even though Sipe did not run a great deal, he had good mobility and moved well in the pocket.

Taking his game up a notch in 1980, Sipe led the Browns to an 11-5 record and their first division title in nine years by finishing second in the league with 4,132 passing yards and 30 touchdown passes, while topping the circuit with a passer rating of 91.4, with his superb play earning him Pro Bowl, First-Team All-Pro, and NFL MVP honors. Leading the Browns and their fans on an incredible journey, Sipe directed the team to several last-minute victories, causing the club to be nicknamed "The Kardiac Kids."

In discussing the uniqueness of that 1980 Browns squad, Sipe said during a 2019 interview, "I think what really set us apart at that time is that the guys could get focused late in the game when they needed to be focused. That's not to say they weren't that way in the first half, but the psyche of a game changes late. This is not to slight the effort by my teammates or whatnot, but coaches get a little funny, teams get a little funny in the fourth quarter when they're protecting leads."

Sipe added, "We were a team playing over our heads. We felt comfortable throwing caution to the wind. The reason we did as well as we did that year is that we simply were a team that refused to lay down. We certainly weren't the most talented team of all time."

Unfortunately, the Browns' magical season ended with a heartbreaking loss to the eventual Super Bowl champion Oakland Raiders in the divisional round of the AFC Playoffs, with a miscue by Sipe in the closing moments proving to be the game's pivotal play.

With the Browns trailing the Raiders by a score of 14–12 and in possession of the football at the Oakland 13 yard line with less than a minute left to play, they needed only a field goal to seal the victory. However, with placekicker Don Cockroft having already missed two field goal attempts earlier in the game, sending him out for a third try represented something of a gamble. Later explaining why he did not consider himself to be a viable option at that point, Cockroft said during a 2006 interview, "What many people don't know about that situation is that I was a long way from being 100 percent physically in 1980. I had two herniated discs and needed four epidurals to just get through the season. I probably should have gone on IR."

That being the case, head coach Sam Rutigliano told Sipe to run a play called "Red Slot Right, Halfback Stay, 88" on first down, also instructing his quarterback to "throw it into Lake Erie" if nobody was wide open in the end zone. However, Sipe misread the Oakland defense and tried to force the ball into Ozzie Newsome. And, with the Browns facing the open end of old Cleveland Stadium on a cold, windy day, Sipe's pass fluttered as it approached Newsome, allowing Raiders safety Mike Davis to cut in front of him and intercept the ball in the end zone. Oakland subsequently ran out the clock and went on to win Super Bowl XV, defeating the Philadelphia Eagles by a score of 27–10. Meanwhile, Sipe spent the rest of his career trying to live down the infamous "Red Right 88" play that brought the Browns' season to an abrupt end.

Looking back on the play years later, Sipe said, "The pass will be with me as long as I'm around football fans. It's the thing that people remind me of from that year."

Sipe then added, "The reason I had an opportunity to make a mistake like that was we had made a lot of those decisions and gotten away with them."

Sipe remained the Browns' starting quarterback for three more years, never again experiencing the same level of success, although he threw for more than 3,500 yards another two times. Performing especially well in 1983, Sipe nearly led the Browns to a wild card playoff berth by throwing for 3,566 yards and 26 touchdowns. However, after engaging in contract negotiations with the New Jersey Generals of the United States Football League throughout the regular season, Sipe decided to leave Cleveland following the conclusion of the 1983 campaign. Sipe, who received a two-year contract worth $1.9 million from the Generals, left the Browns having thrown for 23,713 yards, 154 touchdowns, and 149 interceptions, run for 762 yards and 11 touchdowns, completed 56.5 percent of his passes, and compiled a passer rating of 74.8 as a member of the team. In the 112 games he started at quarterback for the Browns, the team compiled a record of 57-55.

Sipe ended up spending just one year in New York, passing for 2,540 yards and 17 touchdowns in 1984, before being dealt to the Jacksonville Bulls at season's end after the Generals made rookie quarterback Doug Flutie the highest-paid player in football by inking him to a five-year deal worth $7 million. After starting behind center for the Bulls in 1985, Sipe announced his retirement when the USFL folded at the end of the year.

Following his retirement, Sipe returned to San Diego, where he spent some time helping to design custom homes in the nearby cities of Del Mar and Rancho Sante Fe, before returning to the game he loved as quarterbacks coach at Santa Fe Christian School in Solana Beach, California. Describing the events that led to him becoming a coach, Sipe said, "I was friends with former athletic and head football coach [at Santa Fe Christian] Bob Dennison, who was after me for a couple of years to help him out by becoming quarterbacks coach. I did it part-time for a few years. Then I realized that we are put here on Earth to help others."

After eight years at Santa Fe Christian and six years at his alma mater, San Diego State, Sipe decided to focus exclusively on bettering himself as a human being. The father of three, Sipe began attending a local Christian church with his wife and children while still coaching at Santa Fe. Growing increasingly fond of the religion and its teachings after joining a Bible study group, Sipe now says, "The scripture described everything I believe about mankind. After a year or so of attending the study, I was able to surrender my defenses to God."

CAREER HIGHLIGHTS

Best Season

Sipe had easily the finest season of his career in 1980, when he earned Pro Bowl, First-Team All-Pro, and NFL MVP honors by completing 60.8 percent of his passes, leading the league with a passer rating of 91.4, and setting single-season franchise records that still stand by completing 337 passes, passing for 4,132 yards, and throwing 30 touchdown passes.

Memorable Moments/Greatest Performances

Sipe excelled in a relief role on October 27, 1974, when, after replacing an ineffective Mike Phipps behind center in the second half, he led the Browns on two fourth-quarter scoring drives that enabled them to come away with a 23–21 win over Denver, scoring both touchdowns himself on short runs.

Sipe guided the Browns to a 41–20 victory over the Buffalo Bills on October 29, 1978, by completing 12 of 15 pass attempts for 217 yards and three touchdowns.

Sipe led the Browns to a convincing 45–24 win over the Baltimore Colts on November 19, 1978, by throwing for 309 yards and four touchdowns, hooking up with Calvin Hill three times and Reggie Rucker once.

Sipe gave the Browns a dramatic 27–24 victory over the Kansas City Chiefs on September 9, 1979, by hitting Reggie Rucker with a 21-yard touchdown pass in the closing moments. He finished the game with 243 yards passing and three TD passes.

Although Sipe threw three interceptions during a 51–35 loss to the Steelers on October 7, 1979, he also passed for 351 yards and a career-high five touchdowns.

Sipe came up big for the Browns during the latter stages of a 30–24 overtime victory over the Miami Dolphins on November 18, 1979. After sending the game into overtime by hitting Ozzie Newsome with a 34-yard touchdown pass late in the fourth quarter, Sipe gave the Browns the win when he delivered a 39-yard scoring strike to Reggie Rucker in OT. He finished the game with 358 yards passing, three touchdown passes, and no interceptions.

Sipe led the Browns to a 34–27 win over Tampa Bay on September 28, 1980, by throwing for 318 yards and three touchdowns, the longest of which went 43 yards to Calvin Hill.

Sipe performed brilliantly during a 26–21 win over the Packers on October 19, 1980, passing for 391 yards and two touchdowns, which came on a 19-yard connection with Ozzie Newsome and a 46-yard hookup with Dave Logan in the closing moments that enabled the Browns to overcome an eight-point fourth-quarter deficit.

Sipe followed that up by passing for 349 yards and four touchdowns during a 27–26 win over the Steelers on October 26, 1980, with his 18-yard TD pass to Ozzie Newsome late in the final period providing the margin of victory.

Sipe had another big game against Cincinnati on November 23, 1980, throwing for 310 yards and four touchdowns during a 31–7 Browns win.

Sipe continued his magical season by throwing for 340 yards and one touchdown during a 17–14 win over the Jets on December 7, 1980, hitting Greg Pruitt with a game-winning 5-yard TD pass late in the fourth quarter.

Sipe led the Browns to a 42–28 win over the Colts on October 25, 1981, by passing for 444 yards and four touchdowns, the longest of which came on a 40-yard connection with Dave Logan.

Sipe threw another four touchdown passes during a 31–26 win over the Detroit Lions on September 11, 1983, hooking up once each with Ricky Feacher, Mike Pruitt, Ozzie Newsome, and Dave Logan.

Sipe gave the Browns a 30–24 victory over the San Diego Chargers on September 25, 1983, by hitting Harry Holt with a 48-yard touchdown pass in overtime. He finished the game with 327 yards passing and three TD passes.

Sipe led the Browns to a 41–23 win over the Colts on November 27, 1983, by throwing for 313 yards and three touchdowns, the longest of which came on a 66-yard connection with Ozzie Newsome.

Notable Achievements

- Passed for more than 3,500 yards four times, topping 4,000 yards once.
- Threw more than 20 touchdown passes four times, topping 30 TD passes once.
- Completed more than 60 percent of passes once.
- Posted touchdown-to-interception ratio of better than 2–1 once.
- Posted passer rating above 90.0 once.
- Led NFL in touchdown passes once and passer rating once.
- Finished second in NFL in pass completions once, passing yards twice, and touchdown passes once.

- Finished third in NFL in pass completions once, passing yards once, and pass completion percentage once.
- Holds Browns single-season records for most pass completions (337 in 1980), passing yards (4,132 in 1980), and touchdown passes (30 in 1980).
- Holds Browns career records for most pass attempts (3,439), pass completions (1,944), and passing yards (23,713).
- Ranks second in franchise history with 154 touchdown passes.
- 1980 division champion.
- 1980 NFL MVP.
- 1980 Pro Bowl selection.
- 1980 First-Team All-Pro selection.
- 1979 Second-Team All-Pro selection.
- 1980 First-Team All-AFC selection.

35

GARY COLLINS

A gifted athlete who possessed soft hands and outstanding size and speed, Gary Collins spent his entire 10-year career in Cleveland, catching more touchdown passes during that time than any other player in franchise history. Collins, who also ranks extremely high in team annals in receptions and receiving yards, proved to be a significant contributor on special teams as well, serving as the Browns' punter his first six years in the league, with his strong all-around play earning him two Pro Bowl selections and two All-Pro nominations. Yet, despite the many contributions that he made to teams that captured six division titles, Collins is largely remembered today for his singular performance in the 1964 NFL title game that helped the Browns win their last league championship.

Born in Williamstown, Pennsylvania, on August 20, 1940, Gary James Collins starred on the gridiron at Williamstown High School, where, in addition to excelling at wide receiver on offense and linebacker on defense, he displayed the punting skills he developed during his youth. Recruited by several colleges as graduation neared, Collins ultimately accepted a scholarship to the University of Maryland, where he established himself as one of the nation's top wideouts. Performing especially well his senior year, Collins, who also played defensive back and punted for the Terrapins, earned All-America honors and an eighth-place finish in the Heisman Trophy balloting, prompting Maryland head coach Tom Nugent to call him "the finest player I've ever coached" and proclaim, "He produces in the clutch and has never failed me whenever I asked him to do something special."

Subsequently selected by the Browns with the fourth overall pick of the 1962 NFL Draft, and by the Boston Patriots with the sixth overall pick of that year's AFL Draft, Collins chose to go to Cleveland, where he spent his first pro season playing almost exclusively on special teams under Paul Brown, averaging 42.8 yards per punt, while making just 11 receptions for 153 yards and two touchdowns as a backup wide receiver. However, Collins assumed a far more prominent role on offense in 1963 after Blanton

Gary Collins ranks first in franchise history in touchdown receptions.
Courtesy of MearsonlineAuctions.com

Collier replaced Brown at the helm following a disappointing 7-6-1 finish the previous year. Inserted into the starting lineup, Collins helped the Browns improve their record to 10-4 by making 43 receptions, amassing 674 receiving yards, and leading the league with 13 TD catches, which set a new single-season franchise record.

Continuing his solid play in 1964, Collins made 35 receptions for 544 yards and eight touchdowns in an offense that predicated most of its success on the running of Jim Brown, who led the Browns to their first division title in seven years by topping the circuit with 1,446 yards rushing and 1,786 yards from scrimmage. Collins then created headlines when, after listening to several members of the heavily favored Baltimore Colts boast about how they expected to dispose of the Browns rather easily in the NFL championship game, he told the media that he believed his team would win the contest by three touchdowns.

Looking back on his prediction years later, Collins said during a 2016 interview with Fox Sports, "They interviewed me that Wednesday or so, and I said we were going to win. I predicted it, and I got hell from my head coach, but I said, 'Well, why the hell are we playing the game if you don't feel like that?' He [Blanton Collier] paused, and he said, 'Yeah, you've got a point, but you didn't have to say it publicly.'" Collins then added that he told Collier, "But I said it, I meant it, and I'm still not sorry."

Backing up his bold prediction, Collins subsequently gathered in three second-half touchdown passes from quarterback Frank Ryan, in leading his team to a stunning 27–0 victory over the Colts, cementing in the process his permanent place in Browns lore.

Establishing himself as one of the NFL's most productive wide receivers the next two seasons, Collins earned Pro Bowl and Second-Team All-Pro honors in both 1965 and 1966 by catching 50 passes, amassing 884 receiving yards, and scoring 10 touchdowns in the first of those campaigns, before ranking among the league leaders with 56 receptions, 946 receiving yards, and 12 TD catches the following year. Collins also performed brilliantly on special teams in 1965, leading all NFL punters with an average of 46.7 yards per kick.

Standing 6'5" and weighing 215 pounds, Collins had a wide wingspan and a long stride that made him extremely difficult to cover one-on-one, especially close to the opponent's goal line, with Paul Warfield stating, "There was no one who could stop Gary Collins inside of the red zone. He had magnificent hands, and, in the red zone, he was unstoppable."

Warfield then went on to say, "He was probably the best guy I played alongside of throughout my entire career."

An excellent blocker as well, Collins contributed to the Browns' vaunted running game with his willingness to contact defenders at the line of scrimmage and beyond. Collins also proved to be a fearless receiver who often ran crossing patterns and slants over the middle at a time when wideouts typically paid a steep price for doing so. Meanwhile, Collins demonstrated his sure hands by dropping only seven passes his entire career.

Well liked by his teammates, Collins, said Leroy Kelly, was "A great receiver and just a great individual." Kelly then added, "Most of the time, Gary was a good-humored person. I never really saw him get into it, except when Frank [Ryan] wouldn't get him the ball."

Yet, Collins could also be extremely moody, with longtime Cleveland radio talk show host Pete Franklin recalling, "Gary Collins could be a strange cat. One day, he was, 'Hey, how are you? Glad to see you.' He acted as if he were your best friend in the world. The next day, he'd just walk right by you without a word. But say this much for Gary, he was one helluva football player."

Longtime Browns equipment manager Morrie Kono is another who experienced Collins's mood swings, once telling reporters, "I always thought Gary was mad at me. It was from the way he looked. I couldn't tell if Gary was moody, sulking, or angry. But, once I got to know him, what a guy. What a sense of humor."

Later admitting to being an angry player at times, Collins explained that he had been going through a difficult period with his wife, who lived with a man he knew while they were separated in the mid-1960s.

Although Collins's offensive production fell off somewhat in 1967, he earned First-Team All–Eastern Conference honors for the second time by making 32 receptions for 500 yards and seven touchdowns. Plagued by an injured shoulder the following year, Collins appeared in only five games, finishing the season with just nine receptions, 230 receiving yards, and no touchdowns. Collins also willingly surrendered his punting duties in 1968, later saying, "It wasn't easy. We'd have a third-down-and-14 situation, and I'd go out for a long pass. It would be incomplete, and I'd have to come back to the huddle and punt. By the fourth quarter of most games, my legs were starting to tighten up."

Returning to top form in 1969, Collins gained unofficial First-Team All-Pro recognition from three major news sources by making 54 receptions, amassing 786 receiving yards, and finishing second in the league with 11 TD catches. However, the 1969 campaign proved to be Collins's last as an elite wideout. Suffering from multiple rib injuries that he concealed from everyone since he did not wish to make himself a target for opposing defenders, Collins made just 26 receptions for 351 yards and four TDs in 1970. Reaching his nadir during a late-season loss to the Dallas Cowboys, Collins, after being booed off the field by the fans at Cleveland Stadium following a particularly poor performance, responded with an obscene gesture.

Unable to get along with new head coach Nick Skorich the following year, Collins announced at season's end that he intended to retire unless the Browns traded him to either the Washington Redskins or New York Jets. When the Browns failed to work out a deal with either team, Collins announced his retirement, ending his 10-year NFL career with 331 receptions, 5,299 receiving yards, 5,359 yards from scrimmage, a franchise-record 70 touchdown catches, and an average of 41.0 yards per punt.

Collins subsequently sat out the next two seasons, before returning to the game in 1974 as a player-coach with the Florida Blazers of the short-lived World Football League. Retiring from football for good following the conclusion of the campaign, Collins spent the next several years raising horses, owning a small farm, coaching college football, and doing pregame radio reports for the Browns at different times, before becoming an insurance agent. Collins, who is 81 years old as of this writing, now lives with his second wife, Carole, in Hershey, Pennsylvania, where he remains humble about his accomplishments as an NFL player, saying in 2011, "I don't wake up in the morning and think, 'Geez, I was a really good football player, and we shut out the Colts for the NFL championship, and I ought to be in the Hall of Fame.' All of that ego stuff is gone."

CAREER HIGHLIGHTS

Best Season

Collins performed well for the Browns in 1963, catching 43 passes, amassing 674 receiving yards, and leading the NFL with 13 touchdown receptions. But he posted better overall numbers in both 1965 and 1966, earning consecutive Pro Bowl and Second-Team All-Pro nominations by making 50 receptions for 884 yards and 10 TDs in the first of those campaigns, before making 12 TD catches and establishing career-high marks with 56 receptions and 946 receiving yards the following year. When it is considered that Collins also led the NFL with a career-best 46.7 punting average in 1965, he made his greatest overall impact that year.

Memorable Moments/Greatest Performances

Collins contributed to a 38–14 win over the St. Louis Cardinals on November 18, 1962, by making six receptions for 88 yards and scoring his first career TD on a 12-yard pass from Frank Ryan.

Collins helped lead the Browns to a 35–23 victory over the Steelers on October 5, 1963, by making five receptions for 95 yards and two touchdowns, with his 20-yard TD catch in the final period putting his team ahead to stay.

Collins starred during a 37–7 win over the Eagles on October 20, 1963, averaging 51 yards on his two punts and catching five passes for 82 yards and three touchdowns, the longest of which came on a 35-yard connection with Frank Ryan.

Collins topped 100 receiving yards for the first time as a pro on December 1, 1963, making four receptions for 100 yards during a 24–10 win over the Cardinals.

Collins helped the Browns forge a 33–33 tie with the Cardinals on September 20, 1964, by catching six passes for 105 yards and one touchdown.

Collins performed brilliantly for the Browns in the 1964 NFL championship game, earning game MVP honors by making five receptions for 130 yards and three TDs during their 27–0 win over the Colts, collaborating with Frank Ryan on scoring plays that covered 18, 42, and 51 yards.

Collins torched the Philadelphia defensive secondary for eight catches, 128 receiving yards, and two touchdowns during a 38–34 Browns win on November 7, 1965.

Collins contributed to a 49–40 victory over the Giants on December 4, 1966, by making five receptions for 120 yards and one touchdown.

Collins helped lead the Browns to a 38–10 win over the Cardinals in the 1966 regular-season finale by catching five passes for 126 yards and two TDs, which came on hookups of 42 and 44 yards with Frank Ryan.

Collins gave the Browns a 27–23 victory over the Washington Redskins on September 28, 1969, when he gathered in a 15-yard touchdown pass from Bill Nelsen in the closing moments.

Collins had a big day against Pittsburgh on October 18, 1969, making seven receptions for 103 yards and two TDs during a 42–31 win, scoring once on a 48-yard pass from Bill Nelsen.

Notable Achievements

- Surpassed 50 receptions three times.
- Surpassed 800 receiving yards twice.
- Topped 10 touchdown receptions four times.
- Averaged more than 42 yards per punt three times.
- Led NFL with 13 touchdown receptions in 1963.
- Led NFL with punting average of 46.7 yards per kick in 1965.
- Finished second in NFL in touchdown receptions twice.
- Led Browns in receptions four times and receiving yards three times.
- Holds Browns career record for most touchdown receptions (70).

- Ranks among Browns career leaders with 331 receptions (4th), 5,299 receiving yards (5th), 70 touchdowns (3rd), 420 points scored (8th), and 13,764 punting yards (4th).
- Six-time division champion (1964, 1965, 1967, 1968, 1969, and 1971).
- 1964 NFL champion.
- 1964 NFL championship game MVP.
- Two-time Pro Bowl selection (1965 and 1966).
- Two-time Second-Team All-Pro selection (1965 and 1966).
- Two-time First-Team All–Eastern Conference selection (1965 and 1967).

36

MIKE JOHNSON

A versatile defender who excelled for the Browns at three different linebacker positions, Mike Johnson spent eight seasons in Cleveland, leading the team in tackles six times en route to recording the second-most stops in franchise history. A veritable tackling machine, Johnson brought down opposing ball-carriers more than 130 times on five separate occasions, helping the Browns win three division titles in the process. Outstanding at creating turnovers as well, Johnson ranks second in team annals in forced fumbles, with his exceptional all-around play earning him two Pro Bowl selections and one First-Team All-AFC nomination.

Born in Southport, North Carolina, on November 26, 1962, Michael Connan Johnson grew up just outside Washington, DC, in Prince George's County, Maryland, where he spent his youth rooting for the Dallas Cowboys. Drawing the ire of everyone around him by supporting the Redskins' fiercest rival, Johnson recalled, "I was a Dallas Cowboys fan. I was never a Skins fan. My parents were, everybody around me was and still is. They all loved the Redskins so much that I just couldn't take it. I've always been the argumentative type, the person who loves to do the opposite of what everybody else does. Yeah, I've taken a lot of heat over it. But it's no fun just going along with everybody else."

Eventually establishing himself as a standout athlete and student at DeMatha Catholic High School in the Washington suburb of Hyattsville, Maryland, Johnson starred in football and finished in the top 15 percent of his graduating class, prompting such notable schools as Brown University and Carnegie Mellon University to offer him full academic scholarships. Meanwhile, the University of Pittsburgh recruited Johnson for his skills on the gridiron. But, after seriously considering enrolling at Pittsburgh, Johnson decided to attend Virginia Polytechnic Institute and State University (now known as Virginia Tech) in Blacksburg, Virginia, largely because of its excellent program in architecture.

Mike Johnson ranks second in franchise history in tackles and forced fumbles.
Courtesy of MearsonlineAuctions.com

Recalling how his desire to study his primary academic interest affected his decision, Johnson said, "About 10th grade, I just became fascinated with architecture. Nobody in the family was an architect; it was just something I enjoyed, the fascination with structure, continuity. I just really didn't consider professional football to be a priority. I even got into the habit of really downplaying the athletic side of my life. I never believed an education was 'something to fall back on.' But I began to make some All-America teams, and I thought, 'Hmmmm.'"

Lettering in football for four years at Virginia Tech, Johnson often found himself being overshadowed by future Buffalo Bills Hall of Famer Bruce Smith. Nevertheless, Johnson acquitted himself extremely well in his three years as a starter, gaining Honorable Mention All-America recognition twice by recording a total of 429 tackles, with his 135 stops in 1983 helping the Hokies finish first in the nation with an average of just 8.3 points allowed per game.

Subsequently selected by the Pittsburgh Maulers in the second territorial draft held by the United States Football League on January 4, 1984, Johnson headed to Philadelphia when the Maulers traded him to the Philadelphia Stars, whom he helped lead to back-to-back USFL championships in his first two professional seasons. However, just five months after Pittsburgh drafted Johnson, the Browns acquired his NFL rights when they selected him in the first round of that year's NFL supplemental draft of USFL and Canadian Football League players, with the 18th overall pick. Thus, when the USFL folded after the 1985 season, Johnson became the property of the Browns.

Arriving in Cleveland prior to the start of the 1986 campaign, Johnson spent his first year with the Browns playing mostly on special teams, while also filling in for starting linebackers Chip Banks, Clay Matthews, Eddie Johnson, and Anthony Griggs in the team's 3-4 defense. Even though Johnson received a limited amount of playing time, he helped the Browns capture the second of their three straight division titles by making 56 tackles, forcing three fumbles, and recovering two others. Displacing Griggs as the starter at right-inside linebacker the following year, Johnson recorded 98 tackles, one interception, two sacks, and another three forced fumbles, prompting Browns head coach Marty Schottenheimer to say at season's end, "Last season, Mike didn't get to camp until the USFL settlement was well over. But we expected him to be a fine inside linebacker. We had him highly rated from the beginning. He was our second first-round draft pick in the supplemental draft."

Meanwhile, fellow Browns linebacker Eddie Johnson stated, "For a guy to come in from the run-and-shoot that teams played in the USFL, to play well almost right away in the NFL, where intellect and mental preparation are such a big part, is really an accomplishment."

Continuing to perform well after moving to left-inside linebacker in 1988, Johnson registered a team-high 132 tackles and picked off two passes, before spending his remaining time in Cleveland at middle linebacker after the Browns switched to a 4-3 defense the following year. Serving as the focal point of the Browns defense from 1989 to 1993, the 6'1", 230-pound Johnson used his speed, intelligence, and superb instincts to establish himself as one of the NFL's premier inside backers, earning two trips to the Pro Bowl and one All-AFC nomination by consistently placing near the top of the league rankings in tackles, making more than 150 stops on three separate occasions. Strong against the pass as well, Johnson did a solid job in coverage and as an occasional blitzer, picking off three passes one year and recording four sacks in another.

A consummate team player, Johnson discussed the importance of the team concept to him when he said, "One of the big components to being a good player is knowing what everybody else on the field is supposed to be doing. We're 11 different pieces that need to come together in a whole. In order for something good to happen, we all have to come together with some harmony."

But, after recording 974 tackles, 20 forced fumbles, eight fumble recoveries, 10 interceptions, 11 sacks, and two touchdowns over the course of the previous eight seasons, Johnson decided to leave Cleveland and sign as a free agent with the Detroit Lions at the end of 1993. He subsequently spent two years in Detroit, registering more than 100 tackles another two times, before announcing his retirement following the conclusion of the 1995 campaign with career totals of 1,224 tackles, 26 forced fumbles, 13 fumble recoveries, 13 interceptions, 14½ sacks, and three touchdowns. Since retiring from football, Johnson has been honored by being inducted into both the Virginia Tech Sports Hall of Fame and the DeMatha High School Hall of Fame.

BROWNS CAREER HIGHLIGHTS

Best Season

Johnson earned Pro Bowl and All-AFC honors in 1989 by recording 133 tackles, one sack, three interceptions, and three forced fumbles. But he performed just as well in two or three other seasons, finishing second in the NFL with 176 tackles in 1992, while also recording two sacks, forcing four fumbles, recovering five others, and scoring one defensive touchdown, before establishing career-high marks with 181 tackles and four sacks the following year. However, with Johnson earning his second straight trip to the Pro Bowl in 1990 by making 161 tackles, forcing three fumbles, recording two sacks, and scoring a touchdown on a 60-yard interception return, we'll identify that as his finest all-around season.

Memorable Moments/Greatest Performances

Johnson recorded the first sack of his career during a 23–20 overtime win over the Jets in the divisional round of the 1986 playoffs.

Johnson registered his first career interception during a 34–10 victory over the Pittsburgh Steelers on September 20, 1987.

Johnson earned AFC Defensive Player of the Week honors by picking off two passes during a 29–21 win over the Phoenix Cardinals on October 23, 1988.

Johnson lit the scoreboard for the first time in his career when he returned an interception 64 yards for a touchdown during a 24–14 loss to the San Diego Chargers on September 23, 1990.

Johnson helped lead the Browns to a 13–10 win over the Atlanta Falcons on December 16, 1990, by recording two sacks.

Johnson registered another two sacks during a 19–17 victory over the Patriots on October 25, 1992, getting to Hugh Millen twice.

Johnson contributed to a 37–21 win over the Cincinnati Bengals on December 6, 1992, by scoring a touchdown when he recovered a fumble in the end zone.

Notable Achievements

- Scored two defensive touchdowns.
- Recorded more than 100 tackles five times.
- Finished second in NFL with 176 tackles in 1992.
- Finished third in NFL with five fumble recoveries in 1992.
- Led Browns in tackles six times.
- Ranks among Browns career leaders with 974 tackles (2nd) and 20 forced fumbles (2nd).
- Three-time division champion (1986, 1987, and 1989).
- 1988 Week 8 AFC Defensive Player of the Week.
- Two-time AFC Defensive Player of the Month.
- Two-time Pro Bowl selection (1989 and 1990).
- 1989 First-Team All-AFC selection.

37

MYLES GARRETT

The first player selected in the 2017 NFL Draft, Myles Garrett has proven himself to be worthy of that distinction since he arrived in Cleveland, establishing himself as one of the league's premier defensive ends. An outstanding pass-rusher who has finished in double digits in sacks in each of the last four seasons, Garrett has led the Browns in that category five straight times, en route to recording the sixth-most sacks in franchise history. Strong against the run as well, Garrett has gained Pro Bowl and All-Pro recognition three times each with his excellent all-around play, which has made him a huge contributor to an ever-improving Browns defense.

Born in Arlington, Texas, on December 29, 1995, Myles Lorenz Garrett attended Martin High School, where he displayed his exceptional athletic ability by lettering in football, basketball, and track and field, qualifying for the state championships in both the shotput and discus throw. Even more outstanding on the gridiron, Garrett recorded 19½ sacks his senior year, earning in the process a five-star rating from the Rivals.com recruiting network, which also ranked him as the second-best overall player in his class.

After receiving several scholarship offers, Garrett committed to Texas A&M University, where he spent three seasons starring at defensive end for the Aggies, recording a total of 31 sacks, 141 tackles, 47 tackles for loss, and seven forced fumbles. A two-time First-Team All-SEC and First-Team All-America selection, Garrett also gained recognition as the nation's top defensive lineman his sophomore year, when, in addition to leading the conference with 12 sacks, he forced five fumbles and registered 36 solo tackles, 18½ of which resulted in a loss.

Choosing to forgo his final year of college, Garrett declared himself eligible for the 2017 NFL Draft, which he entered as one of the most highly touted prospects in years, with his scouting report reading: "Garrett's biggest strength coming out of college is his ability to get to the QB. He is

Myles Garrett has led the Browns in sacks in each of the last five seasons.
Courtesy of Erik Drost

extremely explosive coming off the edge and a great athlete, to say the very least. Garrett racked up 31 sacks in his three-year career in College Station, 11 coming in his freshman season and 11.5 the following year."

Ranked number one on ESPN analyst Mel Kiper Jr.'s big board after he posted a time of 4.64 seconds in the 40-yard dash and leaped 41 inches in the vertical jump and 128 inches in the broad jump at the NFL Scouting Combine in Indianapolis, Garrett ended up going first overall to the Browns, making him the first Texas A&M player ever to be accorded that honor.

Laying claim to the starting left defensive end job shortly after he arrived in Cleveland, Garrett performed well for the Browns his first year in the league, earning a spot on the 2017 NFL All-Rookie Team by record-ing seven sacks, 31 tackles, nine tackles for loss, one forced fumble, and one fumble recovery, despite missing four games with an ankle sprain and another with a concussion he suffered during a 12–9 overtime loss to the Tennessee Titans in Week 7. Nevertheless, the Browns finished the season 0-16, making them just the second team to go winless since the NFL expanded its schedule to 16 games in 1978.

Named a defensive captain prior to the start of the 2018 season, Garrett helped the Browns compile a record of 7-8-1 by ranking among the league leaders with 13½ sacks, forcing three fumbles, and registering 44 tackles, including 35 of the solo variety, with his outstanding play earning him Pro Bowl, Second-Team All-Pro, and First-Team All-AFC honors. Com-menting on his teammate's ability to impact the outcome of games from his defensive end position, Browns wide receiver Jarvis Landry stated, "He does what he wants. When he puts his hand on the ground, he's coming after you."

Blessed with freakish athletic ability, the 6'4", 272-pound Garrett pos-sesses a unique skill set that makes him extremely difficult to block one-on-one. Capable of beating his man with either his strength or his tremendous quickness, Garrett typically has multiple blockers assigned to him, freeing up other members of the Browns defense to make plays. Still, Garrett fre-quently finds himself in the opponent's offensive backfield, making him one of the most impactful defensive players in the league.

Continuing to perform at an elite level in 2019, Garrett recorded 10 sacks in just 10 games, although the quality of his character came into ques-tion for the first time following his involvement in a pair of unfortunate incidents, one of which caused the league to suspend him for the final six contests.

Garrett's reputation received its first blow after he committed three personal fouls during the first two games of the 2019 campaign, with his roughing the passer penalty against Trevor Siemian during a 23–3 win over the Jets in Week 2 resulting in the quarterback tearing his anterior cruci-ate ligament (ACL). Fined a combined $52,639 for his three infractions, Garrett came under further scrutiny for his poor conduct during a 21–7 victory over the arch-rival Pittsburgh Steelers in Week 11, when, with just eight seconds left in regulation, he pulled quarterback Mason Rudolph to the ground after an admittedly late hit, prompting the Pittsburgh signal-caller to grab and jerk his assailant's helmet. After getting to his feet, Gar-rett forcibly removed Rudolph's helmet and attempted to strike him in the head with it, delivering a glancing blow while being kept at bay by a pair of

Steelers offensive linemen, one of whom, Maurkice Pouncey, punched and kicked him several times.

Ultimately fined $45,623 and suspended by the league for the rest of the season, Garrett subsequently found his actions being called into question by both Browns head coach Freddie Kitchens and Cleveland quarterback Baker Mayfield in interviews conducted immediately after the game, with Mayfield calling his behavior "inexcusable." Although Garrett later apologized for his actions, which he described as "foolish" and "out of character," his words smacked of insincerity months later when, before his reinstatement hearing, he chose to play the race card, alleging publicly for the first time that Rudolph had directed a "racial slur" at him during their on-field confrontation. Yet, even though Garrett claimed that he told former Browns GM John Dorsey, Freddie Kitchens, and his best friend on the team, Larry Ogunjobi, about the alleged slur immediately after the altercation, no one offered an explanation as to why he waited until his reinstatement hearing to make the allegation public for the first time. And a subsequent investigation found no evidence to support his claim, leaving most people to doubt its veracity.

Nevertheless, the Browns displayed their high regard for Garrett prior to the start of the ensuing campaign, when, some five months after the NFL reinstated him from his suspension on February 12, 2020, they signed him to a five-year, $125 million contract extension. Rewarding the Browns for the faith they placed in him, Garrett helped lead them into the playoffs by ranking among the league leaders with 12 sacks and four forced fumbles, while also registering 48 tackles, 33 solo stops, and 18 hits on opposing quarterbacks, with his exceptional play earning him Pro Bowl, First-Team All-Pro, and First-Team All-AFC honors for the first of two straight times. Although the Browns failed to advance to the playoffs in 2021, Garrett performed brilliantly once again, establishing career-high marks with 16 sacks, 51 tackles, and 33 quarterback hits.

Still only 26 years old as of this writing, Garrett will enter the 2022 season with career totals of 58½ sacks, 11 forced fumbles, four fumble recoveries, 203 tackles, and one defensive touchdown, with the first two figures both placing him extremely high in team annals. Since Garrett figures to add significantly to those totals in the years ahead, there is no telling how high on this list he will eventually rise.

CAREER HIGHLIGHTS

Best Season

Although Garrett also performed exceptionally well the previous year, he had his finest all-around season in 2021, when, in addition to scoring the only touchdown of his career, he finished third in the league with 16 sacks and recorded 51 tackles, 17 tackles for loss, and 33 hits on opposing quarterbacks.

Memorable Moments/Greatest Performances

Garrett recorded the first two sacks of his career during a 17–14 loss to the Jets on October 8, 2017.

Garrett helped the Browns forge a 21–21 tie with the Steelers in the opening game of the 2018 regular season by registering two sacks, forcing two fumbles, and making six tackles.

Garrett helped lead the Browns to a 21–17 win over the Jets on September 20, 2018, that marked their first victory since the latter stages of the 2016 campaign by recording two sacks.

Garrett starred against the Jets once again on September 16, 2019, recording three sacks and three tackles for loss during a 23–3 Browns win.

Garrett contributed to a 34–20 victory over the Washington Redskins on September 27, 2020, by registering two sacks and forcing a fumble.

Garrett followed that up by sacking Dak Prescott twice and forcing a fumble during a 49–38 win over the Dallas Cowboys on October 4, 2020, earning in the process AFC Defensive Player of the Week honors.

Garrett turned in an outstanding all-around effort during a 37–34 win over the Cincinnati Bengals on October 25, 2020, recording two sacks, one forced fumble, and one tackle for loss.

Garrett performed magnificently during a 26–6 victory over the Chicago Bears on September 26, 2021, earning AFC Defensive Player of the Week honors by recording seven tackles, four tackles for loss, and a career-high 4½ sacks.

Garrett scored the only points of his career during a 24–22 win over the Baltimore Ravens on December 12, 2021, when he sacked quarterback Tyler Huntley late in the first half, causing a fumble that he subsequently recovered and returned 15 yards for a touchdown.

Notable Achievements

- Has scored one defensive touchdown.
- Has finished in double digits in sacks four times.
- Has finished third in NFL in sacks once and forced fumbles once.
- Has led Browns in sacks five times.
- Ranks among Browns career leaders with 58½ sacks (6th) and 11 forced fumbles (3rd).
- Member of 2017 NFL All-Rookie Team.
- Two-time AFC Defensive Player of the Week.
- October 2020 AFC Defensive Player of the Month.
- Three-time Pro Bowl selection (2018, 2020, and 2021).
- Two-time First-Team All-Pro selection (2020 and 2021).
- 2018 Second-Team All-Pro selection.
- Three-time First-Team All-AFC selection (2018, 2020, and 2021).

38

RAY RENFRO

Nicknamed "The Rabbit" for his exceptional running speed, Ray Renfro proved to be one of the NFL's most dangerous wideouts for much of his 12-year career, which he spent entirely in Cleveland. Settling in at wide receiver full-time in 1955 after also seeing action as a running back and return-man his first few seasons with the Browns, Renfro went on to establish himself as a top deep threat, averaging more yards per reception than any other player in franchise history. Also ranking extremely high in team annals in total receptions, receiving yards, and TD catches, Renfro helped the Browns win five division titles and two NFL championships, earning in the process three Pro Bowl selections and unofficial Second-Team All-Pro honors twice.

Born in Whitesboro, Texas, on November 7, 1929, Austin Raymond Renfro began his journey to the NFL at Leonard High School in Fannin County, where he starred for the Tigers on the gridiron. Continuing to display his superior athletic ability after he enrolled at North Texas State University (now the University of North Texas) following his graduation in 1948, Renfro excelled as a halfback in football and a sprinter in track, earning First-Team All-America honors as a senior in 1951 by rushing for 1,043 yards and scoring 15 touchdowns, with his 207-yard, three-touchdown effort against arch-rival Texas Western making him a North Texas legend.

Impressed with Renfro's outstanding play at the collegiate level, the Browns selected him in the fourth round of the 1952 NFL Draft, with the 48th overall pick, making him the highest drafted player in North Texas State history to that point. Renfro subsequently spent his first year in Cleveland serving the Browns primarily as a kickoff and punt returner, amassing 299 yards on special teams, while gaining another 34 yards on offense as a backup halfback. Assuming a far more prominent role on offense the following year while splitting his time between running back and wide receiver, the speedy Renfro finished second in the NFL with 1,074 yards from scrimmage, carrying the ball 60 times for 352 yards and

Ray Renfro averaged more yards per reception than any other player in team annals.

four touchdowns, and gaining another 722 yards on 39 pass receptions, with his excellent all-around play earning him Pro Bowl honors.

Although the Browns won the NFL title in 1954, Renfro missed nearly half the season with a series of nagging injuries that limited him to just 379 yards from scrimmage and one touchdown. Moved to flanker full-time the following year, Renfro helped the Browns repeat as NFL champions by making 29 receptions, amassing 603 receiving yards, finishing second in the league with eight TD catches, and topping the circuit with an average of 20.8 yards per reception, prompting the Newspaper Enterprise Association (NEA) to accord him unofficial Second-Team All-Pro honors. After posting less impressive numbers in 1956, Renfro totaled 75 receptions, 1,690 receiving yards, and 18 touchdowns over the course of the next three seasons, with his 21 receptions, 589 receiving yards, six TD catches, and career-high average of 28 yards per reception in 1957 gaining him Pro Bowl recognition for the second time. Meanwhile, the *New York Daily News* accorded Renfro Second-Team All-Pro honors in 1959 after he made 30 receptions, accumulated 528 receiving yards, and scored six touchdowns during the regular season.

Even though the 6'1", 190-pound Renfro typically gathered in a modest number of passes each year and never led the league in either receiving yards or touchdown catches, he played a key role in the Browns' offense, which predicated much of its success on the running of Jim Brown. While Brown served as the focal point of the team's offense, Renfro provided an excellent alternative at wide receiver, loosening up opposing defenses with his tremendous speed that made him one of the NFL's most dangerous wideouts. And, once Renfro broke into the open field, no defensive back in the league possessed the quickness or athleticism to bring him to the turf.

Brown remained a starter in Cleveland for three more years, gaining Pro Bowl recognition in 1960 despite making just 24 receptions for 378 yards and four touchdowns, before having his finest statistical season the following year, when he caught 48 passes, amassed 834 receiving yards, and scored six touchdowns. After making 31 receptions for 638 yards and four touchdowns as a player-coach in 1962, Renfro assumed a backup role in 1963, before announcing his retirement following the conclusion of the campaign.

In explaining his decision to retire when he did, Renfro said, "I thought about retiring after my 10th year [1961], but Coach Brown talked me into staying two more years as a player-coach. I had had some knee injuries. If you play pro football, you have knee injuries, particularly running backs and receivers. I had my share. Finally, you wake up one morning, and you can't get out of bed. That's why I retired."

Ending his career with 281 receptions, 5,508 receiving yards, 6,190 yards from scrimmage, 6,569 all-purpose yards, 50 TD catches, 55 total touchdowns, and 682 yards rushing, Renfro continues to rank among the franchise's all-time leaders in all but the last of those categories.

After retiring as an active player, Renfro returned to Cleburne, Texas, a suburb of Fort Worth, where he opened a dry-cleaning business, later saying, "I was well prepared to retire because I had wanted to get out a couple of years earlier, so, I really didn't miss playing. I did miss the fellowship of my teammates, but it was just like someone in your family gets married. It's a change you learn to live with."

But, after remaining away from the game for one year, Renfro, who took rookie receiver Paul Warfield under his wing while serving as a consultant at the Browns' training camp in 1964, became an assistant coach with the Detroit Lions in 1965. After one year in Detroit, Renfro spent two seasons coaching Washington Redskins receivers under former Browns teammate Otto Graham, remembering, "That worked out all right for a while because I could come back after the season and work in the cleaning business. But the second year it was just too hard to be away from the family for six months."

Shortly after resigning his post in Washington, Renfro received a call from Dallas Cowboys head coach Tom Landry, recalling during a 1984 interview, "When I left Washington, Coach Landry called and wanted me to come over and work the passing game as an assistant coach with the Dallas Cowboys. Of course, I had to go full-time because, with Coach Landry's system, there was too much work to be done just on a seasonal basis. I was with the Cowboys from 1968 to 1972. When I left the Cowboys, I went with the Tarrant Concrete Company in Fort Worth as sales manager. I have been in the ready-mix concrete business ever since."

Renfro continued to work in the concrete business for several more years, until a bout with cancer forced him to retire to private life. Renfro ultimately lost his battle with the dreaded disease, passing away at the age of 67, on August 4, 1997.

CAREER HIGHLIGHTS

Best Season

Although Renfro scored six touchdowns and established career-high marks with 48 receptions and 834 receiving yards in 1961, he had his finest all-around season for the Browns in 1953, earning Pro Bowl honors for the first of three times by making 39 receptions for 722 yards, gaining 352 yards on the ground, scoring nine touchdowns, finishing second in the league with 1,074 yards from scrimmage, and ranking among the leaders with 1,127 all-purpose yards.

Memorable Moments/Greatest Performances

Renfro scored the first touchdown of his career when he hauled in a 48-yard pass from Otto Graham during a 27–7 win over the Chicago Cardinals on October 4, 1953.

Renfro contributed to a 30–14 victory over the Washington Redskins on October 18, 1953, by gaining 101 yards on seven carries and making three receptions for 44 yards.

Renfro turned in an outstanding all-around effort during a 34–16 win over the Pittsburgh Steelers on November 8, 1953, catching three passes for 35 yards, running 44 yards for one touchdown, and returning a blocked field goal 79 yards for another TD.

Renfro went over 100 receiving yards for the first time as a pro on November 29, 1953, when he made four receptions for 105 yards during a 27–16 victory over the Chicago Cardinals.

Renfro followed that up by rushing for 66 yards, making two receptions for 71 yards, throwing a 36-yard touchdown pass to Pete Brewster, and scoring a pair of touchdowns during a 62–14 blowout of the Giants on December 6, 1953, with his TDs coming on a 58-yard run and a 60-yard pass from Otto Graham.

Renfro came up big for the Browns in the 1954 NFL championship game, making five receptions for 94 yards and two touchdowns during a 56–10 rout of the Detroit Lions. Looking back on his performance years later, Renfro said, "I remember that as my biggest thrill in pro football, not just because I had such a good day catching the ball, but because we beat the Lions, the team that had beaten us in two previous championship games."

Renfro helped the Browns forge a 35–35 tie with the Giants on November 27, 1955, by making five receptions for 130 yards and one TD, which came on a 42-yard pass from Otto Graham.

Renfro helped lead the Browns to a 35–24 win over the Cardinals in the 1955 regular-season finale by catching six passes for 110 yards and two touchdowns, the longest of which came on a 41-yard connection with Graham.

Renfro proved to be a thorn in the side of the Cardinals once again on December 1, 1957, collaborating with Tommy O'Connell on scoring plays of 65 and 23 yards during a 31–10 win.

Although the Browns lost to the Steelers by a score of 21–20 on November 22, 1959, Renfro had a huge game, making five receptions for 161 yards and three touchdowns, one of which came on a career-long 70-yard hookup with Milt Plum.

Renfro starred in defeat again on November 26, 1951, catching seven passes for 166 yards and two touchdowns during a 37–21 loss to the Giants.

Renfro contributed to a 34–7 win over the St. Louis Cardinals on October 21, 1962, by making six receptions for 152 yards and one TD, which came on a 38-yard pass from Jim Ninowski.

Notable Achievements

- Amassed more than 1,000 yards from scrimmage once.
- Averaged more than 20 yards per reception five times.
- Led NFL with average of 20.8 yards per reception in 1955.
- Finished second in NFL in touchdown receptions once, yards from scrimmage once, and average yards per reception once.
- Finished third in NFL in touchdown receptions once, touchdowns once, and average yards per reception once.
- Led Browns in receptions once and receiving yards three times.
- Holds Browns career record for most yards per reception (19.6).
- Ranks among Browns career leaders with 281 receptions (12th), 5,508 receiving yards (4th), 6,190 yards from scrimmage (8th), 6,569 all-purpose yards (10th), 50 touchdown receptions (4th), 55 touchdowns (5th), and 330 points scored (10th).
- Five-time division champion (1952, 1953, 1954, 1955, and 1957).
- Two-time NFL champion (1954 and 1955).
- Three-time Pro Bowl selection (1953, 1957, and 1960).

39

DOUG DIEKEN

One of the longest-tenured players in franchise history, Doug Dieken spent 14 seasons in Cleveland, establishing himself during that time as the most durable player in team annals. Persevering through countless injuries that included torn cartilage in both knees, broken hands, and broken thumbs, Dieken never missed a game his entire career, starting every contest the Browns played from November 21, 1971, to December 16, 1984, after supplanting Dick Schafrath as the starter at left tackle. Along the way, Dieken helped the Browns win two division titles, earning in the process team MVP and Pro Bowl honors once each.

Born some 100 miles southwest of Chicago, in Streator, Illinois, on February 12, 1949, Douglas Heye Dieken grew up on the city's mean streets, stating years later that "meeting up to fight with the guys from the town 16 miles away [Ottawa] qualified as having fun on a weekend."

Acquiring a strong work ethic from his father, who managed the local farms, Dieken recalled, "He gave me all the lousy jobs he could find, like baling hay. He wanted to see if I could work hard. My mother's family was in the grain commodity market."

Getting his start in organized sports at Streator Township High School, Dieken initially starred in basketball and baseball, before beginning his career on the gridiron at the urging of his basketball coach, with Dieken remembering, "The high school basketball coach said he wanted me to get in shape in the fall before basketball started. He wanted me to run cross country or play football."

Choosing football, Dieken joined the varsity team his freshman year, after which he went on to earn All-State honors twice as a wide receiver. Meanwhile, Dieken continued to excel as a pitcher on the diamond and a center on the basketball court, averaging 12.6 points and 9.5 rebounds his junior year.

Deciding to attend his parents' alma mater following his graduation, Dieken accepted a football scholarship to the University of Illinois, where

Doug Dieken never missed a game his entire career.

he played wide receiver as a sophomore in 1968, before transitioning to tight end the following year. Excelling at both posts for the Fighting Illini, Dieken ended his collegiate career with 89 receptions for 1,246 yards, with his 39 catches, 537 receiving yards, and four touchdown receptions his senior year prompting both United Press International and the Associated Press to accord him All–Big Ten honors.

Subsequently selected by the Browns in the sixth round of the 1971 NFL Draft, with the 142nd overall pick, Dieken recounted how the team informed him of its plans to convert him into an offensive lineman, saying, "On draft day, I was sitting at home waiting for a team to call. I was watching TV. Not the draft. It wasn't on back then. My mother was upstairs with her bridge club. The phone rang. I picked it up. 'This is Nick Skorich, head coach of the Cleveland Browns. We just drafted you in the sixth round as an offensive tackle.'"

After pausing for a moment, Dieken asked Skorich, "Any chance I could play tight end?" In response, Skorich said, "We'll see when you get here."

Dieken continued, "I showed up at the old Fleming Field at Case Western for rookie camp. They handed me jersey No. 73 and pointed me toward the offensive line."

While learning his new position, Dieken spent the first several weeks of his rookie campaign playing mostly on special teams, seeing very little action on offense while serving as a backup to starting tackles Dick Schafrath and Bob McKay. But after McKay suffered an injury, Dieken received his first significant playing time at right tackle, recalling, "I went in, and I'd never played right tackle in my life. I played maybe three quarters at left tackle in the preseason games. No tackle in college."

With Dieken having acquitted himself extremely well in his regular-season debut as an offensive lineman, the Browns inserted him into the starting lineup a few weeks later, replacing the aging Schafrath with him at left tackle. Dieken subsequently started the next 194 games for the Browns at that post, setting in the process an NFL record for most consecutive starts by a left tackle that still stands.

Although the 6'5", 254-pound Dieken developed into one of the league's better players at his position before long, it took some time for him to fully grasp the intricacies of offensive line play, stating, "The biggest adjustment was pass blocking. But then I figured out it was like blocking out your man in basketball. Instead of keeping your body between the man and the rim, it was keep your body between the man and the quarterback. You square him up. Footwork is the key."

Dieken then admitted that he played his position all wrong, explaining, "If you play left tackle, your left hand is on the ground and your left leg is back. But I played with my right hand in the dirt, the right leg back. It was backwards."

Nevertheless, Dieken proved to be extremely effective as both a pass-protector and run-blocker, helping quarterback Brian Sipe earn NFL MVP honors in 1980, four years after serving as the anchor of an offensive line that allowed Browns passers to be sacked just 19 times the entire season. Meanwhile, Dieken helped pave the way for Greg Pruitt to rush for more than 1,000 yards three times and Mike Pruitt to gain more than 1,000 yards on the ground on four separate occasions.

Through it all, Dieken continued to show up week after week, going about his job in workmanlike fashion, no matter how much pain he had to endure. After experiencing discomfort in his right knee his second year in the league, Dieken visited the team doctor, who told him, "You tore a cartilage. You can have the operation and miss the rest of the season. Or you can tape it up and play." Dieken played the rest of the year, delaying surgery until the subsequent offseason.

A similar situation developed with his other knee the following season, and, once again, Dieken postponed surgery until the end of the year. Dieken also sustained broken hands, broken thumbs, torn tendons, strained ligaments, a fractured arm, and, in his own estimation, "a concussion or two. Maybe four or six. Hard to know."

In explaining his ability to continue playing under such trying conditions, Dieken said, "Physical courage is part of the game. You learn to play with pain. Part of what it is is survival."

The camaraderie that Dieken shared with the other members of Cleveland's offensive line also helped keep him going, as he suggested when he said, "It was more like an elite boys club than anything. Our group of linemen, we were close as hell. If you picked a fight with one of us, you picked a fight with all of us. To be able to get into that boys club and to play was a great thing to do. It wasn't for the money."

However, Dieken finally began to wear down in 1984, prompting him to announce his retirement at the end of the year. In addition to his 194 regular-season starts, Dieken started all four playoff games in which the Browns appeared during his career.

Shortly after retiring as an active player, Dieken, who has since had both knees and hips replaced, joined the Cleveland Browns Radio Network, with whom he spent most of the last 37 years doing color commentary for both incarnations of the Browns franchise, before announcing his retirement at the end of 2021. In speaking of his longtime broadcast partner, Browns play-by-play man Jim Donovan said, "He's incredibly vigilant and caring about what's happening in my life. I had a real health scare a while ago, and he was incredible to me, almost like a father to me, and he's a great dad. When [former Browns broadcaster] Casey Coleman had cancer and was away from us, every Sunday we were in the broadcast booth, he made sure to dial up Casey and ask how he was feeling and doing. That's the kind of guy he is. . . . From the very first game we did together . . . the Hall of Fame Game in Canton, it was just two guys sitting around talking football like we had tickets to the game. It's just kind of continued that way. He takes some of the emotion out of it. I can be very emotional. He can clinically say why a play did or didn't work, or why he's throwing the ball here and not there."

Since 1997, Dieken has also co-sponsored various events to support the Cleveland Public Schools Special Olympics Program through the Doug Dieken Foundation, which he created after witnessing the impact that the Olympics had on his developmentally disabled brother. Presented with a Lifetime Achievement Award at the 2012 Greater Cleveland Sports Awards, Dieken received the following words of praise from David Gilbert, the president and CEO of the Greater Cleveland Sports Commission: "Doug Dieken is a great Cleveland icon who has had an enormous impact on our community. Doug has been a positive force in Cleveland from the time he first stepped on the field at Municipal Stadium. His work on the field, in the broadcast booth, and in the community has touched the lives of countless Clevelanders. We are honored to award him the Lifetime Achievement Award at the 2012 Greater Cleveland Sports Awards."

CAREER HIGHLIGHTS

Best Season

Dieken earned Pro Bowl and All-AFC honors for the only time in his career in 1980, when he helped the Browns place near the top of the league rankings in passing yards (2nd), total yards (5th), and points scored (8th), while anchoring an offensive line that allowed just 23 sacks of NFL MVP Brian Sipe.

Memorable Moments/Greatest Performances

Dieken's strong blocking at the point of attack helped the Browns rush for 278 yards and amass 481 yards of total offense during a 40–14 win over the Kansas City Chiefs on December 14, 1975.

Dieken and his line-mates dominated the Chiefs at the line of scrimmage once again on October 30, 1977, with the Browns amassing 526 yards of total offense during a 44–7 win, gaining 322 of those yards on the ground and 204 yards through the air.

Dieken anchored an offensive line that enabled the Browns to rush for 309 yards and amass 532 yards of total offense during a lopsided 41–20 victory over the Buffalo Bills on October 29, 1978.

Dieken and his cohorts controlled the line of scrimmage during a 45–24 win over the Colts on November 19, 1978, with the Browns gaining 309 yards through the air and not allowing a single sack of Brian Sipe.

Dieken and his line-mates dominated the Colts at the point of attack once again on October 25, 1981, with the Browns throwing for 431 yards and amassing 562 yards of total offense during a 42–28 win.

Dieken experienced perhaps the most memorable moment of his career during a 25–19 overtime win over the Houston Oilers on October 30, 1983, when he caught a 14-yard touchdown pass from holder Paul McDonald off a fake field goal attempt. Recalling the play years later, Dieken said, "The pass was supposed to go to the flat. But I was so wide open in the end zone, even Paul McDonald couldn't miss me!"

NOTABLE ACHIEVEMENTS

- Holds franchise records for most consecutive games played (203) and most consecutive starts (194).
- Holds NFL record for most consecutive games started by a left tackle (194).
- Ranks fourth in franchise history with 203 games played.
- Two-time division champion (1971 and 1980).
- Browns offensive MVP in 1975.
- 1980 Pro Bowl selection.
- 1980 Second-Team All-AFC selection.

40

BERNIE KOSAR

An overachiever who established himself as one of the NFL's better quarterbacks even though he possessed somewhat limited athletic ability and an awkward-looking sidearm throwing motion, Bernie Kosar won the hearts of Browns fans with his blue-collar style of play, exceptional leadership ability, and team-first mentality. The Browns' primary signal-caller from 1985 to 1993, Kosar led the team to four division titles, amassing along the way the second-most pass completions, third-most passing yards, and fourth-most touchdown passes in franchise history. A one-time Pro Bowler and one-time All-AFC selection, Kosar remains one of the most popular players ever to don a Browns uniform nearly three decades after he appeared in his last game as a member of the team.

Born in Youngstown, Ohio, on November 25, 1963, Bernard Joseph Kosar Jr. grew up in nearby Boardman, a little more than one hour southeast of Cleveland, where he spent his youth rooting for the Browns. Acquiring his strong work ethic from his parents, Kosar recalled being raised according to the principle of love and exhaustion that suggests: "If you love your children, keep them busy and keep them tired so that you keep them out of trouble."

Eventually emerging as a standout athlete at Boardman High School, Kosar excelled in baseball, basketball, and football, gaining general recognition as the finest quarterback in the state his senior year, when, in addition to being named an All-American by *Parade* magazine, he earned First-Team All-Ohio and Ohio Division I Offensive Player of the Year honors. Yet, despite his outstanding play at Boardman, Kosar did not receive as many scholarship offers as he would have liked due to his poor mechanics, lack of superior athletic ability, and gangly 6'5" frame, with one high school friend later saying, "Basically, he was kind of skinny and geeky for a quarterback."

After his first choice, Ohio State, chose not to recruit him, Kosar decided to enroll at the University of Miami, where he spent just two

Bernie Kosar led the Browns to four division titles.
Courtesy of George A. Kitrinos

seasons playing under head coach Howard Schnellenberger, before electing to turn pro. Accomplishing a great deal those two seasons, Kosar led the Hurricanes to their first National Championship in 1983 and left Miami with then school records for most career pass completions, passing yards (5,971), and touchdown passes (40).

In explaining his decision to leave college early, Kosar, who possessed the ability to decipher defenses quickly, later said, "College football was not challenging. With our passing system at Miami, which was head and shoulders above any other college, after a while it was just too easy. I don't want that to sound wrong, but in games I'd see only one, maybe two coverages. It was so unsophisticated. For me to grow at so slow a pace—what was the point?"

With NFL rules at that time permitting only college seniors and college graduates to turn pro, Kosar accumulated 24 additional credits during the spring and summer of 1985, making him eligible for that year's NFL Supplemental Draft, where, after working out a deal with the Buffalo Bills, the Browns selected him with the first overall pick.

Joining the Browns prior to the start of the 1985 campaign, Kosar spent the season's first month sitting on the bench, before taking over behind center when Gary Danielson suffered a torn rotator cuff in Week 4. Starting the season's final 12 games, Kosar compiled rather pedestrian numbers, passing for 1,578 yards, throwing eight touchdown passes and seven interceptions, completing 50 percent of his passes, and posting a passer rating of 69.3. Nevertheless, with the Browns compiling a record of 8-8 that earned them a first-place finish in the NFL's weakest division and Kosar leading them to victory in four of their final six regular-season contests, team owner Art Modell proclaimed at season's end, "I fully expect Bernie Kosar to be the best quarterback I ever had, ever will have. The intelligence, the leadership, the arm. He has everything. Everything including magnetism I haven't seen since Jimmy Brown. People are attracted to him, something in his presence."

Taking his game up a notch in 1986, Kosar led the Browns to a 12-4 record and their second consecutive division title by ranking among the league leaders with 3,854 passing yards, throwing 17 TD passes and 10 interceptions, completing 58.4 percent of his passes, and posting a passer rating of 83.8. Kosar followed that up with the finest statistical season of his career, leading the Browns to their third straight division title by passing for 3,033 yards, throwing 22 touchdown passes and only nine picks, completing 62 percent of his passes, and posting a passer rating of 95.4 during the strike-shortened 1987 campaign, with his exceptional play earning him Pro Bowl honors and a third-place finish in the NFL AP Offensive Player of the Year voting.

Kosar's passing accuracy, highly competitive nature, confidence in his abilities, and elite football IQ allowed him to overcome his physical shortcomings that included a lack of foot speed and an unorthodox throwing motion that resembled that of a javelin-thrower, with sports columnist Jim Murray once writing, "He doesn't throw the ball, he lets go of it like a guy losing a bar of soap in the shower. The first look at Kosar's delivery, you think it's a gag. I've seen bridal bouquets thrown with more velocity."

The 6'5", 210-pound Kosar also assumed a unique side-saddle position prior to the snap that allowed him to get his feet out of the way quicker once he received the football. Yet, despite his poor mechanics, Kosar proved to be a winner, as the Browns' strength and conditioning coach Dave Redding noted when he said, "Yeah, but the one thing Bernie's always known how to do perfectly is beat you."

Expressing little concern over how he appeared to others, Kosar stated, "The ultimate way of how a quarterback is judged is on the end results. How I look is of no consequence to me. Sometimes I throw underhanded, side-armed, off the wrong foot, all the good stuff. But I've been doing that my whole life."

Coming off his banner year of 1987, Kosar sustained an injury to his elbow in the 1988 regular-season opener that forced him to miss nearly two months of action. Nevertheless, he returned in time to lead the Browns to an overall record of 10-6 and a wild card playoff berth by throwing for 1,890 yards and 10 touchdowns. Kosar subsequently led the Browns to their fourth division title in five years in 1989 by passing for 3,533 yards, throwing 18 touchdown passes, completing 59.1 percent of his passes, and posting a passer rating of 80.3, before setting over the course of the next two seasons an NFL record that stood for almost 20 years by throwing 308 straight passes without being picked off. Compiling some of the best overall numbers of his career in 1991, Kosar passed for 3,487 yards, threw 18 TD passes and nine interceptions, completed 62.1 percent of his passes, and posted a passer rating of 87.8. Yet, despite his strong play, the Browns failed to make the playoffs for the second straight time, going just 6-10 under new head coach Bill Belichick.

After breaking his ankle during the early stages of the 1992 campaign, Kosar ended up appearing in just seven games, before a loss of arm strength, his lack of mobility, and philosophical differences with Belichick caused him to lose his starting job to former Miami teammate Vinny Testaverde the following year. Although an injury to Testaverde allowed Kosar to start six games behind center, Belichick eventually cut ties with him in early November, saying at the time, "This is the most difficult decision I've ever been a part of. Basically, it came down to his production and a diminishing of his physical skills. I'm not going to bad-mouth and bash Bernie. He's done too much for this organization."

However, Kosar and many of his teammates felt that Belichick released him because he viewed the veteran quarterback as a threat to his control of the team, with Kosar, who frequently angered his head coach by calling audibles at the line of scrimmage, saying, "I've known for a while that I don't really fit into their plans. Bill has his way of doing things. That's been shown by the way they've been getting rid of the players who were here before he got here."

Stating the belief that Kosar still had the ability to be a successful quarterback, Browns running back Leroy Hoard said, "I don't think he's lost his skills. I don't think this is about diminishing skills. This is about Bill wanting to go a certain way, and so that's what he chose to do."

Defensive end Rob Burnett said, "Bill's the man. He's got the last word, period. He has been given a lot of power, and he's using it. It's Bill's show. Obviously, it's his way or the highway."

Defensive tackle Michael Dean Perry added, "It doesn't matter what I think, what the media thinks, what the fans think. The only thing that matters is what Bill Belichick thinks. He's the head man. He has the power, and, if he feels like Bernie's skills have diminished, then it's his decision. There's nothing I can say or do to change that."

Expressing their dissatisfaction with the release of Kosar, many Browns fans subsequently carried picket signs outside the team's training complex in Berea, Ohio, that read, "Cut Belichick, Keep Bernie."

Meanwhile, Art Modell stated, "I can't say enough about Bernie Kosar. He has been like a son to me."

Looking back on his decision 10 years later, Belichick said, "The only thing I can say is I did what I thought was best at the time. If things had been different, who knows? Nobody has more respect for Bernie Kosar as a football player, for his preparation, for his love of football, and for his intelligence, than I do."

Following his release by the Browns, Kosar, who passed for 21,904 yards, threw 116 touchdown passes and 81 interceptions, completed 58.8 percent of his passes, posted a passer rating of 81.6, and rushed for four TDs as a member of the team, signed with the Cowboys, with whom he spent the remainder of the year serving as a backup to Troy Aikman on a Dallas team that ended up winning the Super Bowl. Joining the Miami Dolphins prior to the start of the 1994 season, Kosar spent the next three years backing up Dan Marino, before announcing his retirement following the conclusion of the 1996 campaign with career totals of 23,301 passing yards, 124 touchdown passes, and 87 interceptions, a pass-completion percentage of 59.3, and a passer rating of 81.8.

Following his playing days, Kosar became involved in various business ventures that included purchasing a minority share of the NHL's Florida

Panthers in 2001 and a minority stake in the Arena Football League's Las Vegas Gladiators in 2007. After relocating the Gladiators to Cleveland, Kosar assumed the dual role of team president and CEO, before the recession of 2008 left him with almost $10 million of total debt, forcing him to declare for Chapter 11 bankruptcy. The Browns, though, helped him get back on his feet by hiring him as a consultant in 2009.

Unfortunately, Kosar, who suffered numerous concussions during his career, has begun to show signs of CTE (Chronic Traumatic Encephalopathy) the last few years. Plagued by insomnia, slurred speech, and a ringing in his head, Kosar has undergone a unique treatment program called Megadose Vitamin Therapy that has helped to alleviate his symptoms. Kosar also suffers from chronic pain due to his injuries that has left him addicted to pain medication.

BROWNS CAREER HIGHLIGHTS

Best Season

Although the 1987 players' strike prevented Kosar from throwing for as many yards as he did in two or three other seasons, he posted the best overall numbers of his career that year, earning Pro Bowl and All-AFC honors by passing for 3,033 yards, throwing 22 touchdown passes and only nine interceptions, and finishing second in the league with a pass-completion percentage of 62.0 and a passer rating of 95.4.

Memorable Moments/Greatest Performances

Kosar led the Browns to a 21–6 win over the Houston Oilers in his first start as a pro on October 13, 1985, collaborating with Clarence Weathers on a 68-yard scoring play for the first touchdown pass of his career.

Kosar victimized the Oilers again in the second meeting between the two teams on December 15, 1985, earning AFC Offensive Player of the Week honors for the first of five times by running for one touchdown and throwing for three others during a 28–21 Browns win.

Kosar earned that distinction again by throwing for 401 yards during a 26–16 victory over the Miami Dolphins on November 10, 1986.

Kosar gave the Browns a 37–31 overtime win over the Pittsburgh Steelers on November 23, 1986, by delivering a 36-yard touchdown pass to Webster Slaughter in OT. Kosar, who finished the game with 414 yards passing and two TD passes, earned AFC Offensive Player of the Week honors once again for his outstanding performance.

Kosar led the Browns to a 23–20 overtime victory over the Jets in the divisional round of the 1986 playoffs by throwing for a then–playoff record 489 yards and one touchdown.

Kosar had a big game against the Buffalo Bills on November 15, 1987, passing for 346 yards and two touchdowns during a 27–21 Browns win, with the longest of his TD passes going 52 yards to Webster Slaughter.

Kosar earned AFC Offensive Player of the Week honors by throwing for 241 yards and four touchdowns during a 38–24 win over the Cincinnati Bengals on December 13, 1987, connecting twice with Webster Slaughter and once each with Kevin Mack and Derek Tennell.

Although the Browns lost the 1987 AFC Championship Game to the Denver Broncos by a score of 38–33, Kosar performed brilliantly, nearly bringing his team back from two 18-point deficits by passing for 356 yards and three touchdowns.

Kosar led the Browns to a 24–21 win over the Dallas Cowboys on December 4, 1988, by throwing for 308 yards and three touchdowns, the longest of which came on a 73-yard connection with Reggie Langhorne.

Kosar guided the Browns to a 34–30 victory over Buffalo in the divisional round of the 1989 playoffs by completing 20 of 29 pass attempts for 251 yards and three touchdowns, collaborating with Webster Slaughter on scoring plays of 52 and 44 yards.

Kosar earned AFC Offensive Player of the Week honors for the fifth and final time by completing 19 of 23 pass attempts for 239 yards and two touchdowns during a 37–21 win over Cincinnati on December 6, 1992, hooking up with Eric Metcalf for a 35-yard touchdown and delivering a 45-yard scoring strike to Michael Jackson.

Notable Achievements

- Passed for more than 3,000 yards four times, topping 3,500 yards twice.
- Threw more than 20 touchdown passes once.
- Completed more than 60 percent of passes four times.
- Posted touchdown-to-interception ratio of better than 2–1 twice.
- Posted passer rating above 90.0 once.
- Finished second in NFL in pass completions once, pass completion percentage twice, and passer rating once.

- Ranks among Browns career leaders with 3,150 pass attempts (2nd), 1,853 pass completions (2nd), 21,904 passing yards (3rd), and 116 touchdown passes (4th).
- Four-time division champion (1985, 1986, 1987, and 1989).
- Five-time AFC Offensive Player of the Week.
- Finished third in 1987 NFL AP Offensive Player of the Year voting.
- 1987 Pro Bowl selection.
- 1987 Second-Team All-AFC selection.

41

GALEN FISS

A n athletic linebacker who possessed good speed, superb instincts, and outstanding leadership ability, Galen Fiss spent his entire 11-year NFL career in Cleveland, helping to lead the Browns to three division titles and one league championship. One of the team's most durable players, Fiss missed just five games in his 11 years in the league, with his consistently excellent play earning him two Pro Bowl selections and one First-Team All–Eastern Conference nomination. Displaying a nose for the football throughout his career, Fiss recorded 13 interceptions and recovered 18 fumbles, with the second figure representing the third-highest total in franchise history. Yet, despite his many accomplishments, Fiss will always be remembered primarily for the momentum-changing play he made in the 1964 NFL championship game that helped spark the Browns to a stunning 27–0 victory over the heavily favored Baltimore Colts.

Born in the small midwestern town of Johnson, Kansas, on July 30, 1931, Galen Royce Fiss grew up on his family's farm, where he spent much of his youth cultivating the land with his father, grandfather, and brother. Developing a powerful physique from the hard work he did as a youngster, Fiss eventually emerged as a standout athlete at Johnson High School, excelling in baseball, football, and basketball. Particularly outstanding on the gridiron, Fiss received an offer to attend the University of Kansas on a football scholarship, with Kansas coach Don Fambrough recalling, "Galen was one of the first football players that I ever recruited. I don't know how many coaches made it to Johnson. I was probably the only coach that could find it."

Continuing to compete in all three sports in college, Fiss drew national attention for the success he experienced in baseball and football, starring as a catcher on the diamond and a linebacker and fullback on the gridiron, where his jarring hits earned him the nickname "Earthshaker."

Subsequently selected by the Browns in the 13th round of the 1953 NFL Draft, with the 156th overall pick, Fiss did not officially become a

Galen Fiss shifted the momentum of the 1964 NFL championship game with his touchdown-saving tackle of Baltimore's Lenny Moore.

member of the team until three years later. Choosing instead to sign with the Cleveland Indians, Fiss spent one year playing for their farm team in Fargo-Moorehead, before serving a two-year stint in the Air Force, where he attained the rank of lieutenant. However, Fiss finally decided to forgo a potential career in baseball when the Browns offered him $7,500 to sign with them following his discharge early in 1956.

Arriving at his first NFL training camp several months later, Fiss struggled his first few days of practice, causing him to nearly quit camp and head home. But after having his confidence buoyed by Browns' roommate and former college teammate, Mike McCormack, Fiss went on to earn the starting right-outside linebacker job, recording the first interception of his career as a rookie. Moved to the left side of Cleveland's defense the following year, Fiss spent the next five seasons teaming up with Walt Michaels and Vince Costello to form one of the league's finest linebacking units, with Fiss gradually emerging as arguably the best of the three.

An excellent all-around player, the 6-foot, 230-pound Fiss possessed good size, strength, and quickness, making him equally effective against the run and the pass. Extremely intelligent as well, Fiss knew how to use his athleticism to evade would-be blockers, with his ability to take proper angles to the football allowing him to frequently bring down opposing ball-carriers behind the line of scrimmage.

Fiss also proved to be a superb team leader who always did the right thing, both on and off the playing field. Admired and respected by all his teammates, Fiss, who attained the honor of being named team captain in 1961, drew praise for his leadership ability from former Browns defensive tackle Jim Kanicki, who said, "Galen Fiss was a true leader. He wasn't one of those rah-rah guys, but he had an honesty about him. He could talk to everybody—the white guys, the black guys, the city guys, and the farm guys."

Meanwhile, former Browns public relations director Kevin Byrne said during a 1997 interview, "You see Galen now, and he's some balding, chunky insurance man from Kansas City. But his teammates talk about him almost reverently. On the 1964 defensive team, you had three players who became head coaches in Monte Clark, Paul Wiggin, and Dick Modzelewski. You had an evangelist in Bill Glass, defensive end. But who was the captain? Galen Fiss."

After earning Pro Bowl honors in each of the previous two seasons, Fiss helped lead the Browns to the NFL Eastern Division title in 1964, missing just one game the entire year despite suffering a broken left thumb in early December that forced him to wear a cast from his fingers to his elbow the rest of the year. Continuing to display his tremendous heart and determination in the NFL title game, Fiss made a career-defining play against the Western Division champion Baltimore Colts, when, with the contest still scoreless in the second period, he prevented a likely touchdown by tackling Hall of Fame halfback Lenny Moore in the open field with two blockers in front of him and no other defenders between him and the Cleveland end zone. In addition to driving the 79,544 fans at Cleveland Municipal Stadium into a frenzy, Fiss's extraordinary play inspired his teammates, who subsequently went on to defeat the Colts by a score of 27–0.

Fiss spent two more years in Cleveland, serving the Browns primarily as a backup, before age, injuries, and an increasing lack of foot speed prompted him to announce his retirement following the conclusion of the 1966 campaign. In addition to his 13 interceptions and 18 fumble recoveries, Fiss ended his career with an unofficial total of 6½ sacks and countless unrecorded tackles.

Following his playing days, Fiss settled in Kansas City, where he spent more than two decades running his own insurance agency. Eventually retiring to private life, Fiss moved to Overland Park, Kansas, where he remained until July 17, 2006, when he died of cardiac arrest at the age of 74, after spending the previous few years battling Alzheimer's disease.

Speaking of his love for Cleveland and its fans some years earlier, Fiss stated, "I don't know what it was like elsewhere, but I loved Cleveland because the fans really made a fuss over you, and you were part of them, part of the city. It was a loving relationship. The old stadium was a great place to play. It had a lot of history."

On another occasion, when asked if he minded being remembered by so many football fans for making that one pivotal play in the 1964 NFL championship game, Fiss displayed his humility by answering, "It's an honor to be remembered at all."

CAREER HIGHLIGHTS

Best Season

Although Fiss's leadership proved to be invaluable to the Browns throughout his 11-year tenure in Cleveland, he had his finest all-around season in 1962, when, in addition to earning one of his two Pro Bowl nominations and his lone First-Team All–Eastern Conference selection by intercepting four passes and recovering four fumbles, he gained unofficial Second-Team All-Pro recognition from United Press International (UPI) and the Newspaper Enterprise Association (NEA).

Memorable Moments/Greatest Performances

Fiss contributed to a 38–14 victory over the St. Louis Cardinals on November 18, 1962, by recording two interceptions in one game for the only time in his career.

Fiss made easily the most memorable play of his career in the 1964 NFL championship game, when his brilliant ankle-high tackle of Lenny Moore in the open field likely deprived the Baltimore Colts of the game's first points. After Moore gathered in a short swing pass from Johnny Unitas near the Baltimore 30 yard line, he headed upfield with only Fiss standing between him and the Cleveland goal line. Caught somewhat out of position, Fiss approached Moore with All-Pro offensive linemen Jim Parker and Bob Vogel bearing down on him. Somehow avoiding both Parker and Vogel, Fiss cut between the two behemoths and brought down Moore with a diving ankle tackle just as he turned the corner. Praised by his teammates afterwards, Fiss, said Jim Brown, "made one of the most inspirational plays in the history of football." Performing brilliantly throughout the contest, Fiss harassed Unitas all game long, sacking him once and clubbing him in the helmet with his cast on another play. Fiss also tipped a Unitas pass that teammate Vince Costello picked off and did an excellent job of covering Hall of Fame wide receiver Raymond Berry on his shorter routes.

Recalling years later the events that transpired that day, Fiss said, "We had a lot of good teams, but in 1964 it just sort of all came together for us. That season, that one game against Baltimore for the championship, I guess you would have to say that was the highlight of my career. We were underdogs in that game because the Colts really were a great football team. But we were, too, and I'm not exactly sure why people made us such underdogs. . . . I guess everybody looked at the Colts with all their great players and figured we couldn't keep up with them, but we had a good day. Everybody on our team played well. To beat a guy like Johnny Unitas, that's what has to happen, and it did."

Notable Achievements

- Missed just five games in 11 seasons.
- Recorded four interceptions in 1962.
- Finished second in NFL with four fumble recoveries in 1962.
- Ranks third in franchise history with 18 fumble recoveries.
- Three-time division champion (1957, 1964, and 1965).
- 1964 NFL champion.
- Two-time Pro Bowl selection (1962 and 1963).
- 1962 First-Team All–Eastern Conference selection.

42

ERIC METCALF

A dynamic playmaker once described as "a Swiss army knife in an offensive coordinator's toolbox," Eric Metcalf proved to be one of the most versatile players in franchise history during his six seasons in Cleveland, excelling for the Browns as a runner, receiver out of the backfield, and punt and kick returner. Amassing more than 1,500 all-purpose yards four times, Metcalf consistently ranked among the NFL leaders in that category, accumulating more total yards than any other player in the league in 1993. Especially dangerous on special teams, Metcalf ranks among the NFL's all-time leaders in punt-return yards, punt-return touchdowns, and punt- and kickoff-return TDs, returning a total of seven kicks for touchdowns while wearing a Browns uniform. A key contributor to teams that made two playoff appearances and won one division title, Metcalf earned two Pro Bowl selections and one All-Pro nomination during his time in Cleveland, before being accorded Pro Bowl and All-Pro honors once more while playing for the San Diego Chargers.

Born in Seattle, Washington, on January 23, 1968, Eric Quinn Metcalf spent much of his youth being raised solely by his mother, Christina Jefferson, who never married his father, Terry Metcalf, a star running back for the St. Louis Cardinals. Only 16 years old at the time of his son's birth, Terry later explained, "I was too young to get married, but it was almost like we were married because I spent more time at her house than mine."

After his dad left home at the age of 19 to attend Long Beach State University, young Eric grew up with his mother in Seattle, where he watched his father's football career unfold from afar, later saying, "I never really thought about Terry Metcalf as my dad. I thought of him as a football player, and that's what I wanted to be."

Getting his start on the gridiron in the pee wee and little leagues of his hometown, Eric displayed his explosive playmaking ability at an early age, once scoring 10 touchdowns in a single game as a seven-year-old. Recalling that her son excelled away from the playing field as well, Metcalf's mother

Eric Metcalf excelled for the Browns on both offense and special teams.
Courtesy of MearsonlineAuctions.com

stated, "Eric was not only a great athlete, but a great kid. The worst trouble he ever got in was when he pulled a little girl's hair in the fifth grade. I told him it was because he liked her, but he said no. . . . Eric always got A's and B's in school, and everybody liked him. We used to have friends at our house all the time."

Eventually enrolling at O'Dea High School, an all-boys Catholic school in Seattle, Metcalf spent one year playing freshman football and running track, before his desire to compete at a higher level prompted him to move elsewhere, later saying, "They wouldn't let me play varsity ball as a freshman. I told them I would leave, but I guess they didn't believe me."

Joining his father in Arlington, Virginia, Metcalf enrolled at Bishop O'Connell High School, where he spent his final two seasons starring in football and track, scoring a total of 35 touchdowns, while also setting school records in the long jump, triple jump, and 100-, 200-, and 400-yard dashes. Subsequently recruited by several major colleges, Metcalf initially committed to the University of Miami, although both his parents suggested that he attend Notre Dame instead. However, Metcalf balked at the idea, stating years later, "No way was I going there. I had gone to Catholic schools all my life. Besides, they wore black shoes and had nothing on their helmets."

Finally choosing to enroll at the University of Texas at Austin, Metcalf went on to become a Heisman Trophy candidate, a three-time All–Southwest Conference selection, and a two-time NCAA champion in the long jump. After earning SWC Offensive Player of the Year and Second-Team All-America honors as a junior in 1987 by rushing for 1,256 yards, amassing 1,541 yards from scrimmage, accumulating 2,080 all-purpose yards, and scoring 12 touchdowns, Metcalf concluded his college career by gaining 932 yards on the ground, amassing 1,265 yards from scrimmage, accumulating 1,574 all-purpose yards, and scoring 10 touchdowns his senior year, prompting Longhorns head coach David McWilliams, who described him as the best player he ever coached, to later say, "Eric could play any skill position you wanted. He could return punts, return kicks. He could have been a defensive back. He could pass-block. He was tough."

Also excelling in track and field while at Texas, Metcalf won the US Track and Field championship in the long jump in 1988 and the NCAA National Long Jump championship in both 1986 and 1988, en route to earning All-America honors four straight times.

Impressed with Metcalf's extraordinary achievements at the collegiate level, the Browns traded four picks to move up seven spots in the first round of the 1989 NFL Draft, enabling them to select him with the 13th overall pick, with Ernie Accorsi, the team's director of football operations at the time, later saying, "I was obsessed with Metcalf. . . . He was one of my favorite players of my career. He was one of the most electrifying players I've been around."

Making an immediate impact upon his arrival in Cleveland, Metcalf helped lead the Browns to their fourth division title in five seasons in 1989 by rushing for 633 yards and six touchdowns, making 54 receptions for 397 yards and four TDs, and amassing 718 yards returning kickoffs, giving him a total of 1,748 all-purpose yards that placed him sixth in the league rankings. Commenting on his team's new offensive weapon at one point during the campaign, Browns running backs coach George Sefcik said, "I've coached in college and on the pro level, and I've seen few players do what

Eric can do. He can run, he's quick, and he can catch the ball. He'll be a bigger threat once he goes through a full training camp and learns the offense."

Metcalf followed up his outstanding rookie season by accumulating 700 yards from scrimmage, leading the league with 1,052 kickoff-return yards, finishing fourth in the circuit with 1,752 all-purpose yards, and scoring four touchdowns in 1990, before missing half of the ensuing campaign due to injury. However, even though Metcalf amassed just 852 all-purpose yards and failed to score a single touchdown in 1991, the season proved to be a pivotal one in his career since new Browns head coach Bill Belichick began using him as a punt returner.

Fully healthy by the start of the 1992 campaign, Metcalf established himself as easily the Browns' top playmaker, rushing for 301 yards, gaining another 614 yards on 47 pass receptions, amassing 1,501 all-purpose yards, and scoring seven touchdowns, one of which came on a punt return. Metcalf subsequently gained Pro Bowl, First-Team All-Pro, and AFC Special Teams Player of the Year recognition from the NFL Players Association in 1993 by rushing for 611 yards and one touchdown, making 63 receptions for 539 yards and two TDs, gaining another 782 yards on special teams, leading the league with 1,932 all-purpose yards, and scoring twice on punt returns.

Incredibly quick, the 5'10", 188-pound Metcalf had the ability to stop on a dime, accelerate again quickly, and cut back across the field for additional yardage. Extremely elusive, Metcalf also possessed tremendous moves in the open field, making it very difficult for opposing defenders to make solid contact with him. In describing his running style, Metcalf said, "Most of the time, I'm running scared. If I'm running scared, I'm running faster and I'm running around people to avoid the hit. I get those big eyes when I'm running. I don't want to take the big hit. . . . It's like my dad used to tell me: 'It's like a fight. If you run one day, you get to live for the next one.'"

Metcalf remained in Cleveland for one more year, earning Pro Bowl honors again in 1994 by amassing 765 yards from scrimmage, accumulating 1,323 all-purpose yards, and scoring seven touchdowns, before being traded to the Atlanta Falcons in a deal that saw the two teams swap first-round picks in the 1995 NFL Draft. Leaving the Browns with career totals of 33 touchdowns, 2,229 rushing yards, 297 receptions, 2,732 receiving yards, 4,961 yards from scrimmage, 1,341 punt-return yards, 2,806 kickoff-return yards, and 9,108 all-purpose yards, Metcalf continues to rank among the franchise's all-time leaders in each of the last three categories.

Metcalf ended up spending two seasons in Atlanta, where, after being moved to wide receiver, he recorded a total of 158 receptions for 1,788 yards and 14 touchdowns. Continuing to excel on special teams as well,

Metcalf also returned a punt for a TD and amassed more than 1,900 all-purpose yards each season.

Metcalf subsequently split his final five years in the league between the San Diego Chargers, Arizona Cardinals, Carolina Panthers, Washington Redskins, and Green Bay Packers, earning Pro Bowl and First-Team All-Pro honors for the Chargers in 1997 by amassing 1,415 all-purpose yards and returning three punts for touchdowns, before announcing his retirement following the conclusion of the 2002 campaign with career totals of 2,392 rushing yards, 12 rushing touchdowns, 541 receptions, 5,572 receiving yards, 31 TD catches, 7,964 yards from scrimmage, 3,453 punt-return yards, 5,813 kickoff-return yards, 17,230 all-purpose yards, and 12 returns for touchdowns, which ranks as the third-highest total in NFL history, with only Devin Hester and Brian Mitchell having scored more times in that fashion. The only player ever to amass more than 7,000 yards on both offense and special teams, Metcalf displayed his "big play" ability by averaging 36.3 yards on his 55 career touchdowns, with 19 of his TDs covering more than 50 yards.

Following his retirement from football, Metcalf returned to Seattle, where he continued to work with youngsters through the Seatown Express Track Club he established during his playing days. Initially created to help high school boys interested in track obtain a college scholarship, the Seatown Express Track Club, which eventually expanded to include junior high schoolers and girls, has since become an elite track and field club that helps train some of the top sprinters and jumpers in the Puget Sound area. In discussing his operation, Metcalf says, "If the athletes took care of their grades and were serious about track, I could help them by utilizing my connections with college track programs, as well as helping them compete to the best of their abilities. . . . We now start with younger boys and girls, but they have to be serious about the sport and really want to compete."

Metcalf also coached track and football at Rainier Beach High School, before becoming in 2013 the sprint coach at the University of Washington, where he works primarily with sprinters, long jumpers, and triple jumpers. In describing his coaching goals, Metcalf says, "I just want to make sure that, when someone comes to me, they walk out better than they came. My main focus is to make kids better, whether that be on the track, or field, or off."

As for his NFL legacy, Metcalf says that he would like Browns fans to remember that "he could do anything . . . he could do it all . . . that's what makes you a football player . . . the fact that you can play more than one position."

BROWNS CAREER HIGHLIGHTS

Best Season

Metcalf performed brilliantly for the Browns in 1989, 1990, 1992, and 1993, amassing more than 1,500 all-purpose yards all four years. But he made his greatest overall impact in the last of those campaigns, earning First-Team All-Pro honors in 1993 by rushing for 611 yards, making 63 receptions for 539 yards, accumulating 782 yards on special teams, leading the league with 1,932 all-purpose yards, and scoring five touchdowns, two of which came on punt returns.

Memorable Moments/Greatest Performances

Metcalf turned in a tremendous all-around effort against Tampa Bay on November 5, 1989, amassing 239 all-purpose yards and scoring two touchdowns during a 42–31 Browns win. In addition to gaining 87 yards on the ground, Metcalf made seven receptions for 52 yards and returned three kickoffs for 94 yards, scoring his TDs on a 24-yard pass from Bernie Kosar and a 43-yard run.

Metcalf made a huge play in the divisional round of the 1989 playoffs when he returned a kickoff 90 yards for a touchdown during a 34–30 win over the Buffalo Bills.

Although the Browns ended up losing to the Jets by a score of 24–21 on September 16, 1990, Metcalf returned the game's opening kickoff 98 yards for a touchdown.

Metcalf proved to be the Browns' only bright spot during a 58–14 loss to the Houston Oilers on December 9, 1990, returning a kickoff 101 yards for a touchdown and scoring again on a 31-yard pass reception.

Metcalf earned AFC Offensive Player of the Week honors by making five receptions for 177 yards and scoring four touchdowns during a 28–16 win over the Los Angeles Raiders on September 20, 1992, with two of his TDs coming on 69- and 63-yard connections with quarterback Todd Philcox. Praising Metcalf for his brilliant performance afterwards, Browns owner Art Modell said, "This is as good a game as any I've seen from a player on the Browns in many, many years, including the Leroy Kelly and Jim Brown days."

Metcalf contributed to a 27–14 win over the Bears on November 29, 1992, by returning a punt 75 yards for a touchdown.

Metcalf led the Browns to a 37–21 victory over Cincinnati on December 6, 1992, by amassing 210 all-purpose yards and scoring a touchdown on a 35-yard pass from Bernie Kosar, gaining 53 of his yards on nine carries, 73 yards on six pass receptions, and another 84 on special teams.

Metcalf gave the Browns a dramatic 19–16 victory over the Raiders on September 19, 1993, by running the ball in from 1 yard out with just two seconds left on the clock.

Metcalf earned AFC Special Teams Player of the Week honors for the first of three times by returning two punts for touchdowns during a 28–23 win over the Steelers on October 24, 1993, scoring his TDs on returns of 91 and 75 yards.

Metcalf starred in defeat on December 12, 1993, amassing 212 all-purpose yards and scoring a touchdown during a 19–17 loss to the Houston Oilers. In addition to returning two punts for 29 yards, Metcalf gained 82 yards on the ground and made five receptions for 101 yards and one TD, which came on a 49-yard pass from Vinny Testaverde.

Metcalf earned AFC Special Teams Player of the Week honors by returning a punt 92 yards for a touchdown during a 28–20 win over the Bengals in the 1994 regular-season opener.

Metcalf helped lead the Browns to a 21–14 victory over the Colts on September 25, 1994, by gaining 42 yards on eight carries and making five receptions for 74 yards and two touchdowns, the longest of which came on a 57-yard pass from Vinny Testaverde.

In addition to carrying the ball 12 times for 57 yards during a 37–13 win over Cincinnati on October 23, 1994, Metcalf earned AFC Special Teams Player of the Week honors for the final time by returning a punt 73 yards for a touchdown.

Notable Achievements

- Returned five punts and two kickoffs for touchdowns.
- Rushed for more than 600 yards twice.
- Surpassed 50 receptions three times.
- Topped 500 receiving yards twice.
- Surpassed 1,000 yards from scrimmage twice.
- Amassed more than 1,000 all-purpose yards five times, topping 1,500 yards on four occasions.
- Scored 10 touchdowns in 1989.
- Led NFL in all-purpose yards once, kickoff-return yards once, kickoff-return touchdowns once, and punt-return touchdowns twice.

- Finished second in NFL in punt-return average once.
- Led Browns in rushing once and receptions twice.
- Ranks among NFL career leaders with 3,453 punt-return yards (5th), 10 punt-return touchdowns (2nd), and 12 punt- and kickoff-return touchdowns (3rd).
- Ranks among Browns career leaders with 1,341 punt-return yards (4th), 2,806 kickoff-return yards (3rd), and 9,108 all-purpose yards (6th).
- 1989 division champion.
- 1992 Week 3 AFC Offensive Player of the Week.
- Three-time AFC Special Teams Player of the Week.
- October 1993 AFC Special Teams Player of the Month.
- 1993 NFL Players Association AFC Special Teams Player of the Year.
- Two-time Pro Bowl selection (1993 and 1994).
- 1993 First-Team All-Pro selection.
- Two-time First-Team All-AFC selection (1993 and 1994).

43

NICK CHUBB

argely responsible for the Browns' recent return to respectability, Nick Chubb has established himself as one of the NFL's finest all-around running backs since he arrived in Cleveland in 2018, gaining more than 1,000 yards on the ground three times and amassing more than 1,000 yards from scrimmage on four separate occasions. One of just two players in team annals to rush for more than 1,000 yards in three of his first four seasons, Chubb already ranks among the franchise's all-time leaders in rushing yards and rushing touchdowns, with his superb play earning him three trips to the Pro Bowl and two First-Team All-AFC nominations. A consummate team player, Chubb has also contributed to the success of the Browns with his selfless attitude and strong work ethic that have deeply impacted the other players around him.

Born in Cedartown, Georgia, on December 27, 1995, Nicholas Jamaal Chubb owes his name to his great-grandfather, Nicholas, who, along with his seven brothers, helped found Chubbtown, Georgia, a settlement of free Blacks that endured through the American Civil War. One of three brothers who played football in college, Chubb is also the cousin of standout defensive end Bradley Chubb, who the Denver Broncos selected with the fifth overall pick of the 2018 NFL Draft.

Getting his start on the gridiron at Cedartown High School, Chubb performed magnificently for his hometown school from 2011 to 2014, rushing for a total of 6,983 yards and 102 touchdowns. Particularly outstanding his final two seasons at Cedartown, Chubb led the state of Georgia with 2,721 rushing yards and 38 touchdowns as a junior, before amassing 2,690 rushing yards and scoring 41 TDs the following year. Excelling in track and field as well, Chubb won the shotput event at the 2014 4-A Sectionals with a throw of 17.05 meters and finished second in both the 100- and 200-meter dashes with times of 10.69 and 21.83 seconds, respectively.

After fielding offers from several major colleges, Chubb chose to remain close to home and attend the University of Georgia, where he

Nick Chubb has amassed more than 1,000 yards from scrimmage in each of his first four seasons.
Courtesy of Erik Drost

established himself as one of the nation's top running backs over the course of the next four years, rushing for a total of 4,769 yards, amassing 5,130 yards from scrimmage, and scoring 48 touchdowns, despite missing much of his sophomore campaign with a serious knee injury he suffered during a 38–31 loss to Tennessee. Having led the Bulldogs to a 12-1 record and the SEC championship his senior year by rushing for 1,345 yards and scoring 15 touchdowns, Chubb entered the 2018 NFL Draft, where the Browns made him the 35th overall pick when they selected him early in the second round.

Chubb subsequently spent the first few weeks of his rookie season playing behind veteran Carlos Hyde, before becoming a member of the starting unit in Week 7 after the Browns traded Hyde to the Jacksonville Jaguars. Performing exceptionally well the rest of the year, Chubb helped lead the Browns, who had failed to win a game the previous season, to a record of 7-8-1 by rushing for 996 yards and eight touchdowns, making 20 receptions for 149 yards and two TDs, and ranking among the league leaders with an average of 5.2 yards per carry. Continuing his outstanding play in 2019, Chubb earned Pro Bowl and First-Team All-AFC honors for the first time by finishing second in the league with 1,494 yards rushing, placing third in the circuit with 1,772 yards from scrimmage, and scoring eight touchdowns. Despite missing four games the following year due to a sprained MCL in his right knee, Chubb had another excellent season, helping the Browns advance to the playoffs for the first time in nearly two decades by rushing for 1,067 yards and 12 touchdowns, amassing 1,217 yards from scrimmage, and placing near the top of the league rankings with an average of 5.6 yards per carry, with his 1,067 yards and 12 TDs on just 190 carries making him the first player since Miami's Mercury Morris in 1972 to rush for at least 1,000 yards and 12 TDs on 190 or fewer attempts. Meanwhile, Chubb became the first Browns player since Jim Brown to rush for more than 1,000 yards in two of his first three seasons.

Blessed with a rare combination of speed and strength, the 5'11", 227-pound Chubb possesses the ability to run over, or away from, defenders, making him extremely difficult to bring down one-on-one. And, even though Chubb excels at using his outstanding speed to avoid defenders in the open field, he derives more pleasure out of breaking would-be tackles, saying, "It feels good because I know I'm doing good for my team, making explosive plays, getting momentum going. That's just what I pride myself on, being a strong runner, that's just how I run the ball."

In discussing the qualities that he believes make Chubb the league's best all-around running back, one NFL executive told ESPN, "He's the best pure runner in football. I'd take him over [Derrick] Henry because he's a little more explosive."

Also greatly admired for his selflessness, team-first mentality, and strong work ethic, Chubb received high praise from Browns general manager Andrew Berry after he signed a three-year, $36.6 million contract extension with the team prior to the start of the 2021 campaign, with Berry saying at the time, "From the day Nick Chubb first entered our facilities, it was clear to see that he would become a pillar of our organization. Although Nick may be a man of few words whose strong-and-silent demeanor can be easy to overlook from the outside, his actions over the past three years have reverberated within the walls of our building."

Berry continued, "He is a dynamic runner who is on pace to be one of the most accomplished players to ever don an orange helmet at the position. But it's his work ethic, intelligence, toughness, and selflessness that makes us proud that he represents our city. Quite plainly, Nick embodies the soul of our team, and we are thrilled that he will be a Cleveland Brown for years to come."

Browns head coach Kevin Stefanski added, "He doesn't say much, and I think that sometimes seems like he's not a leader in that regard, and that couldn't be farther from the truth. He's a leader in his actions. . . . Nick Chubb is a tremendous football player, but an even better person. He is one of the best examples of a team player that I've been around. Nick always puts the team before himself, and that's why you love seeing a guy like him get rewarded."

Meanwhile, Chubb expressed the joy he felt over inking his new three-year deal when he stated, "It means a lot to me to be able to stay in Cleveland and be a Brown. It's an honor to put on the orange helmet and represent the city of Cleveland and these great fans. I'm happy that I will be able to be here for many more years. The Browns put their faith in me during the draft and I want to say thank you to everyone who believed in me and who has supported me. There is still a lot of work to do to continue to get better and become a better team."

Shortly after Chubb signed his contract extension with the Browns, he exhibited his giving nature and the quality of his character by releasing a new cereal, Chubb Crunch, whose proceeds go to First Candle, an organization that is striving to eliminate sudden infant death syndrome (SIDS). Upon making his announcement, Chubb, who lost his sister to SIDS in 2019, said, "It was a hard time for us. So, any way I can give back to that cause is big."

Chubb had another big year for the Browns in 2021, earning his third consecutive Pro Bowl nomination by finishing second in the league with 1,259 yards rushing, amassing 1,433 yards from scrimmage, scoring nine touchdowns, and averaging 5.5 yards per carry. Heading into the upcoming season, Chubb boasts career totals of 4,816 yards rushing, 92 receptions, 751 receiving yards, 5,567 yards from scrimmage, 36 rushing touchdowns, and 39 total TDs. Since Chubb will not turn 27 until the latter stages of the 2022 campaign, he figures to add significantly to those totals and vastly improve his place in these rankings before his time in Cleveland comes to an end.

CAREER HIGHLIGHTS

Best Season

Chubb performed magnificently for the Browns in 2020, gaining 1,067 yards on the ground, amassing 1,217 yards from scrimmage, and finishing fourth in the league with 12 rushing touchdowns, despite missing four games due to injury. He followed that up with another outstanding season, finishing second in the NFL with 1,259 yards rushing in 2021, while also accumulating 1,433 yards from scrimmage and scoring nine TDs. But Chubb posted the best overall numbers of his career to this point in 2019, when, in addition to scoring eight touchdowns, he placed near the top of the league rankings with 1,494 yards rushing and 1,772 yards from scrimmage.

Memorable Moments/Greatest Performances

Although the Browns lost to the Oakland Raiders in overtime by a score of 45–42 on September 30, 2018, Chubb had a big game, gaining 105 yards on just three carries and scoring the first two touchdowns of his career on runs of 63 and 41 yards.

Chubb helped lead the Browns to a 28–16 win over Atlanta on November 11, 2018, by rushing for 176 yards, making three receptions for 33 yards, and scoring two touchdowns, one of which came on a 13-yard pass from Baker Mayfield and the other on a 92-yard run that represents the longest rushing TD in franchise history.

Chubb starred during a 40–25 victory over the Baltimore Ravens on September 29, 2019, rushing for 165 yards and three touchdowns, one of which came on an 88-yard scamper.

Chubb contributed to a 41–24 win over the Miami Dolphins on November 24, 2019, by making three receptions for 58 yards and rushing for 106 yards and one touchdown.

Chubb led the Browns to a 35–30 victory over Cincinnati on September 17, 2020, by rushing for 124 yards and two touchdowns, the longest of which came on an 11-yard run.

Chubb proved to be the difference in a 10–7 victory over the Houston Texans on November 15, 2020, gaining 126 yards on the ground and scoring what proved to be the game-winning touchdown early in the fourth quarter on a 9-yard run.

Chubb led the Browns to a 27–25 win over the Jacksonville Jaguars on November 29, 2020, by rushing for 144 yards and one touchdown and gaining another 32 yards on three pass receptions.

Chubb contributed to a 48–37 victory over the Pittsburgh Steelers in the wild card round of the 2020 playoffs by rushing for 76 yards and making four receptions for 69 yards and one touchdown, which came on a 40-yard catch-and-run.

Chubb helped lead the Browns to a 31–21 win over the Texans on September 19, 2021, by gaining 95 yards on just 11 carries and sealing the victory with a 26-yard touchdown run late in the fourth quarter.

Chubb starred in defeat on October 10, 2021, rushing for 161 yards and one touchdown during a 47–42 loss to the Los Angeles Chargers, with his TD coming on a 52-yard run on the opening drive of the third quarter.

Chubb contributed to a 41–16 rout of the Bengals on November 7, 2021, by gaining 137 yards on only 14 carries and scoring two touchdowns, one of which came on a season-long 70-yard run.

Notable Achievements

- Has rushed for more than 1,000 yards three times.
- Has amassed more than 1,000 yards from scrimmage four times, topping 1,500 yards once.
- Has scored at least 10 touchdowns twice.
- Has averaged more than 5 yards per carry four times.
- Has finished second in NFL in rushing twice.
- Finished third in NFL with 1,772 yards from scrimmage in 2019.
- Has led Browns in rushing four times.
- Holds Browns record for longest rushing touchdown in franchise history (92 yards vs. Atlanta on November 11, 2018).
- Ranks among Browns career leaders with 4,816 yards rushing (6th), 36 rushing touchdowns (6th), 5,567 yards from scrimmage (12th), and an average of 5.3 yards per carry (2nd).
- 2019 Week 4 AFC Offensive Player of the Week.
- Browns 2020 Ed Block Courage Award winner.
- Browns 2020 Art Rooney Sportsmanship Award winner.
- Three-time Pro Bowl selection (2019, 2020, and 2021).
- Three-time First-Team All-AFC selection (2019, 2020, and 2021).

44

FRANK RYAN

The last quarterback to lead the Browns to the NFL championship, Frank Ryan spent seven seasons in Cleveland, playing for teams that also won four division titles. The Browns' primary signal-caller from 1962 to 1967, Ryan, who ranks among the franchise's all-time leaders in pass completions, passing yards, and touchdown passes, compiled an overall record of 52-22-2 as a starter, with his consistently strong play earning him three Pro Bowl selections and one First-Team All–Eastern Conference nomination. Nevertheless, more than 50 years after he donned a Browns uniform for the last time, Ryan remains one of the most overlooked and underappreciated players in team annals.

Born in Fort Worth, Texas, on July 12, 1936, Frank Bell Ryan never dreamed of playing sports professionally during his formative years, recalling, "I was never very fast or well-coordinated. I never played any sport well. I couldn't hit in baseball. I couldn't dribble in basketball or play tennis or golf. I'm not a natural athlete. I pick up a dart and people start running."

Yet, after spending the early part of his youth drawing sketches of rockets and trying to calculate how fast a space missile would have to travel to break free of the earth's gravitational pull, Ryan began to develop an interest in football in junior high school, remembering, "One thing I was fascinated with was the throwing of a football . . . the spiral. . . . The sense of making that rather awkward object go in a beautiful way."

After getting his start on the gridiron in the ninth grade, Ryan landed a spot on Paschal High School's football team, serving as a backup his first two seasons, before finally breaking into the starting lineup his senior year, when, by his own evaluation, "I was the fifth best of the six quarterbacks in the conference."

Despite the limited amount of success that Ryan experienced in high school, he found himself being recruited by several colleges, including Texas A&M University. Yet, even though Ryan's excellent grades made his father's and brother's alma mater, Yale University, an intriguing option as well, he

Frank Ryan led the Browns to four division titles and their last NFL championship.

ultimately chose to enroll at Rice Institute (now known as Rice University) in Houston, later explaining, "I almost went to Yale. But I chose Rice instead. I was a physics major out of Paschal High School in Fort Worth. No all-state. No big deal. Rice had a program I liked. Besides, the coach, Jess Neely, was after me. No one from Yale was."

Failing to distinguish himself behind center in college as well, Ryan spent most of his time splitting snaps with King Hill, who ended up being the first overall pick in the 1958 NFL Draft. Still, no one appreciated Ryan more than Hill, who told a Philadelphia reporter years later, "I owe a lot to Frank. We beat Texas A&M when A&M was No. 1 in the country. Frank took the club about 70 yards right to the goal. I'll always remember a run he made on the last play of the drive. He spun off tackle, and there was John David Crow waiting for him. Frank stiff-armed him. He really spun his neck back and ran the ball right up to the goal. Then the quarter ended. We changed units, and all I had to do was sneak the thing over for a touchdown. It set me up for All-America. I got a lot of publicity out of the game, but Frank made it possible. You just got to like a guy like that."

Suffering through a difficult senior year, Ryan struggled early in the season and twisted his knee multiple times, forcing him to spend most of the campaign sitting on the bench. Displaying a lack of maturity in dealing with his lack of playing time, Ryan later admitted, "The coach was right, too. I was immature and inconsistent in my play, and very emotional. When we played Clemson early in the season and lost 20–7, I had gotten to play about two series of downs and I was very disgruntled, and that was the low point for me. I was very close to quitting. I can't remember now why I didn't quit, except that I was interested in getting the education."

Entering the 1958 NFL Draft with very little hope of being selected by any of the league's 12 teams, Ryan began to focus exclusively on obtaining his doctorate in mathematics. But much to his surprise, the Los Angeles Rams chose him in the fifth round, with the 55th overall pick, forcing him to alter his plans somewhat. Electing to play pro ball and pursue his PhD at the same time, Ryan began his graduate work at UCLA, before transferring back to Rice, where he spent the next seven years studying during the offseason.

Accomplishing very little with the Rams over the course of his first four NFL seasons, Ryan spent his first three years sitting behind Bill Wade and his fourth season backing up Zeke Bratkowski, starting a total of only 11 games, passing for just 2,674 yards and 15 touchdowns, and throwing 23 interceptions. Frustrated over his inability to garner more playing time, Ryan approached Rams general manager Elroy Hirsch following the conclusion of the 1961 campaign and demanded a trade. Granting Ryan's request, the Rams completed a deal with the Browns on July 12, 1962, that sent the unhappy quarterback and running back Tommy Wilson to Cleveland for defensive lineman Larry Stephens and two picks in the 1963 NFL Draft.

Following his arrival in Cleveland, Ryan spent the first six games of the 1962 season backing up Jim Ninowski, before taking over behind center when Ninowski broke his collarbone during a 41–14 win over the Pittsburgh Steelers in Week 7. Performing well the rest of the year, Ryan led the Browns to an overall record of 7-6-1 by passing for 1,541 yards, throwing

10 touchdown passes and seven interceptions, and ranking among the league leaders with a pass-completion percentage of 57.7 and a passer rating of 85.4. Retaining his starting job when Ninowski returned to full health the following year, Ryan guided the Browns to a 10-4 record and a second-place finish in the seven-team NFL East by throwing for 2,026 yards, completing 52.7 percent of his passes, tossing 25 TD passes and only 13 interceptions, and finishing second in the league with a passer rating of 90.4.

Emerging as one of the league's top signal-callers in 1964, Ryan earned the first of his three consecutive Pro Bowl nominations by throwing for 2,404 yards and topping the circuit with 25 touchdown passes, with his strong play leading the Browns to the NFL championship. Continuing to perform well the next two seasons, Ryan guided the Browns to a composite record of 20-8 and another division title, posting the best overall numbers of his career in 1966, when he led the NFL with 29 touchdown passes and finished second in the league with 2,974 passing yards and a passer rating of 88.2.

Flourishing under the mentorship of Blanton Collier, the 6'3", 200-pound Ryan credited his head coach for much of the success he experienced in Cleveland, saying, "He is the first coach that ever really coached me. He spent days with me, weeks. He taught me those three steps: setting, aiming, throwing. He taught me to pick out a small target on a receiver, rather than just trying to hit a big blob out there with arms. If you're looking at a little pink dot on him, then you're reducing your error. He taught me not to watch the ball. This was a bad habit I used to have, watching my wobbly passes. All of a sudden, you're gonna be watching the flight of the ball before you throw and take your eyes off the target. I still tend to throw wobbly passes, but now I catch myself looking at the receiver and never seeing the ball till it gets there, which to me indicates an improvement."

Ryan added, "I used to put too much responsibility on my own shoulders, and I wasn't relaxed. I used to think that football was much more complicated than it is. There are so many defenses and so many ways you can run this play and hit the defensive weakness. If you let it all overwhelm you, it becomes a big blur. Somewhere along the line, it just occurred to me that I shouldn't concern myself so much with getting it just so, that I should make snap judgments and carry them through. More often than not, football is luck. You can study the defense and call a play that you think'll kill 'em, and all of a sudden they put on a line slant that squashes the play. It occurred to me that a lot of the success or failure depended upon the luck of the situation. My insight was that I shouldn't be tormented or worried or lose sleep over calling exactly the right play because there was such a tremendous variable of luck in it that I couldn't hope to be right every time. So, I've become more relaxed, and when people are more relaxed, they do better."

Noticing the improvement in Ryan's play, Baltimore Colts Hall of Fame defensive end Gino Marchetti commented, "He's come a long way. He has more confidence than he ever did. He's taking more time before getting rid of the ball, and he's more sure of himself. He knows he's good and belongs there. He calls a good game. You can't outguess him because he doesn't type himself."

Meanwhile, Browns guard John Wooten described his quarterback as "Extremely courageous," adding, "He would stand right there and hold that ball until the very last second."

Nevertheless, after a sore elbow and injured arch limited Ryan's effectiveness somewhat in 1965, he spent his remaining time in Cleveland sharing an increasingly contentious relationship with Browns fans, who often booed him during home games. Adding to Ryan's troubles, he needed regular injections of painkillers to help him play after separating his right shoulder in the 1965 Pro Bowl, before finally undergoing surgery on January 25, 1967. And, although Ryan led the Browns to their third division title in four years in 1967 by throwing for 2,026 yards and 20 touchdowns, he suffered through an injury-marred campaign, spraining both ankles during a 21–14 loss to the Dallas Cowboys in the regular-season opener, and sustaining a concussion in a head-to-head collision with Dick Butkus during a 24–0 victory over the Chicago Bears five weeks later.

Replaced behind center by Bill Nelsen after leading the Browns to just one win in their first three games in 1968, Ryan spent the rest of the year sitting on the bench, before being released prior to the start of the ensuing campaign. Ryan, who left Cleveland having passed for 13,361 yards and 134 touchdowns, thrown 88 interceptions, completed 51.7 percent of his passes, posted a passer rating of 81.4, and rushed for 1,032 yards and four touchdowns as a member of the Browns, subsequently signed with the Washington Redskins, with whom he spent the next two seasons serving as a backup, before announcing his retirement following the conclusion of the 1970 campaign. Over the course of his 13-year career, Ryan passed for 16,042 yards, threw 149 touchdown passes and 111 interceptions, completed 51.1 percent of his passes, and posted a passer rating of 77.6.

Revealing years later that his injury woes coupled with the rampant use of drugs throughout the league and illegal bounty programs that rewarded players for inflicting game-ending injuries on their opponents had already soured his view on life in the NFL, Ryan claimed that he welcomed a lifestyle change by the time his playing career ended, saying, "I didn't want to be limited to just being a football player. I wanted to be something beyond that. I was always curious, and most of the time I didn't fulfill my curiosity to the extent I wish I had now. But that always pushed me, and I was becoming more and more confused as to where football was leading me."

Ryan, who received his doctorate in June 1965 and began teaching a variety of courses at Case Institute of Technology in February 1967, assumed many important positions following his retirement, first working as the director of information services for the US House of Representatives, where he developed the first electronic voting system used by Congress. Ryan later spent 10 years serving as the athletic director at Yale University and five years serving as vice president for external affairs and professor of mathematics at Rice University. Entering the private business sector in 1996, Ryan helped design and manufacture cable and interconnect products for the computer and communications industries as president and chief executive officer of Contex Electronics, served as director for America West Airlines, Sequoia Voting Systems, and Danielson Holding Corporation, and assumed the position of advisory director of United Medical Care Inc. Now retired, the 86-year-old Ryan lives with his wife in Grafton, Vermont, where he continues to deal with the numerous injuries he sustained during his playing days, having undergone surgery on both knees, his right elbow, and left pinky, and having had two vertebrae in his neck fused.

Although largely forgotten by most football fans, Ryan received high praise from Mike Tanier of Bleacher Report, who, in assessing his career, wrote:

"Frank Ryan made three Pro Bowls, but All-Pro status was blocked by a couple of guys named Johnny Unitas and Bart Starr. His career was cut short by injuries suffered in the first of those three Pro Bowls. The Colts accused Ryan of running up the score in the 27–0 championship rout of 1964. A Colts defender delivered some payback in the all-star game. Ryan needed surgery and was in constant pain for the rest of his career. Yet he still led his team to the playoffs three more times. . . . There have been many better quarterbacks than Ryan in NFL history. But none accomplished more than Ryan while receiving less acclaim. By being overshadowed by Brown, achieving his greatest success just before the dawn of the Super Bowl era, and getting stuck behind the Tom Brady and Peyton Manning of your grandfather's generation, Ryan earned the title of the NFL's All-Time Most Underrated Player."

BROWNS CAREER HIGHLIGHTS

Best Season

Ryan had an excellent year for the Browns in 1964, earning Pro Bowl honors for the first of three straight times by passing for 2,404 yards, leading the league with 25 touchdown passes, completing 52.1 percent of his passes, and posting a passer rating of 76.7. But he performed even better in 1966, when he led all NFL quarterbacks with 29 touchdown passes, threw just 14 interceptions, completed 52.4 percent of his passes, and finished second in the league with 2,974 yards passing and a passer rating of 88.2.

Memorable Moments/Greatest Performances

Ryan led the Browns to a 35–14 win over the Steelers on November 25, 1962, by throwing for 284 yards and three touchdowns, connecting once each with Jim Brown, Gary Collins, and Ray Renfro.

Ryan had a huge game against Washington in the 1963 regular-season opener, passing for 334 yards and two TDs during a 37–14 win, connecting with Jim Brown from 83 yards out.

Ryan led the Browns to a lopsided 37–7 victory over the Eagles on October 20, 1963, by throwing four touchdown passes in one game for the first time in his career, hooking up with Gary Collins three times and Jim Brown once.

Ryan threw for 256 yards and three touchdowns during a 27–6 win over the Cowboys on October 4, 1964, with the longest of his TD passes going 40 yards to Paul Warfield.

Although Ryan threw the ball just 13 times during a 52–20 rout of the Giants in the final game of the 1964 regular season, he hit on 12 of his attempts, five of which resulted in touchdowns.

Ryan performed well in the 1964 NFL championship game, throwing for 206 yards and three TDs during a 27–0 win over the Baltimore Colts, with all his TD passes going to Gary Collins.

Ryan led the Browns to a convincing 49–17 victory over Atlanta on October 30, 1966, by passing for 223 yards and four touchdowns, the longest of which went 36 yards to Paul Warfield.

Although Ryan had three of his passes intercepted by Spider Lockhart during a 49–40 win over the Giants on December 4, 1966, he brought the Browns back from a 20-point third-quarter deficit by throwing for 326 yards and three touchdowns.

Ryan led the Browns to a 38–10 win over the St. Louis Cardinals in the 1966 regular-season finale by throwing for 367 yards and four touchdowns, connecting twice with Gary Collins and once each with Ernie Green and Clifton McNeil.

Ryan showed his mettle during a 24–0 win over the Bears on October 22, 1967, throwing two TD passes in the second half after being knocked unconscious by Dick Butkus earlier in the game.

Notable Achievements

- Passed for more than 2,000 yards four times, topping 2,500 yards once.
- Threw more than 20 touchdown passes four times.
- Posted touchdown-to-interception ratio of better than 2–1 once.
- Posted passer rating above 90.0 once.
- Led NFL in touchdown passes twice.
- Finished second in NFL in passing yards once, pass completion percentage once, and passer rating twice.
- Finished third in NFL in touchdown passes once.
- Ranks among Browns career leaders with 1,755 pass attempts (5th), 907 pass completions (6th), 13,361 passing yards (5th), and 134 touchdown passes (3rd).
- Four-time division champion (1964, 1965, 1967, and 1968).
- 1964 NFL champion.
- Three-time Pro Bowl selection (1964, 1965, and 1966).
- 1965 First-Team All–Eastern Conference selection.

45

BOBBY MITCHELL

An explosive runner who possessed great speed, tremendous elusiveness, and outstanding open-field running ability, Bobby Mitchell spent the first four years of his career teaming up with Jim Brown to form arguably the greatest running back tandem in NFL history. An extremely versatile player who excelled not only as a runner, but also as a receiver and return-man on special teams, Mitchell surpassed 1,000 yards from scrimmage twice and amassed more than 1,500 all-purpose yards three times as a member of the Browns, while also returning three punts and three kickoffs for touchdowns. The 1958 *Sporting News* NFL Rookie of the Year, Mitchell also earned one Pro Bowl selection, before being traded to the Washington Redskins following the conclusion of the 1961 campaign. Continuing to display his versatility in Washington, Mitchell moved to wide receiver, where he went on to lead the NFL in receiving yards twice, en route to earning a place in the Pro Football Hall of Fame.

Born in Hot Springs, Arkansas, on June 6, 1935, Robert Cornelius Mitchell grew up in the segregated South, although he experienced very little racism as a youth, stating years later, "I rave about Hot Springs. I tell people, 'Everybody lived the same.' I don't even remember riding on the back of the bus. Maybe I did. But Hot Springs was different from most of Arkansas. People came there from all over the country for the baths. But I knew that 20 miles from Hot Springs I'd be hurt."

While growing up in Hot Springs, Mitchell also had the good fortune to meet and become friends with several professional athletes, including Brooklyn Dodger stars Jackie Robinson, Roy Campanella, and Don Newcombe, recalling, "For black players, Hot Springs was like their spring training since they weren't welcome in Florida. We were very fortunate because we got a chance to play baseball and basketball with all these great people. . . . We got to know these guys personally. It was a great situation for all the young kids. To grow up in an area like that was a great advantage for someone like me."

Bobby Mitchell combined with Jim Brown for four years to form arguably the greatest running back tandem in NFL history.
Courtesy of MearsonlineAuctions.com

Developing into an outstanding all-around athlete during his formative years, Mitchell played baseball, basketball, and football with neighborhood friends, remembering, "My older brother didn't want me around, and my younger brother was too young. It's maybe why I turned to sports."

Although Mitchell continued to compete in all three sports while attending Langston High School, he truly made a name for himself on the gridiron, with childhood friend and high school teammate Charles Butler recalling, "Nobody could catch him. He was a threat to break loose on anything. He was hard to get your hands on because he had the instincts to shift his feet. A lot of times we would have plays where they were supposed to go through the tackles, but he bounced outside, and he was so quick that he could pull it off."

After earning All-State honors for the second straight time as a senior in 1953, Mitchell fielded scholarship offers from several colleges, before eventually deciding to enroll at the University of Illinois. Mitchell subsequently established himself as one of the finest backs in the Big Ten over the course of his three-year college career, gaining All-Conference recognition twice, while also excelling as a sprinter in track.

Nevertheless, Mitchell did not thoroughly enjoy his time at Illinois since he encountered far more discrimination there than he had ever experienced in his hometown. Finding particularly objectionable the practice of housing Black players off campus in old Army barracks while the white players lived in the dorms, Mitchell nearly decided to return home to Hot Springs, before All-American halfback J. C. Caroline convinced him to remain in college. However, things finally began to improve in Mitchell's junior year, when the college dean asked him to become the first Black to move into an all-white dorm.

After seriously considering trying to compete for a spot as a hurdler on the 1960 US Olympic track team, Mitchell instead chose to play football for the Browns when they offered him a $7,000 contract after selecting him in the seventh round of the 1958 NFL Draft, with the 84th overall pick. Making an immediate impact upon his arrival in Cleveland, Mitchell gained recognition from the *Sporting News* as its NFL Rookie of the Year by rushing for 500 yards on only 80 carries, gaining another 131 yards on 16 pass receptions, amassing 619 yards on special teams, scoring six touchdowns, ranking among the league leaders with 1,250 all-purpose yards and a rushing average of 6.3 yards per carry, and topping the circuit with an average of 25.2 yards per kickoff return. Impressed with Mitchell's exceptional play, head coach Paul Brown said at season's end, "His long-shot running in several games was responsible for putting us in the playoffs. Everybody thinks of him as a great sprinter, and he is. But more than that, he has unusual balance."

Continuing to perform at an elite level over the course of the next three seasons, Mitchell posted the following numbers from 1959 to 1961:

YEAR	YDS RUSHING	REC YDS	YDS FROM SCRIMMAGE	ALL-PURPOSE YDS	TDS
1959	743	351	1,094	1.507	10
1960	506	612	1,118	1,651	12
1961	548	368	916	1,508	10

Ranking among the NFL leaders in all-purpose yards all three years, Mitchell finished second in the league in that category in both 1959 and 1960, earning Pro Bowl honors for the only time as a member of the Browns in the second of those campaigns. Mitchell also placed near the top of the league rankings in rushing average all three years, finishing second in the circuit in 1959 with an average of 5.7 yards per carry.

Amazingly, Mitchell, who joined the Army National Guard in 1958, performed as well as he did in 1961 even though he spent most of the season away from football. Explaining years later that he received a phone call three games into the campaign stating that he had been summoned into military service because of the Berlin Crisis, Mitchell recalled, "I thought it was a joke and told my wife there was some nut on the phone. About an hour later, there was a knock at the door, and the man told me I would have to leave for Fort Meade [in Maryland] the next day. I called Paul Brown, and he said I had to go, and he reminded me that he didn't have to pay me if I was in the military. I was crying. We had just bought this new house, and I didn't know what we were going to do."

Fortunately, Mitchell's drill sergeant allowed him to leave on weekends to play football, with Mitchell saying, "I'd get there Saturday morning, find out what the game plan was, and play the game the next day."

Proving to be a perfect complement to Jim Brown in Cleveland's offensive backfield, the 6-foot, 192-pound Mitchell used his tremendous speed and elusiveness to outrun opposing defenders, who also found themselves faced with the unenviable task of trying to tackle the powerful Brown. In discussing the qualities that made Mitchell his ideal running mate, Brown said, "Right away, I loved his talent. He was a different kind of runner and had unbelievable track speed. . . . He'd make you stay in your shoes or come out of your shoes because he had the moves and acceleration and speed and the attitude. . . . He only wanted about nine carries, and I needed about 25. That made us very compatible."

One of the league's most difficult players to bring down in the open field, Mitchell, said Detroit Lions Hall of Fame defensive back Dick LeBeau, "was here, he was there, and he was there before you could blink. I've never seen anything like that. It was inhuman."

Former Green Bay Packers and Baltimore Colts center Bill Curry stated, "There's an old thing about 'Give him a leg and take it away.' There would be a leg, but, when the tackler went for it, it was gone."

Meanwhile, in describing Mitchell's running style, Steve Sabol of NFL Films said, "He had sort of loose ankles—almost floppy. He could change directions like a fish. Everything was quick—not necessarily graceful. . . . He was the first one that I ever saw that perfected that sort of high-stepping into the end zone to finish off runs."

Sabol then added, "Bobby was sort of like filet mignon to Jim Brown's sirloin. Bobby was just served up in smaller portions, but they were always very tasty."

Despite Mitchell's brilliant play, the Browns elected to trade him to the Washington Redskins following the conclusion of the 1961 campaign for the rights to select Heisman Trophy–winning running back Ernie Davis with the first overall pick of the 1962 NFL Draft. Leaving Cleveland rather reluctantly, Mitchell headed to Washington having rushed for 2,297 yards and 16 touchdowns, made 128 receptions for 1,462 yards and 16 TDs, amassed 3,759 yards from scrimmage and 5,916 all-purpose yards, and scored 38 touchdowns as a member of the Browns.

Upon his arrival in Washington, Mitchell became the first Black player to don a Redskins uniform, putting him under a great deal of pressure, as he noted years later when he said, "The Redskins owned the Atlantic seaboard at the time . . . there were no other teams [in the Atlantic area] at the time. Their white fans, particularly in North and South Carolina, Alabama, and Florida, weren't used to having a black player on their team. My first year was rather difficult . . . the comments we had to listen to. And there was a lot of pressure on me to perform. So many blacks were counting on me; they wanted me to be a Superman. It was difficult to play and make everybody happy."

Nevertheless, Mitchell went on to establish himself as Washington's best player after moving to wide receiver his first year in the nation's capital, earning three Pro Bowl selections and two All-Pro nominations as a member of the Redskins by consistently ranking among the league leaders in receptions and receiving yards, while also continuing to excel on special teams. Performing especially well in 1962 and 1963, Mitchell amassed 1,794 all-purpose yards, scored 12 touchdowns, and led the NFL with 72 receptions and 1,384 receiving yards in the first of those campaigns, before scoring eight times, topping the circuit with 1,436 receiving yards, and ranking among the league leaders with 69 catches, 1,460 yards from scrimmage, and 1,852 all-purpose yards the following year.

But, after making just 14 receptions for 130 yards in a part-time role in 1968, Mitchell retired during training camp the following year, ending his career with 521 receptions, 7,954 receiving yards, 65 touchdown receptions, 2,735 yards rushing, 18 rushing TDs, 10,689 yards from scrimmage, 699 punt-return yards, 2,690 kickoff-return yards, 14,078 all-purpose yards, and 91 total touchdowns.

Remaining in the Redskins organization as a scout at the insistence of Washington head coach Vince Lombardi following his retirement as an active player, Mitchell eventually worked his way up to assistant general manager, although former Redskins owner Jack Kent Cooke twice passed him over for the position of GM. Finally retiring from professional football in 2003 after spending a total of 41 years serving the Redskins in one capacity or another, Mitchell expressed his dissatisfaction with being known, first and foremost, as the first African American to play for the Redskins when he told his hometown newspaper, the *Hot Springs Sentinel-Record*, "I have to live with people always talking about me as the first black player against all my exploits. I've always been very upset that people always start with it. I don't want to hear that, and yet I have to hear it constantly, and it overshadows everything I've done in the game."

Commiserating with his former teammate, Jim Brown stated, "Bobby was an individual . . . thrown into the arena of being a victim for no reason. He had to suffer for being black more than any person I know that played football at the time I played. With that kind of ability, if he were white, everybody on this earth would know who he was. . . . You can't put up somebody against him and tell me he's better than our Bobby Mitchell."

After retiring to private life, Mitchell remained active in the community and continued to raise funds for the Leukemia & Lymphoma Society through his annual golf tournament until he died at the age of 84 on April 5, 2020. Following his passing, Pro Football Hall of Fame president and CEO David Baker issued a statement that read: "The game lost a true legend today. Bobby was an incredible player, a talented executive, and a real gentleman to everyone with whom he worked or competed against."

Meanwhile, former Redskins running back and return-man Brian Mitchell (no relation) paid tribute to his namesake, saying, "You look at Bobby, his career was a Hall of Fame career, but I know for African American people, he was a social activist, as well. Not only was he a great football player and a guy who would go out there and fight for the rights of his people, but he was also a guy who was a philanthropist, a guy doing everything that you're supposed to do."

BROWNS CAREER HIGHLIGHTS

Best Season

Although Mitchell performed magnificently in each of his four years in Cleveland, he had his finest all-around season for the Browns in 1960, when he earned his only Pro Bowl selection as a member of the team by rushing for 506 yards, gaining another 612 yards on 45 pass receptions, accumulating 533 yards on special teams, scoring 12 touchdowns, and finishing second in the league with 1,651 all-purpose yards.

Memorable Moments/Greatest Performances

Mitchell made an impact in his first game as a pro, rushing for 50 yards and gathering in a 4-yard touchdown pass from Milt Plum during a 30–27 win over the Los Angeles Rams in the 1958 regular-season opener.

Mitchell helped lead the Browns to a 35–28 victory over the Chicago Cardinals on October 12, 1958, by gaining 147 yards on just 11 carries and scoring a touchdown, which came on a 63-yard scamper.

Mitchell followed that up by rushing for 108 yards and making three receptions for 38 yards and one touchdown during a 27–10 win over the Steelers on October 19, 1958.

Mitchell displayed his explosiveness during the first quarter of a 28–14 victory over the Eagles on November 23, 1958, returning a kickoff 98 yards for a touchdown and scoring again on a 68-yard punt return.

Mitchell contributed to a 34–7 win over the Redskins on October 25, 1959, by making three receptions for 107 yards and two touchdowns, the longest of which came on a 76-yard connection with Milt Plum.

Mitchell had another huge game against the Redskins in the second meeting between the two teams on November 15, 1959, carrying the ball 14 times for 232 yards and three touchdowns during a 31–17 Browns win, with one of his TDs coming on a career-long 90-yard run.

Mitchell led the Browns to a convincing 41–24 victory over the Eagles in the opening game of the 1960 regular season by rushing for 156 yards, gaining another 34 yards on five pass receptions, and scoring three touchdowns, two of which came on runs of 31 and 30 yards.

Mitchell turned in a tremendous all-around effort against Dallas on October 16, 1960, leading the Browns to a 48–7 rout of the Cowboys by rushing for 46 yards and one touchdown, scoring once on a 46-yard pass from Milt Plum, and returning a kickoff 90 yards for a touchdown. In addition to his three TDs, Mitchell finished the game with 205 all-purpose yards.

Mitchell turned in a similarly impressive performance against the Giants in the 1960 regular-season finale, amassing 215 all-purpose yards and scoring two touchdowns during a 48–34 Browns win, with one of his TDs coming on a 69-yard pass from Milt Plum.

Mitchell exhibited his tremendous versatility again during a 31–7 victory over the Redskins on October 8, 1961, rushing for 41 yards, making three receptions for 60 yards, and scoring three TDs, which came on a 31-yard run, a 52-yard pass from Milt Plum, and a 64-yard punt return.

Mitchell led the Browns to a 30–28 win over the Steelers on October 22, 1961, by rushing for 119 yards and scoring another three touchdowns, the longest of which came on an 18-yard run.

Mitchell followed that up by rushing for 104 yards and one touchdown during a 21–10 win over the St. Louis Cardinals on October 29, 1961, scoring his TD on a 56-yard run.

Mitchell starred during a 45–24 victory over the Eagles on November 19, 1961, amassing 198 all-purpose yards and scoring two touchdowns, one of which came on a 91-yard kickoff return.

Mitchell excelled in one of his last games as a member of the Browns, gaining 140 yards on just 12 carries during a 38–17 win over the Cowboys on December 3, 1961.

Notable Achievements

- Returned three punts and three kickoffs for touchdowns.
- Rushed for more than 700 yards once.
- Surpassed 40 receptions and 600 receiving yards once each.
- Surpassed 1,000 yards from scrimmage twice.
- Amassed more than 1,000 all-purpose yards four times, topping 1,500 yards on three occasions.
- Scored at least 10 touchdowns three times.
- Averaged more than 5 yards per carry three times.
- Led NFL with average of 25.2 yards per kickoff return in 1958.

- Finished second in NFL in all-purpose yards twice, rushing average twice, and punt-return average once.
- Finished third in NFL in punt-return yards once, kickoff- and punt-return yards once, and rushing average once.
- Led Browns with 45 receptions in 1960.
- Ranks among Browns career leaders with 2,297 yards rushing (12th), 607 punt-return yards (10th), and 1,550 kickoff-return yards (10th).
- 1958 *Sporting News* NFL Rookie of the Year.
- 1960 Pro Bowl selection.
- Member of Cleveland Browns Ring of Honor.
- Elected to Pro Football Hall of Fame in 1983.

46

HORACE GILLOM

The finest punter of his era, Horace Gillom spent his entire 10-year professional career in Cleveland, becoming known during that time for the tremendous hang time and distance he attained on his kicks. A three-time league-leader in punting average, Gillom finished either first or second in the NFL in that category five straight times, averaging more than 45 yards per kick twice at a time when most punters rarely even approached that mark. Giving the Browns a tremendous advantage over their opposition with his ability to drive the ball high and deep downfield, Gillom contributed significantly to teams that won nine division titles and six league championships. More than just an exceptional punter, Gillom also proved to be a valuable backup receiver and a solid performer on special teams as both a return-man and kick coverer. Yet, it is for his punting that Gillom is remembered most, with Paul Brown once saying, "There has never been a better punter than Horace."

Born in Roanoke, Alabama, on March 3, 1921, Horace Albert Gillom grew up in Massillon, Ohio, after moving there with his parents and two older brothers, Jake and Odell, at an early age. Following in the footsteps of his two siblings, Gillom starred on the gridiron at Massillon Washington High School, helping to lead squads coached by Paul Brown to three state championships and an overall record of 30-0 by excelling as a receiver on offense, a linebacker on defense, and a punter and return-man on special teams. Particularly outstanding his final two years at Massillon, Gillom earned First-Team All-County and First-Team All-Ohio honors as a junior by recording six interceptions and scoring seven touchdowns for a team that outscored its opponents by a combined margin of 460–25. Gillom followed that up by scoring a school record 108 points his senior year, prompting the Associated Press to name him Ohio's Most Outstanding Player.

Commenting years later on the all-around brilliance that Gillom displayed at Massillon, school historian Bill Oliver, whose brother, Jack, played alongside the future NFL star, said, "I think if you check the record books,

Horace Gillom proved to be the finest punter of his time.

his name is still in them. He was one of the most outstanding pass catchers of his time. I think he scored more touchdowns than anybody else at that point. He was sure-handed. But he was also a wonderful linebacker on defense. . . . Horace was also the greatest punter Massillon ever had. Paul Brown couldn't believe that Horace could kick the ball as far as he could. When he punted, it would go above the lights, and the poor guy waiting for it had to wait for it to come out of the clouds."

Oliver continued, "I remember sitting out at the stadium one night 20 years ago talking to some people about the great [Massillon] players of the past. We were naming all these great guys. A lady sitting behind me tapped me on the shoulder and said, 'You're forgetting about the greatest of them all, Horace Gillom.' And she was right."

Fellow Massillon historian Phil Glick also shared his memories of Gillom, recalling, "My dad took me to a game, and he said, 'I want you to see this kid punt the ball.' I was only eight years old. I swear, when Gillom kicked it, it was as high as the lights at Tiger Stadium. He was tremendous. . . . The old-timers around here talk about him as a linebacker in Paul Brown's seven-diamond defense. They said it was impossible to throw over top of him. He was so tall and could jump so high."

Glick then spoke of Gillom's tremendous all-around athletic ability, adding, "But he also led them in points scored in track for two years. He was part of their 880-yard relay team that held the school record. And he was a helluva basketball player."

Choosing to follow Paul Brown, who later called him "the greatest high school player I ever coached," to Ohio State University when Brown became head coach of the Buckeyes in 1941, Gillom played on the school's freshman football team, before dropping out because of poor grades. Subsequently drafted into the US Army, Gillom spent the next three years serving his country during World War II, fighting in the Battle of the Bulge and earning three Bronze Stars, with his son, Dennis, revealing that his father described the experience as the "scariest thing he ever saw," recounting, "They were in France, and they were all taking cover in a grape arbor. He said that he had never been so scared. The sky was lit up with bombs, they could hear them right and left, and they didn't know where they were going to hit. But he lived through it, and he made it back."

Following his discharge early in 1946, Motley enrolled at the University of Nevada, Reno, where he led the nation in punting, before dropping out of school once again at the end of the year because of poor grades. Invited by Paul Brown to join his team in the infant AAFC prior to the start of the ensuing campaign, Gillom became one of the first Black athletes to play sports professionally, arriving in Cleveland the same year that Jackie Robinson broke the color barrier in baseball and one year after Bill Willis and Marion Motley became the first African Americans to play for the Browns.

After earning a roster spot, Gillom contributed to the success of a Browns team that won the second of its five straight league championships by finishing third in the AAFC with an average of 44.6 yards per punt, while also intercepting one pass as a linebacker on defense and making two receptions for 24 yards as a backup wide receiver. Although Gillom punted only eight times in 1948, he assumed a more prominent role on offense while filling in for an injured Dante Lavelli for part of the season, making 20 receptions for 295 yards and one touchdown. Doing double duty in 1949, Gillom averaged a career-low 37.2 yards per punt. However, he had his finest offensive season, gaining 359 yards on 23 pass receptions. Even though Gillom occasionally returned kickoffs and lined up as a wide receiver from time to time in subsequent seasons, he served the Browns primarily as a punter the remainder of his career, beginning in 1950 a string of five straight seasons that saw him record either the highest or the second-highest punting average in the league.

Revolutionizing the art of punting, Gillom became one of the first players at his position to emphasize "hang time." Lining up farther behind the line of scrimmage than most to give him more time to drive the ball deep downfield, the 6'1", 221-pound Gillom possessed a powerful right leg that amazed anyone who watched him perform, with former teammate Bob Gain recalling, "I remember Paul Brown yelling at Gillom one time, 'You know how many laces are on it, punt the damn ball.' The ball went over the top of the lights, and the return man said, 'Where is it?' He lost it in the lights."

Several of Gillom's other former teammates sang his praises as well, with Sherman Howard claiming, "With Horace, he would kick it so high that, by the time guys got down, the ball was coming down, so most guys had to fair catch."

Emerson Cole stated, "I never saw any equal in punting. He would tell us in the huddle, 'Go all out, because this one's going to hit going toward the other goal line.' Other times, he would say, 'Be under control, because this one's going to hit and come back.' He could control how the ball bounced."

Lin Houston proclaimed, "Horace was the greatest punter I've ever seen play pro football. They can talk about Ray Guy all they want. He couldn't hold a candle to Horace."

Meanwhile, former New York Giants return-man Otto Schnellbacher said, "We didn't just go back 40 yards, we went back 50, 60 yards because he just kicked it so damn far and so high."

Unfortunately, Gillom's skills began to diminish in 1955, prompting the Browns to release him during the early stages of the ensuing campaign after he developed a sore back. Gillom subsequently retired, ending his career with a punting average of 43.1 yards per kick that placed him second in NFL history at the time only to Sammy Baugh, who posted a mark of 45.1 for the Washington Redskins during his Hall of Fame career.

Eventually moving to Los Angeles with his wife and two children, Gillom worked at the Los Angeles Recreation Department as an assistant athletic director and at a local hospital as a security guard, before dying of a heart attack at only 64 years of age on October 28, 1985.

In discussing his father's unpretentious nature following his passing, Gillom's son claimed that he never outwardly saw himself as a pioneer for other Blacks, despite the pivotal role he played in helping to integrate the game, saying, "He never talked about it. I am sure he knew he was subconsciously. In fact, my father never carried that around, and he really never talked about his football career. He was very normal at home. If you didn't know who he was, you would've never guessed he was a football player. You just wouldn't know. He was such a normal person."

CAREER HIGHLIGHTS

Best Season

Although Gillom earned his lone Pro Bowl nomination in 1952 by leading the league with a career-high average of 45.7 yards per punt, he had his finest all-around season in 1951, when, in addition to topping the circuit with an average of 45.5 yards per punt, he made 11 receptions for 164 yards and returned a fumble 38 yards for a touchdown on defense.

Memorable Moments/Greatest Performances

Gillom displayed his ability to drive the ball far downfield during a 28–0 victory over the Baltimore Colts on September 21, 1947, recording punts of 85 and 80 yards, with his 85-yard kick representing the longest in franchise history.

Gillom contributed to the Browns' 14–3 victory over the New York Yankees in the 1947 AAFC championship game by averaging 45 yards for his five punts.

Gillom scored the first touchdown of his career when he gathered in a 25-yard pass from Otto Graham during a 31–21 win over the Brooklyn Dodgers in the 1948 regular-season finale.

Gillom put the finishing touches on a 45–7 rout of the Pittsburgh Steelers on October 29, 1950, when he hauled in a 38-yard touchdown pass from Cliff Lewis in the fourth quarter.

Gillom played a key role in the Browns' 8–3 win over New York in a one-game playoff to determine the NFL Eastern Division champion on December 17, 1950, consistently forcing the Giants to start deep in their own territory with his long, booming punts.

Gillom recorded the only defensive touchdown of his career when he ran 38 yards to pay dirt after recovering a fumble during a 17–0 win over the Steelers on October 21, 1951.

Gillom contributed to a 34–17 victory over the Chicago Cardinals on November 4, 1951, by making five receptions for 80 yards.

Gillom closed out the scoring of a lopsided 49–7 victory over the Philadelphia Eagles on October 19, 1951, when he caught an 11-yard TD pass from backup quarterback George Ratterman.

Notable Achievements

- Recorded three punts of at least 80 yards.
- Averaged more than 44 yards per punt four times, topping 45 yards per kick twice.
- Led league in total punt yardage once and average yards per punt three times.
- Finished second in league in total punt yardage once and average yards per punt three times.
- Recorded longest punt in NFL three times.
- Holds Browns record for longest punt (85 yards).
- Ranks among Browns career leaders with 492 punts (2nd), 21,206 total punt yards (2nd), and 43.1 punting average (6th).
- Nine-time division champion (1947, 1948, 1949, 1950, 1951, 1952, 1953, 1954, and 1955).
- Three-time AAFC champion (1947, 1948, and 1949).
- Three-time NFL champion (1950, 1954, and 1955).
- 1952 Pro Bowl selection.

47

KEVIN MACK

A powerful runner who acquired the nickname "Mack Truck" for his ability to bowl over opposing defenders, Kevin Mack spent his entire nine-year career in Cleveland, amassing the fifth-most rushing yards and sixth-most yards from scrimmage in franchise history during that time. Starting at fullback for the Browns for seven seasons, Mack led the team in rushing six times, gaining more than 1,000 yards on the ground once and accumulating more than 1,000 yards from scrimmage twice. A complete back, Mack excelled as a blocker and a receiver out of the backfield as well, with his varied skill set making him a key contributor to teams that won four division titles. The 1985 United Press International (UPI) AFC Offensive Rookie of the Year, Mack earned the additional distinctions of being named to two Pro Bowls, before returning to the organization in a front office capacity following his retirement.

Born in Kings Mountain, North Carolina, on August 9, 1962, James Kevin Mack grew up some 30 miles west of Charlotte, North Carolina, where he began competing in Pop Warner football at the age of 11. After enrolling at Kings Mountain High School some years later, Mack initially focused on developing his track skills, posting a personal-best time of 4.4 seconds in the 40-yard dash, before turning his attention to football, later saying, "I was in track mode before my sister and my high school football coach got me to think differently. And the rest, as they say, is history." Starring on the gridiron his final two years at Kings Mountain, Mack rushed for a total of more than 2,000 yards, performing especially well as a senior in 1979, when he earned All-State honors by gaining 1,585 yards on the ground.

Subsequently recruited by several major colleges, Mack chose to attend Clemson University in South Carolina, where he lettered in football for four years. Posting his best numbers for the Tigers in his final season, Mack earned honorable mention All-America honors by scoring eight touchdowns and setting a school record for fullbacks by rushing for 862 yards.

Kevin Mack led the Browns in rushing six times.
Courtesy of MearsonlineAuctions.com

Selected by the Washington Federals in the second USFL Territorial Draft held on January 4, 1984, Mack appeared in just three games with the Federals, before financial problems forced them to trade him to the Los Angeles Express. After finishing out the season in Los Angeles, Mack signed with the Browns, who had selected him with the 11th overall pick of a special Supplemental Draft the NFL held on June 5, 1984, for college seniors who had already signed with either the USFL or the Canadian Football League. Expressing his satisfaction with the acquisition of Mack, Browns head coach Marty Schottenheimer said, "It's a very good sign when a player is eager and ready to go. Kevin Mack knows he will have every opportunity to make this ballclub. He's a hard-nosed runner, a guy that carries his weight well. I expect him to challenge for a spot on the roster."

Although unsure of his ability to compete in the NFL when he first arrived in Cleveland, Mack went on to have a fabulous rookie season, earning Pro Bowl honors and a spot on the 1985 NFL All-Rookie Team by rushing for 1,104 yards, gaining another 297 yards on 29 pass receptions, scoring 10 touchdowns, and ranking among the league leaders with an average of 5.0 yards per carry. And, with halfback Earnest Byner also gaining more than 1,000 yards on the ground, Mack and Byner became just the third 1,000-yard rushing tandem in league history.

Even though Mack failed to reach the 1,000-yard mark in either of the next two seasons, he continued to perform well, rushing for 665 yards, amassing 957 yards from scrimmage, and scoring 10 touchdowns in 1986, before earning his second Pro Bowl nomination the following year by rushing for 735 yards, amassing 958 yards from scrimmage, and scoring six TDs.

In addition to his size and strength, the 6-foot, 230-pound Mack possessed outstanding running speed that enabled him to assume a far more varied role on offense than most fullbacks, who serve primarily as blockers, short-yardage runners, and occasional pass-catchers. While Mack did an exceptional job of blocking for close friend and running mate Earnest Byner, he also excelled as a receiver out of the backfield, twice recording more than 40 receptions. Meanwhile, Mack proved to be a huge contributor to the Browns' running game, gaining more than 500 yards on the ground on six separate occasions.

Troubled by an ailing knee, Mack appeared in only 11 games in 1988, limiting him to just 485 yards rushing, 572 yards from scrimmage, and three touchdowns. Then, after undergoing arthroscopic surgery during the following offseason, Mack ended up missing the first 12 games of the 1989 campaign—not for medical reasons, but because of an error in judgment he made on June 28, 1989, when police arrested him after they found him sitting in a car in a seedy section of Cleveland with 11 packets of cocaine in his possession. After originally being charged with four counts of drug trafficking and possession, Mack eventually pled guilty to using cocaine, a fourth-degree felony. Subsequently suspended by the NFL for the first four games of the regular season, Mack later received a six-month jail sentence, before having his sentence reduced to just 33 days after he agreed to remain on probation for two years, perform community service, and subject himself to frequent drug tests.

Rejoining the Browns for the final four games of the 1989 regular season, Mack received a vote of confidence from running backs coach George Sefcik shortly after he returned to the team, with Sefick saying, "He's a darn good football player. We'd like to put the other stuff in the past. Kevin is on a mission. When he came back with us, he was pointed toward football."

Performing well in a part-time role during the season's final month, Mack helped the Browns capture the division title by rushing for 130 yards and scoring one touchdown. Regaining his starting job the following year, Mack played some of the best ball of his career over the course of the next two seasons, rushing for 702 yards, amassing 1,062 yards from scrimmage, and scoring seven touchdowns in 1990, before gaining 726 yards on the ground, accumulating 981 yards from scrimmage, and scoring 10 TDs in the ensuing campaign. Plagued by injuries the next two seasons, Mack appeared in a total of just 16 games, prompting him to announce his retirement at the end of 1993 with career totals of 5,123 rushing yards, 197 receptions, 1,602 receiving yards, 6,725 yards from scrimmage, 46 rushing touchdowns, and eight TD catches.

Following his playing days, Mack relocated from Cleveland to Houston, Texas, where, among other work, he coached at Texas Southern University. Returning to Cleveland in 2007, Mack assumed the position of assistant director of player programs for the Browns, before later being named head of the organization's Alumni Relations Department. In discussing his job while accepting the Dino Lucarelli Lifetime Achievement Award in 2016, Mack said: "Some of the things that I learned from these guys are amazing. The way they care about the players, the history of this team is just amazing. So, I try to emulate that now. And it's real easy for me because I get to work with guys that I played with and the guys who were blazing the trail before we got into Cleveland. The Jim Browns, Paul Warfields, those guys. So, I'm blessed and I'm lucky to be able to work with gentlemen like that who set the standard for the Cleveland Browns."

CAREER HIGHLIGHTS

Best Season

Mack posted the best numbers of his career as a rookie in 1985, when he earned Pro Bowl honors for the first of two times by rushing for 1,104 yards, amassing 1,401 yards from scrimmage, scoring 10 touchdowns, and averaging 5.0 yards per carry.

Memorable Moments/Greatest Performances

Although the Browns lost the 1985 regular-season opener to the St. Louis Cardinals in overtime by a score of 27–24, Mack performed well in his first game as a pro, gaining 48 yards on nine carries, and scoring the first touchdown of his career on a 13-yard run.

Mack led the Browns to a 21–7 win over the San Diego Chargers on September 29, 1985, by carrying the ball 16 times for 130 yards, making seven receptions for 49 yards, and scoring two touchdowns, scoring once on a 10-yard run and once on a 10-yard pass from Gary Danielson.

Mack earned AFC Offensive Player of the Week honors by amassing 200 yards from scrimmage and scoring a touchdown during a 24–20 victory over the Patriots on October 6, 1985, gaining 115 of his yards on the ground and the other 85 on five pass receptions.

Although Mack rushed for only 27 yards against Miami on November 10, 1986, he helped lead the Browns to a 26–16 win by making six receptions for 94 yards.

Mack contributed to a 37–31 overtime victory over the Steelers on November 23, 1986, by rushing for 106 yards and one touchdown.

Mack followed that up by rushing for a season-high 121 yards during a 13–10 OT win over the Houston Oilers on November 30, 1986.

Mack helped lead the Browns to a convincing 34–3 victory over the Bengals on December 14, 1986, by rushing for 93 yards and two touchdowns.

Mack contributed to a 23–20 overtime win over the Jets in the divisional round of the 1986 playoffs by making five receptions for 51 yards and rushing for 63 yards and one touchdown. Making Mack's performance even more impressive is the fact that he had two teeth knocked out on the game's first play, forcing him to spend the remainder of the contest playing with the teeth wedged against his mouthpiece (the doctor told him not to remove the mouthpiece) and a streak of blood down the middle of his uniform, before undergoing oral surgery afterwards.

Mack helped lead the Browns to a 40–7 rout of the Oilers on November 22, 1987, by rushing for 114 yards and one touchdown, which came on a 5-yard run.

Mack proved to be too much for the Bengals to handle on December 13, 1987, gaining 133 yards on the ground and scoring two touchdowns during a 38–24 Browns win, with one of his TDs coming on a 22-yard run and the other on a 2-yard pass from Bernie Kosar.

Mack carried the ball 16 times for 100 yards during a 19–3 win over the Philadelphia Eagles on October 16, 1988, reeling off a career-long 65-yard run during the contest.

Mack enabled the Browns to advance to the playoffs as AFC Central Division champions in 1989 when he gave them a 24–20 victory over the Houston Oilers in the final game of the regular season by running the ball in from 4 yards out with just 39 seconds left on the clock. Commenting on Mack's TD run afterwards, teammate Mike Johnson said, "They didn't have enough people on the field to tackle Kevin Mack. He fought and fought. He wanted that touchdown as bad as he wanted anything in his life." Meanwhile, Mack, who returned to the Browns during the latter stages of the campaign after undergoing arthroscopic knee surgery and serving 33 days in jail following his cocaine conviction, stated, "I wanted to pay back all the people who believed in me. The touchdown made up for some of what I went through this year, but not a lot of it. This is only a start."

Notable Achievements

- Rushed for more than 1,000 yards once.
- Surpassed 1,000 yards from scrimmage twice.
- Scored 10 touchdowns three times.
- Averaged more than 5 yards per carry once.
- Led Browns in rushing six times.
- Ranks among Browns career leaders with 5,123 yards rushing (5th), 6,725 yards from scrimmage (6th), 6,725 all-purpose yards (9th), 46 rushing touchdowns (4th), 54 touchdowns (6th), and 324 points scored (11th).
- Four-time division champion (1985, 1986, 1987, and 1989).
- Member of 1985 NFL All-Rookie Team.
- 1985 Week 5 AFC Offensive Player of the Week.
- 1985 United Press International (UPI) AFC Offensive Rookie of the Year.
- Two-time Pro Bowl selection (1985 and 1987).

48

DON COCKROFT

The only kicker the Browns carried on their roster for most of his career, Don Cockroft spent 13 seasons in Cleveland, assuming all the team's kicking duties his first nine years in the league. One of the last combination punter/placekickers, Cockroft took on both roles for the Browns from 1968 to 1976, a period during which he set franchise records for most punts and total punt yardage. Also ranking extremely high in team annals in field goals made and points scored, Cockroft proved to be one of the most consistent kickers of his time, leading the NFL in field goal percentage on three separate occasions. A key member of teams that won four division titles, Cockroft earned All-AFC honors twice, although he somehow never gained Pro Bowl or official All-Pro recognition.

Born in Cheyenne, Wyoming, on February 6, 1945, Donald Lee Cockroft grew up in Delta, Colorado, where he spent his early years working on his family's farm. Developing his strong right leg while riding his bicycle to the Little League ballfield some four or five miles from home, Cockroft recalled, "The hill on the way back was a nightmare."

After moving to the Colorado Springs suburb of Fountain, Colorado, in the seventh grade, Cockroft went on to establish himself as a three-sport star at Fort Carson High School, excelling in football, basketball, and track. Particularly outstanding on the gridiron, Cockroft served as the team's quarterback, middle linebacker, and kicker, remembering, "I played every minute of every game. We had only 48 kids in our senior class, and 35 of them were girls. So, I always jokingly say it wasn't hard for me to be the male athlete of the year at my high school."

With Cockroft's first choice, Colorado State University, showing no interest in him, he ultimately decided to enroll at Colorado's Adams State University, whose football team he joined as a walk-on, saying, "I went to Adams State without a scholarship. I wanted to play quarterback but saw right away that there were two quarterbacks who were far better than I was.

Don Cockroft excelled for the Browns as both a punter and placekicker.

That's when I decided to concentrate on kicking. The rest, as they say, is history."

Eventually emerging as a standout kicker at Adams State, Cockroft, who also played strong safety for the Grizzlies, had an exceptional senior year, earning NAIA All-America honors by leading all college punters with an average of 48.1 yards per kick.

Subsequently selected by the Browns in the third round of the 1967 NFL Draft, with the 55th overall pick, Cockroft spent his first season in Cleveland honing his skills as a member of the team's taxi squad, while Lou Groza and Gary Collins retained their respective placekicking and punting duties. However, Cockroft took over for both men the following year, concluding the 1968 campaign with an average of 37.7 yards per punt and a league-leading 75 percent field goal percentage that he attained by successfully converting 18 of his 24 attempts. Later crediting the recently retired Groza for his rapid development into one of the NFL's most accurate kickers, Cockroft said, "Lou was a great guy—and what a great guy to work with. The decision that Blanton Collier made to keep Lou as my coach so I could learn the finer points of kicking helped me to lead the league in field goal percentage during my rookie season."

Cockroft also expressed his appreciation to the Browns head coach for the confidence he placed in him when he stated, "Without Blanton Collier, I probably would have never made the team. He believed in me. I was one of the last players in the NFL to handle both the punting and the kicking. Blanton came to me early in my career and said, 'Don, you can do them both.'"

Cockroft continued, "You have to remember that, when I got to the Browns, there were only 40 players on the roster, and when I left, there were 43. Today, there are 53 players on the active roster, so there is more specialization now."

Cockroft continued to function in his dual role for the next eight seasons, until the Browns signed second-year punter Greg Coleman prior to the start of the 1977 campaign. And over the course of those eight seasons, Cockroft remained one of the NFL's more effective kickers, leading the league in field goal percentage another two times, while also averaging more than 40 yards per punt on six separate occasions. Particularly outstanding in 1972 and 1974, Cockroft gained unofficial First-Team All-Pro recognition from the Newspaper Enterprise Association (NEA) in the first of those campaigns by leading the league with a field goal percentage of 81.5 and finishing fourth in the circuit with a career-high average of 43.2 yards per punt. Two years later, Cockroft led all NFL kickers with a career-best 87.5 field goal percentage.

While those numbers might seem relatively modest by today's standards, they must be viewed within the context of the era in which Cockroft played. In discussing how conditions for placekickers have vastly improved through the years, the 6'2", 195-pound Cockroft, who employed a straight-on style of kicking, explained: "Things have definitely changed over the years when it comes to kicking. Now, you've got a center whose only job is to snap on field goals and punts. You don't have someone who is just coming in and snapping the ball haphazardly anymore. You've got someone who will get the snap perfect 99 percent of the time. Now, the kicker probably never has to kick a lace. The conditions on the field itself have also changed for the better. Phil Dawson, as great as he was and as nasty as the winds are in Cleveland, he never had to kick in the mud. . . . Groza and I did. I remember Jan Stenerud and Garo Yepremian saying almost identical things to me before games in Cleveland in late November, asking me, 'Don, how do you kick in this place?' I also believe the ball has changed. My last year . . . they actually put two bladders in it to help the moisture situation. The softer the ball is, the more it's going to spring off your foot. I kicked the new ball, and I said, 'This ball's going five yards further than the other ball.' . . . When Dawson pushed on that ball, it really caved in. The old ball that we had . . . you could have stood on that ball, and it wouldn't have indented as much as the new one did when Dawson just pushed on it!"

Furthermore, Cockroft's overall numbers do not reflect his ability to deliver in the clutch, something he addressed when he said, "The big trivia question on the radio right at the time I retired was 'How many kicks did Cockroft miss to win games?' I went back and checked it. I was 17-for-17 with the game on the line during my career—most were field goals, but a few were extra points late in the game. I felt confident that I wouldn't have been 17-for-18."

Although Cockroft surrendered his punting duties in 1977, he continued to serve as the Browns' placekicker for four more years, before being waived prior to the start of the 1981 season. Choosing to announce his retirement, Cockroft ended his career with 216 field goals (in 328 attempts), 432 extra points (in 457 attempts), 1,080 points, 26,262 yards punting, and a field goal percentage of 65.9 that ranked as the best in NFL history at the time.

Following his playing days, Cockroft moved back to Colorado, where he spent the next 30 years working in the oil and gas business, primarily in marketing and sales. Now 77 years old, Cockroft, who released in the fall of 2011 the 672-page coffee-table book *The 1980 Kardiac Kids—Our Untold Stories*, looks back in astonishment on his NFL career, saying, "It still amazes me. To look back, coming from a small town, small everything, and go to the NFL from Adams State was pretty special. It was an absolutely unbelievable experience."

CAREER HIGHLIGHTS

Best Season

Cockroft scored a career-high 100 points in 1968, when he successfully converted a league-leading 75 percent of his field goal attempts. He also performed extremely well in 1974, when he established career-high marks with 3,643 yards punting and a field goal percentage of 87.5. But Cockroft had his finest all-around season in 1972, when he earned First-Team All-AFC honors by scoring 94 points, averaging a career-best 43.2 yards per punt, and leading the league with 3,498 yards punting and a field goal percentage of 81.5, successfully converting 22 of his 27 field goal attempts.

Memorable Moments/Greatest Performances

Cockroft kicked four field goals in one game for the first time in his career during a 33–21 win over the 49ers on November 3, 1968, with his longest kick of the day coming from 46 yards out.

Cockroft contributed to a 27–20 victory over the Denver Broncos on October 29, 1972, by kicking two field goals, with his career-long 57-yard third-quarter kick representing the longest in the NFL all season.

Cockroft proved to be the difference in a 26–24 win over the Steelers on November 19, 1972, kicking four field goals, with his 26-yarder with only eight seconds left in the game giving the Browns the victory.

Cockroft once again split the uprights four times on September 30, 1973, giving the Browns all the points that they needed to defeat the Giants by a score of 12–10.

Cockroft had a huge hand in the Browns' 23–21 win over Denver on October 27, 1974, kicking three field goals and completing a 27-yard pass to Van Green off a fake punt.

Although the Browns lost to the Broncos by a score of 16–15 on October 19, 1975, Cockroft kicked five field goals in one game for the only time in his career, driving the ball through the uprights three times from more than 40 yards out.

Cockroft proved to be the difference in an 18–16 victory over the Steelers on October 10, 1976, kicking four field goals, the longest of which traveled 50 yards.

Cockroft gave the Browns a 30–27 overtime win over the Patriots on September 26, 1977, by successfully converting his third field goal of the game, splitting the uprights from 35 yards out.

Cockroft came through in the clutch once again on October 16, 1977, giving the Browns a 24–23 win over the Houston Oilers by kicking a 30-yard field goal as time expired.

Cockroft provided further heroics on September 10, 1978, when he gave the Browns a 13–10 overtime victory over the Cincinnati Bengals by driving the ball through the uprights from 27 yards out.

After sending the 1979 regular-season opener into overtime by kicking a 35-yard field goal late in the fourth quarter, Cockroft gave the Browns a 25–22 win over the Jets by splitting the uprights from 27 yards out in OT.

Cockroft helped clinch the division title for the Browns in 1980 by kicking a 22-yard field goal in the fourth quarter of the regular-season finale that gave them a 27–24 win over Cincinnati.

Notable Achievements

- Recorded two punts of more than 70 yards.
- Averaged more than 42 yards per punt twice.
- Scored 100 points in 1968.
- Converted more than 80 percent of field goal attempts twice.
- Led NFL in field goal percentage three times and total punt yardage once.
- Finished second in NFL in field goal percentage once.
- Holds Browns career records for most punts (651) and most total punt yards (26,262).
- Ranks among Browns career leaders with 216 field goals (3rd) and 1,080 points scored (3rd).
- Four-time division champion (1968, 1969, 1971, and 1980).
- 1972 First-Team All-AFC selection.
- 1978 Second-Team All-AFC selection.

49

MILT MORIN

One of the finest all-around tight ends of his era, Milt Morin spent 10 seasons in Cleveland excelling for the Browns as both a receiver and blocker. A forerunner of the modern-day tight end, Morin possessed size, speed, and outstanding open-field running ability, making him a significant contributor to teams that won four division titles. Surpassing 40 receptions twice and 750 receiving yards once, Morin ranks 10th in franchise history in the second category, with his outstanding play earning him two Pro Bowl selections and three All-Conference nominations.

Born in Leominster, Massachusetts, on October 15, 1942, Milton Denis Morin grew up with his seven siblings about one hour west of Boston, where he began his athletic career at an early age, with his sister, Deanne, recalling, "He was quite an athlete. He was a busy boy. He played all the sports, and he played all the time. . . . They called him a gazelle in high school because he was so fast for his size. . . . He was big and fast."

Starring in multiple sports at St. Bernard's Central Catholic High School in nearby Fitchburg, Morin established school records in track and field and served as co-captain of the football team, before attending Brewster Academy, an independent boarding school in Wolfeboro, New Hampshire, from which he graduated in 1962. Sharing his memories of Morin years later, Brewster Academy athletic director Matt Lawlor said, "In the 1960s, Milt Morin was one of the better athletes in all of New England. According to his teammates, he was one of the most physically imposing players they had ever seen. Milt didn't say much. He did his talking with his pads, but, when he spoke, everyone listened."

Offered a football scholarship to the University of Massachusetts in Amherst, Morin continued to excel on the gridiron in college, earning All-America honors twice and All-Conference recognition three times with his outstanding two-way play for teams that won two Yankee Conference championships. While at UMass, Morin also lettered in lacrosse and

Milt Morin proved to be a forerunner of the modern-day tight end.

wrestling, winning the New England heavyweight wrestling championship as a senior in 1965.

Claiming that his background in wrestling helped make him a better football player, Morin later said, "Wrestling gave me a mental discipline and an inner toughness. . . . It taught me the concept of individual responsibility. When you lose a match, there's no one to turn to but yourself. This attitude readies you for football, where they expect you to get the job done and not be looking around to blame the other guy."

Selected by the Browns in the first round of the 1966 NFL Draft, with the 14th overall pick, and by the San Diego Chargers in the third round of that year's AFL Draft, with the 24th overall pick, Morin chose to sign with the Browns for $6,000 after also weighing the option of pursuing a career in teaching. Earning a starting job immediately upon his arrival in

Cleveland, Morin spent his first year in the league serving as a fourth option in the Browns offense behind star running back Leroy Kelly and veteran wide receivers Paul Warfield and Gary Collins, concluding his rookie campaign with 23 receptions for 333 yards and three touchdowns. Troubled the following year by an injured back that required surgery, Morin appeared in only six games, making just seven receptions for 90 yards and failing to score a touchdown.

Fully healthy by the start of the 1968 campaign, Morin emerged as one of the Browns' most potent offensive weapons, earning Pro Bowl and First-Team All–Eastern Conference honors by finishing second on the team to Warfield with 43 receptions, 792 receiving yards, and five TD catches. Although Morin posted less impressive numbers the following year, finishing the season with 37 catches, 495 receiving yards, and no touchdowns, he helped the Browns capture their third straight division title by making several clutch third-down grabs and excelling as a lead blocker for running backs Leroy Kelly and Ron Johnson.

One of the NFL's better-blocking tight ends, the 6'4" Morin, who weighed 238 pounds when he first entered the league, before gradually increasing his playing weight to 255, did an outstanding job of securing the edge on the famous Browns sweep, using his size, strength, and quickness to drive his opponent off the line of scrimmage. Equally proficient as a pass receiver, Morin had good hands, the ability to use his sturdy frame to ward off his defender in tight coverage, and the speed to beat his man deep. An outstanding runner once he gathered in the football, Morin proved to be particularly effective at breaking tackles in the open field, once saying, "When I catch the ball in the middle of the field, I try and make it a physical thing."

Although Morin never ranked among the league leaders in pass receptions, he attributed his relatively modest numbers to the wealth of riches the Browns had on offense, stating, "You can't catch 100 passes if people throw you 45 passes. I always felt that I had the potential to catch 100 passes a year, but it really wasn't my part to play in the system. We had other weapons that were better than me. So, let's use all the weapons and share it."

Morin remained a key cog in the Cleveland offense for four more years, performing especially well in 1970 and 1971. After making 37 receptions for 611 yards and one TD in the first of those campaigns, Morin earned Pro Bowl and First-Team All-AFC honors the following year by catching 40 passes, amassing 581 receiving yards, and scoring two touchdowns for the Central Division champion Browns.

Plagued by injuries, Morin lost his starting job to Oscar Roan in 1975, although he appeared in every game the Browns played for the eighth straight season, giving him a string of 112 consecutive contests in which he made an appearance. Choosing to announce his retirement following the conclusion of the campaign, Morin ended his career with 271 receptions, 4,208 receiving yards, 4,249 yards from scrimmage, and 16 TD catches.

Following his playing days, Morin worked as a carpenter, owned an antiques store, and spent 15 years serving as a corrections officer at the Hampshire County House of Corrections in western Massachusetts, before retiring in 2003.

While awaiting induction into the College Football Hall of Fame in 2010, Morin died of a heart attack at the age of 67, passing away at Cooley Dickinson Hospital in Northampton, just one week before the scheduled ceremonies. Upon learning of his former teammate's passing, Paul Wiggin said, "He was a complete player, a prototype tight end. Back then, they had 240-pound tight ends who couldn't catch the ball and 200-pounders who couldn't block. Milt did both."

Paul Warfield also spoke of Morin's unique skill set and tremendous versatility, stating, "He could have played tight end in this era. He'd be worth his weight in gold because most teams have a tight end who can catch, or a tight end who can block. Milt was such a good blocker we ran Leroy Kelly's sweeps around his end. He could run precise patterns, and he could blow you off the ball with his blocks."

Warfield then added, "He came back from a very serious back injury that required surgery. He was just a great teammate, a big fellow, a wonderful guy."

Meanwhile, Sheriff Robert Garvey raved about Morin's work as a corrections officer, telling the *Hampshire Gazette*, "He had the respect of his colleagues as well as the inmates. You would think someone with his background would be just a tough guy, but he was a gentle man, tremendously understanding of people who were incarcerated."

CAREER HIGHLIGHTS

Best Season

Although Morin gained All-AFC recognition in both 1971 and 1973, he played his best ball for the Browns in 1968, when he established career-high marks with 43 receptions, 792 receiving yards, and five touchdown catches.

Memorable Moments/Greatest Performances

Morin scored the first touchdown of his career on a 20-yard pass from Frank Ryan during a 28–7 win over the Giants on October 2, 1966, finishing the game with four receptions for 88 yards and that one TD.

Morin starred in defeat on October 13, 1968, catching eight passes for 151 yards and one touchdown during a 27–21 loss to the St. Louis Cardinals.

Morin helped lead the Browns to a 33–21 victory over the 49ers on November 3, 1968, by making six receptions for 71 yards and two touchdowns, collaborating with Bill Nelsen on scoring plays of 32 and 15 yards.

Morin turned in another strong performance two weeks later, making five receptions for 103 yards and one TD during a 45–24 win over the Pittsburgh Steelers on November 17, 1968.

Although Morin made just two receptions during a 47–13 rout of the Philadelphia Eagles on November 24, 1968, he amassed a total of 108 receiving yards, with one of his catches resulting in a career-long 89-yard gain.

Morin contributed to a 24–21 victory over the Washington Redskins on December 8, 1968, by amassing 133 yards on six pass receptions.

Morin feasted against the Pittsburgh defensive secondary on October 10, 1971, making eight receptions for 126 yards and one touchdown during a 27–17 Browns win.

Morin helped the Browns forge a 20–20 tie with the Kansas City Chiefs on December 2, 1973, by making three receptions for 86 yards and one touchdown, which came on a 51-yard connection with Mike Phipps late in the final period that deadlocked the contest.

Notable Achievements

- Surpassed 40 receptions twice.
- Surpassed 750 receiving yards once.
- Averaged more than 18 yards per reception twice.
- Led Browns with 611 receiving yards in 1970.
- Ranks 10th in franchise history with 4,208 receiving yards.
- Four-time division champion (1967, 1968, 1969, and 1971).
- Two-time Pro Bowl selection (1968 and 1971).
- 1968 First-Team All–Eastern Conference selection.
- 1971 First-Team All-AFC selection.
- 1973 Second-Team All-AFC selection.

50

CLARENCE SCOTT

Aversatile defensive back who played both cornerback and safety for the Browns, Clarence Scott spent 13 seasons in Cleveland, recording the third-most interceptions in franchise history during that time. Excelling at cornerback his first eight years in the league before moving to safety for his final five seasons, Scott registered a total of 39 interceptions, two of which he returned for touchdowns. A member of Browns teams that won two division titles, Scott missed just one game his entire career, with his consistently strong play earning him one Pro Bowl selection and two All-AFC nominations.

Born in Atlanta, Georgia, on April 9, 1949, Clarence Raymond Scott Jr. grew up in the nearby suburb of Decatur, where he developed a love for football at an early age. Spending his Saturday mornings listening to the older guys in his neighborhood talk about the high school players who had competed the night before, Scott became fascinated with the game, recalling, "I developed within me something that I could reach for, and it turned out to be a real good life."

Spending his youth rooting for the Cleveland Browns, Scott remembered, "I was a Cleveland Browns fan from the time I was a boy. There were no Atlanta Falcons, no Miami Dolphins, no New Orleans Saints, no Carolina Panthers, no Jacksonville Jaguars at the time, so on Sundays we got on television NFL games involving the Browns, Baltimore Colts, Washington Redskins, and New York Giants. The Browns were my favorite team because Jim Brown was my favorite player. I wanted to be a Cleveland Brown from sixth grade on."

Since organized sports did not begin in Decatur until the eighth grade (the first year of high school there), Scott spent his formative years playing football, baseball, and basketball with other neighborhood boys in backyards, playgrounds, and schoolyards, although, as he said, "Football was always my favorite." Making up for lost time, Scott began competing in all three sports as soon as he entered Trinity High School, the region's all-Black

Clarence Scott starred for the Browns at both cornerback and safety.
Courtesy of MearsonlineAuctions.com

school. However, in order to play football, Scott had to alter his earlier plans somewhat, explaining, "At the beginning of my sixth-grade year, the kids who wanted to join the band for training to be in the marching band in high school would go down to the band room at the high school and meet the band director and hear a message from him. And I did that because I was the kind of guy who would play in the band. When I came home from the meeting, I told my mother I was going to be in the band and that we needed to order a trumpet for me. Then one of my buddies who knew how much I liked football and knew how good I was at it told me, 'Well, if you're gonna be in the band, it's gonna be a problem for you playing football because the band and the football team perform at the same time.'"

Scott continued, "I hadn't thought about that. It hadn't crossed my mind. I was only in the sixth grade, and you couldn't play football until high school in the eighth grade. But I knew, even as a sixth grader, that football was my priority. So, I came home and told my mother to forget about that trumpet. And she'd tell you that she never heard me talk about a trumpet again. Once that buddy of mine told me I wouldn't be able to play football because it operates at the same time the band operates, that closed the door. My dream of being the next Louie Armstrong . . . that door was closed."

Excelling at shooting guard in basketball and wide receiver and cornerback in football at Trinity High, Scott proved to be particularly outstanding on the gridiron, earning All-State honors his final two seasons. Recruited by several major colleges, including Kansas State, Michigan State, Wake Forest, and Northwestern, Scott ultimately chose to enroll at KSU, recalling, "My high school coach wanted me to go to Kansas State. He told me, 'If you go there, you'll open up another door for guys behind you.' Then the Kansas State coaches told me, 'If you come to Kansas State, we've got a quarterback here named Lynn Dickey. He's 6-4 and 200 pounds, he's got a strong arm who's breaking all the records in Kansas high school football, and he's gonna be throwin' you the ball.' So, I said, 'Okay, great.'"

However, much to Scott's surprise, when he arrived at Kansas State University in the summer of 1967, he discovered that the coaching staff had penciled him in at left cornerback, later saying, "I never played one single down at receiver in four years at Kansas State. I started at cornerback all four years."

Nevertheless, Scott performed extremely well for the Wildcats, picking off a total of 12 passes, en route to becoming the first KSU player in two decades to earn All-America honors. Impressed with Scott's outstanding play at the collegiate level, the Browns selected him in the first round of the 1971 NFL Draft, with the 14th overall pick, disappointing in the process their fanbase, which would have preferred Ohio State defensive back Jack Tatum. Recalling the initial rancor he faced as a result, Scott said, "Cleveland fans didn't know who I was. The Browns needed a cornerback, though. Tatum was a safety. Erich Barnes was in his last year, and I replaced him. So, when I ran out onto the field before our only preseason home game, the fans booed. I wasn't upset about it either. I understood. Tatum was from Ohio State, and I was from Kansas State."

Scott, though, quickly silenced the boobirds after laying claim to the starting left cornerback job, picking off two passes in his very first game and intercepting four passes as a rookie, while also making significant contributions on special teams. Although Scott failed to record an interception the following year, his outstanding cover skills gained him Second-Team All-AFC recognition. Meanwhile, Scott displayed his mettle by starting all 14 games after dislocating his right thumb in the regular-season opener, later saying, "They popped it back into place, and it was never a problem again."

Emerging as one of the league's top cornerbacks in 1973, Scott picked off five passes, which he returned for a total of 71 yards and one touchdown, earning in the process Pro Bowl, First-Team All-AFC, and unofficial Second-Team All-Pro honors from the Newspaper Enterprise Association. Continuing to perform well at left corner the next five seasons, Scott recorded another 16 interceptions and scored his second touchdown on defense, before moving to strong safety in 1979.

Equally effective at his new post, Scott used his many intangible qualities to establish himself as one of the league's better safeties. Although the 6-foot, 190-pound Scott lacked elite running speed, he possessed superior instincts, an innate ability to anticipate the opposing quarterback's next move, and outstanding leadership skills that made him a steadying presence in the Browns defensive backfield. In explaining the success that he experienced over the course of his career, Scott said, "I just knew how to play football. I had the instincts to play."

Scott continued to man the strong safety position in four of the next five seasons, also spending one year at free safety, before announcing his retirement at the end of 1983 with career totals of 39 interceptions, 407 interception-return yards, 11 fumble recoveries, and three sacks. After missing one game as a rookie, Scott appeared in every contest the Browns played in each of the next 12 seasons, appearing in 186 out of 187 contests, 166 of which he started.

Thanking Scott for his many years of service at his retirement press conference, Browns owner Art Modell described him as a player "who conducted himself professionally both on and off the field," and stated, "He was, and is, a credit to the Browns."

Browns head coach Sam Rutigliano added, "Clarence influenced by example. He is a role model for both rookies and veterans. His retirement is a tremendous loss."

Following his playing days, Scott returned to Atlanta, where he operated a travel agency for six years, before partnering in a cleaning company for almost two decades. Scott then worked as an independent contractor for an energy company for several years, before finally retiring to private life.

Now 73 years old, Scott claims that playing for the Browns fulfilled all his childhood dreams, saying, "My heart's desire was to be a Cleveland Brown. What were the chances of me being drafted by the Browns? Even being available? Or even that they'd want me? Everything that's happened to me has been because God has said, 'This is what you want and I'm willing to give it to you,' and I have no complaints. The only thing I ever wanted to do was to be a football player . . . and to be a football player for the Browns. And I did that. So that, in and of itself, has provided me with just a wonderful life. My connection and contact with the Browns and their fans, and everything about them both, have been a big part of it. I'm glad to have lived the life of a Cleveland Brown."

CAREER HIGHLIGHTS

Best Season

Scott performed extremely well in 1981, picking off four passes and recovering three fumbles. But he played his best ball for the Browns in 1973, earning First-Team All-AFC honors by recording a career-high five interceptions, one of which he returned 45 yards for a touchdown.

Memorable Moments/Greatest Performances

Scott recorded the first two interceptions of his career in his very first game as a pro, picking off two passes during a 31–0 shutout of the Houston Oilers in the 1971 regular-season opener.

Although the Browns lost to the Packers by a score of 26–10 in the opening game of the 1972 regular season, Scott returned a blocked field goal 55 yards for a touchdown.

Scott lit the scoreboard again in the 1973 regular-season opener when he returned his interception of a Bert Jones pass 45 yards for a TD during a 24–14 win over the Baltimore Colts.

Although the Browns suffered a 17–9 defeat at the hands of the defending Super Bowl champion Miami Dolphins on October 15, 1973, Scott made a memorable play during the contest, recalling years later, "Mercury Morris broke free for a long run, and I caught him before he got to the end zone. I wouldn't say I was faster than Mercury Morris, but I made football plays and did whatever it took to do that."

Scott helped lead the Browns to a 7–0 win over the 49ers on December 1, 1974, by recording a pair of interceptions.

Scott scored the last of his three career touchdowns when he ran 49 yards to pay dirt after picking off a John Hadl pass during a 24–23 win over the Houston Oilers on October 16, 1977.

Scott helped preserve a 17–14 victory over the Oilers on November 30, 1980, by intercepting a Ken Stabler pass deep inside Browns territory with just over a minute left in the final period.

Notable Achievements

- Missed just one game in his entire career, appearing in 186 out of 187 contests.
- Recorded at least four interceptions five times.
- Returned two interceptions for touchdowns.
- Led Browns in interceptions twice.
- Ranks among Browns career leaders in interceptions (3rd), interception-return yards (8th), and fumble recoveries (tied for 7th).
- Two-time division champion (1971 and 1980).
- 1973 Pro Bowl selection.
- 1973 First-Team All-AFC selection.
- 1972 Second-Team All-AFC selection.

SUMMARY
AND HONORABLE MENTIONS
(THE NEXT 25)

Having identified the 50 greatest players in Cleveland Browns history, the time has come to select the best of the best. Based on the rankings contained in this book, the members of the Browns' all-time offensive and defensive teams are listed below. Our squads include the top player at each position, with the offense featuring the three best wide receivers, one tight end, and the two best running backs, tackles, and guards. Meanwhile, the defense features two ends, two tackles, two outside linebackers, one middle linebacker/guard, two cornerbacks, and a pair of safeties. Special teams have been accounted for as well, with a placekicker, punter, kickoff returner, and punt returner also being included.

OFFENSE		DEFENSE	
Player	Position	Player	Position
Otto Graham	QB	Myles Garrett	LE
Jim Brown	FB	Bob Gain	LT
Leroy Kelly	HB	Michael Dean Perry	RT
Ozzie Newsome	TE	Len Ford	RE
Dante Lavelli	WR	Jim Houston	LOLB
Mac Speedie	WR	Bill Willis	MG/MLB
Paul Warfield	WR	Clay Matthews	ROLB
Joe Thomas	LT	Frank Minnifield	LCB
Jim Ray Smith	LG	Warren Lahr	SS
Frank Gatski	C	Thom Darden	FS
Gene Hickerson	RG	Hanford Dixon	RCB
Mike McCormack	RT	Horace Gillom	P
Lou Groza	PK	Eric Metcalf	PR
Josh Cribbs	KR		

Although I limited my earlier rankings to the top 50 players in franchise history, many other fine players have worn a Browns uniform over the years, some of whom narrowly missed making the final cut. Following is a list of those players deserving of an honorable mention. These are the men I deemed worthy of being slotted into positions 51 to 75 in the overall rankings. Where applicable and available, the statistics they compiled during their time in Cleveland are included, along with their most notable achievements while playing for the Browns.

51—ALEX MACK (C; 2009–2015)

Courtesy of Erik Drost

Notable Achievements

- Started 80 consecutive games from 2009 to 2013.
- Member of 2009 NFL All-Rookie Team.
- Three-time Pro Bowl selection (2010, 2013, and 2015).
- 2013 Second-Team All-Pro selection.
- NFL 2010s All-Decade Team.

52—WEBSTER SLAUGHTER (WR; 1986–1991)

Courtesy of MearsonlineAuctions.com

Browns Numbers

305 Receptions, 4,834 Receiving Yards, 27 Touchdown Receptions.

Notable Achievements

- Surpassed 50 receptions three times.
- Surpassed 1,000 receiving yards once.
- Amassed more than 1,000 all-purpose yards twice.
- Finished third in NFL with average of 19 yards per reception in 1989.
- Led Browns in receptions three times and receiving yards four times.
- Ranks among Browns career leaders in receptions (9th), receiving yards (8th), and touchdown receptions (10th).
- Three-time division champion (1986, 1987, and 1989).
- 1989 Week 8 AFC Offensive Player of the Week.
- October 1989 AFC Offensive Player of the Month.
- 1989 Pro Bowl selection.
- 1989 Second-Team All-Pro selection.
- 1989 First-Team All-AFC selection.

53—DON COLO (DT; 1953–1958)

Browns Numbers

1 Interception, 11 Fumble Recoveries.

Notable Achievements

- Ranks among Browns career leaders in fumble recoveries (tied for 7th).
- Four-time division champion (1953, 1954, 1955, and 1957).
- Two-time NFL champion (1954 and 1955).
- Three-time Pro Bowl selection (1954, 1955, and 1958).
- Three-time Second-Team All-Pro selection (1955, 1956, and 1957).
- Pro Football Reference All-1950s Second Team.

54—CHIP BANKS (LB; 1982–1986)

Courtesy of MearsonlineAuctions.com

Browns Numbers

27½ Sacks, 5 Interceptions, 117 Interception-Return Yards, 6 Fumble Recoveries, 1 Touchdown.

Notable Achievements

- Recorded three interceptions in 1983.
- Recorded 11 sacks in 1985.
- Led Browns in sacks twice.
- Two-time division champion (1985 and 1986).
- Member of 1982 NFL All-Rookie Team.
- 1982 NFL Defensive Rookie of the Year.
- Four-time Pro Bowl selection (1982, 1983, 1985, and 1986).
- 1983 First-Team All-Pro selection.
- Three-time First-Team All-AFC selection (1983, 1985, and 1986).
- 1982 Second-Team All-AFC selection.

55—JOEL BITONIO (G: 2014–2021)

Courtesy of Erik Drost

Notable Achievements

Member of 2014 NFL All-Rookie Team.
Four-time Pro Bowl selection (2018, 2019, 2020, and 2021).
2021 First-Team All-Pro selection.
Three-time Second-Team All-Pro selection (2018, 2019, and 2020).
Three-time First-Team All-AFC selection (2014, 2020, and 2021).

56—ERNIE GREEN (RB/KR; 1962–1968)

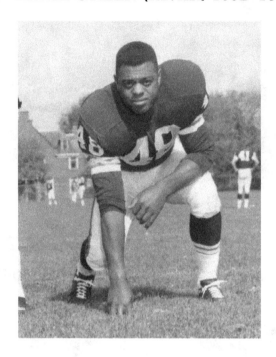

Career Numbers

3,204 Yards Rushing, 195 Receptions, 2,036 Receiving Yards, 5,240 Yards from Scrimmage, 648 Kickoff-Return Yards, 6,008 All-Purpose Yards, 15 Rushing TDs, 20 TD Receptions, 35 TDs, 4.8 Rushing Average.

Notable Achievements

- Rushed for more than 700 yards twice.
- Amassed more than 1,000 yards from scrimmage twice.
- Amassed more than 1,000 all-purpose yards three times.
- Scored 10 touchdowns in 1964.
- Averaged more than 5 yards per carry twice.
- Finished second in NFL with average of 4.9 yards per carry in 1967.
- Finished third in NFL with average of 5.2 yards per carry in 1966.
- Ranks among Browns career leaders in rushing yards (9th).
- Four-time division champion (1964, 1965, 1967, and 1968).
- 1964 NFL champion.
- Two-time Pro Bowl selection (1966 and 1967).

57—JOHN WOOTEN (G; 1959–1967)

Notable Achievements

- Never missed a game in nine seasons, appearing in 122 straight contests.
- Three-time division champion (1964, 1965, and 1967).
- 1964 NFL champion.
- Two-time Pro Bowl selection (1965 and 1966).
- 1965 First-Team All–Eastern Conference selection.

58—PAUL WIGGIN (DE; 1957–1967)

Career Numbers

60½ Sacks, 3 Interceptions, 19 Fumble Recoveries, 2 Touchdowns.

Notable Achievements

- Never missed a game entire career, appearing in 146 straight contests.
- Recorded at least 8 sacks in a season four times.
- Led NFL with four fumble recoveries in 1967.
- Ranks among Browns career leaders in sacks (5th) and fumble recoveries (2nd).
- Four-time division champion (1957, 1964, 1965, and 1967).
- 1964 NFL champion.
- Two-time Pro Bowl selection (1965 and 1967).

59—DON PAUL (DB/PR; 1954–1958)

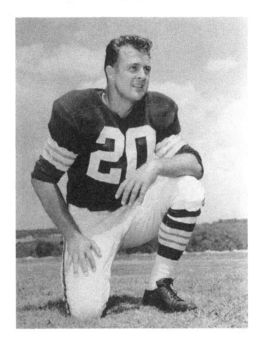

Browns Numbers

22 Interceptions, 389 Interception-Return Yards, 6 Fumble Recoveries, 106 Fumble-Return Yards, 383 Punt-Return Yards, 3 TDs.

Notable Achievements

- Returned one interception, one fumble, and one punt for touchdowns.
- Led NFL with 89 fumble-return yards in 1957.
- Finished third in NFL with 190 interception-return yards in 1956.
- Finished fifth in NFL with seven interceptions in 1956.
- Led Browns in interceptions three times.
- Ranks among Browns career leaders in interceptions (12th) and interception-return yards (10th).
- Three-time division champion (1954, 1955, and 1957).
- Two-time NFL champion (1954 and 1955).
- Three-time Pro Bowl selection (1956, 1957, and 1958).
- Two-time Second-Team All-Pro selection (1955 and 1957).
- 1958 First-Team All–Eastern Conference selection.
- Pro Football Reference All-1950s First Team.

60—PHIL DAWSON (PK; 1999–2012)

Courtesy of Erik Drost

Browns Numbers

1,271 Points Scored, 363 Field Goal Attempts, 305 Field Goals Made, 358 Extra-Point Attempts, 350 Extra Points Made, 84.0 Field Goal Pct.

Notable Achievements

- Scored at least 100 points six times, tallying 120 points once.
- Converted more than 90 percent of field goal attempts twice.
- Finished second in NFL in field goal percentage three times.
- Holds Browns career records for most field goals made and highest field goal percentage (minimum 50 attempts).
- Ranks second in Browns history in points scored.
- Ranks third in Browns history in games played (215).
- Two-time AFC Special Teams Player of the Week.
- 2012 Pro Bowl selection.
- Two-time Second-Team All-Pro selection (2007 and 2012).

61—BERNIE PARRISH (DB; 1959–1966)

Browns Numbers

29 Interceptions, 557 Interception-Return Yards, 5 Fumble Recoveries, 4 TDs.

Notable Achievements

- Recorded at least five interceptions three times.
- Amassed more than 100 interception-return yards once.
- Returned three interceptions and one fumble recovery for touchdowns.
- Recorded longest touchdown interception in NFL in 1960 (92 yards).
- Recorded three interceptions vs. Dallas on December 3, 1961.
- Led NFL with 238 interception-return yards in 1960.
- Led Browns in interceptions three times.
- Ranks among Browns career leaders in interceptions (7th), interception-return yards (4th), and touchdown interceptions (tied for 3rd).
- Two-time division champion (1964 and 1965).
- 1964 NFL champion.
- Two-time Pro Bowl selection (1960 and 1963).
- 1964 Second-Team All-Pro selection.
- 1964 First-Team All–Eastern Conference selection.

62—BOB GOLIC (NT; 1982–1988)

Courtesy of MearsonlineAuctions.com

Browns Numbers

14 Sacks, 1 Interception, 1 Fumble Recovery, 1 Touchdown.

Notable Achievements

- Three-time division champion (1985, 1986, and 1987).
- Three-time Pro Bowl selection (1985, 1986, and 1987).
- 1985 Second-Team All-Pro selection.
- 1985 Second-Team All-AFC selection.

63—ROSS FICHTNER (DB; 1960–1967)

Browns Numbers

27 Interceptions, 581 Interception-Return Yards, 3 Fumble Recoveries, 3 TDs.

Notable Achievements

- Recorded at least seven interceptions twice.
- Amassed more than 100 interception-return yards twice.
- Returned three interceptions for touchdowns.
- Recorded three interceptions vs. Dallas on October 23, 1966.
- Finished second in NFL with eight interceptions in 1966.
- Finished third in NFL with seven interceptions in 1962.
- Finished fourth in NFL with 152 interception-return yards in 1966.
- Led Browns in interceptions three times.
- Ranks among Browns career leaders in interceptions (tied for 8th), interception-return yards (2nd), and touchdown interceptions (tied for 3rd).
- Three-time division champion (1964, 1965, and 1967).
- 1964 NFL champion.
- 1966 Week 7 NFL Defensive Player of the Week.
- 1966 Second-Team All-Pro selection.

64—LOU RYMKUS (OT/DT; 1946–1951)

Notable Achievements

- Six-time division champion (1946, 1947, 1948, 1949, 1950, and 1951).
- Four-time AAFC champion (1946, 1947, 1948, and 1949).
- 1950 NFL champion.
- Two-time First-Team All-AAFC selection (1947 and 1949).
- 1948 Second-Team All-AAFC selection.
- 1951 Second-Team All-NFL selection.

65—EARNEST BYNER
(RB/KR; 1984–1988, 1994–1995)

Courtesy of MearsonlineAuctions.com

Browns Numbers

3,364 Yards Rushing, 276 Receptions, 2,630 Receiving Yards, 5,994 Yards from Scrimmage, 515 Kickoff-Return Yards, 6,564 All-Purpose Yards, 27 Rushing TDs, 10 TD Receptions, 38 TDs, 3.9 Rushing Average.

Notable Achievements

- Rushed for more than 1,000 yards once (1,002 in 1985).
- Surpassed 50 receptions three times and 500 receiving yards twice.
- Amassed more than 1,000 yards from scrimmage twice.
- Amassed more than 1,000 all-purpose yards four times.
- Scored 10 touchdowns twice.
- Averaged more than 5 yards per carry once.
- Finished third in NFL with eight rushing touchdowns in 1987.
- Led Browns in rushing once and receptions three times.
- Ranks among Browns career leaders in rushing yards (8th), rushing TDs (8th), yards from scrimmage (9th), and all-purpose yards (11th).
- Three-time division champion (1985, 1986, and 1987).
- 1987 Week 9 AFC Offensive Player of the Week.
- 1987 Second-Team All-AFC selection.

66—KEN KONZ (DB/PR; 1953–1959)

Career Numbers

30 Interceptions, 392 Interception-Return Yards, 6 Fumble Recoveries, 32 Fumble-Return Yards, 556 Punt-Return Yards, 5 TDs.

Notable Achievements

- Never missed a game entire career, appearing in 84 straight contests.
- Returned four interceptions and one punt for touchdowns.
- Recorded at least five interceptions three times.
- Amassed more than 100 interception-return yards twice.
- Led NFL with two touchdown interceptions in 1954.
- Finished second in NFL with 133 interception-return yards in 1954.
- Finished third in NFL in punt-return yards once and punt-return average once.
- Led Browns in interceptions five times.
- Ranks among Browns career leaders in interceptions (tied for 5th), interception-return yards (9th), and touchdown interceptions (2nd).
- Four-time division champion (1953, 1954, 1955, and 1957).
- Two-time NFL champion (1954 and 1955).
- 1955 Pro Bowl selection.
- 1955 Second-Team All-Pro selection.
- Two-time First-Team All–Eastern Conference selection (1956 and 1957).

67—VINCE COSTELLO (LB; 1957–1966)

Courtesy of MearsonlineAuctions.com

Browns Numbers

18 Interceptions, 245 Interception-Return Yards, 8 Fumble Recoveries, 2 TDs.

Notable Achievements

- Returned two fumbles for touchdowns.
- Finished fifth in NFL with four fumble recoveries in 1964.
- Led Browns with seven interceptions and 118 interception-return yards in 1963.
- Three-time division champion (1957, 1964, and 1965).
- 1964 NFL champion.

68—JOE DELAMIELLEURE (G; 1980–1984)

Courtesy of MearsonlineAuctions.com

Notable Achievements

- 1980 division champion.
- 1980 Pro Bowl selection.
- Two-time Second-Team All-Pro selection (1980 and 1983).
- 1980 First-Team All-AFC selection.
- 1981 Second-Team All-AFC selection.
- Elected to Pro Football Hall of Fame in 2003.

69—TOMMY JAMES (DB; 1948–1955)

Browns Numbers

34 Interceptions, 309 Interception-Return Yards, 5 Fumble Recoveries, 44 Fumble-Return Yards, 2 TDs.

Notable Achievements

- Returned one interception and one punt for touchdowns.
- Recorded at least five interceptions twice.
- Finished second in NFL with 37 fumble-return yards in 1953.
- Finished fourth in NFL with nine interceptions in 1950.
- Led Browns in interceptions twice.
- Ranks fourth in Browns history in interceptions.
- Eight-time division champion (1948, 1949, 1950, 1951, 1952, 1953, 1954, and 1955).
- Two-time AAFC champion (1948 and 1949).
- Three-time NFL champion (1950, 1954, and 1955).
- 1953 Pro Bowl selection.

70—DUB JONES (RB; 1948–1955)

Browns Numbers

1,910 Yards Rushing, 171 Receptions, 2,874 Receiving Yards, 4,784 Yards from Scrimmage, 5,030 All-Purpose Yards, 20 Rushing TDs, 20 TD Receptions, 40 Touchdowns, 4.2 Rushing Average.

Notable Achievements

- Surpassed 500 receiving yards twice.
- Amassed more than 1,000 yards from scrimmage once.
- Scored more than 10 touchdowns twice.
- Finished second in NFL in rushing TDs once and touchdowns twice.
- Finished third in NFL with 1,062 yards from scrimmage in 1951.
- Led Browns with 492 yards rushing in 1951.
- Holds share of NFL record for most touchdowns scored in one game (six vs. Chicago Bears on November 25, 1951).
- Eight-time division champion (1948, 1949, 1950, 1951, 1952, 1953, 1954, and 1955).
- Two-time AAFC champion (1948 and 1949).
- Three-time NFL champion (1950, 1954, and 1955).
- Two-time Pro Bowl selection (1951 and 1952).
- 1951 First-Team All-Pro selection.

71—CODY RISIEN (OT; 1979–1983, 1985–1989)

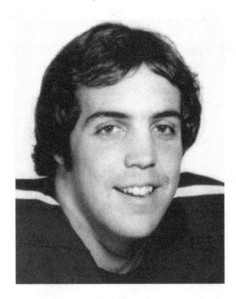

Notable Achievements

- Five-time division champion (1980, 1985, 1986, 1987, and 1989).
- Member of 1979 NFL All-Rookie Team.
- Two-time Pro Bowl selection (1986 and 1987).
- 1983 First-Team All-AFC selection.
- Two-time Second-Team All-AFC selection (1986 and 1987).

72—D'QWELL JACKSON
(LB; 2006–2009, 2011–2013)

Courtesy of Jeffrey Beall

Browns Numbers

824 Tackles, 11½ Sacks, 8 Interceptions, 85 Interception-Return Yards, 5 Forced Fumbles, 7 Fumble Recoveries, 1 Touchdown.

Notable Achievements

- Recorded more than 100 tackles five times, surpassing 150 stops twice.
- Led NFL with 154 combined tackles in 2008.
- Led NFL with 116 solo tackles in 2011.
- Finished third in NFL with 158 combined tackles in 2011.
- Led Browns in tackles five times.
- Ranks fourth in Browns history in career tackles.
- 2012 Week 12 AFC Defensive Player of the Week.
- September 2011 AFC Defensive Player of the Month.

73—TOM DELEONE (C; 1974–1984)

Courtesy of MearsonlineAuctions.com

Notable Achievements

- Missed just one game from 1975 to 1980, starting 89 out of 90 contests.
- 1980 division champion.
- Two-time Pro Bowl selection (1979 and 1980).
- 1980 Second-Team All-AFC selection.

74—JOE HADEN (DB; 2010–2016)

Courtesy of Erik Drost

Browns Numbers

19 Interceptions, 231 Interception-Return Yards, 370 Tackles, 4 Forced Fumbles, 4 Fumble Recoveries, 2 Sacks, 1 TD.

Notable Achievements

- Recorded six interceptions and amassed 101 interception-return yards in 2010.
- Returned one interception for a touchdown.
- Finished second in NFL with 20 passes defended in 2014.
- Finished third in NFL with 20 passes defended in 2013.
- Led Browns in interceptions three times.
- Member of 2010 NFL All-Rookie Team.
- Two-time Pro Bowl selection (2013 and 2014).
- 2013 Second-Team All-Pro selection.

75—REGGIE RUCKER (WR; 1975–1981)

Browns Numbers

310 Receptions, 4,953 Receiving Yards, 32 Touchdown Receptions.

Notable Achievements

- Finished second in NFL with 60 receptions in 1975.
- Finished fourth in NFL with average of 20.8 yards per reception in 1978.
- Finished sixth in NFL with 893 receiving yards in 1978.
- Led Browns in receptions three times and receiving yards four times.
- Ranks among Browns career leaders in receptions (8th), receiving yards (7th), and touchdown receptions (7th).
- 1980 division champion.

GLOSSARY

ABBREVIATIONS AND STATISTICAL TERMS

ALL-PURPOSE YDS. All-purpose yards.

C. Center.

COMP %. Completion percentage. The number of successfully completed passes divided by the number of passes attempted.

DB. Defensive back.

DE. Defensive end.

DT. Defensive tackle.

FB. Fullback.

FS. Free Safety.

G. Guard.

HB. Halfback

INTS. Interceptions. Passes thrown by the quarterback that are caught by a member of the opposing team's defense.

KR. Kickoff returner.

LB. Linebacker.

LCB. Left cornerback.

LE. Left end.

LG. Left guard.

LOLB. Left-outside linebacker.

LT. Left tackle.

MLB. Middle linebacker.

NT. Nose tackle.

OT. Offensive tackle.

P. Punter.

PK. Placekicker.

PR. Punt returner.

QB. Quarterback.

QBR. Quarterback rating.

RB. Running back.

RCB. Right cornerback.

RE. Right end.

RECS. Receptions.

REC YDS. Receiving yards.

RG. Right guard.

ROLB. Right-outside linebacker.

RT. Right tackle.

SS. Strong Safety.

TD PASSES. Touchdown passes.

TD RECS. Touchdown receptions.

TDS. Touchdowns.

TE. Tight end.

WR. Wide receiver.

YDS FROM SCRIMMAGE. Yards from scrimmage.

YDS PASSING. Yards passing.

YDS RUSHING. Yards rushing.

BIBLIOGRAPHY

Books

Grossi, Tony. *Tales from the Cleveland Browns Sideline: A Collection of the Greatest Browns Stories Ever Told.* New York: Sports Publishing, 2012.

Jones, Danny. *More Distant Memories: Pro Football's Best Ever Players of the 50s, 60s, and 70s.* Bloomington, IN: AuthorHouse, 2006.

Loede, Matt. *Game of My Life: Cleveland Browns: Memorable Stories of Browns Football.* New York: Sports Publishing, 2016.

Pluto, Terry. *When All the World Was Browns Town: Cleveland's Browns and the Championship Season of '64.* New York: Simon & Schuster, 1997.

Video

Greatest Ever: NFL Dream Team. Polygram Video, 1996.

Websites

Biographies, online at *Hickoksports.com*
(www.hickoksports.com/hickoksports/biograph).

Biographies from *Answers.com*
(www.answers.com).

Biographies from *Jockbio.com*
(www.jockbio.com).

BrownsNation.com
(www.brownsnation.com).

CapitalNewYork.com
(www.capitalnewyork.com).

CBSNews.com
(www.cbsnews.com).

ESPN.com
(http://sports.espn.go.com).

Hall of Famers, online at *profootballhof.com*
(www.profootballhof.com/hof/member).

Inductees from *LASportsHall.com*
(www.lasportshall.com).

LATimes.com
(http://articles.latimes.com).

Newsday.com
(www.newsday.com).

NYDailyNews.com
(www.nydailynews.com/new-york).

NYTimes.com
(www.nytimes.com).

Pro Football Talk from *nbcsports.com*
(http://profootballtalk.nbcsports.com).

SpTimes.com
(www.sptimes.com).

StarLedger.com
(www.starledger.com).

SunSentinel.com
(http://articles.sun-sentinel.com).

The Players, online at *Profootballreference.com*
(www.pro-football-reference.com/players).

CPSIA information can be obtained
at www.ICGtesting.com
Printed in the USA
BVHW092311310722
643446BV00003B/3

9 781493 062799